Management for Professionals

The Springer series *Management for Professionals* comprises high-level business and management books for executives. The authors are experienced business professionals and renowned professors who combine scientific background, best practice, and entrepreneurial vision to provide powerful insights into how to achieve business excellence.

More information about this series at http://www.springer.com/series/10101

Oliver Gassmann · Martin A. Bader ·
Mark James Thompson

Patent Management

Protecting Intellectual Property and Innovation

Springer

Oliver Gassmann
Institute of Technology
Management
University of St. Gallen
St. Gallen, Switzerland

Martin A. Bader
THI Business School
Technische Hochschule Ingolstadt
Ingolstadt, Germany

Mark James Thompson
IP Australia
Canberra, Australia

ISSN 2192-8096   ISSN 2192-810X (electronic)
Management for Professionals
ISBN 978-3-030-59008-6   ISBN 978-3-030-59009-3 (eBook)
https://doi.org/10.1007/978-3-030-59009-3

© Springer Nature Switzerland AG 2021

This work is subject to copyright. All rights are reserved by the Publisher, whether the whole or part of the material is concerned, specifically the rights of translation, reprinting, reuse of illustrations, recitation, broadcasting, reproduction on microfilms or in any other physical way, and transmission or information storage and retrieval, electronic adaptation, computer software, or by similar or dissimilar methodology now known or hereafter developed.

The use of general descriptive names, registered names, trademarks, service marks, etc. in this publication does not imply, even in the absence of a specific statement, that such names are exempt from the relevant protective laws and regulations and therefore free for general use.

The publisher, the authors, and the editors are safe to assume that the advice and information in this book are believed to be true and accurate at the date of publication. Neither the publisher nor the authors or the editors give a warranty, expressed or implied, with respect to the material contained herein or for any errors or omissions that may have been made. The publisher remains neutral with regard to jurisdictional claims in published maps and institutional affiliations.

This Springer imprint is published by the registered company Springer Nature Switzerland AG.
The registered company address is: Gewerbestrasse 11, 6330 Cham, Switzerland

Preface

Innovation is paramount to gaining a competitive advantage because innovation creates and captures value. In difficult times like the COVID-19 crisis in 2020, many companies have realized the pressure to innovate. But only a company that can effectively appropriate its innovation can sustain its profitability. In the global competition for innovation, managing intellectual property (IP), especially patents, is becoming much more important than the management of factories. Control over key technologies and innovations cannot be easily replaced, but factory suppliers can. Moreover, the locus of IP generation has shifted eastward with China and Korea now ranking at top positions alongside the USA, Japan, and Europe. China became the global leader in patent applications, having filed more patents in 2018 than the all the countries from second to tenth place taken together. Leading companies have been *Huawei* (telecom), *Oppo* (smartphone), *BOE* (LCD panels), *Lenovo* (computer), *Tencent* (gaming), and *ZTE* (telecom). The geocentric gravity has shifted in terms of intellectual property notwithstanding that, regarding foreign applications, US companies have filed more than three times as many patents as Chinese ones have.

In addition to the quantitative increase, both the legal effectiveness and strategic nature of patents are also gaining in importance. On the one hand, there is a need for experts who, in close cooperation with research and development, are able to apply for these patents and enforce them legally, while on the other hand, the challenges in managing a patent portfolio in a given competitive environment are becoming evermore taxing as the volume of IP increases. A comprehensive patent management, adapted to the company's specific situation, is therefore becoming essential so as not to be technologically blindsided. Patents have also become a major reason for mergers and acquisitions, most prominently in the pharmaceutical industry, but increasingly so in telecom and computer science.

Although the importance of patent management for corporate competitiveness has increased precipitously, there is still little literature on the subject from a management perspective. As our German book *Patent Management* has been very successful—being now in its fourth edition—we have decided to create an English version. Rather than offer a mere translation, we have chosen illustrative examples, cases, and anecdotes that better reflect the international dimension of patents. We also take a much deeper look at current industries and their specific practices, as well as likewise looking at future technologies such as artificial intelligence in the context of patents.

Our research has taken place mainly at the Institute of Technology Management at the University of St. Gallen, Switzerland; this research centers on, and is conducted in cooperation with, companies and organizations from Europe, China, Japan, India, Canada, and the USA, and it encompasses:

- Global benchmarking studies on strategic technology and intellectual property management, and research and transfer projects on the management of patents in different industries
- Several PhD studies on patent management, the role of patent aggregating companies, and value capturing with patents.
- In-depth studies on patent management, patent generation, licensing, and patent trading together with *BGW, European Commission (EC), Audi/Volkswagen, Dennemeyer, PricewaterhouseCoopers (PwC), Swiss Federal Institute of Intellectual Property (IPI), European Patent Office (EPO),* and *World Intellectual Property Organization (WIPO).*
- Our many industry partners on projects in intellectual property strategy and management. We learned a lot by working on real-life challenges and supporting solutions in leading companies worldwide.

A key element of this book is also the main basis of our own leadership and consulting experience in the management of innovation and intellectual property. We work hard for our motto "from insight to impact" but have really also learned a lot from our partners and clients in the different industries and from different regions of the world.

We would very much like to thank Prof. Dr. Felix Addor and Dr. Kamran Housang Pour from the Swiss Federal Institute of Intellectual Property, Bern, Switzerland, Michael Kucher from Slater & Matsil, Dallas, USA, Julien Lacheré and Tuba Yamaç from BCF Business Law, Montréal, Canada, Dr. Christoph Meister and Dr. Ute Konopka, BGW AG Management Advisory Group, St. Gallen, Switzerland, and Morris Campbell as well as Lutz Brinkmann, for their contributions to this edition. A special thank you goes to THI Business School at Technische Hochschule in Ingolstadt and the Free State of Bavaria, as well as to the University of St. Gallen and its ITEM-HSG Foundation for their support. We would also like to thank Dr. Prashanth Mahagaonkar and Ruth Milewski of Springer for managing the overall publication process. Last but not least, we would like to thank our research donors and partners, project partners, and interview partners as well as PhD researchers and students at the University of St. Gallen, whose commitments have made an important contribution to this book.

We wish you success in creating value and capturing value through innovation using intellectual property with your company or institution.

St. Gallen, Switzerland Oliver Gassmann
Ingolstadt, Germany Martin A. Bader
Canberra, Australia Mark James Thompson
June 2020

Endorsements

"Not only a must-read for every IP specialist but also an exciting introduction for the non-professional with great examples and insights into the business world and its use of the patent system."
—Dr. jur. Catherine Chammartin, *Director General, Swiss Federal Institute of Intellectual Property (IPI), Bern, Switzerland*

"The reader will learn about all aspects of successful patent management: protection, defense, as well as exploitation, valuation, and organization. A core of the book that should be in the reference library of every innovation and IP management are the practical examples from different industries."
—Dr. Beat Weibel, *Chief IP Counsel, Siemens*

"IPR is not limited to "intellectual property rights"; it is more about "innovation," "patents," and "relationship." This book provides in-depth studies on patent management in all respects, to highlight the core value of IPR by the art of management."
—Dr. Li Tian, *Director of IPR & Standardization Department, ZTE Corporation*

"This book not only provides comprehensive guide and best practices for all aspects of enterprise patent management but also highlights several interesting opportunities for patent practitioners, such as patent protection scheme for artificial intelligence-based business method and block chain solution for patent transactions. Overall an excellent read."
—He Sidan, *Managing Director of Strategy, HiSilicon, Huawei*

"An accessible guide and roadmap for how best to navigate the complex world of IP – whether you are a student or practitioner."
—Dr. Carola Weil, *Dean of Continuing Studies, McGill University/ Université McGill, Montréal, Canada*

"An excellent book for professionals working in the field of the intellectual property management."
—Michael Kucher, *Attorney at Law, Partner at Slater & Matsil, Dallas, USA*

"The book is packed with great examples, and invites the reader to explore beyond your own immediate sphere, and always with a mind to assisting with how to manage what is a business critical asset—intellectual property."
—Benjamin Mitra-Kahn, *Chief Economist & General Manager Policy & Governance Group, IP Australia, Phillip/Canberra, Australia*

"A must-read for every technology and innovation manager, who is active in the patent race. The international author team provides valuable insights, many examples, and strong managerial recommendations."
—Dr. Amir Bonakdar, *Senior Director Customer Innovation, SAP Labs Palo Alto, USA*

"The book gives very good and structured insights into the crucial topic of patent management; especially helpful are the numerous examples."
—Prof. Dr. Thomas Kropf, *President Corporate Research and Advance Engineering, Bosch*

"Essential reading on patent management. A comprehensive and practical overview covering everything from the fundamentals to the development of a corporate patent strategy."
—Stephen Albrecht, *Director Corporate Technology, Liebherr International*

"A comprehensive overview of IP management, with a focus on patents. A must-read for anyone involved in creating and managing IP for competitive advantage."
—Dr. Matthias Kaiserswerth, *President of the Board, Abraxas*

"Well-written introduction to IP management for business and innovation managers."
—Dr. Hermann Bach, *SVP, Innovation Management & Commercial Services, Covestro*

"A structured overview of IP strategy considerations, along with a comprehensive teaching of the fundamental principles, terminologies, and processes relating to the world of IP."
—Charles Jeffries, *Group Intellectual Property, Novartis*

"An outstanding textbook on intellectual property protection in innovation management. Explanations are immediately to be understood. Examples confirm the closeness to daily practice. Perfect for use in industry and academia. I wish all textbooks were as great as this one."
—Prof. Dr. Thomas Müller-Kirschbaum, *Senior VP Innovation & Sustainability, Henkel*

"The book provides an easy-to-use framework, how to develop and implement a holistic IP strategy. Insights into different industries as well as on the impact of disruptive technologies (e.g., blockchain) make it a great guide and reference."
—Dr. Thorsten Mueller, *Head Global Product Group Building, ABB;former CTO Osram*

Endorsements

"*Intellectual Property Management for Professionals* is a great book for engineers to leverage and implement their IP strategy and learn about best practices."
—Dr. Oliver Mayer, *fm. Senior Principal at General Electric Research Center*

"A value-driven IP strategy is the key to effectively protect the business of the future. Many companies are struggling implementing the appropriate strategy. This book provides the right tools to implement the necessary processes."
—Dr. Thomas Jetzfellner, *Lead IP Counsel Blockchain, Siemens*

"A great book for IP professionals to leverage and implement their IP strategy and learn about best practices. An experienced handling of IP challenges is essential presently. This book supports all IP professionals to improve their IP strategy and to learn about best practices."
—Dr. Jörg Friedhofen, *Co-Head Patent Department, Vorwerk*

"Very comprehensively written, well-illustrated with examples, and directly applicable for real-life business. A must-read for every innovator who is in patent-intensive industries."
—Nicolas Durville, *CEO & Partner, Zühlke*

"*Intellectual Property Management for Professionals* is a good book that supports IP specialists both in their training and during their work. But also experienced readers will benefit from the book, as they find overviews and best practices that help them optimize IP strategy and IP processes."
—Alexander Poledna, *Head of Intellectual Property Rights, Standards & Journals, voestalpine stahl, Linz, Austria*

"A comprehensive practical guide to effective patent management that takes into account the rapidly changing technological environment of companies and the increasing complexity of the patent system. This book offers a great match between general insights and practical implications."
—Prof. Dr. Martin Woerter, *KOF Swiss Economic Institute, ETH Zürich, Zurich, Switzerland*

"Managing intellectual property as the core values of a firm is much more than IP protection. This book addresses the importance and relevance of IP topics for business success. In addition, up-to-date examples and benchmarks, presented tools, and frameworks are very useful for IP professionals and applicants."
—Prof. Dr. Sevim Süzeroglu-Melchiors, *OTH Regensburg, Germany and fm Global Head of Consulting, Dennemeyer Group*

"Whether you are an executive who wants to understand the business logic of patenting, an IP consultant who wants to provide legal advice better tailored to your clients' strategies, or a student of business and technology, this book offers in-depth and timely answers to your questions about patent management. It is packed with real-world examples, from all major industries as well as from new and emerging technologies."
—Prof. Dr. Marcus Holgersson, *Associate Professor in Intellectual Property Management, Chalmers University of Technology, Gothenburg, Sweden*

"This is a very timely book with IP management gaining increasing importance among executives. The book goes beyond an overview of protection strategies, providing valuable insights into commercialization practices, how to successfully organize patent management followed by important considerations of how patent management varies across industries. Given the applied perspective the authors take, this book will be of particular value to practitioners."
—Dr. Frank Tietze, *Lecturer in Technology and Innovation Management, Institute for Manufacturing, University of Cambridge, Great Britain*

"A great book that does fill a niche on the market. Its value lies in combining theory and practice of patent management. The book does provide a comprehensive overview of patenting trends. Its clear structure in combination with many practical examples is of great help for both practitioners and scientific scholars alike."
—Dr. Nikolaus Thumm, *Senior Fellow at the Joint Research Centre of the European Commission, Seville, Spain*

"This comprehensive book is the perfect mix between theory and practice and the ultimate reading for anyone interested in a real-world picture of patent management. Definitely a must-read."
—Prof. Dr. Massimiliano Granieri, *Professor of Law, University of Brescia, Italy*

"An engaging and useful book, rich of examples that help illustrate the protection of innovation to a wide audience, including postgraduate students, innovation scholars, and practitioners. Besides explaining the fundamentals of patent management in plain words, the book introduces the reader to the nuances of patent strategy in different industries and technological fields."
—Prof. Dr. Salvatore Torrisi, *Professor of Strategic Management, University of Milano-Bicocca, Italy*

"A must-read for all those involved with transforming innovation into intangible company assets, for its comprehensive coverage of all industry sectors and its didactic approach to managing and exploiting these assets."
—Philippe Therias, *Avocat au Barreau de Paris, BCF Global, France*

"A comprehensive and accessible book on patent fundamentals and practice, from a practical management perspective. It offers both a comprehensive and deep analysis of the most important current industries and technologies, its important implications, and specific practices. I recommend it both as a reference manual, to clarify basic concepts on the subject, and for consultation in professional practice related to the protection of specific inventions and technology."
—Reyes Campello Estebaranz, *Arbitrator in Intellectual Property, Managing Partner, CEALAW, Alicante, Spain*

"A great overview of how to manage and protect patent and intellectual property. This book will serve as a very important tool to encourage those who dedicate their time to innovation in every field. I am looking forward to be delighted with this book, which I will certainly use in my routine."
—Ramon Fernandez Aracil Filho, *Partner at Mourão Campos, São Paulo, Brazil*

"An excellent tool for those who aim for professional and planned management of the intangible assets of companies and other organizations, such as public research institutions."
—Prof. Gustavo Schötz, *Universidad Austral, Intellectual Property Center, Buenos Aires, Argentina*

"A practical yet comprehensive handbook on patent management. It is the reference text I wish I had, when starting out in research commercialization!"
—Dr. Luke Krieg, *Digital Innovation Lead, GHD, Auckland, New Zealand*

Contents

1 Fundamentals of Intellectual Property Rights   1
   1.1   Creating Value by Generating Innovation   1
   1.2   Capturing Value by Protecting Innovation   4
   1.3   Types of Intellectual Property Rights 14
   References 23

2 Protection Strategies 27
   2.1   Patent Strategies in General 27
   2.2   Offensive and Defensive Patent Strategies 30
   2.3   Core Dimensions of Patent Strategies 32
   2.4   Cost of Patents 39
   2.5   Complementary Strategies to Patenting 42
   References 49

3 Evaluating and Valuing Patents 51
   3.1   Evaluating Patents 52
   3.2   Valuing Patents 61
   3.3   Managing the Patent Portfolio 75
   References 91

4 Successful Practices in Commercializing Patents 95
   4.1   Licensing 96
   4.2   Cross-Licensing 97
   4.3   Sale 98
   4.4   Strategic Alliance 99
   4.5   Spin-Off and Call-Back 100
   4.6   Joint Venture 101
   4.7   Patenting for Access to Finance 102
   4.8   Litigation for Value 105
   4.9   Complex Strategies 107
   4.10 Commercialization Concepts and Conclusions 108
   References 113

5 Organizing Patent Management ... 115
- 5.1 Governance vs. Service Patent Department ... 115
- 5.2 Costs and Benefits of a Patent Department ... 117
- 5.3 Core Processes of Patent Management ... 121
- 5.4 Inventor Culture as a Catalyst ... 129
- 5.5 Preventing Product Piracy ... 136
- References ... 141

6 Patent Management by Industry ... 143
- 6.1 Pharma ... 144
- 6.2 Chemistry ... 146
- 6.3 Crop Science ... 148
- 6.4 Life Sciences ... 151
- 6.5 Consumer Goods ... 153
- 6.6 Machinery ... 155
- 6.7 Electronics and Electrical Equipment ... 161
- 6.8 Automotive ... 166
- 6.9 Information and Communications Technology ... 172
- 6.10 Computer Science ... 178
- 6.11 Financial Services and Fintech ... 182
- 6.12 Transport and Logistics ... 185
- 6.13 Start-Ups and SMEs ... 188
- References ... 190

7 Patent Management in New Technology Environments ... 193
- 7.1 Biotechnology ... 194
- 7.2 Nanotechnology ... 203
- 7.3 Industry 4.0 and Internet of Things ... 208
- 7.4 Software and Business Methods ... 212
- 7.5 Artificial Intelligence-Based Business Models ... 221
- 7.6 Blockchain and Distributed Ledger Technologies ... 230
- References ... 236

8 Useful Information for Practitioners ... 241
- 8.1 Patent Growth Worldwide ... 242
- 8.2 Structure of a Patent ... 243
- 8.3 Patent Document Codes ... 246
- 8.4 Patent Classification ... 247
- 8.5 Notes on Patent Search ... 248
- 8.6 Member States of the European Patent Organisation ... 250
- 8.7 EUIPO/Unitary Patent/Unified Patent Court ... 251
- 8.8 IP Tax Regimes ... 253

	8.9	Brief Comparison of Patent Legislation	254
	8.10	The World Intellectual Property Day	256
	References		257

Glossary 259

Index 261

About the Authors

Oliver Gassmann is Professor of Technology and Innovation Management at the University of St. Gallen (HSG) and also Chairman of the Board of the Institute of Technology Management there. He is a keynote speaker for several Executive MBA programs aside from being the author and editor of 20 books and of over 400 international papers in technology and innovation management. Oliver is a member of the board of the Swiss Federal Institute of Intellectual Property, a board member of several international companies, as well as co-founder of several spin-offs. Until 2002, he was the head of research and pre-development at Schindler. His research focuses on success factors for innovation and business models.

Oliver has received numerous awards and honors for his work, including the RADMA Prize (1998, Manchester), and in 2013 was ranked as the Top Economist of Germany (2013, FAZ). Also listed as being among the Top 50 Researchers (2014, IAMOT), he became the recipient of the prestigious Scholarly Impact Award (2014, *Journal of Management*). According to Google Scholar, he is the most frequently cited authority in the field of "R&D Management" worldwide (2020).

Martin A. Bader is a European and Swiss Patent Attorney. As well as being Partner and Co-Founder of the specialized innovation and intellectual property management advisory group BGW AG St. Gallen, he has, since March 2016, been Professor for Technology Management and Entrepreneurship at the University of Applied Sciences Ingolstadt (THI). Previously, he was Head of the Intellectual Property Management Competence Center at the Institute of Technology Management at the University of St. Gallen (HSG) and was, until 2002, Vice President and Chief Intellectual Property Officer at Infineon Technologies, Munich.

Martin is a mediator at the Mediation Center for Alternative Dispute Resolution at the World Intellectual Property Organization (WIPO) and has for many years been regarded as being among the top 300 intellectual property strategists worldwide according to the *Intellectual Asset Management* magazine's IAM strategy 300 index. He is also a long-standing author of numerous specialist publications and an internationally sought-after speaker in the field of intellectual property management.

Mark James Thompson is Assistant Director of the Center for Data Excellence at the Australian patent office (IP Australia) and CEO of Arêté Statistics AG, an inferential statistical consultancy. He was Chief Economist of the Austrian Patent office and worked for several years at the Swiss office as an economist on patent reform legislation.

Mark did his PhD specifically on statistical and econometric patent valuation and competition and uses that knowledge to run a long-short equity fund for the pharmaceutical sector where patents add the most value.

Fundamentals of Intellectual Property Rights

1.1 Creating Value by Generating Innovation

Since the beginning of the twenty-first century, innovation has had unique conditions: the entrepreneurial environment has been characterized by a high degree of dynamism, complexity, and competition due to globalization, which has reduced the probability of success—or has finally enabled it through new niches that continually emerge. Only 0.6% of all innovations are commercially successful (Stevens, Burley 1997). In pharmaceuticals, the probability of success is even lower at 1:10,000 (Gassmann et al. 2018; Schuhmacher et al. 2018). The demands placed on innovation management have thus compounded: globalized competition, an explosion of technical knowledge, rapid and accelerating technological diffusion, decentralization of knowledge, the escalation of innovation costs, business model innovations, and shorter innovation cycles.

Globalization of Competition

The power of economies of scale in production, combined with dramatically declining transport and information costs, is forcing companies into global activities. This became particularly clear in 2009 after the economic crisis. Despite the protectionist actions of nations, like the trade war between China and the USA in 2020, overall competition has become global. Companies like *Amazon* and *Alibaba* have brought globalization into the consumers' living rooms. At the beginning of the new decade, important transformations and global power shifts are on the horizon.

Explosion of Technical Knowledge

The amount of available knowledge doubles every 13 months (Buckminster Fuller 1982) and the growth and expansion of the "internet of things" might soon reach a point from where on knowledge doubles every 12 h (IBM 2006). While the number of scientific journals at the beginning of the nineteenth century was still 100, it grew to 1000 in 1850, to 10,000 around the year 1900, and to approximately 300,000 in 2010. Approximately 80% of the technical knowledge has been published in the form of patent specifications. Over 90% of the information disclosed in patent documents is unprotected because it has either expired, been rejected, withdrawn, or not renewed (Ehrat 1997). Most of the technical knowledge from patent specifications are thus not only openly accessible but can even be used freely.

Technological Fusion

The major breakthroughs in mapping and identifying the human genome are the result of a close cooperation between computer science and genetic engineering. *IBM* already ranks seventh in the world in terms of the amount of patents in the field of biotechnology. "Software eats the world" as the *Wall Street Journal* boldly proclaimed in 2012. Software and algorithms are entering every industry—from healthcare and machinery to the automotive industry. With these developments, a new innovation and patent protection behavior is also entering into these industries. For example, the automotive industry has made 2020 the year of the connected car, since this has been defined as one of their three main focal areas of innovation. As a result, it has entered into the complex and dynamic patent wars over connectivity, traditionally the realm of major ICT players.

Decentralization of Knowledge

Information technology, free global movement of highly skilled labor, regional research specializations, and wage arbitrage have led to integrated network structures with clearly defined R&D competence centers: European Businesses spend 30% of their R&D budget abroad; for Swiss firms, the portion is even higher, namely at over 50%, despite being innovation champions. New innovation hotspots are all located in economically emerging countries such as China and India.

Increase in the Cost of Innovation

Due to the dynamic technology and its increased research requirements, R&D costs are rising dramatically. An increasingly large share of the R&D budget is spent on intellectual property rights (IPRs). In technology-intensive industries, up to 5% of the R&D budget is spent on generating and maintaining industrial property rights, and on the costs of enforcing or defending one's own IPRs. Some industries are challenging this model of IPRs because of the very high costs involved.

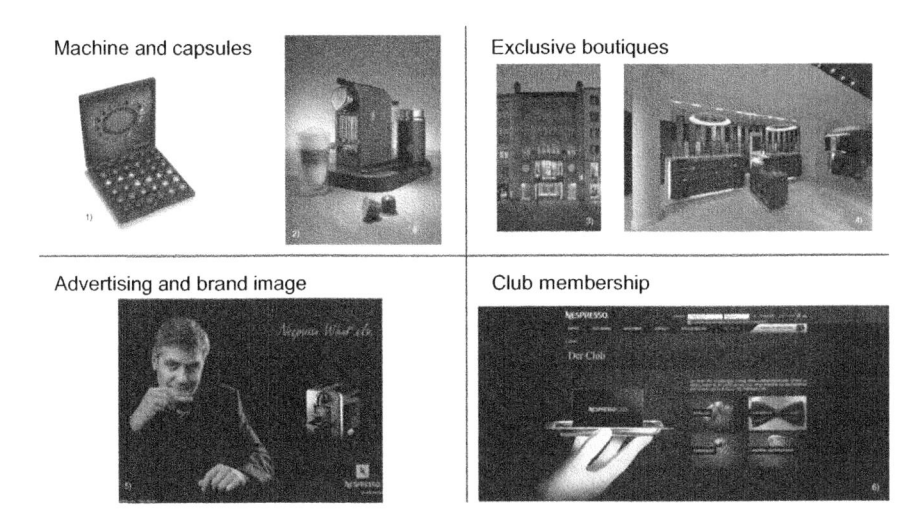

Machine and capsules	Exclusive boutiques
Advertising and brand image	Club membership

Fig. 1.1 Nespresso protection through branding (Brem et al. 2016) (Used with kind permission by Emerald Publishing Limited. All rights reserved)

Innovations in Business Models

In the last 15 years, increasingly systematic ways of creating new business model innovations meant to achieve more sustainable, profitable competitive advantages than could be reached through product, technology or process innovations alone have been discovered (e.g., Gassmann et al. 2020; Winterhalter et al. 2017). *Skype* became the world's largest telecommunications provider without needing its own network infrastructure. *Amazon* is the largest bookseller even without running a single physical bookstore. *Alibaba*, *TenCent*, and *WeChat* are Chinese business model innovators, which have not just imitated Silicon Valley companies, but radically developed their own business models. What does this mean for IPRs? Business models as such used to be patentable only in the USA (if "concrete" and "useful"), but the products and technologies relevant to the business model can be protected very well (e.g., *Nespresso's* capsule principle; see Fig. 1.1).

Shorter Innovation Cycles and Faster Diffusion

The diffusion of innovation has accelerated as a result of globalized competition, shorter innovation cycles, and the constant tightening of cost constraints. The innovation cycle of a mechanical typewriter, for example, was 25 years, while today that of a microprocessor-controlled typewriter is 5 years. In the electronics industry, it now takes a few months for Chinese competitors, for example, to launch a product innovation on the market as a low-cost imitation. In the toy industry, this time span can be brought down to just a few weeks. Innovation and technology leadership, despite rising R&D costs, have become the decisive competitive factor.

This means that protecting innovation is becoming increasingly important for technology-intensive companies to amortize investments in product development, as lead time is no longer an entry threshold. The risks of a delayed market launch are increasing.

The main challenges for the management of innovation in companies can be summarized in terms of complexity, dynamics, and costs. After the intensive restructuring waves of recent years, forward-looking companies are now trying to get a head start through innovation. In order to escape fierce cost competition, their aim is to differentiate themselves to their customer. New products in the electrical, telecommunications, and software industries are usually associated with performance increases, and cost reductions at the same time. An essential part of innovation management is therefore to make continued product differentiation as sustainable as possible and to constantly renew it.

1.2 Capturing Value by Protecting Innovation

Innovations are responsible for half of the economic growth in highly industrialized countries and are therefore of great economic importance. On the one hand, innovative companies generate on average more profit than imitators, and then, generics, one example, currently shows the highest annual growth rates, 10%, in the pharmaceutical industry (Gassmann et al. 2018). An important aspect of innovating is therefore not just creating an innovation, but also how its value is captured (Bader and Stummeyer 2019). In order to be able to afford high investments in the future, monopoly profits achieved must be maintained in the form of temporary competitive advantages. Suitable, situation-appropriate protection strategies for one's own innovation are therefore necessary. *De facto* protection strategies are increasingly being supplemented by *legal* ones (see Fig. 1.2).

There has been an evolution in research, starting with Teece (1986) who is considered to be one of the first to describe the mechanisms of value capture in the context of technological innovation. Other researchers have also included product and process innovation (Chesbrough and Rosenbloom 2002) and have discussed the protection of intellectual property (IP) in the economic context (Cohen et al. 2000; Dosi et al. 2006). For example, the knowledge-intensive business service firms protect their inventions through a joint use of informal and formal protection strategies (Amara et al. 2008; Bader 2008). In general, *formal* (i.e., legal) and *informal* (i.e., de facto) protection mechanism have to complement each another and are both fundamental for capturing value from innovation (Arora and Ceccagnoli 2006; Hall and Ziedonis 2001; McGahan and Silverman 2006; Pisano 2006; Rivette and Kline 2000).

Also, with regard to business models, value capturing has been discovered as being key to the sustainable profitability of companies (Chesbrough 2007; Teece 2010; Zott et al. 2011). There are two main reasons for this (Lepak et al. 2007): First, value creation is no longer limited just to a company and the industry boundaries (Amit and Zott 2001), and it has become important for the individual market player

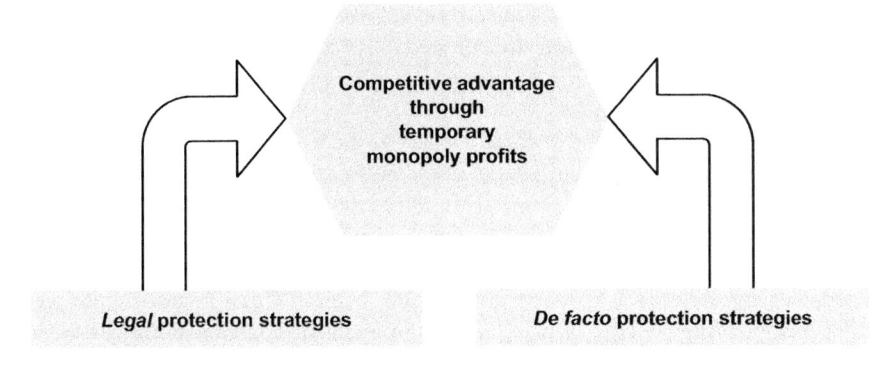

1.2 Capturing Value by Protecting Innovation

Competitive advantage through temporary monopoly profits

Legal protection strategies
- Patents
- Utility models
- Designs
- Trademarks
- Plant breeders' rights
- Copyrights
- Trade secrets

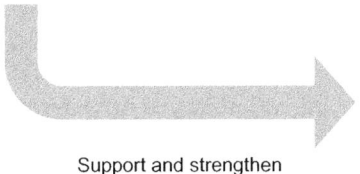

Support and strengthen *de facto* protection strategies

De facto protection strategies
- Shorter time-to-market strategies in fast-pace industries, e.g. *Zara*
- Secret processes / ingredients, e.g. *Coca-Cola*
- Strong business model, e.g. *Nespresso* (lock-in business model)
- High customer loyalty, e.g. via direct sales, e.g. *Hilti, Salesforce*
- Quasi-monopolistic market domination, e.g. *Microsoft, Google*
- Economies of scale, e.g. *Haier*
- Network effects, e.g. *Facebook, LinkedIn*
- Strong branding, e.g. *Apple*
- Stickiness in the ecosystem, e.g. *Amazon*

Fig. 1.2 *Legal* (formal) and *De facto* (informal) protection strategies complement one another (authors' own figure)

to understand where value creation takes place (Gassmann et al. 2020). Second, the question has arisen on how to protect the created value. Profiting from innovation framework (Chesbrough et al. 2006; Teece 2006) Desyllas and Sako (2013) indicates that formal IP right protection methods and strategies should be complementary. While formal IP strategies are mainly effective for short-term purposes, specific complementary assets are needed to capture long-term value. For example, the fast-moving consumer goods giant *Nestlé* applied, for its coffee capsule business *Nespresso*, formal IP protection methods in the short term to build up a premium position and today is mainly relying on informal IP protection strategies long term (Brem et al. 2016).

Which protection strategy to choose also depends on factors such as the type of innovation, the size and market share of the firm, and the firm's R&D activities. In that context, Gallié and Legros (2012) evaluated seven forms of formal and informal protection strategies: patents, design rights, trademarks and copyrights as *formal* protection strategies and trade secrets, and then the complexity of products and the manufacturing process, and lead-time advantage—as an *informal* protection mechanism. They define the protection strategies as follows:

Formal Protection Strategies

1. *Patents:* an inventor, who registers a patent, receives the right to prohibit the imitation or use (apart from his/her own use or selling it) of her invention by others for a limited period of time. This allows the inventor to realize monopolistic prices when exploiting the innovation. However, when registering a patent, the inventor must disclose the information pertaining to the innovation and hence enables competitors to "invent around" the patent. This drawback may well overshadow the benefits of being able to implement monopolistic prices for an innovation.
2. *Design rights:* design rights protect the visual appearance of objects such as the shape, the colors, and the materials. To register a design, two requirements must be met. First, it has to be new, which means that no identical design was published before the registration. Second, it has to be unique, which means that the overall appearance must differ from other designs.
3. *Trademarks:* a trademark is a sign, a symbol, a design, or expression that distinguishes the products or services of a company from those of other companies. Although a trademark is not limited in time, the registering company needs to renew it periodically.
4. *Copyrights:* a firm that registers copyright receives exclusive rights for original work and hence obtains the power to determine who may financially benefit from it.

Informal Protection Strategies

1. *Trade secrets:* trade secrets cover non-public information and enable firms to obtain a competitive advantage over companies that do not own the information. This includes formulas, methods, techniques, processes, and instruments. Firms have to take action to keep secret regarding the information.
2. *The complexity of products and manufacturing processes:* the complexity of products and manufacturing processes constitutes an instrument to capture value from innovation. If a product or service consists of complex processes, technologies or components that are necessary to build and distribute it, this complexity grants the firm a competitive advantage, since the offerings are made more difficult to imitate.
3. *Lead-time advantage:* in this context, the lead-time advantage is established if firms innovate faster than their competitors. This leads to competitive advantages that enable them to capture value from their innovation.

The complementary use of intellectual property rights is also increasingly affecting small and medium-sized enterprises (SMEs). Seventy percent of all patent applicants at the European Patent Office hold only 1 patent. In the furniture supply industry, which is dominated by SMEs, a new competitive component has established itself: since the beginning of the 1990s, patents and utility models have seen an increase in being applied for. The industry is under high price and performance pressure. Design alone is no longer enough to survive in the longer run, and certainly not anymore if in the form of prototypes manufactured shortly before the trade fair. Today, the timely identification of trends, and the development of corresponding technical solutions, each play an important role in the furniture and furniture supply industry. This raises the problem of how to prevent complex and sales-relevant technical functionalities from being taken over directly by the competition.

Looking beyond just creating high-performance R&D organization, protecting the outcomes of those innovation processes legally with intellectual property has thus become a central part of innovation management. Only those firms, which can effectively protect their innovations from competitors can retain their competitive advantage; and the costs of acquiring and managing those rights are minimal compared to the opportunity cost of not maintaining them.

Patents and the Economy

According to Joseph Schumpeter, the father of modern innovation economics, the purpose of patents for innovative companies is the attainment of temporary monopoly power, through which incentives for inventions and technical development are created. These in turn lead to economic growth and the wealth of an economy (Schumpeter 1934). From a macroeconomic perspective, patents foster innovation (Landes and Posner 2003). In a study, the OECD finds that the effects of patents on the innovativeness and on the economic capacity of companies are not that clear and has therefore to be viewed in a more nuanced way (OECD 2004).

Studies find that biotechnology, pharmaceuticals, as well as the chemical industry benefit the most in that patent protection plays a strong role in securing their comparative advantage. To a certain extent, this is also the case for the computer and machinery industries. Companies from other industries often primarily use other protection mechanisms, as for example the use of secrecy, market leadership, technical complexity, and control over commentary advantages (Cohen et al. 2000). Protection strategies can also be based on credibility as it is often the case in *consumer electronics*, or use stronger customer ties by controlling distribution channels, like *Hilti* does with direct distribution.

However, patent protection can also hinder innovation by making access to important knowledge more difficult. This is particularly the case with emergent technologies, if basic patents exist on which further developments are dependent, and the patent holders refuse licenses on reasonable terms. This type of a situation exists partly in genetic engineering (Bar-Shalom and Cook-Deegan 2002; OECD 2003) and also in the software sector (Jaffe and Lerner 2004).

However, patents have a *positive effect on competition* and company start-ups by giving small and young companies the opportunity to penetrate existing markets through using their own patents, to assert themselves against larger companies, and to persuade financial investors (Gans et al. 2002). *Gore-Tex*™ is so successful because their breathable textile products have been protected by patents and

Table 1.1 Economic advantages and disadvantages of the patent system

Effect	Advantages	Disadvantages
Innovation	Incentive for R&D activity through a reward	Higher transaction costs for subsequent innovations
Competition	Reduction of barriers to entry especially for small and young firms	Temporary monopolies, in networks often with a long-term effect Danger of cartel formation
Diffusion of knowledge	Revealing of technical information	Insecurity whether and which published knowledge is available for reasonable conditions

Source: Based on Hall (2003)

trademarks. The patent portfolio has traditionally been one of *Gore's* strongest competitive factors. In the biotechnology sector, patents represent the largest, secured share of the company value for most start-ups.

A *positive effect on the dissemination of knowledge* through patents can be seen in the intensive use of patent documents to obtain technical information: 80% of the technical knowledge published worldwide is only published in patent specifications. By far the largest part of this knowledge is no longer covered by patent protection, since the patents have already been dropped or have already expired. On the other hand, a common reason for companies to not apply for a patent is its subsequent publication (Sheehan et al. 2003).

Table 1.1 summarizes the advantages and disadvantages of the patent system with regard to innovation competition, and the use of knowledge.

Patents Leverage Competitive Advantage

Numerous studies have found a positive influence of patent protection on the company's success (see Fig. 1.3). This has shown that patent protection and thus patent management are of great importance for the company's success, with the quality of patents and patent portfolios in particular being decisive for success (Gassmann and Bader 2017).

Thus, a company's patents and frequently cited patents have a positive influence on its market value (Deng et al. 1999). Patents with a broad technological patent claim also increase company valuation (Lerner 1994). Companies with systematic patenting behavior have proven more successful than companies with unsystematic patenting behavior (Ernst 1996), with significant sales increases based on this showing after a delay of 2–3 years (Ernst 2001). The probability of commercialization in the form of business start-ups or licensing agreements increases with the quality of the underlying patents. The quality can be determined on the basis of the breadth of claims and the citation frequency (Shane 2001).

Amongst patents, the following trends are discernible:

- The number of patents continues to increase.

1.2 Capturing Value by Protecting Innovation

Strategic patent management

Creation of competitive advantages through targeted patent management

- Strategy
- Processes
- Methods
- Structure
- Culture

Capture of competitive advantages by the company

- Industry specifics
- Resources
- Product specifics
- Technological maturity
- Country specifics

Patent portfolio
1. Strategic position
2. Quality
3. Quantity

Commercial success

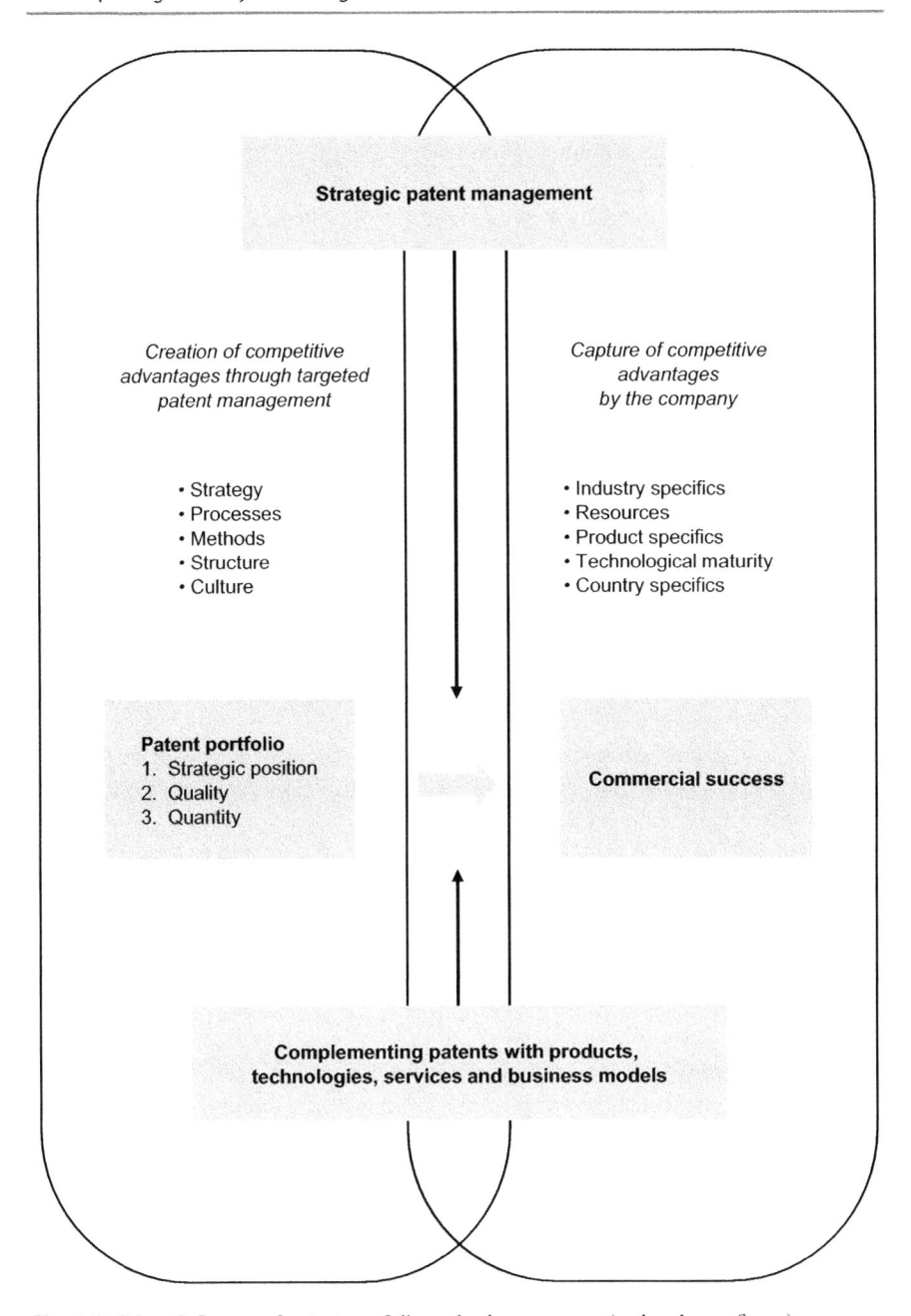

Complementing patents with products, technologies, services and business models

Fig. 1.3 Direct influence of patent portfolio on business success (authors' own figure)

- The quality of patents is likely decreasing over time (Squicciarini et al. 2013), due to patent office backlogs under ever larger patent documents, and a relative erosion of fees in real terms (Thompson 2017).
- Individual patents are attaining astronomical values, e.g., *RIM* for *BlackBerry* and *NTP* at USD 612.5 m.
- Individual regions, like China, still exhibit specific characteristics (Zeschky et al. 2014).
- Patents are becoming increasingly like commodities through pricing.

The goal of patent management is to contribute to the company's success by optimizing not only the simple number of patents but also their quality and effectiveness—and to attain the strongest possible patent position.

There are many ways by which to influence the success of a company with patents. Patents can have the following effects on companies:

- *Securing market revenues for the invention*: In practice, patent applications are often derived from inventions that arise as a "by-product" from in-house development. In this context, the desired legal protection through patents often concentrates primarily on securing market revenues: its own products are protected against counterfeiting, as in the example of Aventis, whose patents are often valid in more than a hundred countries. The fields of activity of competitors then play a secondary role in the invention generation phase. Nevertheless, companies are generally interested in achieving the broadest possible scope of protection for inventions in order to make it more difficult for competitors to circumvent them.
- *Access trade goods to technologies*: A company can also gain access to technology patent pools by owning patents that are relevant to them. This is playing an increasingly important role in cross-licensing negotiations and technical standardization procedures. In the late 1980s, Siemens cleverly used its own patent portfolio to make the leap ahead at a relatively late stage to the already established GSM standard, which was protected by numerous patents.
- *Comparative competitive advantages by blocking competitive technology*: From a policy perspective economically questionable, but often sensible from a business perspective, intellectual property rights filed with the intent purely to block others. The Rheintal-based company *Leica Geosystems*, today part of the *Hexagon Group*, is active in the field of geomatics in about 25 fields of technology (e.g., laser distance measurement, GPS surveying, and microsystems). The international competitive environment is also active on a similar scale. Leica Geosystems must, therefore, monitor and analyze more and more carefully so that its own products are not blocked by the intellectual property rights of competitors having perhaps only a very small market share, thus hindering its own further technological development.
- *Direct revenue from external technology commercialization*: In this context, own research shows that the thrust of legal protection strategies is directed not only at protecting intellectual property against counterfeiting but also at generating

licensing revenue through external marketing. *Schindler* has applied for over 20 patents during its development of an aramid rope for elevators. The total pre-development project costs of several million Swiss francs have already been refinanced through the granting of licenses and the sale of patents in non-elevator areas. Today, one in two companies already markets intellectual property rights externally. Pioneer *IBM* generates over $1 billion in annual licensing revenue.
- *Image enhancement and marketing of innovation*: Patents are often also used for marketing purposes. This is especially the case in the Swiss watch industry, where technology and marketing represent the core of the product appeal. In the mechanical engineering industry, for example, patents are also used to emphasize the innovativeness of products or that of the company. The textile fiber manufacturer *Gore* pursues a consistent brand and patent policy in order to retain customers.

Strategic Management of Patents

The generation, evaluation, and commercial exploitation of patents are part of strategic technology and innovation management. In recent years there has been a strong, so far unbroken trend toward open innovation processes and external technology commercialization. Open innovation has meanwhile developed into an established business model, which is actively used not only by multinational corporations but also by SMEs (Gassmann et al. 2020).

Generation
The generation of a company's own patent portfolio can take place internally through its own patent applications. In addition, a company can also obtain external industrial property rights or the corresponding rights through purchase or in-licensing. Joint ventures and cooperation in which internal and external generation merge are a special case.

Valuation
An essential part of patent management is the evaluation of patents and patent portfolios. Already in the generation phase, an evaluation provides the basis for necessary decision-making. The question is whether a patent should be filed for an invention, or whether the renewal fees for an existing patent should continue to be paid, or whether the license should be priced for an external patent portfolio. Due to their information function, evaluation methods can also be used for the early detection of technology in order to pursue competitive activities.

Exploitation
The company's own patent portfolio can be exploited internally by directly supporting the company's primary business, i.e., products, technologies, and processes. On the other hand, external exploitation aims at generating value through second parties' capacities rather through an own business model, since an additional

financial value creation arises. These include the sale and out-licensing of intellectual property; in the USA, tax benefits can even be claimed (donation) by donating patents and other property rights to nonprofit organizations such as universities, another example would be *IBM's* donations to the open-source community. In addition, patents are often used by companies as trading goods to "buy" their way into comparable or other technologies. When designing technology standards, it is often even necessary for companies to contribute their own relevant intellectual property (IP), such as trademarks or patents, in order to be able to participate in the standard without license payments.

Creation of Competitive Advantages

With the help of patent management, competitive advantages are aimed to be attained by optimizing the patent portfolio. The way in which companies can systematize and implement patent management can be analyzed using five categories, namely: strategy, processes, methods, structure, and culture.

Strategy
Does a company's management and do its employees use intellectual property as protection, or, to gain access to new business domains? Are actual property rights strategies systematically combined with patent and trademark protection? Are alternative ways of securing freedom to operate being examined under cost–benefit considerations? Are patents actively commercialized externally? Is there an intellectual property strategy that is closely linked to the business and innovation strategy?

Processes
Does a company rely on only a few singletons or is it able to use its full network for patent management? Does a systematic idea and knowledge management take place, which is joined with the patent management? Are there clear milestones for drafting invention announcements? Do inventors and engineers systematically coordinate with patent attorneys? What other interfaces exist, for example to the marketing department, and are these kept up?

Methods
Are systematic methods used to generate patents? According to which evaluation criteria are patents selected? How is the value of patents determined? Which software is used to manage patents? Which portfolio technology is used to evaluate patents?

Structure
Are patent applications handled by a separate patent department or outsourced to external patent attorneys? Where is the patent department organizationally located? Is the organization of the patent management system structured top-down or bottom-up? Does the broad organization have access to relevant information regarding patents? Is the creative potential used in the company?

Culture
How are routine processes and change processes handled? What degree of willingness to share knowledge early and to file strategic patents is there? What is the interaction between the inventor and the patent department? How much does the company value intellectual property?

> **Competitive Advantages**
> Companies can gain enormous competitive advantages through active patent management, which addresses the five categories already mentioned: strategy, processes, methods, structure, and culture.

Capture of Competitive Advantages

The realization and utilization of competitive advantages are subject to numerous business conditions specific to the respective companies. In this context, the following characteristics of patent management must be taken into account.

Industry Specifics
In which industry does the company operate? How fast is the rate of change in the industry in question? Is temporary monopolization through intellectual property rights feasible or is there a high degree of standardization? How mature is the industry? What are the barriers to entry in this industry? What is the competitive structure of this industry (duopolistic, oligopolistic, polypolistic) and what are the power and market share ratios?

Resources
Is the company a global corporation or a small or medium-sized company with a strong niche focus? What resources are available within the company? What is the degree of complexity? Can a patent also be defended in a dispute if the legal costs, as in the USA, have to be borne by the patent holder?

Product Specifics
The type of products affected plays an important role, especially the question in which stages of the value chain the company is active. Is the product highly diversifiable? Which technological alternatives exist? How attractive is the product at the moment (fashion, trend products)?

Technological Maturity
Depending on the maturity of a technology, a product, or a service, the so-called first-mover or second-mover advantages are decisive when it comes to taking advantage of emerging trends. How many basic technologies are already protected

by patent rights held by competitors? Does the company have technological core competencies in the potential area?

Country Specifics
The scope within which the company and its competitors operate or intend to operate is crucial for the necessary preventive and relevant measures to be taken. Is there a market, and if yes, is it perhaps a key market? Do the competitors have production capacities in the respective country? How strong is the enforcement of patent law, for example in China?

Aligning with Products, Technologies, Services, and Business Models

Without aligning the intellectual property generated to real products, technologies, services, and business models that create direct value for a company, the best patent portfolio is a toothless tiger. In other words, the competitive advantages created by patent management must also be used by the company.

This is only possible if the patent strategy is consistently aligned with the corporate strategy and actively supports it. In innovative companies, intellectual property must be consistently integrated into R&D and marketing strategies. *Gore* demonstrates this particularly well, as IP is the company's core value driver. A portfolio of lucky hits may be successful in individual cases; however, this is usually cost-intensive and less effective. The patent strategy must be aligned with the strategic directions and existing core competencies of the company. Especially R&D-intensive companies typically achieve major competitive advantages via patents.

1.3 Types of Intellectual Property Rights

A general overview of various types of intellectual protection rights (IPRs) is given in Table 1.2, which will be elucidated further.

Patents

> **What Is a Patent?**
> A patent grants its owner the right to prevent others from:
>
> - Commercially producing, using, offering, storing, importing, or selling the invention.
> - For a specific jurisdiction.
> - For a limited period.

1.3 Types of Intellectual Property Rights

Table 1.2 Overview of the main types of intellectual property rights

IPR	Subject	Application	Examination	Max duration
Patent	Technical invention	Yes	Yes	20
Supplementary Protection Certificate	Pharmaceuticals or regulated chemicals	Yes	No	5/5.5 years
Utility Model	Technical invention (no processes)	Yes	No	10 years
Design Patent	Visual arrangements, smells	Yes	No	25 years
Topography	Semiconductor circuits	Yes	No	10 years
Plant Breeders'/ Plant Variety Right	Plant varieties	Yes	Yes	25/30 years
Trademark	Brand, acoustic sign, color, scent, 3D-shape	Yes	Yes	Extendable every 10 years
	Business name	No		
	Origin	No		
Geographic Designation of Origin	Local goods, foods, and products	No	No	Indefinite (typically legislated)
Trade Dress	Packaging	No	No	During life of product
Copyright	Software / Writing, architecture, art, music	No	No	50 years / 70 years after death of author
Trade Secret	Proprietary processes and information	No	No	Indefinite

Source: Table compiled by authors

In Europe, an invention in the legal sense solves a technical problem with technology. However, a granted patent does not necessarily confer on its owner the right of unlimited use for the invention. For example, other industrial property rights or other regulations may prevent the use of the invention by the inventor or the patent holder. Patents are therefore also referred to as exclusionary rights or prohibitive rights. The other types of industrial property rights also have this characteristic.

The European Patent Office (EPO), for example, grants patents for inventions which (EPC, Art. 52):

- Are new.
- Are based on an inventive step.
- Are commercially applicable.

The criteria for novelty and for what is inventive are "absolute" and apply worldwide, i.e., they are independent of the territorial origin of the knowledge available at the time of the priority date, the so-called state of the art. The priority date is usually the date of the first filing of the invention application at a patent office. The USA is still an exception since the principle of the invention date (first-to-invent) used to apply there, rather than the first-to-file principle. Under certain circumstances, in case of doubt, this can be used to substantiate the priority date.

> **Prior Art**
> Anything published prior to the filing date in written or oral form, through overt usage, or otherwise made known. There are no restrictions with regard to object, language, space, or time.

During the patent application procedure, the patent applicant must determine for which countries he needs patent protection. The decision on the subsequent application must be made within 1 year of the priority date. Since there are various official and translation fees for each country/region named, the selection of countries or regions is typically based on the expected economic benefit that patent protection can potentially achieve in that country. The duration of patents is controlled by the patent applicant through the payment of annual fees, which are usually collected by the patent offices on an annual basis (not in the USA). In most countries, the maximum term of a patent is 20 years after the filing date. In the USA, patents filed after June 8, 1995 also have a term of 20 years.

If patent protection is intended in several countries, patent application procedures can be bundled internationally via the Patent Cooperation Treaty (PCT), and grant procedures for numerous European states via the European Patent Convention (EPC).

> **Patents Are Exclusionary Rights**
> Patents are not permissive rights—unfortunately a still widespread misconception, which often leads to erroneous investments in the millions. Patents are exclusionary rights that prohibit the imitation of the protected invention by third parties.
>
> When it comes to the question of what is ultimately accessible to patent protection—products, systems, processes, procedures, software, or even business models—regional legal areas play a major role.

Supplementary Protection Certificates for Pharmaceuticals (SPCs)

The marketing of medicinal products, and of some chemicals, can only take place after relatively lengthy approval procedures, which severely restrict the effective patent term, have been completed. After the statutory term of the basic patent has expired, the supplementary protection certificate provides the possibility of extending the effectiveness of patent protection by a maximum of 5 years with a maximum remaining term of 14 years after approval (EC Regulation No. 1768/92; 35 U.S.C. §§ 155, 156).

Utility Models

Utility models or innovation patents are also sometimes called *petty patents* because they have a shorter duration, and also cover a more limited range of inventions. The exact legal definition of the utility model varies by jurisdiction more than by patents. In Germany, the *"Gebrauchsmuster"* are technical inventions based on an inventive step and its industrial application, and not on processes. The 8-year Australian innovation patent requires an "innovative step" rather than an "inventive step." Utility models, typically have a 10-year term, like in Austria, and can nevertheless serve as priority applications in order to file subsequent patent applications in other countries.

However, compared to patent protection, there are lower requirements for the required inventive step of a utility model. Utility model applications can, e.g., be filed in Austria, Australia, Brazil, China, the Czech Republic, Denmark, Finland, France, Germany, Hungary, Italy, Japan, Mexico, Poland, Russia, Spain, and South Korea. Not every jurisdiction offers a utility model: Switzerland and the USA do not have a national utility model, and Australia is rethinking whether to convert their "innovation patent."

Design Patents

Two- or three-dimensional manifestations of a product or parts thereof may be protected as designs (Sec. 1 (1) GeschmMG). In the fashion industry, for example, fabric samples are often protected, while in the consumer goods industry packaging, such as beverage bottle shapes, is often protected. A protectable design must be new, and it must exhibit a sufficient degree of peculiarity. The maximum term of protection is 25 years, starting from the filing date.

Legal Dispute About Design: Apple versus Samsung
In 2012, there were numerous legal disputes between the technology groups *Apple* and *Samsung* over the alleged infringement of protected designs.

The iPad manufacturer *Apple*, for example, sued Samsung, a competitor, before the Düsseldorf Regional Court with an application for an injunction for infringement of a registered European Community design. According to *Apple*, *Samsung* infringed *Apple*'s registered Community design No. 000.181.607–0001 with its tablet "Galaxy Tablet 10.1." The Düsseldorf court ruled in favor of *Apple* on the ground that the design of the Galaxy Tablet gives the same overall impression even to informed users and is therefore worthy of protection. *Samsung* filed an appeal, but the appeal was rejected because the Higher Regional Court found that *Samsung*'s tablet was an imitation of the iPad (see Fig. 1.4).

In response, *Samsung* published a successor model which, with a different design, differed from its predecessor model and thus also from the iPad. *Apple* reacted with a renewed application for an injunction and again claimed infringement of its Community design. The Düsseldorf court rejected this claim on the grounds that the design of the successor model left the user with a different overall impression and was therefore outside the scope of protection (Bartenbach et al. 2013).

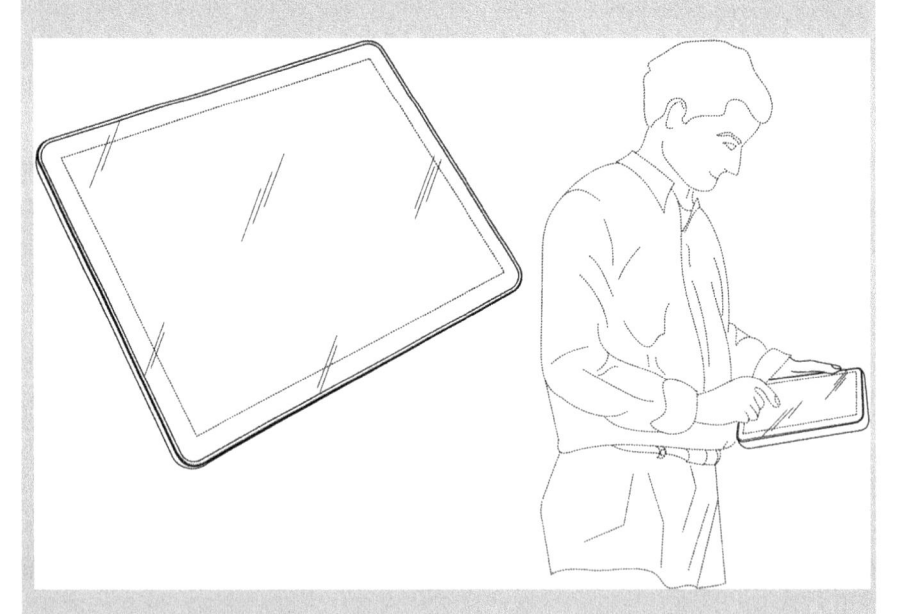

Fig. 1.4 Excerpt from Apple US-Design Patent US D504,889 S

In addition to the national procedure, there is also the possibility of depositing designs internationally in the more than 50 member countries of the Hague Agreement, including Germany and Switzerland, via the *Hague Model Convention (HMA)*.

If design protection is to be obtained exclusively in EU countries such as Germany or Austria, an EU Community design, valid for the entire Community territory, can also be registered. In contrast to German law, it is irrelevant whether the design has an aesthetic content or is functional.

Design protection is also possible in the USA and Japan. In both countries, a cost- and time-intensive, computer-aided novelty examination is carried out, whereby in principle no protection against infringers exists until a grant has been given. In the USA, however, the enforcement of designs has generally proved to be difficult in practice, as more than 70% of designs have so far been declared invalid in infringement proceedings.

Topography

Topographies are three-dimensional structures of microelectronic semiconductor products and are protectable similarly to inventions. However, a topography can only be protected if it has a "peculiarity." Similar to utility models, topography registration does not involve any substantive examination by the patent office. Although numerous topographies have been registered to date, this type of property right has not yet had any significant effect in the practice of law enforcement.

Plant Breeders' Rights (PBRs)/Plant Variety Rights (PVRs)

Plant variety protection rights are exclusionary rights comparable to patent protection, with the aim of protecting intellectual property rights in new plant varieties in order to aid progress in breeding in agriculture and horticulture. Breeders or discoverers of new plant varieties can apply for protection for varieties of the entire plant kingdom at the respective national plant variety protection offices. A plant variety is in principle eligible for protection if it is distinct, homogeneous, stable, and new, and if it is also designated by a registrable variety denomination. Plant variety protection has the effect that only the owner of the plant variety protection or his legal successor is entitled to market, produce or import propagating material (plants and parts of plants, including seeds) of a protected variety for commercial purposes.

Trademarks and Similar Rights

A trademark is a registered right which is suitable for distinguishing the products or services of one entity from those of other entities, and which fulfills the purpose of indicating origin. Trademarks can be registered at the national, regional (e.g.,

EUIPO), or international level (WIPO). The most relevant criterion in practice is the distinctiveness from other trademarks, and it should also not be descriptive; the word "Apple" can be trademarked for computers, but not for a type of apple. The term of protection can then be extended as often as desired. Trademarks can be protected as:

- Words, e.g., Persil *(Henkel)*.
- Letter combinations, e.g., *ABB*.
- Number combinations, e.g., 501 *(Levis)*.
- Pictorial representations and logos, e.g., the *Mercedes* star *(Daimler)*.
- Three-dimensional shapes, e.g., *Coca-Cola* bottle.
- Slogans, e.g., "Vorsprung durch Technik" *(AUDI)*.
- Combinations of these elements as word/picture marks, e.g., *Continental*.
- Contourless colors and color combinations as visually perceptible signs, e.g., magenta/gray of *Deutsche Telekom*.
- Acoustic signs, e.g., *twentieth century Fox* melody.
- Position mark, e.g., red stripe in *Lloyds* men's shoe heel.

In addition to classic trademarks, there are a number of other similar rights meant for protecting the symbols of organizations, groups, or for enabling special protection (discussed below).

> **Trademarks: Some Special Cases**
> **Established Trademarks**
> Descriptive signs can obtain protection if they become generally known on the market for goods or services of a certain company, if they have "prevailed" in technical jargon, in Switzerland, e.g., *Valser* for mineral water.
> **Public Domains**
> Due to their presence over many years, trademarks can mutate into designations for entire product categories, make their way into the general vocabulary, and lose their defensibility—no American today any longer says "paper facial tissue," the expected term is "*Kleenex*"; in Great Britain people say "*to hoover*" when they mean "to vacuum." The legal test for this entry into the public domain is whether general reference works have the term (MSchG 231.11 Art. 16).
> **Famous Brands**
> Brands like *Nestlé* or *Nike* enjoy, as an example, in case there is a risk of exploitation by third parties, protection as well for goods and services for which they were not even registered.
> **Internet Domain Names**
> The domain and hosting provider *Swizzonic* (formerly *switchplus*) is responsible for the allocation of domain names with the country codes CH

(continued)

and LI and their registration. Domain names can also be registered as trademarks in accordance with the usual principles.
  Declaration of Origin
  Declarations of Origin distinguish certain goods or services from each other, but not with regard to the manufacturer of the goods, instead rather with reference to a particular geographical origin. A distinction is made between direct indications of source, e.g., *Swiss chocolate*, indirect indications of source, e.g., *William Tell chocolate*, and qualified geographical indications, e.g., *Geneva* for watches.
  Protected Appellations of Origin (AOP) / Protected Geographical Indications (IGP)
  Protected appellations of origin, e.g., *Tête de Moine AOP*, and protected geographical indications, e.g., *St. Gallen Kalbsbratwurst IGP*, are registered in Switzerland in the Register of Agriculture. They can only be registered as a trademark, or as a trademark component under certain conditions.
  Source: IPI (2020)

Domain Names

The Domain Name System (DNS) is coordinated by the Internet Assigned Numbers Authority (IANA—www.iana.org/) and the Internet Corporation for Assigned Names and Numbers (ICANN—www.icann.org/). Allocation and registrations take place via the respective national, central registries for top-level domain names, as is exemplified below:

- Germany (.de): www.denic.de
- Austria (.at): www.nic.at
- Switzerland (.ch): www.switchplus.ch
- Generic top-level domains (e.g., .com, .net): www.verisign.com

Trade Dress

Trade dress is a narrower intellectual property right than trademarks in that it typically applies to packaging, boxes, and the visual appearance. The visual elements combine in such a way as to evoke a feeling of knowing the source in the consumer's perception.

Copyrights

The only condition is that the intellectual property has to be detectable by the senses. Direct embodiment or publication is not required. Software as such is also protected by copyright. However, the protection only applies to the software as such, not to the ideas.

> **Copyright Law**
>
> The legal prerequisite of copyright law is that a personal creative achievement is present. No official procedures or other formal requirements are typically required for the creation and enforcement of protection.[1] Works in the copyright sense are creations that have a unique character. These include in particular:
>
> - Literary works of any kind, e.g., novels, scientific treatises, newspaper articles, advertising brochures.
> - Works of music and other acoustic works.
> - Works of fine art, e.g., painting, sculpture, graphics as well as applied art, e.g., objects with a utility value, whereby the deposit as a design patent does not exclude copyright protection.
> - Source code or programming text.
>
> Works of personal intellectual creation may be marked with a copyright notice. The © label should then be used in conjunction with the name of the copyright holder and the year of the first publication.

Trade Secrets

Trade Secrets cover any confidential business information which provides an enterprise with a competitive edge. Trade secrets encompass manufacturing or industrial secrets and commercial secrets. The unauthorized use of such information by persons other than the holder is regarded as an unfair practice and a violation of the trade secret. Depending on the legal system, the protection of trade secrets forms part of the general concept of protection against unfair competition or is based on specific provisions or case law on the protection of confidential information. The

---

[1] In addition, a voluntary registration of the protected work with the United States Copyright Office—The Library of Congress—makes sense. This makes the work public on the one hand and the Office issues a certificate of registration on the other. In the context of the judicial enforcement of copyrights, registration is even a prerequisite for being able to assert a flat-rate claim for damages provided for by law and for being able to demand reimbursement of lawyer's fees in the event of success.

subject matter of trade secrets is usually defined in broad terms and includes sales methods, distribution methods, consumer profiles, advertising strategies, lists of suppliers and clients, and manufacturing processes. While a final determination of which information it is that specifically constitutes a trade secret will depend on the circumstances of each individual case, practices that are clearly unfair in respect of secret information include industrial or commercial espionage, breach of contract, and breach of confidence (WIPO 2020).

References

Amara, N., Landry, R., & Traoré, N. (2008). Managing the protection of innovations in knowledge intensive business services. *Research Policy, 37*(9), 1530–1547.
Amit, R., & Zott, C. (2001). Value creation in e-business. *Strategic Management Journal, 22*(6/7), 493.
Arora, A., & Ceccagnoli, M. (2006). Patent protection, complementary assets, and firms incentives for technology licensing. *Management Science, 52*(2), 293–308.
Bader, M. A. (2008). Managing intellectual property in the financial services industry sector: Learning from Swiss Re. *Technovation, 28*, 196–207.
Bader, M. A., & Stummeyer, C. (2019). The role of innovation and IP in AI-based business models. In R. Baierl, J. Behrens, & A. Brem (Eds.), *Digital entrepreneurship – Interfaces between digital technologies and entrepreneurship* (pp. 23–56). Heidelberg: Springer.
Bar-Shalom, A., & Cook-Deegan, R. (2002). Patents and innovation in cancer therapeutics: Lessons from CellPro. *The Milbank Quaterly, 80*(4), 637–676.
Bartenbach, K., Jung, I., & Renvert, A. (2013). Apple vs. Samsung – Zu den Grenzen von Geschmacksmusterschutz und ergänzendem wettbewerbsrechtlichen Leistungsschutz. *Mitteilungen der deutschen Patentanwälte, 104*(1), 18–24.
Brem, A., Maier, M., & Wimschneider, C. (2016). Competitive advantage through innovation: the case of Nespresso. *European Journal of Innovation Management, 19*(1), 133–148.
Buckminster Fuller, R. (1982). *Critical path*. New York: St. Martin's Press.
Chesbrough, H. (2007). Business model innovation: It's not just about technology anymore. *Strategy and Leadership, 35*(6), 12–17.
Chesbrough, H., & Rosenbloom, R. S. (2002). The role of the business model in capturing value from innovation: Evidence from Xerox Corporation's technology spin-off companies. *Industrial and Corporate Change, 11*(3), 529–555.
Chesbrough, H., Birkinshaw, J., & Teubal, M. (2006). Introduction to the research policy 20th anniversary special issue of the publication of 'profiting from innovation by David J. Teece'. *Research Policy, 35*(8), 1091–1099.
Cohen, W. M., Nelson, R. R., & Walsh, J. P. (2000). *Protecting their intellectual assets: Appropriability conditions and why US manufacturing firms patent or not*. NBER Working Paper, No. 7552.
Deng, Z., Lev, B., & Narin, F. (1999). Science and technology as predictors of stock performance. *Financial Analysts Journal, 55*(5), 20–32.
Desyllas, P., & Sako, M. (2013). Profiting from business model innovation: Evidence from pay-as-you-drive auto insurance. *Research Policy, 42*(1), 101–116.
Dosi, G., Marengo, L., & Pasquali, C. (2006). How much should society fuel the greed of innovators? On the relations between appropriability, opportunities and rates of innovation. *Research Policy, 35*(8), 1110–1121.
Ehrat, M. (1997). *Kompetenzorientierte, analysegestützte Technologiestrategieerarbeitung*. Dissertation University of St. Gallen (HSG), St. Gallen, No. 1981.

Ernst, H. (1996). *Patentinformationen für die strategische Planung von Forschung und Entwicklung*. Gabler: Wiesbaden.

Ernst, H. (2001). Patent applications and subsequent changes of performance: Evidence from time-series cross-section analyses on the firm level. *Research Policy, 30*, 143–157.

Gallié, E. P., & Legros, D. (2012). French firms' strategies for protecting their intellectual property. *Research Policy, 41*(4), 780–794.

Gans, J., Hsu, D. H., & Stern, S. (2002). When does start-up innovation spur the gale of creative destruction? *RAND Journal of Economics, 33*(4), 571–586.

Gassmann, O., & Bader, M. A. (2017). *Patentmanagement: Innovationen erfolgreich nutzen und schützen* (4th ed.). Berlin: Springer.

Gassmann, O., Frankenberger, K., & Choudury, M. (2020). *The Business Model Navigator*. FT Publishing.

Gassmann, O., Schuhmacher, A., Reepmeyer, G., & von Zedtwitz, M. (2018). *Leading pharmaceutical innovation – How to win the life science race* (3rd ed.). Berlin: Springer.

Hall, B. H. (2003). *Business method patents, innovation and policy*. NBER Working Paper, No. 9717.

Hall, B. H., & Ziedonis, R. H. (2001). The patent paradox revisited: an empirical study of patenting in the US semiconductor industry 1979–1995. *RAND Journal of Economics, 32*(1), 101–128.

IBM. (2006). *The toxic terabyte: How data-dumping threatens business efficiency*. IBM Global Technical Services white paper. Accessed on March 9th, 2020, https://archive.org/stream/TheToxicTerabyte/The%20Toxic%20Terabyte_djvu.txt

IPI. (2020). *Envisioned. Created. Protected. A concise guide to trade marks, patents and co.* (10th ed). Bern: IPI Swiss Federal Institute of Intellectual Property.

Jaffe, A. B., & Lerner, J. (2004). *Innovation and its discontents: How our broken patent system is endangering innovation and progress, and what to do about it*. Princeton, NJ: Princeton University Press.

Landes, W. M., & Posner, R. A. (2003). *The economic structure of intellectual property law*. Cambridge, MA: Belknap Press of Harvard University Press.

Lepak, D. P., Smith, K. G., & Taylor, M. S. (2007). Value creation and value capture: A multilevel perspective. *Academy of Management Review, 32*(1), 180–194.

Lerner, J. (1994). The importance of patent scope: An empirical analysis. *RAND Journal of Economics, 25*(2), 319–332.

McGahan, A. M., & Silverman, B. S. (2006). Profiting from technological innovation by others: The effect of competitor patenting on firm value. *Research Policy, 35*(8), 1222–1242.

OECD. (2003). *Genetic inventions, IPRs and licensing practices: Evidence and policies*. Paris: OECD.

OECD. (2004). *Patents and innovation: Trends and policy challenges*. Paris: OECD.

Pisano, G. (2006). Profiting from innovation and the intellectual property revolution. *Research Policy, 35*(8), 1122–1130.

Rivette, K. G., & Kline, D. (2000). Discovering new value in intellectual property. *Harvard Business Review, 79*(1), 54–66.

Schuhmacher, A., Gassmann, O., McCracken, N., & Hinder, M. (2018). Open innovation and external sources of innovation. An opportunity to fuel the R&D pipeline and enhance decision making? *Journal of Translational Medicine, 119*(16), 1–14.

Schumpeter, J. A. (1934). *Theorie der wirtschaftlichen Entwicklung* (8th ed.). Berlin: Dunker und Humblot.

Shane, S. (2001). Technological opportunities and new firm creation. *Management Science, 47*(2), 205–220.

Sheehan, J., Guellec, D., & Martinez, C. (2003) Business patenting and licensing: Results from the OECD/BIAC survey. In: *Proceedings of the OECD Conference on IPR, Innovation and Economic Performance*, 28–29 August 2003. Paris: OECD.

Squicciarini, M., Dernis, H., & Criscuolo, C. (2013). *Measuring patent quality*. Paris: OECD.

References

Teece, D. J. (1986). Profiting from technological innovation: Implications for integration, collaboration, licensing and public policy. *Research Policy, 15*(6), 285–305.

Teece, D. J. (2006). Reflections on "profiting from innovation". *Research Policy, 35*(8), 1131–1146.

Teece, D. J. (2010). Business models, business strategy and innovation. *Long Range Planning, 43*(2), 172–194.

Thompson, M. (2017). The cost of patent protection: Renewal propensity. *World Patent Information*, Vol. 49.

Winterhalter, S., Zeschky, M., Neumann, L., & Gassmann, O. (2017). Business models for frugal innovation in emerging markets: The case of the medical device and laboratory equipment industry. *Technovation* 66–67.

WIPO. (2020). *What is a trade secret?* Geneva: WIPO. https://www.wipo.int/sme/en/ip_business/trade_secrets/trade_secrets.htm. Accessed on January 8th, 2020.

Zeschky, M., Widenmayer, B., & Gassmann, O. (2014). Organizing for reverse innovation in Western MNCs: The role of frugal product innovation capabilities. *International Journal of Technology Management, 64*(2–4), 255–275.

Zott, C., Amit, R., & Massa, L. (2011). The business model: Recent developments and future research. *Journal of Management, 37*(4), 1019–1042.

Protection Strategies

2.1 Patent Strategies in General

Industrial property rights make it possible to influence, if not control, to a greater extent one's own corporate strategic position, and affect the activities of competitors. The guidelines for patent strategy must be determined by corporate strategy so that the contribution to the whole is thereby ensured. A strategy should explicitly address, in particular, the existing and desired products, technologies, and applications.

> **Strategy**
> A *strategy* defines base and guidelines within which a company operates. It shows the direction and goals of a company and points out possible ways to achieve them.
>
> A *patent strategy* provides answers to questions such as those about which invention areas are patented for which purpose, also: which market and production areas are covered by patent protection, and what means, expenses, and risk-taking appetite are used to defend this protection; and how far this risk propensity of this protection will be carried.

Positioning of the firm happens in relation to:

- Products and technologies
- Markets
- Financial framework

It is often the case in small and medium enterprises (SMEs) that the strategy is made implicit by the running of the company. According to Mintzberg et al. (2005), five ways of exercising strategy can be distinguished:

- Plan: Path/goal description—What is to be achieved and how is the goal to be achieved?
- Chess move: Presentation of the strategy as a game move in competition with and against competitors.
- Patterns: Decision and action patterns typical of a company.
- Position: Market and competitive position of a company in relation to its environment.
- Perspective: Perception and reconstruction of the environment.

Implementing a strategy requires management, which itself requires feedback ("You can't manage what you can't measure"). A patent strategy must not only consider the company as a whole, but also see the individual business areas, and be at the same time production- and product-oriented, setting a financial framework. In doing so, the following questions arise:

- What specifications do I need from other areas of strategy, for example, from the corporate, technology, product, or innovation strategy?
- What minimum requirements or minimum statements are required for intellectual property portfolio management to be carried out?
- What are the target figures for which statements must be made, for example, whether there is a general willingness to license, and to what extent, and also by what means, license revenues should be generated?

The reformulation of a patent strategy can be set in motion by a general strategic business reorientation or an internal restructuring.

> **Preconditions for a Patent Strategy**
> For a well-embedded patent strategy, clear statements on the corporate strategy are a prerequisite. How do we create and capture value for customers? What are our core competencies? What is it that creates a comparative competitive advantage? In which countries are we active, in which of these do we want to be active in the near future, and also: in which countries are our core competitors active? What is the core of the business model of the company?
> The main question here is: "How should the company create and capture value by means of the patent strategy?"

However, external pressure leading to the initiation of a patent strategy is often caused by resource and budget adjustments requiring a realignment and optimization of the existing approach. On the one hand, this raises the question of which technologies and products should be protected while on the other hand asking what this protection should look like. Which characteristics should be protected and for how long a time in which countries? When developing a new product generation, a successful approach lies in defining the desired patent protection of certain technology, and defining also the product characteristics as a concrete goal, and lastly to measure this continuously in accordance with the progress of the project.

The requirement for a successful patent strategy and, in particular, the value of *freedom-of-action* or *freedom-to-operate* as a strategic asset of the company generally becomes very clear when the latter, i.e., freedom-to-operate, is lacking. This is the case, for example, when disputes related to or caused by patents cause a blockade and obstruct current business activities. This can result in a decline in sales or profits (*Siemens*, pacemakers) or a severe impairment of market capitalization or market capitalization (*Adobe vs. Macromedia*).

When initiating a patent strategy, coordination between the Intellectual Property, R&D, and Corporate Development departments is important, whereby consistency and ultimately maintaining consensus are critical success factors. While the patent department should be the process owner for the initiation of the patent strategy, clear support by management is required.

Endress+Hauser, a medium-sized Swiss manufacturer of measurement instruments and automation solutions, has attached particular importance to the invention, and the protection of inventions, through patents since the end of the 1990s, getting there after successfully defending itself against a patent infringement suit filed by an American competitor.

Critical success factors are having sufficient resources, a common understanding of the necessity for a patent strategy, the support of middle management, and having made a sufficient analysis of the current situation. The preferred tools for bringing this about are good communication and visualization, such as, for example, meaningful patent statistics, possibly with the aid of external patent databases. Important stakeholders who should be involved in the initiation phase of a patent strategy are a company's management, inventors, technical experts, and patent attorneys or patent managers.

> **Patent Strategy**
> The initiation of a patent strategy is essential when starting a technology-based venture. In many companies, such a patent strategy is only initiated when its own action of freedom has been blocked by a competitor's patent or when the company has experienced patent infringement.
>
> Important factors for a patent strategy proving successful are:
>
> - Consistency with corporate strategy
> - A clear market view
> - Thinking in terms of competitive advantages
> - Technological competence in-house
> - Patenting expertise in the team
> - Managerial commitment

2.2 Offensive and Defensive Patent Strategies

Depending on their orientation and aggressiveness, patent strategies can be subdivided into offensive and defensive patent ones:

Offensive Patent Strategies

This orientation is based on the strategic planning of intellectual property use within the framework of corporate and business activities, in addition to which patent rights are then proactively and aggressively enforced. This strategy is rounded off by active participation in various interest groups in the legal development of intellectual property legislation.

For years, the American semiconductor memory company *Rambus* has pursued an aggressive marketing strategy for its patent portfolio with licensing requirements for a specific clock and bus process for SDRAM memory chips. For several years, numerous patent infringement cases have been pending in the *USA* and *Europe*, causing irritations within the semiconductor memory industry. *Rambus*, one example, reached a settlement with *Samsung*, which secured for the company a large compensation payment.

As a tactical maneuver, some companies also apply for patents to lure their competitors down a wrong path. These patents involve little effort, and the examination fees are also not paid. The only desired effect of this measure is to deliberately mislead competitors as to the technological direction being taken. However, the value of this maneuver should not be overestimated, especially if used too frequently.

US-based patent aggregating companies having no products of their own, which business leaders often characterize as "patent trolls," are companies characterized by the most aggressive use of patent strategies, since defending patents *is* the business model. These strategies also make sense for the reason that most patent litigations end in a settlement (Krech et al. 2015). Trolling is most practicable where the cost of litigation is enormous, especially in the USA, or where a process of uncovering is part of the legal action (Thompson 2013).

Defensive Patent Strategies

This strategy aims to minimize the impact of third-party IP strategies on your business. The medium-sized furniture supplier Hettich pursues an aggressive defense strategy. Through excellent handling of state-of-the-art information, numerous confrontational proceedings against competitive patents are engaged in, and attacks by competitors are leveraged.

Offensive/Defensive Patent Strategies

Large companies in particular often pursue hybrid patent strategies with both offensive and defensive components. Although *Siemens* and *Microsoft* both pursue offensive strategies in the abovementioned sense. One particular tactic is always directed at minimizing the effects of third parties on their own companies. At *Siemens*, this is driven by the broad diversity of its products and services. For example, competitors of one division are often customers of another. *Microsoft*, on the other hand, is very sensitive to attacks coming from third parties; this is due to the company's high global market share based on a comparatively limited product and service offering.

Companies characterized by such an activity and competition configuration therefore increasingly conclude exchange contracts for patent licenses in order to reduce their own exposure. As a result, lighting manufacturer *Osram*, and electronics manufacturer *Sharp* concluded a far-reaching agreement on the reciprocal licensing of patents in 2013. This agreement covers patents of both companies in the field of optoelectronic semiconductor components as well as products in which these are contained. It thus encompasses LED and laser diode chips and modules, as well as luminaires. *Osram* had previously to this entered into patent exchange agreements with other major opto-semiconductor manufacturers such as *Nichia*, *Philips*, *Toyoda Gosei*, *Cree*, *Samsung,* and *LG* to reduce the risk of unintentionally using the intellectual property rights of other companies (Osram 2013).

> **The 10 Patent Management Principles of *Geberit***
> *Geberit* is active in sanitary technology and has over 6000 subsidiaries worldwide; the tenets of its patent policy are:
>
> 1. *Application policy:* *Geberit* applies for protectable inventions consciously and in a targeted manner. Before applying the positioning of the patents is decided upon.
> 2. *Collision avoidance:* For each development project, a patent analysis is conducted.
> 3. *Portfolio review:* The *Geberit* patent portfolio is evaluated annually in terms of cost-benefit. The application criteria serve as a decision basis for dropping or maintaining each individual patent.
> 4. *Invention offerings:* *Geberit* examines inventions made by other companies in terms of their technical and commercial viability. The patent legal analysis becomes part of the corporate decision process.
> 5. *Competitor surveillance:* *Geberit* follows a strict publication policy in its own domain and also for adjacent technical ones; this is to prevent competitors from being able to ease in on their territory.

(continued)

6. *Competitive and Technology Analyses:* For specifically defined competitors, systematic patent and technology analyses are conducted.
7. *Licensing:* Through an internal *Geberit* licensing system, R&D activities are financed, but *Geberit* does not actively license its patents to third parties.
8. *Enforcement:* *Geberit* robustly enforces its patents against all possible infringers.
9. *Information systems:* *Geberit* ensures the necessary flow of information for its own patents using a periodic report, suited for its level and business units.
10. *Organization:* The patent activities are centrally led and coordinated; the decentralized R&D units protect their own market-specific developments themselves.

2.3 Core Dimensions of Patent Strategies

Most leading international technology companies pursue a patent strategy aimed at securing their own freedom of action, such as *Siemens* or *IBM*. A further aspect of this strategy is wanting to prevent the imitation of their own products and to thereby sustainably strengthen their competitive differentiation. Especially in the pharmaceutical and chemical industries, the development of new active ingredients would not be affordable without effective patent protection. Some companies successfully defend their own products with patents, for example, *Bayer* versus *Barr Laboratories*, *Ruby*, and *Hoechst-Marion-Roussel*. Relatively few companies still focus their patent strategy on generating licensing revenues, such as is done by *Philips*.

A patent strategy aimed at the protection of innovations demonstrates the following core dimensions (Gassmann and Bader 2017; see Fig. 2.1):

- Goal 1: Ensuring Freedom-to-Operate (FTO)
- Goal 2: Differentiation by applying one's own intellectual property
- Goal 3: Multiplier effect by generating licensing revenues

A comprehensive patent strategy already in itself provides for an initial situation in which the company can be attacked as little as possible by third parties. The less vulnerable a company is, the greater its *freedom-to-operate* vis-à-vis patents of third parties, and the stronger its own products can be defended, and have intellectual property rights enforced vis-à-vis competitors. Three types of activity can be distinguished:

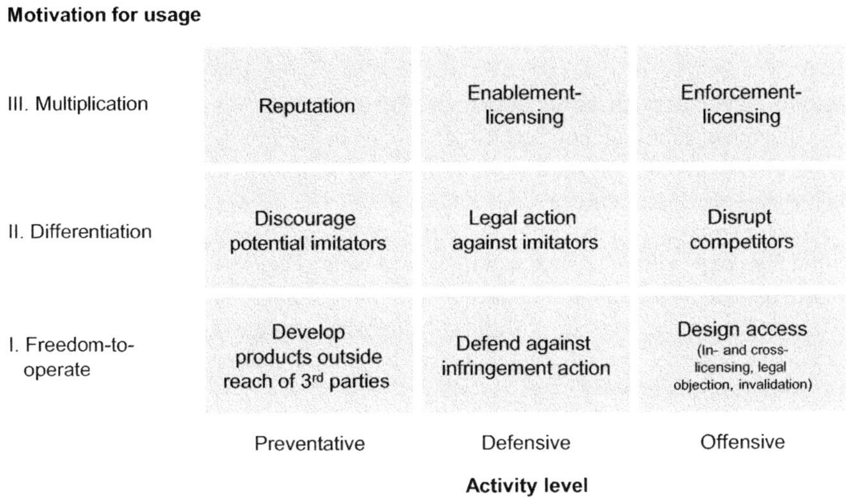

2.3 Core Dimensions of Patent Strategies

Motivation for usage

III. Multiplication	Reputation	Enablement-licensing	Enforcement-licensing
II. Differentiation	Discourage potential imitators	Legal action against imitators	Disrupt competitors
I. Freedom-to-operate	Develop products outside reach of 3rd parties	Defend against infringement action	Design access (In- and cross-licensing, legal objection, invalidation)
	Preventative	Defensive	Offensive

Activity level

Fig. 2.1 The core dimensions of a patent strategy (authors' own figure)

- *Prophylactic* measures for prevention
- *Defensive* measures to defend one's own competitive position
- *Offensive* measures for the self-initiated attack on competition

Goal 1: Ensuring Freedom-to-Operate

Here, the focus is on securing one's own freedom-to-operate vis-à-vis third parties. As a rule, European companies attach great importance to this dimension and try to develop products and technologies that do not collide with the intellectual property rights of third parties. The own freedom of action can already be underpinned by the quantity of own patents and patent applications. On the one hand, competitors can be deterred and on the other, products can potentially get covered by potential attackers.

Freedom-to-operate (FTO) can thus be achieved through preventive, *prophylactic* measures in the development of one's own products and technologies.

Defensive measures must be initiated if one company is attacked by another on the grounds of a patent infringement. In practice, the attacked company tries to use its own protective rights against products and business activities of the attacking company in addition to other measures.

Offensive measures that serve to obtain or maintain freedom of action can also be carried out on the company's own initiative. This includes, in particular, proactive in-licensing or cross-licensing of interesting patents, but also the destruction of interfering patents, for example, through opposition or nullity proceedings.

The Swiss elevator manufacturer *Schindler* strives to use the best possible technology for its products and services without infringing on them and also strives for the successful destruction of interfering third-party patents, for example, through opposition proceedings before the patent offices.

Develop Products Outside Reach of Third Parties
This objective should be pursued by companies in general. In practice, this means that the IP activities of third parties must be monitored and analyzed and, if necessary, specific circumvention solutions have to be developed.

This process, known as Product Clearing or Patent Clearing, is often associated with a high expenditure of time and money as well as a continuous qualification of employees. A disregard or negligence can be punished in the USA in patent infringement proceedings by a tripling of damages (treble damages). In general, intellectual property rights are monitored with regard to the specifics and granularity of the relevant markets.

For example, the telecommunications equipment manufacturer *Alcatel* (now *Alcatel-Lucent*) monitored different sources of information: Publications and disclosures were used to prepare the technical information. Patents were mainly monitored for risk assessment with reference to the USA, Europe, and Germany. Patent searches were carried out by *Alcatel* using contract services, proprietary data profiles, and statistical evaluation methods. Typically, *Derwent's WPIDS, Inpadoc, EUROPatfull,* and *USPatfull* were queried and the data further analyzed. Furthermore, the patent administration system *Memotech* of *CPA* was available. Further processing of the data, including statistical processing, was carried out using Excel and structured according to business areas, keywords, and other criteria. The results were released by the Senior IP Counsels and made available via the internal intranet site Quick-Place. *Alcatel* used a specially configured Lotus Notes database. Alcatel had by then found that the own preparation of the data was ultimately more cost-effective than purchasing evaluations via information service providers. In addition, researchers and developers were able to conduct patent searches themselves via the intranet.

Defending Against Infringement Action
An earlier OECD study on Business Patenting and Licensing showed that 70% of the companies surveyed reported growing involvement in patent infringement proceedings. The following applies to those affected: "Attack is the best defense." The basic strategy of defense against attacks by third parties is based on four pillars:

- Counter-attack on the legal validity of the action patents, for example through nullity actions
- Counter-determination as to whether an infringement of property rights exists at all, for example through negative declaratory relief
- Counter-attack on the product, technology, and service range of the aggressor with his own intellectual property rights
- Further procedural, legal, and possibly even political steps to influence the infringement proceedings in one's own sense

Nevertheless, the high costs that can generally arise in the enforcement of intellectual property rights should be taken into account: The costs of patent litigation in the USA amount to an average of 1.2 m US dollars—in most cases this is a zero-sum game (Cotropia et al. 2017). In the end, most litigation ends up with a settlement in order to prevent massive litigation costs. Furthermore, innovative SMEs have to consider in particular the consequential costs and resource commitment in a possible legal dispute; this applies in particular to the USA. In this respect, legal protection strategies must always be based not only on legal but also on financial and political considerations.

Cultural aspects have also changed. While pharmaceutical companies such as *Bayer Pharma* or *Sanofi* were generally able to reach an out-of-court agreement with third parties in the past, there has now been an increase in court-supported disputes, not least due to the influence of American companies.

Design Access
Anyone wishing to avoid the latent risk of knowingly infringing third-party patents must proactively seek access to these rights or at least attempt to nullify them.

Licensing-In
In many cases, the complete development of workarounds is not possible, too costly, or undesirable for other reasons, reasons such as required adherence to technical standards. Then licensing or the acquisition of the IP right offer a solution for the exploitation of the rights.

Many companies, such as *IBM*, are already pursuing an open licensing strategy and offering licenses to third parties on fair, reasonable, and non-discriminatory terms. However, as a rule, there is no general obligation for a company to license to third parties. Especially for large companies, the granting of licenses to third parties is often additionally tied to security being offered in return, for example, in the form of back-licenses. The in-licensing company is to be prevented from later being able to approach the licensing company for patent infringement. The licensing company could then only defend itself with great difficulty because the relevant patents have already been licensed and can no longer be used for a counter-attack.

Licensing at Google
The foundations of *Google's* search technology were developed by the founders Page and Brin in 1998 during their studies at *Stanford University* (California). The patent rights have been held by the university ever since. However, *Google* was able to acquire the exclusive license rights until 2011.

In 2002, *Google* was sued in the USA by *Yahoo!* subsidiary *Overture* for patent infringement. The core patent (U.S. Patent US 6,269,361) protects a process that affects an essential function for the advertising market—*Google's* main source of income: the process allows the order of automatically

(continued)

generated search results to be subsequently changed and ads to be placed. The patent dispute was settled shortly before the IPO in 2004: *Google* received a license. In return, *Google* paid 2.7 million shares with an issue value of around 100 US dollars and also paid license fees to *Yahoo!* subsidiary *Overture* for permission to use it.

One of the more controversial decisions is when the US Federal Trade Commission (FTC) sued *Qualcomm* for its unfair licensing practices. The US circuit court ruled that the company's infamous "no license, no chips policy" was anti-competitive. The company had essentially forced companies, which needed its hardware in the form of specialized modem chips for mobile networks, to license its technology. *Qualcomm's* biggest profit center had been the patent licensing rather than the manufacturing. Judge Koh ruled that the royalty agreement, which was 5% of the value of the phone, had to be assessed off the price of the chips instead. *Apple* had been battling *Qualcomm* in court over the same issue for years before (Wallstreet Journal 2019).

Cross-Licensing

If back-licenses are granted in return for the in-licensing of industrial property rights, a cross-licensing exists. In particular, companies with large market shares have the problem of high vulnerability in the respective market segments due to third-party patents. In addition, if there is a high level of competition and innovation in these segments with a high volume of intellectual property rights, many companies try to increase their degrees of freedom by gaining access to other intellectual property right portfolios, as *Siemens* and *Microsoft* do, which two companies have concluded a patent license exchange. Whereas in the past there were often pure barter transactions of reciprocal rights of use, in recent years a balancing out of the mutual benefits has increasingly been compensated by monetary compensation.

The technology group *OC Oerlikon* has so far primarily used cross-licensing agreements to settle disputes. According to the head of the *Emch* legal department, however, in the future, these procedures will increasingly also be used for the economically viable procurement of intellectual property, for example, as a substitute for the pure acquisition of property rights, for company acquisitions or for the precautionary safeguarding of access to certain property rights.

Patent License Exchange Between SAP and Microsoft
During negotiations with *Microsoft* on a joint partnership to develop Internet services, *SAP* confirmed that it had already been approached in 2003 regarding a possible merger with *Microsoft*. The preliminary discussions stalled, but in

(continued)

> 2004 both parties entered into a joint collaboration to develop Internet services. The agreement also included a patent license exchange agreement to improve the development framework of the two companies.

Opposition and Invalidation Actions

The opposition procedure gives the public not previously involved in the patent grant procedure the opportunity to have the patent re-examined by the patent office. The adversary is involved in the opposition procedure. If the opposition is successful, the patent is either restricted or revoked. The effect of the patent is accordingly retroactive. In the European and German proceedings, a period of 9 months is available for filing an opposition. In the *USA*, the 1-party procedure *Ex Parte Reexamination* and the 2-party procedure *Inter Partes Reexamination* for examination of the patent are available. After that, only the usually expensive and costly nullity proceedings are available at the national level in many legislations.[1]

With these legal instruments, the emergence of new protective rights can thus be restricted or even prevented at an early stage. In practice, the legal uncertainty existing until the conclusion of the proceedings is usually problematic. If the European procedure involves two instances, it will take about 4 years before the final decision is reached. In addition, the patent owner is made aware by the opponent that he is disturbed by the patent, otherwise the costs for the procedure would not be invested. The proportion of patents challenged by oppositions before the European Patent Office has been at a low level for years, 3.2 % in 2018 (2014: 4.7%) (EPO 2019). In many sectors, however, such as the consumer goods industry or the furniture supply industry, a real culture of objection is still lived. The consumer goods manufacturer *Henkel* alone lodges around 80 appeals a year in Europe.

Goal 2: Differentiation by Applying Own Intellectual Property

Deterrence requires credibility: A legal protection strategy only retains its deterring effect vis-à-vis third parties if the fundamental willingness to enforce property rights is also believable. The real value of patents decreases if competitors infringe them and the patent holder knowingly or unknowingly tolerates this. In addition to the purely prophylactic deterrent effect of a patent portfolio, it is therefore important for

---

[1] While the opposition procedure also exists at the national and regional European level, the nullity procedure is only possible at the national level. Furthermore, nullity proceedings are not possible in many legislations as independent proceedings, but only in connection with infringement proceedings.

companies to take offensive measures and also to use their own intellectual property rights to block infringers.

This behavior, which is questionable from an economic point of view, makes sense if companies in duopolistic or oligopolistic markets want to gain comparative advantages over competitors or gain access to other third-party technologies. The extension of the disruption option, therefore, consists in building up intellectual property rights whose restricted area is primarily geared to competitors' products, technologies, and services—irrespective of the focus of the notifying company itself. Competitors can be approached in an even more focused manner or future markets can be opened up if corresponding competitive products are analyzed within the framework of systematic reverse engineering and potential improvements are then patented themselves—this makes it possible to sustainably improve one's own starting and negotiating position. In this way, leverage can be gained over competitors, for example, to gain access to other technologies or to control substitution technologies.

From the customer's point of view also, products get better if the competitor has to technologically circumvent the other's products in the same area. Comparative competitive advantages in *Porter's* sense not only aim to improve relative customer benefits but are also deliberately directed against competitors.

The *Gore* company, known by the *Gore-Tex* brand, is unique, and it consistently secures its products and technologies based on fluoropolymers through patents and brands against imitation and substitutes. In this way, prices and margins can be maintained and further developments made possible. However, *Gore* verifies that the cost of legal protection is economically justified.

However, the motivation to disrupt the market reaches its limits when companies achieve outstanding market dominance. It can then happen that the public sector is required to "open up" patents to competitors within the framework of compulsory licenses. In the relevant areas, the question arises as to whether patents should be granted at all or not. However, it is not only US companies that are affected by such a stalemate: The telecommunications group *Swisscom*, for example, suffers from its dominant market position in Switzerland and the resulting "deregulation activities" of the Swiss regulatory authority. The then *Swisscom* CEO Jens Alder already warned: "As a result of this uncertainty, investments in innovation are at risk!"

Goal 3: Multiplier Effect Through Licensing Revenues

The commercialization of intellectual property rights via licenses takes place under profit/loss aspects. The licensing policy, therefore, exerts a strong influence on the desired patent generation: If exclusivity is the sole objective, or if the company's own patents are generally available to third parties for an appropriate licensing fee, for example, to avoid conflicts with competition and trade administrations due to the company's positioning.

The formation of alliances also has a major influence on the generation of patents. In the case of standardization alliances or competitive alliances, the alliance participants usually have a looser arrangement for dealing with the specific intellectual property among themselves than for third parties who are not members of the alliance. The latter are either excluded altogether or have to pay (higher) license fees.

Therefore, the reputation of a company in this area plays an important role in generating license revenues; reputation especially with regard to technical, financial, and procedural experience in the licensing business and the assertiveness achieved in this respect vis-à-vis third parties. In principle, a distinction is made between enablement and enforcement licensing in the generation of licensing income.

Case Study: Julius Blum GmbH

The example of the Austrian kitchen and furniture fittings manufacturer *Julius Blum* shows the importance of a functioning patent strategy. The Austrian company generated sales of nearly two billion euros and employed over 6500 people at production sites close to the headquarter, the USA, Poland, and Brazil. *Blum* holds over 1000 patents and attaches great importance to patent management after the company had a negative experience in the 1960s when a competitor's patent prevented it from entering the market. One example of this: the success of the innovative "Blumotion®" damping system, which was introduced at the turn of the millennium and is now the standard in the furniture industry, was secured.

Blum's patent strategy focuses on preserving freedom of action, i.e., ensuring unrestricted market access regarding the main European markets and their competitors. Thanks to this strategic focus and the active management of the patent portfolio, patent disputes with Asian patent infringers were also successfully resolved (BMWFJ 2013).

2.4   Cost of Patents

Patents legally preclude the imitation of an innovation only in those countries, in which the patent has been granted and is maintained *(Territoriality principle)*. With the international *Patent Cooperation Treaty (PCT)* procedure, patent protection can be sought in over 148 countries with a single patent application. Additional regional patent offices include the *European Patent Office (EPO)* as well as the *Eurasian Patent Organization (EAPO)*. The inter-governmental *African Regional Intellectual Property Organization (ARIPO)* and the *Organisation Africaine de la Propriété Intellectuelle (OAPI)* cover Africa.

Central criteria for the selection of the jurisdictions to maintain a patent are:

- Location of the company's markets and competitors
- Production location of the company and those of the competitors
- Country-specific legislation, for example, enforceability
- Cost aspects, for example, translation and maintenance

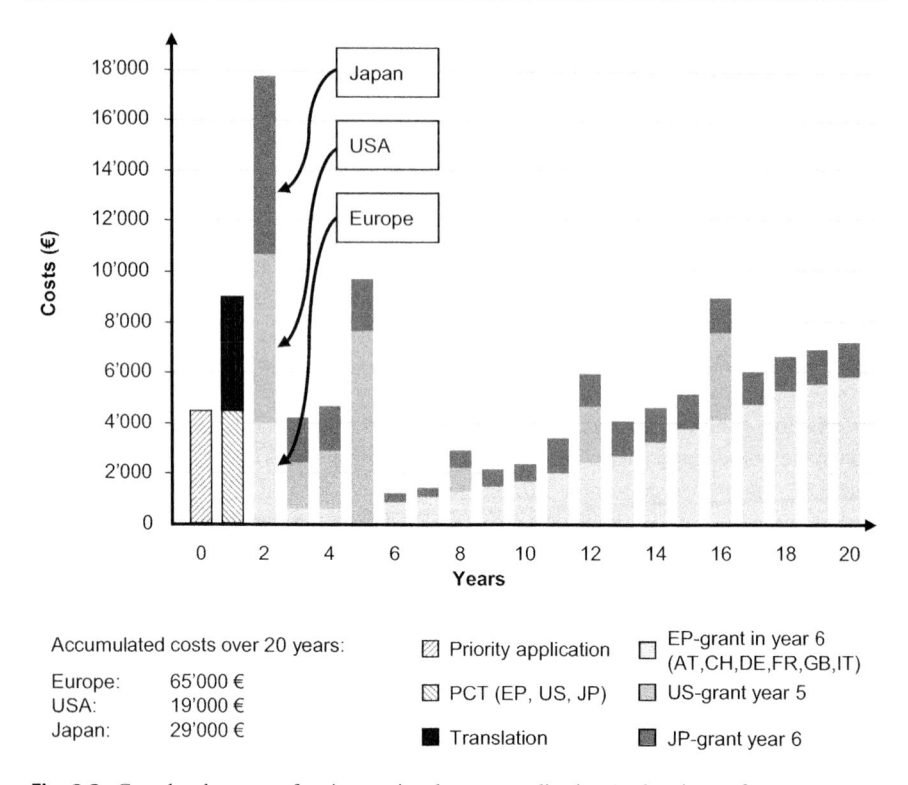

Fig. 2.2 Cost development of an international patent application (authors' own figure)

Accumulated costs over 20 years:
Europe: 65'000 €
USA: 19'000 €
Japan: 29'000 €

Legend: Priority application; PCT (EP, US, JP); Translation; EP-grant in year 6 (AT,CH,DE,FR,GB,IT); US-grant year 5; JP-grant year 6

The optimal selection of countries depends on the industry and company-specific configuration and flexibility of the value chain. The guidelines for the selection of countries are derived from the competitive strategy. Important criteria are the locations of the competitors and the current and potential markets.

The acquisition and maintenance of a patent family in Europe cost about 25,000 € for a multi-country portfolio for 10 years. These costs arise over the course of the proceedings and show peaks mainly when there are transfers of proceedings, as lawyers and translation costs are incurred. This is particularly the case when the international Patent Cooperation Treaty patent application procedure (PCT procedure) passes into the regional or national phase and whenever the European patent application procedure passes into the national phase (Gassmann and Bader 2017).

In the case of granted patents, the annual fees increase depending on the service life achieved (see Fig. 2.2). With this regulation, the legislator intends to increase the opportunity costs for the non-use of a patent. However, many companies still neglect a regular review of the existing patent portfolio and overlook the creeping increase in expenses due to patents no longer required. These are hidden costs that do not create a competitive advantage.

Since the fees and costs also depend on the specificities of the respective countries, a company must carefully consider in which countries patent protection

2.4 Cost of Patents

```
10 years accumulated – in kEUR
(Scenario: EP, US, JP)
```

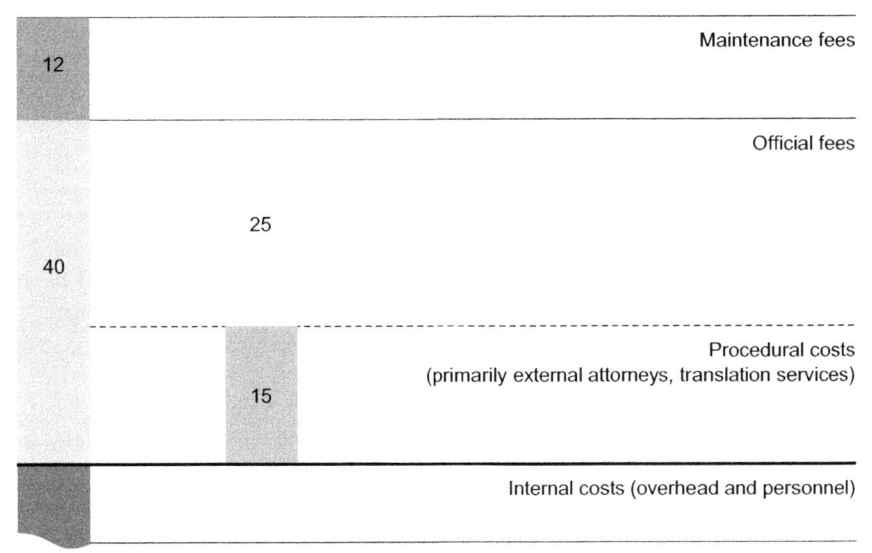

12	Maintenance fees
40 / 25	Official fees
15	Procedural costs (primarily external attorneys, translation services)
	Internal costs (overhead and personnel)

Fig. 2.3 Average patent costs for a patent family over 10 years (authors' own figure)

will later become valid. Although the bundled international PCT procedure is usually more expensive and takes longer than an individual procedure, total costs can be saved with large patent portfolios. Due to the longer international application and search procedure, more time is available for the selection of those procedures which should be continued in the first place due to the state of the art as well as due to the company's and the competition's activities. The "international" phase of the procedure enables the applicant to initially conduct a formally relatively manageable and bundled application procedure and to use this time for the final country selection before further translation and legal costs are incurred. Expensive wrong decisions for unnecessary patent applications can thus be avoided and the portfolio can be optimized at a very early stage at low cost.

Covering a period of 10 years, a larger patent portfolio in North America (USA, Canada) will cost around 15,000 € per invention, in Europe (Germany, Austria, Switzerland, Great Britain, France, and Italy) around 25,000 €, and in Asia (Japan, South Korea, China, and Taiwan) around 25,000 €. This sum results from the costs of obtaining a granted patent on the one hand and from the costs of maintaining patent protection on the other (see Fig. 2.3):

- The costs for obtaining a patent grant consist of internal costs, such as those for personnel in the patent department, as well as external costs. The latter include costs for external patent attorneys, translations, and official fees.
- The costs for maintaining patent protection are essentially the annual fees. Many companies also use the services of external organizations or law firms to pay

annual fees worldwide. As a rule, a lump sum per country and annual fee is charged as a retainer.

The costs for obtaining the granted patent and thus for obtaining patent protection, excluding internal expenses, amount to approximately 75% of the accumulated total costs. It is therefore an expensive error, if it turns out only after the grant that the originally applied for patent protection is actually no longer needed.

If the patents are enforced at a later date, further high costs may arise. For example, the average cost of an infringement suit in the USA is US$ 2.6 million median to the end of the discovery phase and US$ 4.7 million to the end of the proceedings (AIPLA 2019; Litigation Patent Infringement) for amounts in dispute in excess of US$ 25 million. It should be noted, however, that each party must bear its own cost.

IP outsourcing partners are often used to save costs in patent management and at the same time reduce the risks of global applications. In the early 1960s, the Luxembourg company *Dennemeyer* specialized in paying patent fees for its customers. Today, *Dennemeyer* is one of the world's largest IP service providers with over 180 employees and offers comprehensive IP services such as portfolio management, IP software solutions, and legal IP consulting.

> **Cost-Benefit-Ratio**
> Cost-benefit consideration should also include robustness of patent enforcement: A large block of costs often goes back to pay for defense in patent infringement proceedings. As a golden rule: if you do not have the budget for a fight through court, the patent has only half the value claimed. Important is that the potential patent violators believe that you will maintain one hundred percent strictness in prosecuting violators.

2.5 Complementary Strategies to Patenting

Although this book focuses mainly on patents, we must stress that using IP alone, in most cases, is not the best strategy. In some cases, IP-based strategies are even the wrong choice to make. One of the better studies done on a basically firm choice was conducted by UKIP (Athreye and Fassio 2018). In a large survey, it found that some of the strategic reasons for why it may be wise *not* to patent are:

- The innovation is not new to the market.
- The cost of a patent application was too high.
- A patent would have disclosed too much.
- Patent infringement cannot be well detected.
- A patent would be difficult to enforce.

2.5 Complementary Strategies to Patenting

More essential than perhaps lording an innovation over competitors, is ensuring that the core business model can operate. A company's own patent is a method of ensuring the firm's own freedom to operate, though being not the only one or even necessarily the best. In addition to filing patents, there are four other alternatives—or better—*complementary actions* to patenting:

- Defensive publication (Prior Art publications)
- Secrecy
- Speed and time to market
- Designed complexity

Table 2.1 presents an overview of protection strategies with five typical strategies that firms use to protect innovation. Patenting and IP are the obviously known ones. Sometimes used are defense publications, which can permit the firm the freedom-to-operate quickly. Secrecy is often used by smaller firms. Speed and first-mover advantage are classic strategies that are used for innovations where economies of scale and network effects can create their own monopolistic rent. Designed complexity includes a collective set of strategies like black box technologies, knowledge-intensive applications, process know-how, or a strong brand.

Defensive Publication

In order to minimize the risk of "unwanted" patent applications by third parties, and to ensure future freedom of action, publications of all kinds, which in this context are also referred to as *"defensive publications"* or *"defensive disclosures,"* are helpful.[2] Once published, the competitor can no longer patent at least the invention described. In addition, the company's image as a technology leader is promoted. *Swisscom* publishes inventions that cannot be patented, for example, on the Internet at *ip.com* and in technical journals. *Roche Diagnostics* takes a very differentiated approach: where appropriate, publication may take the form of a special publication sheet published every 2 weeks. *Microsoft* and *Siemens* use technical reports or conference papers that reach numerous interest groups. Use of special publication media that conceal the origin but are still available to patent offices for examination, such as *priorartpublishing.com*. Publications are safeguards against possible later patenting and blocking attempts by competitors.

Prior Art publications can be overt, for example in a journal, and sometimes even covert. Swiss pharma firms occasionally take out advertisements in regional papers, and publish formulae—thus ensuring the freedom to operate without tipping off competitors! Today, publishing in paper form would be a good way of doing this since it would not then be searchable via the Internet.

---

[2]Pre-emptive publication must also be developed and thought through. There are some costs associated with it, and there is a certain level of dependence on the publisher's discretion.

Table 2.1 Innovation protection strategies: capturing value (table compiled by authors)

	Patenting	Defensive publication	Secrecy	Speed	Designed complexity
Exclusivity	Max 20 years	Until publication	Until the secret is made known	Until being copied	Limited
Defense against others' protection rights	Unlimited once disclosed (latest after 18 months); Limited from day of application	Unlimited	Sometimes internal grandfathering of usage; Illicit usage remains unknown	Unlimited	Depends on level of public disclosure
Defense against previous protection rights	Identification through official or internal search enables early defense possible	No	No protection; Illicit usage remains unknown	No	No
Possibility for cooperation	Cross-licensing; Patent pools; Reduction of licensing royalties or unit price; Influence over standards	No	Exchange of know-how	Product specific possibility to influence standards	Strong (through use of licensing)
Applicability	Guarantee of temporary monopoly profits through exclusivity of the products; Possibility to prohibit competitors and new market entrants	Ensuring freedom to operate for a very low cost; SMEs with a small war chest; Establishing standards through the diffusion of knowledge	Procedures, processes, based on internal knowledge; Inventions for which patent violation is hardly provable, algorithms and production processes	Highly attractive products, e.g., trendy products with short life-cycles or highly dynamic technical fields	Good for products where there is a large amount of complementary knowledge or IP (like design and trademarks)

Loss of Novelty

The flip-side is that the premature revelation of an invention jeopardizes its patentability. Publications, trade-fair appearances, and the construction of pilot plants must, therefore, be strategically managed and coordinated with patent application activities. The legal validity of patents has more than once been vitiated because pilot plants were installed in publicly accessible buildings, or because some extroverted project manager presented technical innovations in a public lecture before these had been patented.

> **"Guerilla Strategy" for Freedom-to-Operate**
> Publications in specialist media also make sense in terms of technological progress. The disadvantage, however, is that this procedure often enables the competitor to draw helpful conclusions regarding patent and product strategy as well as current R&D activities. There are more creative alternatives, especially for SMEs:
>
> The Swiss company *Kern*, now part of the Swedish company *Hexagon*, used the Aarau Cone magazine as a publication medium for inventions. These were special inventions that were not strong enough for cost-intensive patents but were in danger of potentially appearing in the form of competitive patents.
>
> Their guerilla strategy to guarantee their freedom of operation was: publish in such a way that nobody reads it! The main competitor was unlikely to find them. The publication is then stored in the company's own archives, constituting a cheap insurance against unwanted patents by third parties. Swiss pharmaceuticals used to do the same thing by publishing their formulae in the local penny-saver papers.

Secrecy

An important alternative to patent applications in the protection of one's own technology and products is secrecy. Indeed, a solid and sophisticated econometric study found that "The results of these analyses show that a higher percentage of R&D-performing firms in all size classes find secrecy to be a more effective means of appropriation than patents" (Arundel 2001).

Secrecy is particularly useful if it is difficult or impossible to determine whether the subject matter of the IP right has been used or if the enforceability of the IP rights is generally questioned.

Many manufacturing companies, therefore, keep production processes secret and apply for patents for invention objects that can be easily proven only on the product or on the technology. *Coca-Cola* keeps the recipe of the well-known *Coca-Cola* lemonade secret in order to avoid imitations. Looking back, it can be said that this was the more effective protection strategy because patents would have expired long ago. There is still no identical imitation of *Coca-Cola*, despite numerous attempts having been made by competitors.

The elevator manufacturer *Schindler* keeps the control algorithms of its elevator systems secret. It would be difficult to prove a patent infringement because the source code of elevator control algorithms is generally not accessible to competitors, which is why the company opted for secrecy as a protective measure.

If secrecy is to be maintained, supplementary measures are advisable in order to avoid the outflow of knowledge via other channels. The most frequently used methods for keeping technical innovations secret are, in particular, the following:

- Implementation of internal confidentiality guidelines[3]
- Control over presentations and publications given and written by researchers and employees
- Absolute IT security control over critical documents and plans so that no employee can take them
- Decentralized access to the innovation by keeping data, teams, and personnel segregated from the entire development (most applicable to larger firms)

Trade secrets, or tacitness, is a common tactic used to prevent imitation. A core technological advantage may even be protected this way, and effectively so. Even with perfect formal knowledge of some technology, it may not be operationalized without highly specific knowledge, or impossible to transfer. Tacit knowledge can and does move between companies through the transfer of key personnel with intimate knowledge of the technology. In this sense, non-compete agreements and various legal and contractual measures have to be taken to safeguard secrets. Filing patents immediately alert competitors to new products. Tacitness is especially effective for highly specialized installed, non-mass-market products. For example, building specialized forklift attachments—filing a patent would immediately make competitors worldwide aware of a new invention.

Speed

The faster innovation cycles move, the more difficult it is to achieve sustainable competitive advantages through intellectual property rights, since patent protection only provides effective protection against imitation after a certain time delay. A CEO of a consumer electronics company put it succinctly: "Our innovation competition is 'blitzkrieg'—realizing it faster is the match-deciding factor. Strategy is important, but patents only help us in a few platform and key technologies."

---

[3]These should, in particular, provide for the use of confidentiality agreements which are agreed before the start of a conversation with external parties. Supplementary minutes of the discussion are useful.

The effect that patents can have also depends on the range of manufacture that a company aims to achieve, and the position and share that the company occupies in the entire value chain. The more a company succeeds in influencing, not only its own, but also other stages of the value chain via patents, the stronger their effect will be. Conversely, dependency and risk increase if a company is directly or indirectly dependent on other value chains to develop and market its own products.

At the transitions from semiconductor to electrical engineering products, *semiconductor* companies are expanding their value chains due to the continuously progressing integration of functionalities on the integrated circuits, and are coming into collision with the value creation stage of their current customers. Often, cross-licensing agreements are common between *IBM*, *Siemens*, and *Infineon Technologies* in order not to block each other.

Designed Complexity

The natural goal of engineers is to design something in as simple a way as possible. Simplicity goes with creating lean products that are easy to be manufactured. All simultaneous engineering and design-for-manufacturing philosophies subscribe to simplicity. However, adding an artificially designed complexity to a product or its related processes prevents products from being imitated. Keeping complex technology in a black box within one critical module is what enables this strategy. Often the black box module is designed and manufactured in the central R&D lab close to the headquarter. In the international R&D literature, it is therefore also called the "national treasure strategy" (von Zedtwitz and Gassmann 2002). Complexity can be also achieved through highly specific maintenance requirements. Elevator companies such as Otis, Thyssen, and Schindler earn most of their revenues by maintenance and services. This is especially true when it comes to high-rise elevators. Here the maintenance of an elevator is highly specific, the investments in the installation of the elevator are mostly monetized by the maintenance business following it.

In the machinery industry, it has become more difficult to patent. Chinese low-cost competitors have often caught up to European companies. However, one way to protect the intellectual property is the tacit knowledge regarding the application and parametrization of the product. The Swiss food processing company Buehler, a world market leader and hidden champion of the industry, keeps the process as the real differentiating factor inside its walls. The complexity of system optimization and parametrization lies in a deep knowledge about how to process food. This process know-how is much more difficult to imitate than the machine itself where reverse engineering makes it easy to manufacture the components.

> **Complexity**
> Firms often use the design of complexity as a source of protection from imitation. Complexity can be designed in:
>
> - *Products*, e.g., high-tech modules as a black box, typically developed and manufactured in a secure location
> - *Processes*, e.g., service integration, cryptographic protocols
> - *Systems*, e.g., IT-security on all levels, firewalls, segmented IT-network
> - *Organization*, e.g., highly integrated patterns of job rotation, loyalty programs, decentralized R&D teams with the critical technologies located close to the headquarter (von Zedtwitz and Gassmann 2002)
>
> These measures of creating complexity by design are typically applied in countries with a weak appropriability regime, such as in China, India, or Russia (Gassmann et al. 2012).

Alternative Techniques of Value Appropriation

Aside from the major techniques listed above there are further complementary alternatives to appropriate value and ensure freedom-to-operate. In a comprehensive survey firms in two technologically advanced and innovative countries with strong IP regimes, the USA and Japan, researchers found that only about 36% of companies find patents effective in protecting and appropriating innovation (Cohen et al. 2002). Lead time/first-mover advantage was more important, with secrecy being especially important to US firms.

There are other motives, more ancillary in importance:

- Control over complementary assets: there may be some strategic resources necessary to produce an invention. Perhaps a common example is *Tesla's* battery high-capacity lithium–cobalt battery technology, which allows for higher discharge rates. *Tesla* has moved to secure a lot of the supply making it more difficult for competitors wanting to use the same known technology.
- Retention of strategic personnel: keeping loyal personnel is perhaps the most critical aspect of IP protection. There is an old saying: *"Know-how travels with people."* The diffusion of technology amongst firms takes place mostly through this channel. Disclosures concerning a patent are strategic and intentionally opaque; any patent attorney worth her salt discloses only as much as is necessary when having to circumscribe the invention. However, critical R&D personnel know much more details about how to use and implement the invention, and thus much of the knowledge resides in employees; important are incentive systems and, most important, a strong corporate culture.

- NDAs (non-disclosure-agreements) and traditional licensing contracts are often much more enforceable in court than intellectual property: start every critical meeting with an NDA; too often this is neglected.
- Open source: one alternative in the software and hardware spaces has been to open up the key technologies, and build the business model off of services and specialized applications. If the technology is attractive enough people will use it thus growing it to the very market size the business intends to target; making this success possible are bundles of chargeable services around the open core.
- Service contracts that tie into the technology.
- Branding, naming, and advertising: a strong brand can be stronger than a patented technology; see, e.g., *Red Bull*.
- Strict control over distribution channels: build your own distribution channels, e.g., through direct sales, as is done by *Hilti*, *Vorwerk*, or *Nespresso*.
- Complementary manufacturing is an important technique whereby certain bits of the technology are kept in-house so that no supplier and no other manufacturer can replicate the product without having the core manufacturing technology.

References

AIPLA. (2019). *Report of the Economic Survey*. Arlington, Virginia: AIPLA American Intellectual Property Law Association.

Arundel, A. (2001). The relative effectiveness of patents and secrecy for appropriation. *Research Policy, 30*(4), 611–624.

Athreye, S., & Fassio, C. (2018). *When do firms not use patents and trademarks to protect valuable innovations? Evidence from the SIPU 2015 survey*. UK Intellectual Property Office.

BMWFJ. (2013). *Immaterielle Vermögenswerte – geistiges Eigentum als Wachstumstreiber*. Vienna: Bundesministerium für Wirtschaft, Familie und Jugend.

Cohen, W. M., Goto, A., Nagata, A., Nelson, R. R., & Walsh, J. P. (2002). R&D spillovers, patents and the incentives to innovate in Japan and the United States. *Research Policy, 31*(8-9), 1349–1367 (p. 1354).

Cotropia, C. A., Kesan, J. P., Rozema, K., & Schwartz, D. L. (2017). *Endogenous litigation costs: An empirical analysis of patent disputes* (January 3, 2017). Northwestern Law & Econ Research Paper 17-01; University of Illinois College of Law Legal Studies Research Paper No. 17-14. Available at SSRN: https://ssrn.com/abstract=2893503 or https://doi.org/10.2139/ssrn.2893503.

EPO. (2019). *Annual report 2018*. Munich: European Patent Office.

Gassmann, O., & Bader, M. A. (2017). *Patentmanagement: Innovationen erfolgreich nutzen und schützen* (4th ed.). Berlin: Springer.

Gassmann, O., Beckenbauer, A., & Friesike, S. (2012). *Profiting from innovation in China*. Heidelberg: Springer.

Krech, C.-A., Rüther, F., & Gassmann, O. (2015). Profiting from invention: Business models of patent aggregating companies. *International Journal of Innovation Management, 19*(3), 1–26.

Mintzberg, H., Ahlstrand, B., & Lampel, J. (2005). *Strategy safari: A guided tour through the wilds of strategic management*. New York: Simon and Schuster.

Osram. (2013). *Osram GmbH und Sharp Corporation schließen Patentlizenzaustauschvertrag*. Munich: Osram. http://www.osram.ch/osram_ch/de/presse/pressemeldungen/_fachpresse/2013/osram-gmbh-und-sharp-corporation-schliessen-patentlizenzaustauschvertrag/index.jsp.

Thompson, M. (2013). Costs of Swiss patent litigation. *Sic!* June, 6|2013, pp. 332–345.
von Zedtwitz, M., & Gassmann, O. (2002). Market versus technology drive in R&D internationalization: Four different patterns of managing research and development. *Research Policy, 31*(4), 569–588.
Wallstreet Journal. (2019). *Qualcomm's practices violate antitrust law, judge rules*, 2019-05-22.

Evaluating and Valuing Patents

A basic problem of patent management in most companies is that there are more ideas than a patent can be applied for operationally. Getting and maintaining a patent is associated with high costs, and so firms are required to both *evaluate* their patents and to *value* their patents. We use *evaluation* to refer to the business logic and strategic impact of the patent, and the term *valuation* to refer to the monetary number assigned to a patent. Therefore, a solid evaluation and valuation of ideas worth patenting, along with the regular supervision of existing patent applications and patents is essential. Hence, an important goal of both evaluation and valuation is to help focus on internal firm resources.

An important objective of an evaluation is to provide assistance in focusing resources on activities that are expected to make the greatest contribution to the market success. On the one hand, this can be done anticipatively and top-down by applying standardization strategies to build and optimize patent portfolios, while on the other hand, retrospectively and bottom-up by applying valuation methods to existing patent portfolios. An evaluation can be *qualitative*, i.e., strengths and weaknesses of a patent are determined and evaluated on the basis of value levels, or *quantitative* by assigning a monetary value to patents or patent portfolios.

The following dimensions influence the value of a patent and are therefore more or less taken into account in the portfolio and valuation method:

- Market factors (market potential, market volume, market growth)
- Competition (intensity of competition, product life cycle, products of other market players)
- Research and Development (R&D) criteria (technical risks, resources, investments, time)
- Production criteria (capacity, manufacturing costs)
- Overlap criteria (synergies with other products, probability of follow-up projects, effects on infrastructure and organization, learning effects)
- Legal criteria (validity, scope of protection, dependency, remaining patent life)

Due to the strong time reference of the evaluation, several evaluations have to be carried out in the patent process. Ideally, the times at which cost-effective decisions are to be made in the patenting process are suitable for this:

- Selection of the invention disclosures that are to be pursued as industrial property rights
- Decision on subsequent applications (within priority year period)
- Transition from international or regional examination phase to national phases
- Maturity of annual fees

> **Key Components of Patent Strategies**
> - *Evaluation:* Finding the qualitative value of the protection right using different levels.
> - *Valuation:* Finding the quantitative value of the protection right using recognized valuation methods.
> - *Portfolio management:* Values the right from the point of view of the market and technology positions, and normative action in relation to the entire portfolio.

3.1 Evaluating Patents

The qualitative evaluation of patents, also called patent evaluation, analyzes the strengths and weaknesses of a patent. This evaluation is carried out on the basis of criteria, each of which is assigned a specific value number. The result of a qualitative evaluation is usually a statement from which direct recommendations for action can be derived. A qualitative evaluation of a patent could, for example, be formulated as follows: "The patent protects a technology of strategic importance in a semi-attractive market. It can be enforced efficiently."

A qualitative evaluation, therefore, supports patenting decisions, allows for portfolio comparisons to be made, and supports patent management decisions.

Valuation methods can be classified (see Fig. 3.1).

Monovariate Patent Evaluation

For one-dimensional patent evaluation, criteria are defined on the basis of which the quality and value of a patent are assessed. These criteria can be both *subjective* (e.g., difficulty in circumventing a patent for competitors, the attractiveness of use for competitors), and *objective* (e.g., frequency of citation, geographical scope).

With the patent value number method, the criteria are assigned a value number, e.g., from 0 to 6 or from A to E. The criteria are then used to calculate the patent value. Table 3.1 gives an overview of criteria that are frequently used in practice for

3.1 Evaluating Patents

Approach	Monovariate patent-evaluation	Bivariate patent-evaluation	Trivariate patent-evaluation
Methods	Patent value number e.g. Gassmann/Bader	Ernst approach	Brockhoff approach
	Bader et al. approach	Kuckartz approach	Faix approach
	Barney/Barney approach	Pfeiffer et al. approach	Hofinger approach
	Breitzman/Narin approach	Poredda/Wildschütz approach	Schulze approach
	Ernst/Omland patent citation approach	Comparison of expositional value	Wurzer approach
	IPscore®		

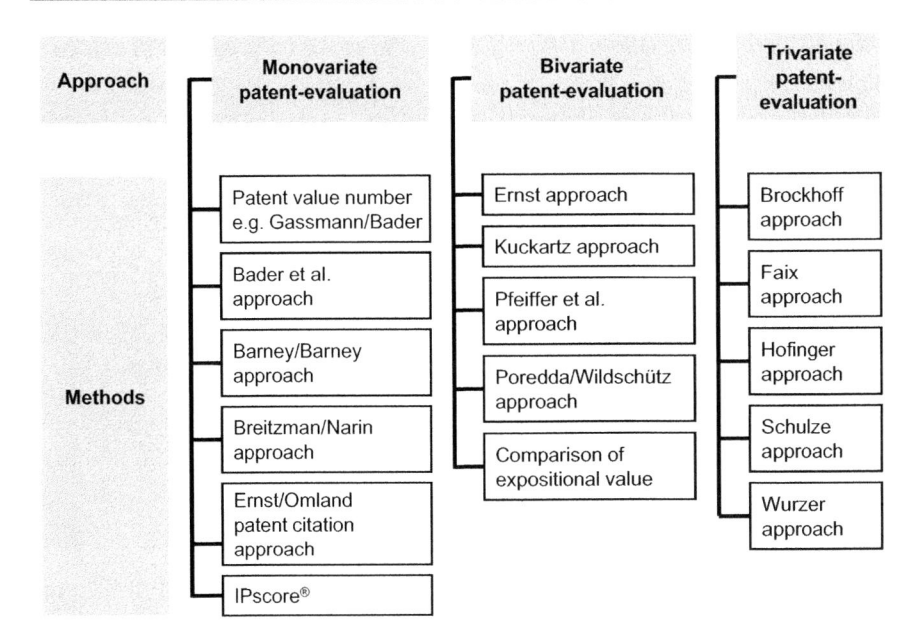

Fig. 3.1 Qualitative patent evaluation methods (authors' own figure)

the qualitative evaluation of inventions, patent applications, and patents. For each criterion, a value number is defined between "0" (worthless) and "6" (excellent). The overall result can be obtained either by averaging or by a weighted evaluation of the individual results.

Objective Evaluation methods are often used for ratings. These objective criteria are so-called empirical indicators (Reitzig 2002 provides an overview of empirical indicators). Statistical studies confirm a correlation between patent value and these indicators. The advantage of these indicators is that they can be easily determined from databases.

Ratings are often carried out by professional providers. One rating provider, for example, is *PatentRatings*, which was part of *Ocean Tomo* for some time, which patented its rating process (US 6,556,992). Another patent for a rating method was filed by *1790 Analytics* (US 6,175,824). Patent ratings are also offered in German-speaking countries. According to Ernst and Omland (2010), the approach evaluates the current extent of worldwide patent protection and the relevance of the patent for subsequent developments.

The *St. Gallen Patent Index (SGPI)* developed by Bader et al. (2012) evaluates both the relevance of the patent and the strength of the markets in which the patent is applied for. A particular advantage is that not only individual patents are evaluated, but also the strength of the portfolio, taking into account that the value of a portfolio is more than the sum of its individual patents.

Statements about the patent value are made by one-dimensional valuation methods over previously defined ranges or the direct comparison of several patents.

Table 3.1 Monovariate portfolio evaluation: Patent value number (table compiled by authors)

Criterion		Value number (0...6)
Difficulty of circumvention for competition:		
Direct substitutes	Pract. impossible	5...6
	Requires effort	2...4
	Easily achieved	0...1
Attractiveness for competitors:		
Competitive interest	Strong	5...6
	Average	2...4
	Minimal	0...1
Discovery of competitive usage:		
Proof	Easily obtained	5...6
	Difficult to obtain	2...4
	Impossible to obtain	0...1
Direct usage in production:		
	Probable	5...6
	Possible	2...4
	Improbable	0...1
Size of respective patent portfolio segment:		
	Too small	5...6
	Appropriate	2...4
	Too big	0...1
Additional criteria:		
Future technology or future products		...
Ensuring important R&D results		...
Supporting sales		...
Strengthening negotiation position		...
Public funding for project		...
Contributes to a standard		...
Other		...
Total value number:		...

Patent Evaluation at Eastman Kodak

Kodak evaluates patents in connection with acquisitions, maintenance, and licensing. It recognizes the value of intellectual property primarily in terms of the market advantages of protection and for licensing purposes. *Kodak* uses the following criteria:

- Proven or expected internal use
- Proven or expected external use
- Breadth of patent claims
- Identification of the use of proprietary technologies or products

The review for internal purposes is based on a qualitative evaluation and does not include a financial one.

Patent Evaluation at Schindler

Schindler has outsourced the management of intellectual property to a subsidiary, *Inventio*. The latter uses an internally developed IP database as the basis for evaluating patents. The patents are classified within the database. The classification is carried out by the R&D team, the sales team, and by *Inventio* itself. The keywords of the classifications are defined by all of these deciding together and takes place about every 2 years.

The evaluation of individual property rights and bundles of property rights is also carried out by *Inventio* after consultation with the product managers. The patents are evaluated qualitatively with the help of a uniform evaluation sheet making use of a point system. The evaluation sheet takes into account both the economic perspective (market success) and the legal perspective (sustainability). In addition, an evaluation is carried out according to technical aspects. *Inventio*'s patent evaluation criteria guiding the technology process consist of the creative phase, the development phase, and the maturity phase (see Fig. 3.2).

The addressees of the evaluation are indicated in the phases above. Below the process, evaluation criteria are assigned to each phase. Market success is assessed on the basis of cost advantage, customer benefit, and turnover. The demands on the technology reveal the *strength of the patent claims, clarity, completeness,* and the *scope of protection*. The criteria for evaluating sustainability are *chances of being granted, circumventability, territorial scope of the protection* as well as *validity* and *enforceability* of the patent.

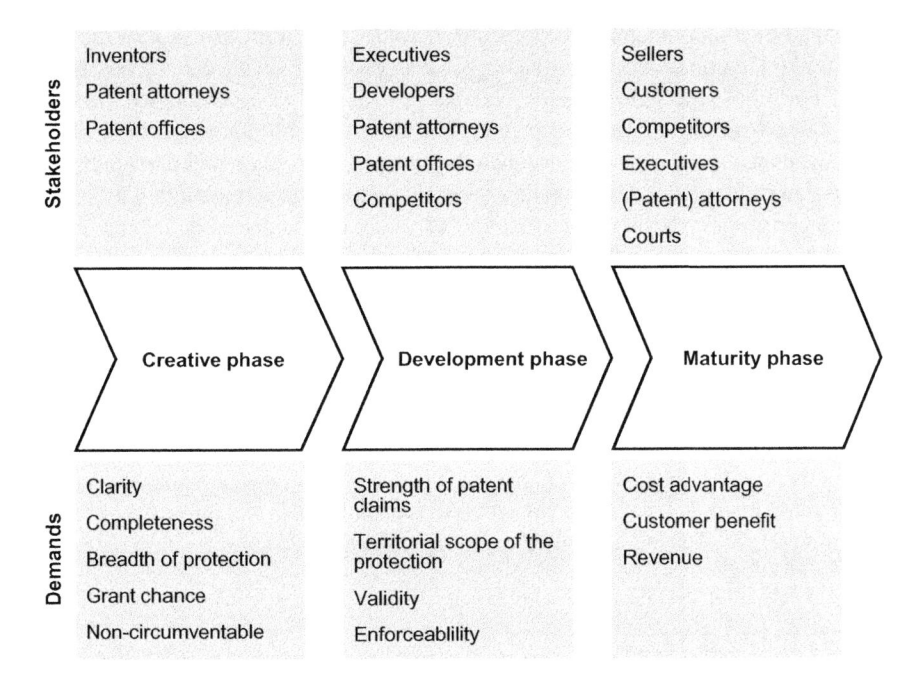

Stakeholders	Creative phase	Development phase	Maturity phase
	Inventors	Executives	Sellers
	Patent attorneys	Developers	Customers
	Patent offices	Patent attorneys	Competitors
		Patent offices	Executives
		Competitors	(Patent) attorneys
			Courts
Demands	Clarity	Strength of patent claims	Cost advantage
	Completeness	Territorial scope of the protection	Customer benefit
	Breadth of protection		Revenue
	Grant chance	Validity	
	Non-circumventable	Enforceablility	

Fig. 3.2 Database concept for patent evaluation at *Schindler* (authors' own figure)

Bibliometric Patent Quality

The value of a patent can be inferred by its apparent quality. Patent quality indicators are, for example, citation rate, international scope, i.e., foreign applications file, duration, and opposition rate against the patent. While none of these itself causes patent value, high-value patents often have more family members, get cited, and are legally attacked (see Figs. 3.3 and 3.4).

Bivariate Patent Evaluation

Within the framework of patent license negotiations or in preparation for them, risk and reward assessments between companies are often conducted. A proven practical concept is a comparison of the respective *exposure* of one company with the other and vice versa.

Exposure is determined on the basis of two variables: the turnover of one enterprise, and the number of patents and patent applications of the other enterprise relevant to its turnover.[1] In the simplest case, exposure is the product of the two variable values. In comparison, it can then be determined whether risks and opportunities are evenly balanced or whether one of the companies has a higher exposure value and is therefore disadvantaged compared to the other (see Fig. 3.5).

If, for example, a cross-licensing agreement is to be concluded between two companies, the agreement could be concluded in a financially neutral manner due to the balance out. In the latter case, the company with the lower exposure could additionally demand financial recompense or some other form of compensation to make up for the imbalance. The advantage is that, especially in the case of very large patent portfolios, the values of the variables can initially be determined without information from the negotiating partner, and the exposure values can be qualitatively estimated: sales can be determined through market studies, and the number of patents can be found out through patent searches. If the valuation method is accepted by both partners as a basis for negotiation, the values can be discussed in a mutually comprehensible manner. The disadvantage of this method, however, is that it is generally assumed that one company's sales will at first be evenly covered by the intellectual property of the other company and vice-versa. This is therefore only plausibly justifiable in the case of large patent portfolios.

An important supplementary criterion is therefore the hit rate. This is the proportion of intellectual property rights that are ultimately also used by the products and technologies of the negotiating partner and can, therefore, be introduced into patent infringement proceedings. A comparison of the exposure values only makes sense if both parties assume a balanced hit rate and can prove this credibly. For smaller portfolios, it is advisable to calculate and compare exposure values for each patent or

---

[1] There may be other types of protection rights, like utility models, that can be incorporated into this analysis.

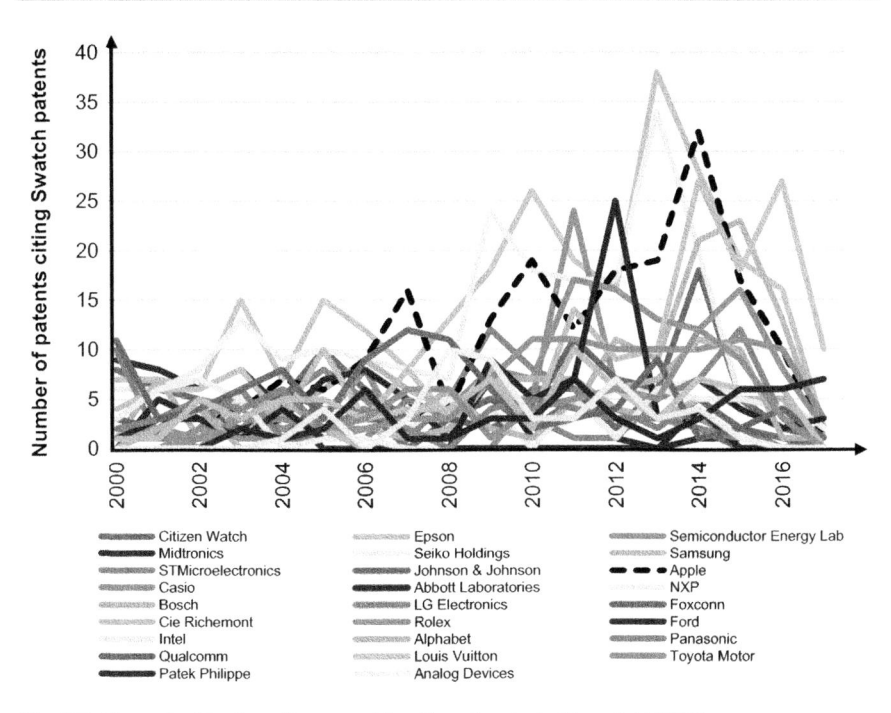

Fig. 3.3 Example: Number of patents citing *Swatch* patents (Econsight 2020)

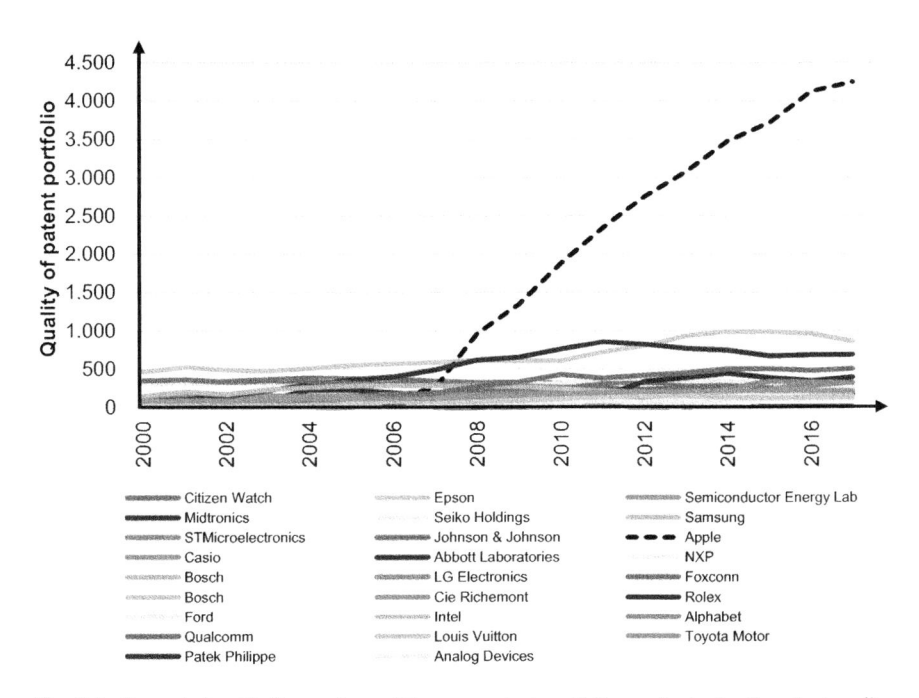

Fig. 3.4 Example (cont.): Comparison of the same patent portfolios on the basis of a patent quality approach (Econsight 2020)

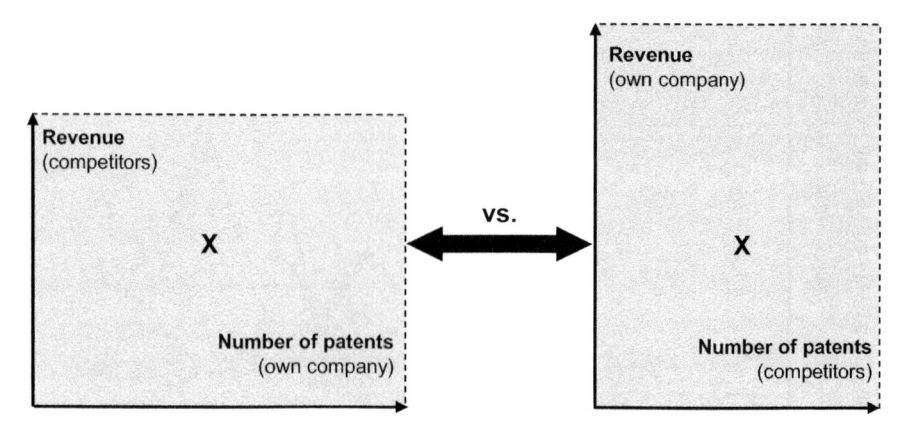

Fig. 3.5 Bivariate portfolio evaluation: exposure comparison (authors' own figure)

clearly defined portfolio. A total exposure value can then be determined for each company by summing up the exposure values.

For example, a company A has a turnover of 150 million euros and 20 patents. Company B, on the other hand, has a turnover of 20 billion euros and 1000 patents.

Exposure value company A: $150 \times 1000 = 150{,}000$
Exposure value company B: $20{,}000 \times 20 = 400{,}000$

Although the larger company B holds many more patents, it is subordinate to the smaller company A in the exposure value comparison.

In addition to comparing exposure values, patent portfolio approaches are also used to evaluate patents. Known bivariate patent portfolio approaches are the Ernst approach (1996), the Kuckartz approach (2007), the Pfeiffer et al. approach (1989), and the Poredda and Wildschütz approach (2004).

The Poredda and Wildschütz approach considers both the individual patents and the patent portfolios that are assigned to a defined product or product area. The basic idea of this qualitative valuation method is that there is a correlation between the value of the patent and the market share of the patented product. The dimensions of patent valuation are:

- Market value of the patent
- Legal value of the patent

Starting from the consideration of individual patents, a two-dimensional patent portfolio representation can be generated (see Fig. 3.6). In addition, recommendations for action can be derived for individual patents.

Market Value of the Patent
Indicators for the market value of a patent are the relative attractiveness of patented technical solution, the total profit of the product category, and its effective blocking duration.

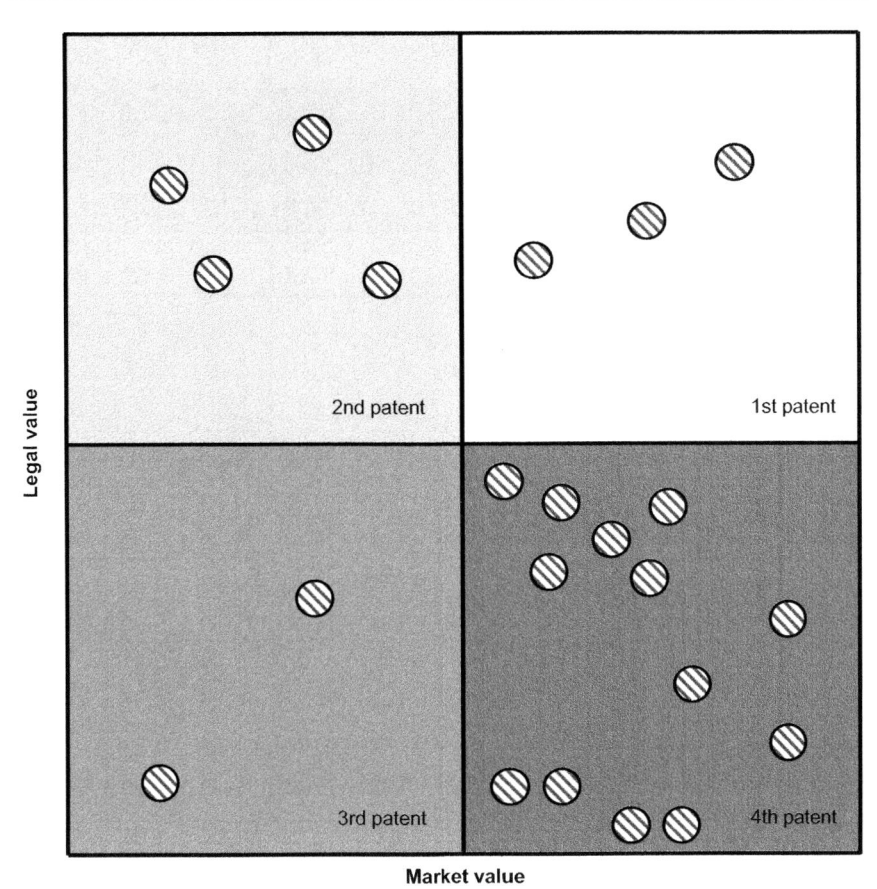

Fig. 3.6 Bivariate portfolio evaluation according to Poredda and Wildschütz

Legal Value of the Patent
Indicators for the legal value are patentability, ease in identifying patent violation, the dependency of other protection rights, and territorial coverage. These indicators are established in cooperation with patent, market, and technology experts.

Trivariate Patent Evaluation

Well-known trivariate approaches are the Brockhoff approach (1999); the Faix approach (2001); the Hofinger approach (1997); the Schulze approach (2005); and the Wurzer approach (2005). The Brockhoff approach (1999), for example, compares technologies and patent portfolios on the basis of the following three variables (Brockhoff 1999; Ernst 1998, 1999, 2002):

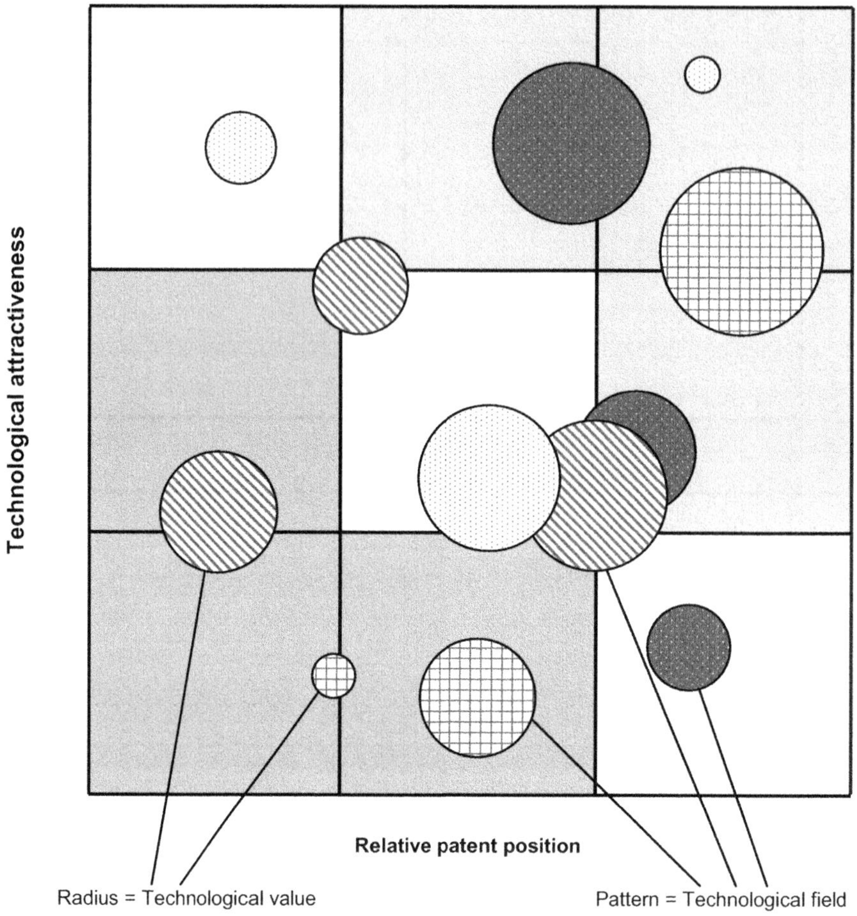

Fig. 3.7 Trivariate portfolio evaluation according to Brockhoff

- Relative patent position
- Technological attractiveness
- Technological significance

A three-dimensional patent portfolio representation can be generated on the basis of certain technology fields of companies (Fig. 3.7). In this way, technologies or technology groups can be classified and qualitatively compared with each other. For example, the abscissa represents the relative patent position, the ordinate represents the technology attractiveness, and the circle's diameter represents the technological significance. Standard strategies can then be derived from the positions.

Relative Patent Position
Calculation of the relative patent position of a company in relation to other companies. For example, the ratio of a company's own patents to the (quality-adjusted) total number of patents relating to the field of technology under investigation is calculated. The maximum value is therefore one.

Technological Attractiveness
Technological attractiveness is calculated for example out of the relationship between the growth in the patent applications of the respective technological field, and the growth of patent applications of all observed technological fields.

Technological Significance
The significance of a technology for a company is calculated out of the relation of the number of patents of a technological field of a company, and the entire number of patents of the company.

> **Evaluation of Patents**
> Qualitative patent evaluation is a suitable tool to support patent management decisions. The following points have to be considered:
>
> - *Strategic recommendations for action:* in order to identify strategic recommendations for action and to support decisions, there is a multitude of analytic methods.
> - *Communicability of the results:* A good communicability is given by systematized scales or graphical preparation of the results.
> - *Subjective value indicators:* These help to depict the value more realistically, but also make the assessment dependent on the person making the assessment.

3.2 Valuing Patents

While the evaluation aims to analyze the strengths and weaknesses of a patent and to make a statement about the quality of the patent on the basis of certain criteria along with subsequent options for action, valuation determines the monetary value of a patent.

However, no strategic recommendations for action can be derived directly from the valuation (Bader et al. 2008).

In spite of a diverse set of methods, the determination of a patent's value is complex because the term "value" does not have a clear definition. Depending on the point of view and the perception, the value can take on the following forms:

- Value in the sense of *meaning*: a thing having meaning for a certain person
- Value in the sense of *price*: the monetary amount that a seller demands for the good offered
- Value in the sense of *cost*: the monetary amount actually paid in a transaction

If one explains this by using as an example an invention, it is evident that the product is often of great importance to the inventor because he has invested a lot of time, including some of his leisure time, into it. So, if the invention is then to be sold, the inventor might demand, say, 50,000 € for it. The company that is willing to buy the invention assesses the invention differently from the inventor and eventually both agree on a transaction price of 25,000 €. Patents are always context-specific due to their dependence on their use in and for the company, their age, and other factors. Therefore, there is no such thing as objective patent value.

However, in order to estimate the value of a patent, the future benefit of the patent can be taken into account. The economic benefit results in particular from the products for which the patent is granted, or on the basis of which these are manufactured. The influencing variables of the patent value are divided into technical, economic, and legal factors (Moser and Goddar 2007).

Technological factors are, for example, the uniqueness of the technology, its degree of novelty, the status of R&D relating to it, the level of innovation, or the life cycle of the technology. The technology of the underlying invention influences the positioning of a product in different ways. For example, a product can be differentiated by patents. The manufacturer can charge a surcharge for the product. The development of a new technology can result in lower production costs and competitive advantages. A patent can also enable exclusive production or guarantee freedom of production.

The market factor reflects the economic dimension and is described, for example, by market potential, market volume, market growth, industry structure, or product life cycle.

However, only legal protection enables the various forms of use of patents, and therefore, it has a great influence on the value of a patent. The legal protection is influenced by the factors: validity, scope of protection, dependencies with other patents, or the remaining patent life. If the patent is not valid, or if it is unenforceable, the property right has no value, even if the market grows exponentially or the product can be produced particularly cost-effectively. On the other hand, a patent that blocks competitors can guarantee high sales.

In contrast to patent evaluation, which is mainly conducted in order to optimally control the strategic management of patents, patent valuation is carried out for a large number of different business transactions. The general conditions determine whether a valuation is done voluntarily or due to external compulsion, for example, in the case of company takeovers. In M&A, patents are evaluated more extensively than in purely internal considerations. This is one more reason why valuation plays an important role.

Reasons for a monetary patent evaluation are:

3.2 Valuing Patents

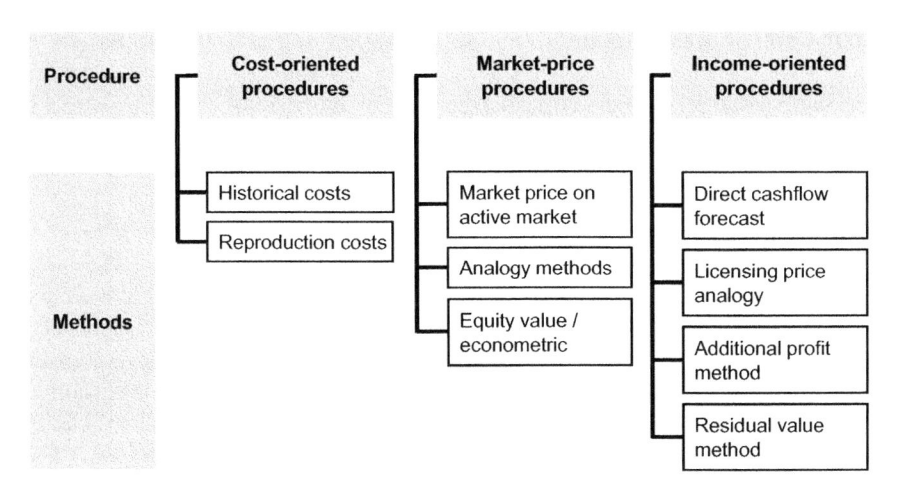

Fig. 3.8 The trichotomy of quantitative patent valuation procedures (authors' own figure)

Procedure:
- Cost-oriented procedures
- Market-price procedures
- Income-oriented procedures

Methods:
- Cost-oriented: Historical costs; Reproduction costs
- Market-price: Market price on active market; Analogy methods; Equity value / econometric
- Income-oriented: Direct cashflow forecast; Licensing price analogy; Additional profit method; Residual value method

- Management-oriented events: patent portfolio maintenance, budget allocation, monitoring of R&D, inventor remuneration, risk analyses, patenting decisions
- Corporate actions: due diligence, joint venture, initial public offering, company sale, company valuation
- Financing and balance-sheet-oriented events: patent as loan collateral, accounting, debt and equity financing, voluntary capital market information
- Transfer-oriented events: licensing, cross-licensing, strategic alliances, technology transfer
- Conflict-oriented events: liquidation, insolvency, transfer prices, determination of damages

More than 100 quantitative patent valuation methods are now discussed in the literature. For this reason, it is often assumed that the valuation methods can be divided into three main valuation methods (including Smith and Parr 2019; DIN 77100 2011; IDW S 5 2013), namely:

- Cost-oriented procedures
- Market-oriented procedures
- Income-oriented procedures

Figure 3.8 (see also Table 3.5) shows an overview of this trichotomy and the most frequently cited patent evaluation methods in the literature. Smith and Parr are probably the most frequently cited representatives of this trichotomy. They argue that any method they have identified in their extensive literature research can basically be traced back to one of the above methods (Smith and Parr 2019). In order to do justice to their complexity or their use in practice, further methods are explained at the end of this section in addition to the methods of the three methods mentioned here.

Cost-Oriented Procedures

The basic assumption of the cost-oriented procedure is that the value of a patent is best represented by the costs incurred during the lifetime of the patent. The two most commonly used methods are the historical cost method and the replacement cost method.

(1) Historical Costs

In practice, the historical cost method is often used when the amount of information available is still relatively small. This is often the case in the R&D phase of a patented technology (Turner 2000) because an R&D project undergoes a constant stream of cash outlays. Using a theoretical example, Turner shows that the historical costs [C] (for example, the costs involved in creating and filing a patent) can be derived from the corporate cost of capital [r]:

$$\text{Value} \cong \text{Cost (C)} = \text{Investment (I)} + \text{total cost of carry (R)}$$

The total time cost of money is the carry cost of the amount spent up until time (t).

$$R = I_1 * r + (I_1 * r + I_2 * r) + (I_1 * r + \cdots + I_t * r)$$

So, for a 3-million-dollar project (I=3m) over 3 years (I_1=1m; I_2=1m; I_3=1m) with a 10% corporate cost of capital (r=0.1), we would compute the approximate patent value as:

$$\text{Value} \cong 3m + (1m * .1) + (1m * .1 + 2m * .1) + (1m * .1 + 2m * .1 + 3m * .1)$$
$$= 4 \text{ million dollars}$$

Another disadvantage of this method is that it is often difficult to determine the start and end times of R&D for a particular technology and to determine what proportion of total R&D expenditure is attributable to a single patent.

The example was divided into five phases. The first phase is the R&D phase, and it includes personnel, material, and search costs incurred in the development of the patented technology and attributable to the patent. This attribution is the most difficult to carry through because it is strongly based on estimates. Further R&D costs were not incurred in later phases. Defining the costs in the later subsequent phases is easier. Costs incurred for the application are defined by the Patent Office and can be clearly attributed to the patent. The same applies to possible costs that would be incurred in patent disputes. In Table 3.2, these costs were waived. By simply adding up all costs incurred, a patent value of 965,100 € is obtained.

(2) Reproduction Costs

In this method, the patent value is calculated by adding all the costs that would be incurred if the existing patent were recovered. Replacement does not mean the exact reproduction of the existing patent, but the development of a patent with exactly the same functionalities as the existing one (Smith and Parr 2019). It may happen that the new patent is more advantageous than the existing one in some respects.

3.2 Valuing Patents

Table 3.2 Simplified example of method of historical costs (in Euro)

Type of cost	t_4[a]	t_3[b]	t_2	t_1	t_0[c]
R&D costs					
Personal costs	750,000				
Material costs	150,000				
Search cost	50,000				
Sum R&D cost	950,000	0	0	0	0
Filing costs					
Application fee		100	0	0	0
Examination fee		1565	0	0	0
Search fee		1035	0	0	0
Translation(s)		0	0	0	4000
Annual fee		0	0	0	400
Monitoring		600	600	600	600
Opposition		0	0	0	0
procedure		0	0	0	0
Nullity procedures		300	250	300	250
Searches		0	0	0	0
Patent litigation		3000	500	500	500
Patent attorney costs					
Sum patent office costs	0	6600	1350	1400	5750
Sum of patent costs	950,000	6600	1350	1400	5750
Patent value	965,100				

Source: Table compiled by authors
[a]R&D phase
[b]Time of patent application
[c]Time of valuation

Although the development and methods used to create the new patent may differ greatly from those used for the present patent, the basic functions of both patented technologies are the same. It should be noted that the costs used are virtual costs.

Advantages and Disadvantages of Cost-Oriented Procedures

The biggest advantage of the cost-oriented method is its ease of use. In order to obtain a patent value, only the costs have to be added. In addition, relatively little information is required, which can often be queried by R&D controlling. On the other hand, information is required that is very specific and often cannot be generated at the push of a button (Ensthaler and Strübbe 2006).

The cost-oriented procedure is based on the assumption that costs are equal to value. This is classified as problematic (Smith and Parr 2019; Wurzer and Reinhardt 2010). There is also no empirical evidence that there is a correlation between the value of a patent and its costs (Bertolotti 1996; Dressler 2006). Patents that do not generate any economic added value but have cost a lot of money in R&D (e.g., classic undesirable developments) are categorized here as very valuable. On the other hand, patents that have low development costs but generate high market returns could then be classified as worthless.

Application of Cost-Oriented Procedures

The cost-oriented method is a simple tool to calculate the ranges of prices for patent sales or licensing negotiations. It is also used by cost-based accounting or in cases where taxation is necessary. In technology and patent management, this approach is particularly suitable for make-or-buy decisions. However, strategic decisions in which the future utility of the patent plays a central role should not be made on the basis of this procedure since it is largely an accounting technique.

Market-Oriented Procedures

The market-based methods rely on the assumption that the precise value of a patent is the value that the market would be willing to pay for a similar patent in similar circumstances. There are two methods in this procedure. The patent value can be determined either by the market price in an active market or by analogy.

(3) Market Price on Active Market

The simplest way of a market-price-oriented patent valuation is to offer the patent on the open market and thereby find out what price potential buyers would be willing to pay. This simple description also includes the most important condition for the application of market-price-oriented procedures. In order to obtain a precise value, the existence of a market must be guaranteed. *ICAP Patent Brokerage* offers auctions of patents and patent portfolios (formerly *Ocean Tomo*).

(4) Analogy Methods

Another valuation method is to collect information on comparable transactions (comparable patent, technology, situation of participants, etc.) and to determine the value of one's own patent through a detailed comparison.

Using a simplified numerical example, Table 3.3 shows how a patent was evaluated using the analogy method. The comparator patent should be comparable to your own patent and should be reviewed for relevant product and market sizes.

Table 3.3 Simplified example of the analogy method (in Euro)

	t_1	t_2	t_3
Comparator patent			
Revenue Licensing: 3% per year (patent protection: 2 years)	100,000	100,000	
Patent to value			
Revenue Licensing: 3% per year (patent protection: 3 years)	80,000 2400	80,000 2400	80,000 2400
Discount rate: 8%/year	2222	2058	1905
Patent value	6185		

Source: Table compiled by authors

These variables can include the actual and possible scope of use of the patent, extent of the innovation, property right situation (e.g., nullity actions), territorial scope of protection, achieved and achievable competitive advantages through the patent, remaining useful life, market growth, size, potential, share, possibilities of subsequent inventions, industry specifics, etc. (Rings 2000). In the example below, the settlement patent transaction implies a licensing royalty rate of 3%. This 3% is applied then used. The patent value is now determined by forecasting the turnover for the next 3 years (the previously determined remaining useful life). The license rate is calculated on the basis of the revenue and the royalty. The fictitious license payments are discounted to reflect the time value of money. The patent value then results from the addition of all potential discounted license payments. As can be seen from the example, only the license rate of the comparable patent is used. Remaining useful life and possible revenues are based on the estimate of the own patent.

(5) Equity Value/Econometric

Since this is a management book, most of the valuation approaches here take on a business perspective. Yet, it is worth mentioning that there is also an econometric way of valuing patents. The basic premise of the market value approach is to predict the excess value of a firm beyond its book value using the company's patents as a regressor. This approach, first pioneered by Griliches in 1981, uses *Tobin's q* as a dependent variable, and past patenting to predict the value of a company in excess of its book value.

A series of articles refining and extending the same basic approach in that pilot study were conducted using Bayesian methods (Connolly and Hirschey 1988), incorporating appropriability (Cockburn and Griliches 1987); addressing technological opportunity (Connolly and Hirschey 1988). Hall et al. (2005) further refined this approach adding patent quality to the mix. In addition to these variants on the same basic approach, the technique has been applied to specific industries like those of semiconductors (Megna and Klock 1993), as well as local markets like the UK (Otto Toivanen and Bosworth 2002), Malaysia (Ghapar et al. 2014), Australia (Bosworth and Rogers 2001), and Europe (Hall and Mairesse 2007). This technique has likely been so appealing because it is intuitive and uses public market pricing requiring, in its simplest form, only three variables: market capitalization, book value, and patents.

Thompson (2016) then extends this approach by incorporating all global stocks in order to assess the local market valuation of patents—different investors pay different amounts for technological growth firms; he finds that patenting stocks tends to outperform the market by about 83 bps beyond the standard risk-adjust 4-factor equity model. Using this technique, he estimates the median patent to be worth about 123,000 USD, and the average value to be higher at 316,000 USD.

Pros and Cons of Market-Oriented Procedures

There are four basic conditions for an efficient patent valuation based on market pricing methods (Smith and Parr 2019): the most important condition is that an active market exists in the first place. In addition to this, the transaction partners must act according to the arm's length principle. This means that they must not allow themselves to go for political transfer prices but must instead negotiate prices as between neutral market participants. Sufficient information from a sufficiently large number of past comparable transactions is also necessary. This condition implies that access to the information must be available. If one assesses the conditions listed here on the basis of the current situation on the patent transfer market, it can be seen that not even the first condition is fulfilled. Compared to stocks or commodities, there is still no active market for patents. Most patent deals are bilateral transactions and are thus in direct opposition to the concept of perfect markets without transaction costs, high liquidity, no arbitrage opportunities, and many market participants. Even though an active market is a central prerequisite for the application of market-based approaches, the most important requirement for these approaches is the comparability of transactions and the availability of information. Due to the bilateral nature of patent transactions mentioned above, information on details or prices of patent deals is often not publicly available. Comparability is also often difficult to achieve, as patents are already, by definition, IP rights for new and often unique inventions. Since there are still relatively few transactions at present, this quantity is severely limited by the requirement that the information must be publicly accessible and the transferred patents must be comparable. One method used extensively in the academic literature is using stock-market price changes to evaluate the value of a patent, either using key events like publish date or grant or as stock variables. Econometric inferences from real-world equity data are a good thing when wanting to capture the IP value at the level of the economy, but not necessarily just as good for explaining the value of any particular patent.

Market-based approaches are often used to determine price estimates for sales or licensing negotiations. Tax authorities, in particular, prefer these methods, as the inherent concept has already been established by their application to other assets. In the case of patents, it is difficult to determine a meaningful value due to unknown transaction values.

Income-Oriented Procedures

The income-based method relies on the concept of *Discounted Cash Flows (DCF)*. In this method, the value is determined by the economic benefit associated with the internal or external commercialization of the patent (cash flow). In addition, the cash flows are discounted using an appropriate interest rate. This interest rate also reflects the risk associated with generating the cash flows. By discounting the cash flows, the fair value of the money is taken into account, and the final value of the patent corresponds to the present value concept.

Figure 3.9 describes the basic concept of discounted cash flows graphically. The first step is to predict how high the cash flows resulting from the patent are and how long they will last. Then an interest rate is determined which reflects the capital costs of the company, possible capital costs of the patent or product, and the risk associated with the patent (consisting of legal risks, technical risks, and economic

3.2 Valuing Patents

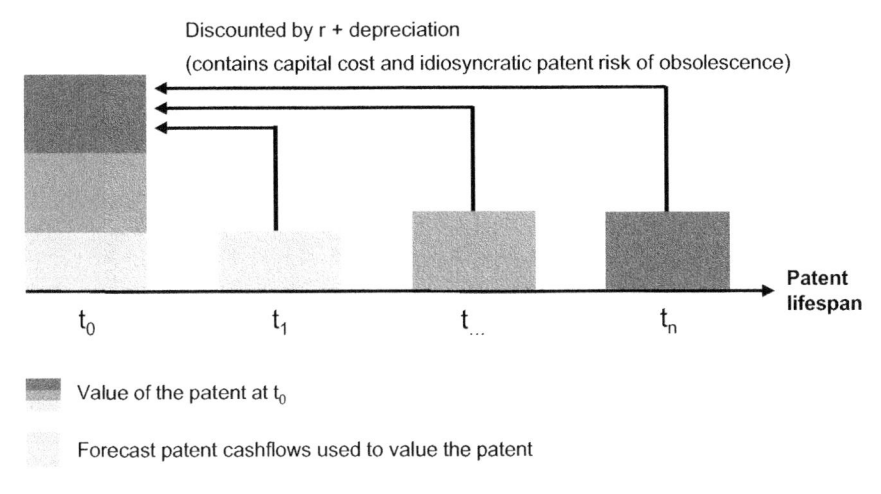

Fig. 3.9 The basic concept of Discounted Cash Flows (DCF) (authors' own figure)

risks). To obtain the patent value, each cash flow per period of time is discounted using the discount rate. In the end, the sum of all discounted cash flows results in the patent value.

The *method of direct cash flow forecasting* is described below, the *method of license price analogy*, the *surplus profit method*, and the *residual value method* are all based on this concept (see Fig. 3.9). They differ above all in the way in which cash flows are determined.

(6) Direct Cash Flow Forecast

The direct cash flow forecasting method assumes that the cash flow generated by a patented product can be attributed to certain value drivers, such as the business model, marketing or patent protection. In order to calculate the patent value, the cash flows directly attributable to the patent are discounted using the patent-specific, risk-adjusted discount rate. The main prerequisite for this is that the cash flows directly attributable to the patent can be determined.

(7) Licensing Price Analogy

With the license price analogy method (also known as *Relief From Royalty* method), the payment flows of a patent are approximated by means of license fees using an analogous patent or invention. These license fees are fees that the owner of the patent does not have to pay because he owns the patent and does not have to license it in. It is, therefore, determined which royalty payments would fictitiously have to be paid if the patent in question had been owned by a third party. These notional royalty payments are derived on the basis of normal market royalty rates for comparable patents, which relate, for example, to sales revenues. Here, too, comparable license rates are chosen that have been negotiated according to the arm's length principle. Reference values for license rates are also published (for example, in Hellebrand

Table 3.4 Simplified example of the License Price Analogy method (in Euro)

	t_1	t_2	t_3
Patent-specific revenue	100,000	110,000	120,000
Licensing fee: 3% per year			
Licensing savings before taxes	3000	3300	3600
Tax: 25%	750	825	900
Licensing savings after taxes	2250	2475	2700
Discount: 8% per year (1% risk-free rate + 7% legal risk and technical risk)			
Cash value	2083	2122	2143
Patent value	6348		

Source: Table compiled by authors

et al. 2007). The license rate must then be multiplied by the planned revenues attributable to the patent to be valued. After the deduction of the corporate taxes that have to be taken into account, the fictitious license payments determined are to be discounted to the valuation date using the patent-specific risk-adjusted discount rate.

Table 3.4 shows a simplified example of a patent valuation using the license price analogy method. A comparable patent was identified that was licensed out at a license rate of 3%. In order to determine the economic benefit of the patent to be valued, patent-specific revenues are forecast for 3 years. The license rate of 3% is calculated using these revenues. Since it is its own patent, the company can save between 3000 € and 3600 € in license fees. These saved royalties are now used to calculate the patent value. First, taxes are deducted. The license savings are then discounted at 8% and then added. There are several ways the discount rate can be estimated. For example, a basic component is the inter-temporal risk-free rate, usually proxied by a government bond. Patent risk comprises both the legal risk and technical risk. These can both be expressed by an annualized probability that the patented invention is obsoleted or the patent is invalidated in any given year (Köllner 2009). We could also take various factors, such as the firm's opportunity costs into account.

(8) Additional Profit Method

Under the additional profit method, the expected future cash flows from the company including the patent to be valued are compared with the corresponding cash flows from a fictitious peer company excluding the corresponding patent. It is assumed that the comparable company either does not own this patent or waives its use completely. The additional cash flows can result from additional payments that were realized through the patent or from saved payments and/or costs from the utilization of the patent. The difference between the cash flows of the two companies shows the additional cash flow attributable to the patent being valued. To determine the value, these additional cash flows are discounted to the valuation date using the patent-specific risk-adjusted discount rate.

(9) Residual Value Method

As a rule, patents only generate cash flows in combination with other tangible or intangible assets. Under the residual value method, fictitious payments for these supporting assets are deducted from the total cash flow when determining the cash flows generated by the patent. These payments can be regarded as fictitious usage fees for the supporting assets.

The remaining cash flows, which can now be attributed to the patent, are discounted to the valuation date using the patent-specific risk-adjusted discount rate.

The residual value method is generally reserved for the patents with the greatest influence on the overall cash flow of the company, so that the assets for which usage fees are deducted are actually only supportive. If the residual value method is used for several patents, it must be ensured that multiple allocations of the same cash flows to different assets are excluded.

Identification of the Value-Determining Parameter

The problem in the application of income-oriented methods lies in determining the basic idea itself, since the three essential input parameters (level of cash flows, duration of cash flows, and risk associated with the patent) are crucial for a correct calculation of the patent value.

The first challenge of income-oriented methods is to quantify the amount of cash flows and to consider all exploitation possibilities that make sense from a business point of view. There are direct and indirect methods of calculating income flows. If sufficient information about specific economic benefits that can be generated by the patent is available, the direct method can be used. Price premiums through higher customer benefits or cost savings through greater efficiency are typical examples of such specific economic benefits. The indirect method tries to quantify the economic benefits through general economic or financial information. To calculate cash flows using the indirect method, the difference between the turnover of companies with and without the legal protection of the patent under assessment is often determined (Smith and Parr 2019).

In order to obtain an adequate patent value, it is also necessary to determine the trajectory of the economic benefits. The determination of a realistic time frame is just as important as the level of the cash flows themselves (Parr 1999). Since the legal patent life is often much longer than the economic patent life, the estimation is complex. The economic patent life ends either when it becomes unprofitable to maintain the patent or when another patent becomes more profitable and replaces the old one. The economically useful existence can be terminated for a variety of reasons: One of the most important reasons is the speed of technological change. The duration of payment flows is therefore of great importance for the income-oriented process, as younger patents have more time to generate economic benefits.

Another central element of the income-based method is that the risk associated with the patent is included in the calculation of the patent value. The risk results from the fact that information about the future can only be estimated. The longer the time frame in which forecasts are made, the higher the risk due to insufficient information.

The literature distinguishes three types of risk that are important when using a patent: economic risks, technical risks, and legal risks. In order to take these risks into account in the income-oriented procedure, they are estimated and transformed into a percentage value. The application of the risk specific percentage then depends on the design of the valuation model. Either the risk-specific percentage discounts the determined cash flows directly or the risk-specific percentage is added as a premium to the company's standard cost of capital. In their search for an appropriate discount rate, most companies choose either *Capital Asset Pricing Model (CAPM)* or *Weighted Average Cost of Capital (WACC)*.

Pros and Cons of Income-Oriented Procedures
Due to the well-founded concept and the general acceptance of the concept of value, the income-oriented procedure can be applied to most valuation problems. In theory, they are very useful for patent management, as the use of future economic benefits can well support patent management decisions. However, the method is error-prone in the context of patents, and one should not be underestimating the numerous parameters that need to be determined, and assumptions that need to be made.

Further Methods of Patent Valuation

All the patent evaluation methods listed below can be traced back to one of the methods already mentioned. They are listed separately due to their being of high practical importance:

(10) 25%-Rule
The royalty rate is 25% of the gross profit before or after taxes of the company using the intellectual property rights (*25%-rule*).

This procedure has the advantage that it can be applied as a simple "rule of thumb." Therefore, it is particularly suitable if fundamental estimates are to be made, if only a small amount of data is available, or if it is to be disclosed. The disadvantage is that neither future profitability nor the relationship between the opportunities and risks of the license business model are included in the valuation. The method is therefore only suitable for stable industries having low growth.

(11) Profit Share
The valuation takes place in the form of the determination of a certain license rate in relation to the profit. Valuation by pro rata profit can be applied if the future revenue to be expected on the basis of the underlying industrial property rights can be easily estimated.

Despite the simple calculation method, however, the proportional factor must be negotiated. For this reason, a threshold value is often agreed upon which the expected turnover must reach as a minimum. The valuation result thus depends on the respective negotiating partner.

(12) Technology Factor

This valuation method was developed by the management consultants *Arthur D. Little* and the chemical company *Dow Chemical*. The cash flow is determined using a technology factor. The technology factor is based on the contribution of the protected technology to the total revenue of the technology.

In addition to the business risk, the technology factor is derived from application, competitive, and legal positions and can, therefore, be used for internal valuations and combined with other valuation methods.

At the same time, agreement on the technology valuation is reached within the framework of the valuation. However, numerous experts from various disciplines must work together on the basis of detailed knowledge of the competitive environment and the underlying business plans.

In recent years, evaluation methods based on possible future events have become increasingly important. From the basic idea, the new methods are based on the idea that the patent value can best be determined by future economic benefits (cash flows). Compared to the simple income-oriented valuation method, however, real options and decision tree analyses in particular have the advantage that they take into account the patent owner's options for action when exploiting a patent (Rudolf and Witt 2002).

(13) Real Options Method

This method is also based on the basic idea of discounted cash flows. However, it takes into account the fact that if the net present value is negative, the owner has the option of abandoning the patent or postponing a project. Therefore, the ownership of a patent can also be compared with an option that includes the monopoly to exploit a patent. The value of such an option basically results from the inherent asymmetric peculiarity, which protects against the risk of a price drop and at the same time offers the possibility to benefit from larger price increases (Wu and Tseng 2006).

The real options method assumes there is a constant timeline between the time of valuation and the expiration of the patent; it is based on the concept used for financial options. The parameters used to value a patent are the present value of cash flows resulting from the exploitation of the patent, investment costs, economic patent life, standard deviation of project value due to technical, economic and legal risks, and risk-free interest. If one of these parameters changes, it has a direct influence on the value of the option (Pitkethly 1997). The real options method is often used in the pharmaceutical industry (Bogdan and Villiger 2010, see Sects. 6.1 and 6.2).

The specific advantage of the real options method lies in the fact that both initially weak cash flows and high risks can be taken into account as well as future decisions, such as further investments in business conditions.

(14) Decision-Tree Analysis

Another possibility of taking into account the flexibility of the patent owner with regard to decisions about patent valuation is the so-called decision tree analysis. Decision-tree analysis recognizes the possibility of postponing decisions beyond the future of a project until the end of a certain period is reached. The owner can wait until a defined milestone has been reached before postponing, exercising, or discontinuing a project (in the pharmaceutical industry, for example, a milestone can be the result of clinical phases). However, only a limited number of possibilities can be included in the model. In addition, decisions must be made at specific, predefined points in time. The decision tree is determined by all significant occasions and possible decisions en route to commercializing a patent (Razgaitis 2003b).

As with all methods of the income-oriented procedure, however, the determination of the parameters cannot be objectified in decision tree analysis. The required probabilities of occurrence even add another estimated parameter.

(15) Monte Carlo Method

Monte Carlo simulation is a technique to simulate the behavior of stochastic systems (Howell et al. 2001). Many random experiments are carried out. The outcome of each random experiment is observed and summarized in a distribution. In order to obtain a large number of possible future patent values, a sequence of random numbers is first generated, which forms the basis for the uncertainty. In addition, for each variable (remaining patent life, turnover, costs) both upper and lower limits as well as distributions within these limits are defined.

Based on this, the computer program simulates individual cash values for thousands of combinations of variables and summarizes them in a distribution. This type of patent evaluation does not calculate a patent value but gives out a range of possible values and the probability with which they occur (Razgaitis 2003a).

This distribution is an advantage of the Monte Carlo method because in reality it is unlikely that the future will occur exactly as it was modeled with discount factor and input parameters. The output of a distribution also gives one a feeling for the respective project, because the range gives values for the best possible and worst possible project developments (Brealey and Myers 2003).

Even though the Monte Carlo method is more realistic in that it generates a distribution, it is also very dependent on the input parameters. Since the Monte Carlo method is very complex and correct input parameters are prerequisites for determining a correct distribution, this method is even more prone to errors. Due to the high complexity, the calculation effort is enormous and relatively expensive, even in the case of perfect information. Therefore, it is rarely appropriate to use it in most enterprises. The importance of patent evaluation also lies in its practicality.

While it does not apply in many situations, it certainly does apply very well in the pharmaceutical sector because the parameters are well known and are also repeatedly measured. Perhaps it is best use is to simulate patient outcomes where the parameters and costs can easily be ascertained from healthcare records—simulations using those data can then be used to value alternate courses of treatment, and thereby very directly value the patent that covers the new treatment.

> **Valuation of Patents**
> If quantitative patent valuation methods are used for patent management, the following things have to be considered (overview see Table 3.5):
>
> - *Patent value:* The value of a patent is idiosyncratic, i.e., it strongly depends on who owns the patent, uses it, and in what context this happens. So, there is not "one" or absolute patent value.
> - *Valuation method:* The chosen valuation approach and the valuation method to be used strongly depend on the reason for the valuation.
> - *Subjective value:* Especially in patent management, not only objective but also subjective values of a patent or *subjective input parameters* are important. However, this subjectivity makes the evaluation susceptible to misjudgments.

3.3 Managing the Patent Portfolio

Portfolios are instruments for the analysis and visualization of strategic positioning and thrust directions. The variety of the portfolio techniques is immense, each technique has its own weakness when it comes to the selection of the dimensions. The *St. Gallen Approach to Managing Technologies and Patents* from Gassmann and Bader (2017) goes back to a method developed at the Institute of Technology Management at the University of St. Gallen, Switzerland, in the early 1990s (Boutellier et al. 1995). It has been continuously refined through numerous practical projects and introduced in numerous European and international companies (Boutellier et al. 2008).

We developed the *St. Gallen Patent Portfolio Management Model* further to strategically manage patents. It derives the patent strategy per core dimension from the corporate strategy or from the technology and innovation strategy.

Via portfolio management, action measures are derived from evaluated market and technology positions which serve to implement the corporate strategy. The vision and mission of the corporate strategy form the basis for evaluating the challenges posed by customers, the market, competitors, and substitutable technologies. The company's competencies, technology, and product fields are evaluated and positioned, taking into account the company's resource strength. This forms the basis for deriving standardization strategies. On the basis of the strategies developed, the necessary measures for dealing with intellectual property rights in these areas to build up and secure potential are finally derived (see Fig. 3.10).

Table 3.5 Overview of quantitative patent valuation methods

Method	Description
Cost-oriented:	
(1) Historical costs	Sum of costs needed to generate the patent.
(2) Reproduction costs	All costs needed to reproduce it.
Market-oriented:	
(3) Market price on active market	Valuation of patents based exclusively on how much would be willing to be paid on an open market.
(4) Analogy methods	Value of the patent of an analogous known in the market.
(5) Equity value/ econometric	Marginal contribution to equity market value of the patent, usually ascertained econometrically.
Income-oriented:	
(6) Direct cash flow forecast	Cash value based on directly calculable cash flows.
(7) Licensing price analogy	Cash value based on licensing (analogous) payments.
(8) Additional profit method	Cash value based on the difference compared to a fictional company without patent protection.
(9) Residual value method	Cash value based on payments after subtracting pro forma costs of firm.
Further methods of patent valuation:	
Profit-oriented:	
(10) 25%-rule	25% of gross profit before or after taxes.
(11) Profit share	Value in the form of licensing as a fraction (%) of profit.
Future-value-oriented:	
(12) Technology factor	Cash value in assessing the technology's contribution to cash flow.
(13) Real options method	Cash value based on the value of potential business options over time.
(14) Decision-tree analysis	Cash value incorporating future decisions at pre-defined milestones.
(15) Monte Carlo method	Simulation of a patent's value based on random draws.

Source: Table compiled by authors

Step 1: Vision and Mission

Vision and mission reflect the normative framework of the corporate strategy; they are supplemented by medium-term objectives and general corporate values. Such a guiding corridor is necessary in order to be able to assess the challenges that arise in relation to corporate competencies. It is important that the vision and mission are concrete and thus groundbreaking. Exchangeable statements such as "No. 1 in the market," "Customer orientation," or "Employee development" are generally not sufficient.

A *vision* answers the question "Where do we want to go by when?" and is based on the following elements:

3.3 Managing the Patent Portfolio

1. Vision & mission

2. Challenges for the company
1. Customer / Market
2. Competitors
3. Substitution technologies

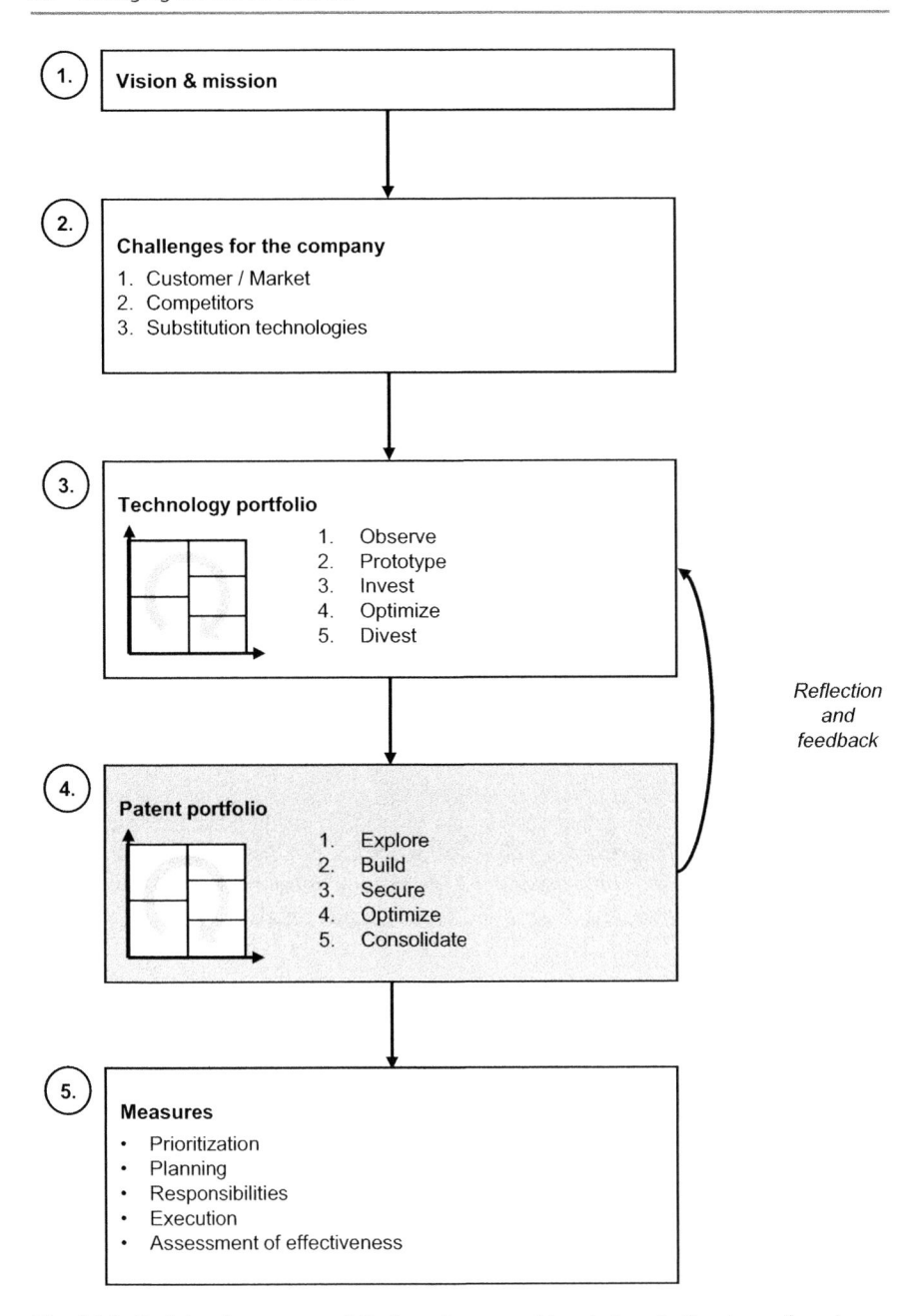

3. Technology portfolio
1. Observe
2. Prototype
3. Invest
4. Optimize
5. Divest

4. Patent portfolio
1. Explore
2. Build
3. Secure
4. Optimize
5. Consolidate

Reflection and feedback

5. Measures
- Prioritization
- Planning
- Responsibilities
- Execution
- Assessment of effectiveness

Fig. 3.10 Deriving the patent portfolio from the overarching strategy (authors' own figure)

- The central idea of the desired development
- Feasible utopia
- Future orientation
- Time reference with regard to realization

A *mission* addresses the question "How and with what do we want to achieve the vision" and considers the following aspects:

- Guard rails of the desired development
- Instrumental focus on implementation: task at the center
- Orientation to the present

Step 2: Challenges for the Company

In this step, the technological challenges that the company has to face are determined. Three perspectives have to be considered with regard to corporate competencies:

- Customer/market
- Competitors
- Substitution technologies

Customer/Market
The customer and market perspectives take the requirements placed by customers and markets on the competencies, skills, technologies, products, and services available from the company, into account. A distinction must be made between the requirements of individual lead users and broad market trends.

Competitors
The competitive perspective makes relativize the comparison to the activities of the competition and takes into account the comparative advantages and disadvantages, strengths, and weaknesses. If, for example, the company is not a technology or competence leader in one area, the question arises as to whether the company should adopt a fast follower or better a differentiation position.

Substitution Technologies
On the one hand, the importance of in-house competences in terms of substitutability with new, external technologies, products, or services must be assessed. On the other hand, the question of replacing existing technologies with new internal technologies arises. Even if the introduction of new technologies does not bring new advantages to the market or even should it provide additional functions that are not required, the introduction of substitution technologies makes sense if internal costs can be saved or internal logistics processes can be optimized. Taiwanese light-emitting diode

manufacturer *Huga Optotech*, for example, is replacing conventional neon tube lighting in offices with light-emitting diodes.

Step 3: Technology Portfolio

The basic orientation of the technology portfolio can be derived from a two-dimensional portfolio representation. Based on the competencies to be classified, their strategic significance is determined on the basis of the challenges posed by customers, the market, competition, and substitution technologies, and then mapped on the vertical axis. For each competence, the relative resource strength of the company is determined as well, which is mapped on the horizontal axis: The technological capabilities of the company, such as infrastructure, employees, available knowledge, and experience are also taken into account and evaluated in comparison to the competition.

The *St. Gallen Approach* distinguishes between five technology portfolio sectors and the resulting norm strategies, which correspond, in chronological order, to a typical product development life cycle (see Fig. 3.11): *observe, prototype, invest, optimize,* and *divest* (Boutellier et al. 2008).

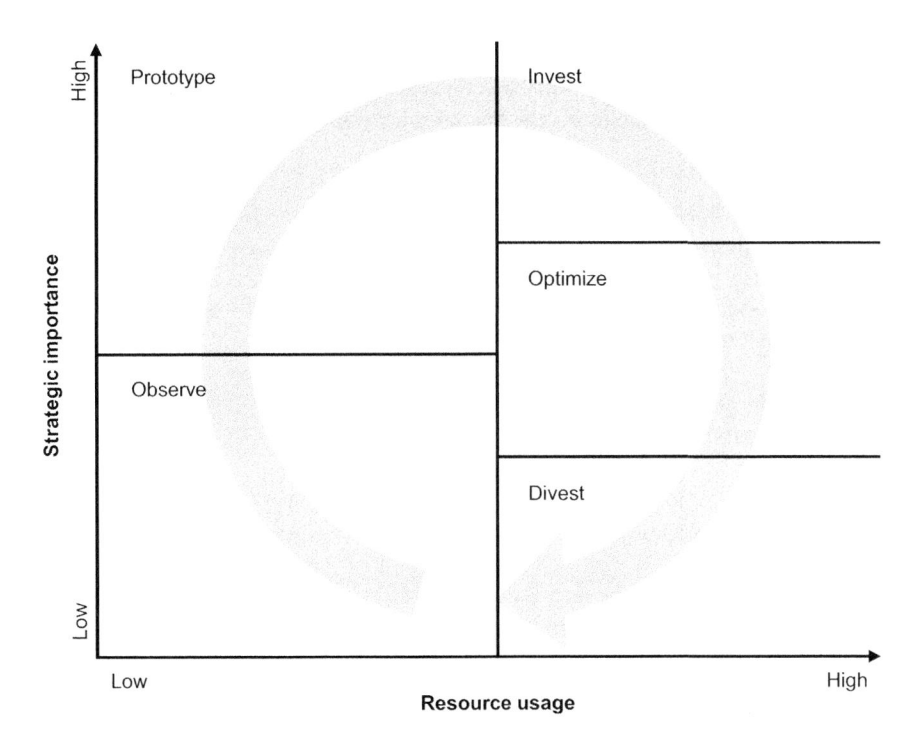

Fig. 3.11 Normative strategies for strategic technology portfolio management. Source: Boutellier et al. (2008)

Observe

Competencies in this segment are characterized by a strategic importance that is still perceived as low. The corresponding competence, technology, product, or service fields should be actively monitored, for example, by attending exhibitions and congresses, by studying magazines, journals, and the Internet, and cooperating with universities.

Prototype

If the strategic importance grows from the perspective of customers, markets, competitors, or substitution technologies, the initial trials must be conducted and skills have to be built up, for example, through prototypes. In addition, external partners are sought and integrated in order to thereby develop internal competencies as efficiently as possible.

Invest

High internal resource strength contrasts with high long-term strategic importance. Long-term investments in the core competence area are therefore necessary and reasonable in order to secure existing technologies and investments and to further expand competitive advantages.

Optimize

If, despite high internal resource strength, there is only medium strategic importance or if it is foreseeable that this will even decrease, no larger investments are meaningful any more, but an optimization becomes necessary.

Divest

If no competitive advantage becomes visible over the next 5–10 years, resources previously tied up must be reduced in good time to make it available for realizing new technology potential. A continuation of the technologies and products only makes sense as long as revenues can still be generated. However, further investments in the expansion of competencies are not expected.

Step 4: Patent Portfolio

The patent strategy to be derived from the corporate strategy should serve both to build up business potential, and on the other hand also to secure existing and realized potential. Accordingly, it makes sense to derive appropriate *patent standardization strategies* on the basis of the technology portfolio structure already described.

The *patent standardization strategies* make general statements about the control of the development as well as the dismantling of intellectual property rights under corporate strategic aspects. The portfolio can be expanded, for example, by filing its own patent applications, purchasing or acquiring intellectual property rights, or by taking out a license. The portfolio is reduced by dropping patents, selling them, or selling them in the context of spin-offs.

3.3 Managing the Patent Portfolio

The scope of protection can often already be derived from the claim categories. For example, the chemical industry differentiates between claims relating to processes for the manufacture from the claims relating to substance compositions. While infringing manufacturing processes are usually difficult to prove, infringing substance compositions can be proven relatively easily.

By categorizing products and countries, country-specific legal requirements can later be taken into account. Furthermore, a strategic evaluation of the countries must be incorporated into the portfolio management, for example, determining which countries are relevant for the market and production—not only from the point of view of the own company but also from the point of view of the competitors.

A further criterion in portfolio management is the potential for own use and use by third parties, an important prerequisite for licensing projects.

Particularly in the *pharmaceutical industry, life cycle management* plays an important role, one in which attempts are made to build up product-related succession protection rights beyond the basic patents; this is often the only way to maintain an effective blocking effect even after the basic active ingredient patent has expired. This is of great importance due to the rapidly growing generics market.

The phases of the technology portfolio serve as the basis for the respective measures of the patent strategy along the technology life cycle. The *St. Gallen Patent Portfolio Management Model* therefore has five phases (see Fig. 3.12):

- Explore
- Build
- Secure
- Optimize
- Consolidate

The norm strategies address the three core dimensions of the patent strategy.[2] In the portfolio presentation, the dimension of *strategic impact* also reflects the *external perspective* (customers/competitors/substitution technologies) just as the dimension of *resource intensity* indicates the *internal perspective* (capabilities/competencies).

In the first phase, i.e., *Explore*, patent scanning can be used to identify potential across industries. Based on the technology portfolio and the technology roadmap, for example, a decision must be made in this phase as to whether broad conceptual patents should be applied for. In the development phase of the patent portfolio life cycle, i.e., *Build*, targeted patent searches are then initiated. Selected competitors are analyzed in order to be able to take strategic competitive advantages into account when filing patent applications. In the further phase, i.e., *Secure*, patent clusters should be formed systematically in order to provide the best possible protection. On the basis of the technology portfolio and the technology roadmap, broad basic patents and patents on specific design variants *(growing and pruning)* can be

---

[2]For the core dimensions of patent strategy see Chap. 2.

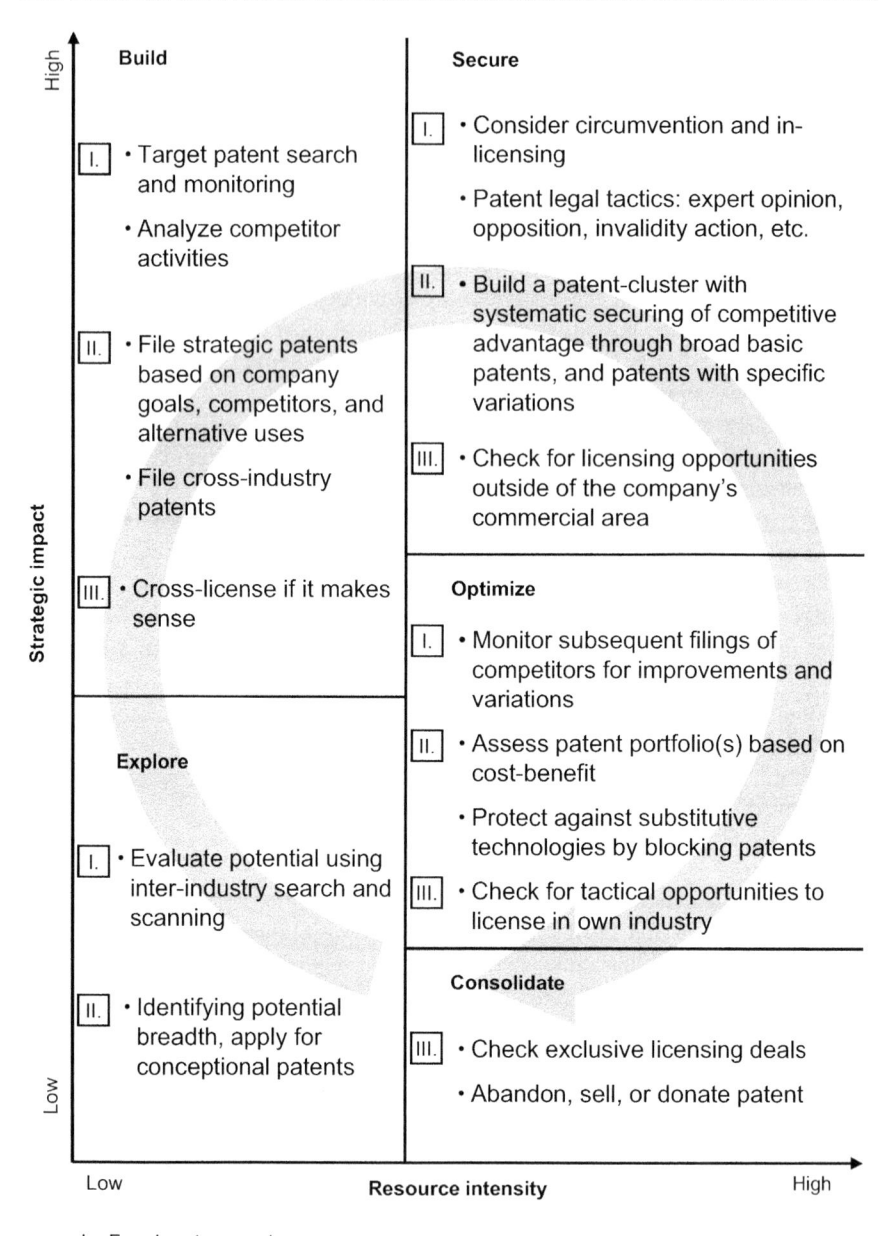

Build

I. • Target patent search and monitoring
 • Analyze competitor activities

II. • File strategic patents based on company goals, competitors, and alternative uses
 • File cross-industry patents

III. • Cross-license if it makes sense

Secure

I. • Consider circumvention and in-licensing
 • Patent legal tactics: expert opinion, opposition, invalidity action, etc.

II. • Build a patent-cluster with systematic securing of competitive advantage through broad basic patents, and patents with specific variations

III. • Check for licensing opportunities outside of the company's commercial area

Explore

I. • Evaluate potential using inter-industry search and scanning

II. • Identifying potential breadth, apply for conceptional patents

Optimize

I. • Monitor subsequent filings of competitors for improvements and variations

II. • Assess patent portfolio(s) based on cost-benefit
 • Protect against substitutive technologies by blocking patents

III. • Check for tactical opportunities to license in own industry

Consolidate

III. • Check exclusive licensing deals
 • Abandon, sell, or donate patent

Axes: Strategic impact (Low–High) vs. Resource intensity (Low–High)

I. Freedom-to-operate
II. Differentiation
III. Multiplication

Fig. 3.12 Normative strategies for strategic patent portfolio management (authors' own figure)

considered for better protection. Out-licensing potential to secure long-term financial returns may be conceivable in other application areas and should be reviewed. In order to optimize the patent portfolio, i.e., during the phase *Optimize*, licensing opportunities in one's own field can also be considered for short-term financial returns. Furthermore, the patent clusters should be reviewed in particular on the basis of cost-benefit considerations. Depending on the competitive situation, blocking patents can protect against substitutions. In the final phase of the patent portfolio life cycle, i.e., the phase *Consolidate*, the abandonment or exclusive exploitation of patents may be considered (sale, exclusive out-licensing, possibly donations).

Explore

The contribution of a patent strategy in this phase of the technology life cycle, therefore, focuses primarily on broadly based searches, which are intended to examine whether earlier inventions exist *(patent scanning)*.

The underlying inventions should be continuously further developed, and the protection of improvements and variants should also be considered.

DSM Nutrition (formerly Roche Vitamins) systematically uses patent searches to identify trends in manufacturing process technologies, and also to identify efficient substitution technologies in good time. With researchers and marketing specialists, search profiles are defined on the basis of keywords in order to narrow down relevant areas of interest. A special focus of the trend analyses are the life cycle curves. The time horizon is 5–10 years.

Publicly accessible platforms are available for initial research. Relatively quick overviews can be obtained, individual documents can be downloaded, and simple questions can be answered.

> **Explore Checklist**
> - Evaluation of risks and potential by means of cross-industry patent searches *(patent scanning)*
> - Use of further analysis methods, e.g., scenario technique or road mapping
> - Understanding of trends and future markets, for example, service innovations
> - In the case of identified potentials, registration of broad, conceptual patents

Build

As soon as topics and areas of competence of growing strategic importance are identified, focused patent searches must be carried out (patent monitoring). The aim is to monitor further developments in certain fields of technology and also to monitor certain competitors through patent searches. It should be noted that most patent documents are only published 18 months after the priority application. In a company, it is advisable to determine specialists for certain competitors and areas of competence who will carry out these searches and analyze any prototypes already available.

The medium-sized company *Erbe Elektromedizin* systematically monitors its competitors:

- Every month, the patent department receives the new publications of the previous month from the IP rights monitoring department. The monitoring of intellectual property rights is largely carried out by the search department of an external patent attorney, who prepares these on the basis of a defined filter. In urgent cases, it is also possible to conduct searches yourself.
- The patent department checks and pre-selects the documents. The documents are then sent to the respective R&D experts. An engineer receives precisely those documents that relate to his technical areas.
- The technical experts prepare short presentations of the publications submitted to them. Three minutes are available for this purpose.
- Within the framework of a monthly patent round, the short presentations of the technical experts are shown. A short discussion is held afterward, and the next steps are decided upon, for example, a decision to file an opposition or to be included in the monitoring of publications. Since the patent round meets once a month, there is in principle the possibility of an opposition for all documents discussed there.[3]
- The patent department draws up minutes that are distributed to the participants of the patent round.

Advantages of this procedure: The fixed date of the patent round guarantees a high degree of regularity, which in turn ensures that the specialist engineers have constant knowledge of the intellectual property rights situation. The obligation to give short presentations guarantees that the engineers deal with the patent specifications on time (opposition deadline), while the direct feedback to the patent department and colleagues brings a lively discussion of the documents, concrete suggestions to each R&D working group, and it also avoids having duplicate developments and applications.

The highly innovative Swiss hearing aid manufacturer *Phonak (today: Sonova)* makes intensive use of patent information to support its internal technology early warning system. The patent disclosure documents of all relevant competitors, such as Siemens Audiology, are collected, broken down by technology and core competence fields, and analyzed under the responsibility of the head of the research department. A time horizon of 3–5 years is achieved for the identification of trends.

The focus should not only be on the company's own activities, but also on the expected directions of existing and potential competitors. This is the only way to build up an effective blocking potential through intellectual property rights in good time.

---

[3]The German and European opposition deadline is 9 months after publication of the intent to grant.

Patent claims should aim for the broadest possible protection corridor, address solution architectures, and concepts and be formulated in a cross-sectoral manner. In this phase, the foundations are laid for later patent license exchange options. Even if a direct confrontation with competitors only takes place after a further maturity phase of the competencies, groundbreaking intellectual property rights generally date back to this technology phase. *Endress+Hauser* specifically develops intellectual property rights in order to avoid later disputes with major competitors.

If R&D activities are carried out with external partners, it is necessary to weigh up which exploitation and commercialization requirements will be sought later. Accordingly, cooperation negotiations must be conducted appropriately.

CeramTec, a group of companies within the *Dynamit Nobel Group*, developed a cylinder head for engines in cooperation with an automotive supplier. Negotiations on the handling of the resulting industrial property rights were conducted carefully. While joint use was agreed on for the engine area, *CeramTec* received the exclusive rights for the ceramics area.

Build Checklist
- Conduct targeted patent search (patent-monitoring)
- Analysis of competitors' activities
- Applying for patents of strategic importance
- Flesh out patent families
- Targeted patent to block competitors
- Alternative areas outside of the field of activity
- Application for patents applicable to multiple industries
- Investigate cross-licensing possibilities

Secure

In this phase, a company has already built up its own resources in a field of competence of high strategic importance. At the same time, however, one's own activities increase the risk of conflict with competitors' patents. Securing one's own freedom to operate is therefore of great importance in this phase. If, however, signs of disruptive patents from third parties become more frequent, these should be investigated as quickly as possible and with high priority. Only in this way can suitable countermeasures be introduced in good time and investment decisions be made accordingly:

- Disturbing patent applications can be monitored and, if necessary, expert opinions prepared or opposition proceedings considered when granting a patent.
- Technical circumvention solutions can still be developed.
- Make-or-buy decisions can be made on the basis of cost-benefit considerations and in- or cross-licensing and cooperation options can be examined and tackled if necessary.

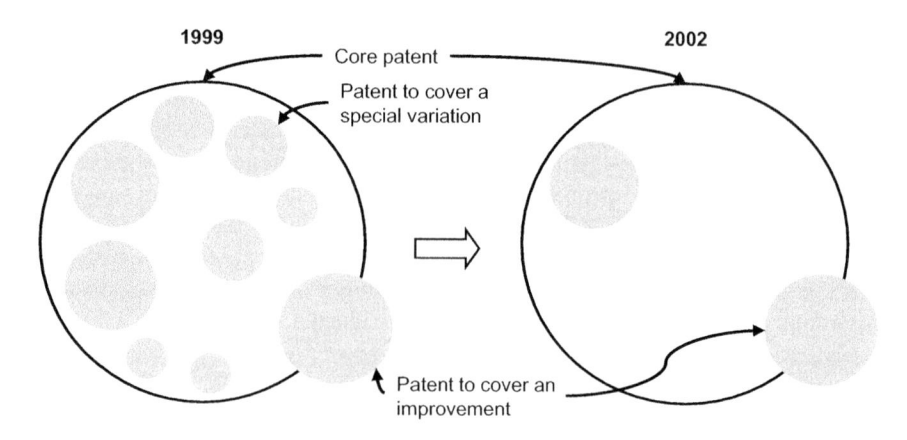

Fig. 3.13 Growing and pruning: *Henkel's* "Megaperls©" patent portfolio (authors' own figure)

The potential for applying for broad basic patents is declining, since public knowledge, the *state of the art*, has grown considerably in all areas. The focus of patent applications is increasingly on more detailed, very concrete forms of execution. It is therefore important to systematically examine the subject areas for solution and execution variants or for workarounds.

Within the framework of patent portfolio optimization, companies are therefore increasingly endeavoring to create *patent clusters* in strategically important technology fields: initially, broadly covering patent portfolios are built up *(growing)*, but at a later point in time, when it is easier to assess which ideas are technically and commercially relevant, they are thinned out again *(pruning)*. It is advantageous to make cost-effective decisions according to the benefit aspect already in the current patent application procedure. The German consumer goods manufacturer *Henkel* successfully uses this method to protect as many variants as possible at an early stage and to avoid excessive costs for the patent portfolio later on (see Fig. 3.13).

Particularly in the case of competences that have been developed with external cooperation partners, it should be examined to what extent out-licensing possibilities are possible in other technical areas or other markets in order to be able to generate licensing income in the long term.

BMW cooperated with the small Californian software company *Immersion* in the cooperative development of the central, multifunctional control element "iDrive." This company had already developed relevant competencies in the field of force feedback technology, a technology used in joysticks, operating devices in the design sector, and in medical technology. It was agreed that *BMW* would be granted limited, exclusive rights to the development results for the automotive sector, but that *Immersion* would be entitled to independent use and marketing outside the automotive sector.

> **Secure Checklist**
> When there are signs of disruptive third-party IP rights:
>
> - Check for ways of circumventing, in-licensing, and cross-licensing
> - Patent procedural measures (opinions, opposition)
> - Development of patent thickets to systematically protect strategic advantage:
> - Wide basic patents
> - Patents for specific refinements and features
> - Check licensing to other domains and industries:
> - Long-term return on investment (ROI)

Optimize

In this case, the company has high competencies in these fields, but its strategic importance is declining from the customer, market, competitive, or technological point of view. Now at the latest, existing patent clusters must be thoroughly reviewed for cost-benefit considerations. This includes the monitoring of competition activities with regard to the (re-)registration of improvements and variants. If there is possibly even the danger that competences could be replaced at an early stage by substitution technologies, consideration should be given to using patents of one's own, patents relating to these areas as blocking protection rights, in order to prevent a one-sided decline in the value of the existing core technologies.

The sports car manufacturer, Porsche, for example, uses intellectual property rights on substitution technologies in a targeted manner in order to avoid a premature decline in value, and a dilution of existing technologies. If necessary, exclusive licenses are even taken and kept in stock for this purpose.

In addition to this, out-licensing opportunities must be examined, which, unlike potential protection, also encompass the Group's own technical areas or markets in order to generate licensing income in the short term. Sometimes even a market segment can be stimulated by means of a greater openness to such an extent that substitution tendencies can be further delayed by greater standardization and price reductions.

For example, after a patent dispute with *3M*, the Danish hearing instrument manufacturer *ReSound* was able to purchase a strong patent portfolio that *ReSound* contributed to the hearing instrument patent pool *HIMPP (Hearing Instrument Manufacturers Patent Partnership)*. This pool, which was formed with other companies such as *Danavox, Oticon, Phonak, Starkley,* and *Widex*, can now be joined by companies willing to pay a membership fee. In practice, this creates barriers to entry for potential new competitors.

> **Optimize Checklist**
> - Competition monitoring by means of patent searches
> - Review patent clusters according to cost-benefit considerations
> - Protection against substitution technologies through blocking patents
> - Investigate out-licensing possibilities also in own field; short-term return on investment (ROI)

Consolidate

If the strategic importance of a technology or competence has decreased considerably, it must be examined whether the patent claim versions permit a reassessment with an allocation to other fields of competence or competition. The possibility of an *exclusive* out-licensing should be considered, as far as this is possible due to other, already existing license agreements. Otherwise, a low benefit can be assumed, which is offset by high costs. If there are no other reasons, such as the necessity of a large patent portfolio, such patents can be abandoned, sold, surrendered, or donated.[4]

Endress+Hauser, for example, segregates or sells all patents if the subject areas concerned are not incorporated into its own products or manufacturing processes within a period of about 7 years.

> **Consolidate Checklist**
> - Check exclusive licensing to an active firm
> - Investigate partial licensing to a patent pool
> - Resign patent, sell, or sell/donate

Step 5: Measures

Once the technology and patent strategies have been derived, the final step is to implement the portfolio measures. In order to implement the developed strategies in the over-burdened patent departments, the first step is to prioritize the directions of action. The most important measures *(vital few actions)* must be planned in detail with the business units or developers and implemented with them.

Case Study: Patent Portfolio Management at Daimler

With its intellectual property strategy, the *Daimler Automotive Group* pursues the following two main objectives:

---

[4]In the USA, donating patents to universities or charitable organizations can be taken as a tax deduction.

3.3 Managing the Patent Portfolio

1. Securing its own monopoly positions
2. Protecting against monopoly positions of third parties

According to Mr. Einsele, the former Head of Intellectual Property, *Daimler* is committed to project-integrated patent work in order to achieve these goals: "At the beginning of development projects, the relevant state of the art and external property rights are searched for, and the respective property right status is recorded and evaluated."

A separate patent strategy is defined for each development project. During the course of the project, the assessment of the property right situation is regularly updated and project-related information on third-party property rights is made available. This reduces the chance of duplicate developments and of possible collisions. Additionally, this phase is used to determine protectable results. During projects, the acquisition of intellectual property rights of third parties is an increasingly important aspect, but the marketing and licensing of one's own know-how is also gaining in importance. In the case of cooperation or R&D partnerships, the search for suitable partners also begins with patent portfolio analyses. The Intellectual property department later accompanies the drafting of cooperation and development agreements as well as bringing about confidentiality agreements to safeguard know-how. At the end of the project, final project reviews are carried out, in which final statements about the state of the art, third-party property rights, own property right position, contractual situation, and standards are recorded.

Patent management at *Daimler* consists of nine elements:

- Early involvement of the Intellectual Property department in the innovation process
- Accompanying support of the R&D projects by the intellectual property department, in particular also important project reviews
- Definition of strategic priorities
- Support of the developers on site
- Monitoring competitor activities
- Avoidance and minimization of risks
- Protection of protectable results
- Checking the transferability and marketability of development results
- Enforcement of own intellectual property rights against third parties

The importance of proactive patent management was demonstrated with the introduction of the "BAS" brake assistant. *Daimler*, then *Daimler-Benz*, began developing its own brake assist system in 1989. Based on a German basic patent application, over 30 further patent applications in the areas of BAS function, on/off criteria, brake system, and vehicle properties were generated in succession thanks to the intensive support provided by the intellectual property department during the project.

Almost a decade later, the decisive importance of these early patent applications for *Daimler* became apparent: In 1997, *Toyota* approached *Daimler* and applied for a license for *Daimler's* basic patent for the series introduction of a brake assist system. It besides this turned out that *Toyota* had also filed a basic patent application for a brake assistance system in Japan in 1990—albeit 5 days later. *Daimler* agreed to the granting of the license: *Toyota* paid licenses for the basic patent for Germany and the USA, and for the subsequent patents in France, Italy, Great Britain, and even Japan. In return, however, *Daimler* also received a license to *Toyota's* basic patent for the Japanese market.

Managing the Patent Portfolio

Finally, the three core dimensions of patent strategy (see Sect. 2.3) and their connection with the five patent management process phases of the *St. Gallen Patent Portfolio Management Model* are summarized below. It is of great importance that the company is aware of the five standard strategies Exploring, Constructing, Securing, Optimizing, and Divestment. More important than the perfect classification, which can hardly exist in practice, are the regularity of the implementation, and the consistency with the corporate strategy.

Checklist for Managing the Patent Portfolio

Measures for freedom-to-operate:

- Patent searches (patent scanning, patent monitoring)
- Development of circumvention solutions
- In-licensing, exchange of patent licenses, design access
- Patent law measures (e.g., expert opinions, oppositions, nullity proceedings)

Measures against imitators:

- Establishment of patent clusters to systematically secure competitive advantages
- Registration of broad, conceptual basic patents
- Protection of specific design variants
- Analysis of competitive products or processes, and registration of improvement solutions based on them
- Patenting or in-licensing of substitution technologies
- Consistent legal action against piracy

(continued)

Measures for commercialization:

- Treatment of patents as a "real material product" (including a business model)
- Development of the company's own patent portfolio from the point of view of competitive attractiveness, i.e., the potential for use by third parties
- Examination of out-licensing possibilities depending on the technology life cycle (long-term or short-term orientation in other fields or in one's own field)
- Consideration of exchange transactions as an alternative or supplement to cash license payments (e.g., exchange license agreements, purchase or sales obligations, design access)

References

Bader, M. A., Beckenbauer, A., Gassmann, O., König, T., Lohwasser, E., & Menninger, J. (2008). *One valuation fits all? – How Europe's most innovative companies valuate technologies and patents*. PricewaterhouseCoopers: Munich.

Bader, M. A., Vogel, H., Tobias, M., Rüther, F., & Gassmann, O. (2012) *Intellectual property right valuation index and a method and a system for creating such an index*. US 20120303537 A1.

Bertolotti, N. (1996). *The valuation of intellectual property*. Geneva: World Intellectual Property Organization (WIPO).

Bogdan, B., & Villiger, R. (2010). *Valuation in life sciences*. Heidelberg: Springer.

Bosworth, D., & Rogers, M. (2001). Market value, r&d and intellectual property: An empirical analysis of large Australian firms. *The Economic Record, 77*(239), 323–337.

Boutellier, R., Hallbauer, S., & Locker, A. (1995). *Technologiestrategie für kleinere und mittlere Unternehmen*. St. Gallen: University of St. Gallen (HSG).

Boutellier, R., Gassmann, O., & von Zedtwitz, M. (2008). *Managing global innovation* (3rd ed.). Berlin: Springer.

Brealey, R. A., & Myers, S. C. (2003). *Principles of corporate finance* (7th ed.). New York: McGraw-Hill.

Brockhoff, K. (1999). *Forschung und Entwicklung: Planung und Kontrolle* (5th ed.). Munich: Oldenburg.

Cockburn, I., & Griliches, Z. (1987). Industry effects and appropriability measures in the stock market's valuation of r&d and patents. *American Economic Review, 78*, 419–423.

Connolly, R. A., & Hirschey, M. (1988). Market value and patents: A Bayesian approach. *Economics Letters, 27*, 83–87.

DIN 77100. (2011). *Patentbewertung – Grundsätze der monetären Patentbewertung*. Berlin: DIN Deutsches Institut für Normung e.V..

Dressler, A. (2006). *Patente in technologieorientierten Mergers & Acquisitions. Nutzen, Prozessmodell, Entwicklung und Interpretation semantischer Patentlandkarten*. Wiesbaden: DUV.

Econsight. (2020). Difference between quantitative and qualitative patent analysis – Citation of Swatch patents by third parties (number of cited patents vs. cumulative value of cited patents), 2000-2017. In: *Green Technologies – A new approach for investment strategies*, Basel.

Ensthaler, J., & Strübbe, K. (2006). *Patentbewertung. Ein Praxisleitfaden zum Patentmanagement*. Berlin: Springer.

Ernst, H. (1996). *Patentinformationen für die strategische Planung von Forschung und Entwicklung*. Wiesbaden: Gabler.

Ernst, H. (1998). Patent portfolios for strategic R&D planning. *Journal of Engineering and Technology Management, 15*(4), 279–308.

Ernst, H. (1999). Evaluation of dynamic technological developments by means of patent data. In K. Brockhoff, A. K. Chakrabarti, & J. Hauschildt (Eds.), *The dynamics of innovation. Strategic and managerial implications* (pp. 107–132). Berlin: Springer.

Ernst, H. (2002). Patentmanagement. In D. Specht & M. G. Möhrle (Eds.), *Lexikon Technologiemanagement* (pp. 214–218). Wiesbaden: Gabler.

Ernst, H., & Omland, N. (2010). The patent asset index – A new approach to benchmark patent portfolios. *World Patent Information, 33*(1), 34–41.

Faix, A. (2001). Die Patentportfolio-Analyse – Methodische Konzeption und Anwendung im Rahmen der strategischen Patentpolitik. *Zeitschrift für Planung, 2*, 185–208.

Gassmann, O., & Bader, M. A. (2017). *Patentmanagement: Innovationen erfolgreich nutzen und schützen* (4th ed.). Berlin: Springer.

Ghapar, F., Brooks, R., & Smyth, R. (2014). The impact of patenting activity on the financial performance of malaysian firms. *Journal of the Asia Pacific Economy, 19*(3), 445–463.

Griliches, Z. (1981). Market value, r&d, and patents. *Economic Letters, 7*, 183–187.

Hall, B., Jaffe, A., & Trajtenberg, M. (2005). Market value and patent citations. *RAND Journal of Economics, 36*(1), 16–38.

Hall, B. H., & Mairesse, J. (2007). Empirical studies of innovation in the knowledge-driven economy. *Economics of Innovation and New Technology, 15*(4-5), 289–299.

Hellebrand, O., Kaube, G., & Falckenstein, R. (2007). *Lizenzsätze für technische Erfindungen* (3rd ed.). Cologn: Carl Heymanns.

Hofinger, S. (1997). Portfolio-Analyse als Instrument unternehmerischer Patentpolitik. *epi Information*, No. 4, pp. 100–104.

Howell, S., Stark, A., Newton, D., Paxson, D., Cavus, M., Pereira, J., & Patel, K. (2001). *Realoptions. Evaluating corporate investment opportunities in a dynamic world*. London: Financial Times Prentice Hall.

IDW S 5. (2013). *IDW Standard: Principles of the Valuation of Intangible Assets (IDW S 5)* (p. 5/ 2011). Düsseldorf: IDW.

Köllner, M. (2009). Due diligence or discount monetary effect of legal aspects in patent valuation. *LES Nouvelles*, March 2009, 24–37.

Kuckartz, M. (2007). *IPC-Patentportfolio-Bewertung: Patentmanagement speziell für den Mittelstand*. 5. Patentforum Nordbayern 2007.

Megna, P., & Klock, M. (1993). The impact of intangible capital on Tobin's q in the semiconductor industry. *The American Economic Review, 83*(2), 265–269.

Moser, U., & Goddar, H. (2007). Grundlagen der Bewertung immaterieller Vermögenswerte am Beispiel der Bewertung patentgeschützter Technologien. *Finanzbetrieb, 10*, 594–609.

Otto Toivanen, P. S., & Bosworth, D. (2002). Innovation and the market value of uk firms, 1989-1995. *Oxford Bulletin of Economics and Statistics, 64*(39), 0305–9049.

Parr, R. L. (1999). *IP valuation issues and strategies*. Geneva: World Intellectual Property Organization (WIPO).

Pfeiffer, W., Schäffner, G. J., Schneider, W., & Schneider, H. (1989). *Studie zur Anwendung der Portfolio-Methode auf die strategische Analyse und Bewertung von Patentinformationen*. Nürnberg.

Pitkethly, R. (1997). *The valuation of patents*. Working paper, University of Oxford, Said Business School.

Poredda, A., & Wildschütz, S. (2004). Patent valuation – A controlled market share approach. *Les Nouvelles – Journal of the Licensing Executives Society, 34*(2), 77–85.

Razgaitis, R. (2003a). *Dealmaking using real options and monte carlo analysis*. Hoboken, NJ: Wiley Finance.
Razgaitis, R. (2003b). *Valuation and pricing of technology-based intellectual property*. Chichester: Wiley.
Reitzig, M. (2002). *Die Bewertung von Patentrechten. Eine theoretische und empirische Analyse aus Unternehmenssicht*. Wiesbaden: DUV.
Rings, R. (2000). Patentbewertung – Methoden und Faktoren zur Wertermittlung technischer Schutzrechte. *GRUR, 10*, 839–848.
Rudolf, M., & Witt, P. (2002). *Bewertung von Wachstumsunternehmen: Traditionelle und innovative Methoden im Vergleich*. Wiesbaden: Gabler.
Schulze, A. (2005). Patent-Portfoliomanagement für große Unternehmen. *Mitteilung der deutschen Patentanwälte*, No. 9/10, pp. 416–421.
Smith, G. V., & Parr, R. L. (2019). *Intellectual property. Valuation, exploitation and infringement damages* (5th ed.). Hoboken, NJ: Wiley.
Thompson, M. (2016) Estimating global patent rents from public market data. Paper presented *IP Statistics for Decision Makers*, OECD, Sydney 2016.
Turner, J. (2000). *Valuation of intellectual property assets; valuation techniques: parameters, methodologies and limitations*. Geneva: World Intellectual Property Organization (WIPO).
Wu, M., & Tseng, C. (2006). Valuation of Patent – a real options perspective. *Applied Economics Letters, 13*(5), 313–318.
Wurzer, A. (2005). Wertorientiertes Patentportfolio. *Mitteilung der deutschen Patentanwälte*, No. 9/10, pp. 430–439.
Wurzer, A., & Reinhardt, D. F. (2010). *Handbuch der Patentbewertung* (2nd ed.). Cologn: Carl Heymanns.

Successful Practices in Commercializing Patents 4

When it comes to patenting, much of the strategic focus is on protecting the products and processes from imitation and on ensuring one's own freedom of action. This enables companies to create quasi-monopolies on the market and generate returns. This chapter shows another side to patents which is generating value through proactive commercialization rather than building up a static defense against technological and commercial encroachment. When patents are exploited commercially, the focus shifts away from simply protecting the product to generating added value through the patent in a myriad of manners.

Patents have traditionally been embedded in a product that a company sells. Increasingly complex supply chains, cross-border trade, tax rules, and a competitive landscape have led to many different ways of exploiting a patent commercially. This chapter presents an overview of these techniques to give the IP manager a toolbox. Exactly how firms go about deriving value is quite idiosyncratic since technologies and competitive environments are often highly specific. Yet there are a host of common strategies: sale, licensing, cross-licensing, etc. Cross-licensing, which works well in the semiconductor industry, may not work well in the pharmaceutical industry. So rather than be prescriptive, we hope to show the essential techniques for a successful commercialization of patents.

In broad strokes, there are two main motives for commercialization. A distinction can be made between *monetary* and *strategic* motives. Monetary motives refer to directly measurable financial income. Monetary motives include the generation of income, the increase of returns, and the reduction of costs. The strategic motives are more diverse. They can be divided into motives with a focus outside the company, i.e., with external effects, and motives with focus and effects within the company. Commercialization often involves deep strategic questions about the business model, and what it means to "give away" acquired knowledge and patents.

The most common form of patent exploitation is licensing. Other types of patent exploitation include cross-licensing, selling patents, setting up spin-offs or joint ventures, and forming strategic alliances for joint research, and also the development and marketing of an innovation (Parr and Sullivan 1996; Ziegler et al. 2011; Bader and Liegler 2013). While "patenting to protect" typically does not change the core business model, commercialization has broad implications since (cross-)licensing, financing, spinning-off often touch on the core business model.

In the following different forms of patent commercialization are elaborated:

- Licensing
- Cross-licensing
- Sale
- Strategic alliance
- Spin-off and call-back
- Joint venture
- Patenting for access to finance
- Litigation for value
- Complex strategies

Rather than discuss implications theoretically, we present a series of case studies illustrating how exactly firms go about balancing deriving value from patents without destroying the original business model.

4.1 Licensing

In principle, licensing means that the patent holder grants one or more parties permission to use the technology described by the patent. In return, the licensee pays the patent holder (licensor) a license fee. The patent remains in the possession of the licensor. However, licenses differ in various characteristics. Three important characteristics of licenses are described below.

First, a license differs in its degree of exclusivity: An exclusive license means that the patentee licenses out the right to use the patent to only one licensee. If licenses of a patent are granted to several licensees, it is called a nonexclusive license.

Secondly, licenses differ in the scope and content of the transaction. If only the patent is transferred in the form of the patent specification, it is a license without knowledge transfer. In the case of a license with knowledge transfer, know-how and technical expertise are transferred in addition to the patent specification:

- License agreements without know-how include patents or patent applications, worldwide or regional, exclusive or nonexclusive use, and the term of the license.
- License agreements with know-how include research and test reports, samples, prototypes, market studies, and competitive analyses; and they may even include cooperation partners and customers. In addition, technical experts are often made available to support the transfer of knowledge and for further developments. This raises the question of which components can be commercialized in which way: On the one hand, a complete business model can be externally out-licensed, while on the other hand, an in-house spin-up could deliver faster and more sustainable

profits. Although some patents could be out-licensed, they would have to be aggressively enforced in other markets at great expense.

A *third* characteristic is the type of licensing, i.e., *enablement* vs. *enforcement* licensing:

- Enablement licensing, also known as opportunity or carrot licensing: It seeks a licensee who is interested in using the subject matter of the license. Since use only begins after the license has been taken, negotiations are usually characterized by the design of a joint business model.
- Enforcement licensing, also known as assertion or stick licensing: A potential infringer of the intellectual property to be licensed is sought. It is therefore assumed that intellectual property rights are used by third parties before the actual licensing. Since the potential infringer has usually already invested and become active on the market, negotiations usually focus on clarifying whether an infringement has occurred, whether the intellectual property rights are legally valid and, if so, how high the license payments should be.

In the USA, and increasingly in Europe as well, a new business model already exists here, according to which patent attorneys track down patent infringements, buy up the patent in question, sue the infringer, and demand license payments. In economic terms, however, these models must be strongly questioned.

Licensing Master: Qualcomm

The American mobile technology company *Qualcomm* generates a substantial part of its revenues from license revenues. One of the three business units is exclusively engaged in the marketing of intellectual property. One hundred and thirty patents alone relate to the American mobile communications standard *CDMA*. In addition, obvious users of the patent portfolio are convinced of the "necessity" of taking out a license. The patent portfolio is also open to potential licensees.

4.2 Cross-Licensing

Cross-licensing is a licensing agreement in which the consideration of the cooperation partner is not the license fee but also a license. The cooperation partners thus grant each other the right to use their respective patents for further development or product marketing. Depending on the agreement, an additional license fee may nevertheless be payable. Cross-licensing agreements serve in particular to ensure freedom of action and keep open access to external knowledge.

In principle, cross-licensing agreements can be divided into two types:

- The intellectual property rights affected by the agreement remain mutually licensed for their *lifetime*
- The intellectual property rights affected by the contract remain mutually licensed for a certain *period of time* only. After this period, the license expires and new negotiations may be necessary *(guillotine approach)*

Cross-Licensing: Siemens and Microsoft

In 2004, *Siemens* and *Microsoft* entered into a patent license exchange agreement by which they gave each other extended access to their respective patent portfolios. This also gave both companies the opportunity to expand their offerings to their customers and provide them with comprehensive solutions. Although the companies spent a similarly large research and development budget of about 5 billion euros, *Microsoft* had to pay *Siemens* an additional license fee.

4.3 Sale

When a patent is sold, all rights are transferred to the buyer, who also becomes the new owner of the patent. The sale of a patent may be appropriate if the developed technology is outside the business area of a company. If there are no plans to develop the new business area, it is still possible to generate added value by selling the patent portfolio. The sale process is usually completed when the contract is signed, which means that the seller does not incur any further expenses in the form of know-how transfer or—as in the case of licenses—fee monitoring or enforcement activities.

A Market for IP: IPXI

The example of *Intellectual Patent Exchange International (IPXI)* shows the obstacles that have to be overcome in establishing IP marketplaces. The marketplace founded by *Ocean Tomo* in 2008, according to its own statement, was the first worldwide marketplace for licensing and trading intellectual property rights. It saw itself as a market-based alternative for private licensing and IP commercialization. By introducing the concept of a Unit License Rights (ULR), *IPXI* wanted to ensure nonexclusive licensing with market-based prices and standardized terms that could be traded on an electronic trading platform. *IPXI*'s goal was to provide patent owners with an efficient and transparent monetization opportunity. For investors, the added value of this marketplace was the ability to speculate on future technologies and invest directly in IP rights rather than in the proprietary companies. The marketplace was to be financed by an annual membership fee and a 20% share of the transactions to cover running costs (Bader et al. 2012a, b).

Following approval by the U.S. Department of Justice in 2013, the marketplace opened for the first time in 2014 with the trading of *JP Morgan Chase* patents. After

1 year, however, *IPXI* ceased trading in March 2015. In a press release, *IPXI* blamed various market obstacles, such as requirements from potential licensees, and complained that the time was not yet ripe for its idea (IPXI 2015). The high number of high-ranking companies that have been part of the IP marketplace until recently, including numerous companies from technology sectors as well as universities and research institutions, shows that there is a great deal of interest in such an institutionalized IP marketplace. In the end, *IPXI* had over 70 members, including ones such as *JP Morgan Chase*, *Philips*, *Hewlett-Packard*, and *Sony*.

4.4 Strategic Alliance

Especially for early developments and technologies that are not yet ready for the market, strategic alliances between companies and/or research institutions can be beneficial for all parties involved. The alliance partners contribute complementary know-how and patents to the alliance in order to advance research and development activities more efficiently and achieve the goal of market entry or market share expansion. At the same time, risks and costs are shared. In contrast to joint ventures, the alliance partners remain legally independent, i.e., there is no capital commitment underlying the contracts.

Strategic Alliance: IBM and Philips

IBM began formulating licensing strategies in the 1980s. Today, *IBM* has an established licensing program that pursues a strategy of issuing nonexclusive licenses to third parties. In addition, a complementary relationship with the licensee is to be established. Over the past few years, the company, which holds over 40,000 active patents, has generated annual license revenues of approximately $1 billion.

Philips has defined its most important strategic goal in licensing to be: setting standards. *Philips'* intellectual property has been organized into a holding company, *Philips Intellectual Property and Standards (IP&S)*, since 1924. Today, *IP&S* has about 450 employees and holds over 55,000 patents. In its licensing program, the company offers patents, technologies and services, and grants nonexclusive licenses to a broad target group.

Until a few years ago, *Microsoft* focused its licensing activities on the enforcement of intellectual property rights through stick licensing. Following a change in strategy, *Microsoft* is now focusing on a cooperative approach through cross-licensing. In addition, the IP exploitation program *Microsoft Intellectual Property Ventures* was born; the company expects the new approach to strengthen the network and reduce risk.

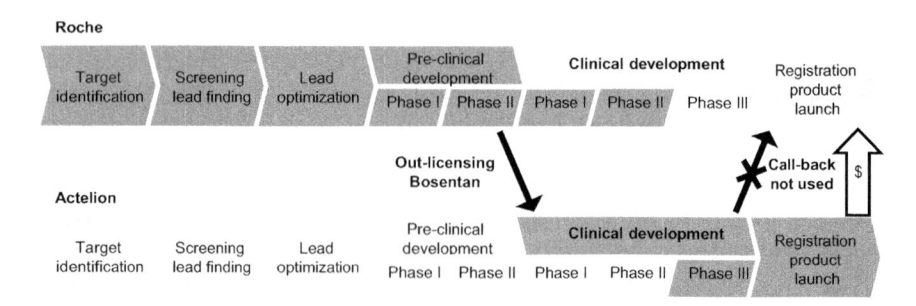

Fig. 4.1 Licensing agreement between *Roche* and *Actelion* (Gassmann et al. 2016) (Used with kind permission by Wiley-VCH, Weinheim. All rights reserved)

4.5 Spin-Off and Call-Back

Spin-offs are another way of exploiting research and development results. The formation of spin-offs also allows the company to further develop innovations that meet with little interest from existing business units and to also generate income from them through equity investments or licensing income. This is also illustrated by two examples from *Roche* and *Novartis*.

Spin-Off: F. Hoffmann-La Roche and Actelion

As part of restructuring measures in the mid-1990s, *Roche* decided not to pursue the research and development of the substance "Bosentan" after Phase II trials. Despite this decision, the spin-off *Actelion*, which included four former *Roche* managers, was set up to exploit the potential of the substance, which was traded as a potential active ingredient for the treatment of heart defects. In 1998, *Roche* licensed the substance Bosentan to *Actelion*, but reserved a call-back option. During the Phase III trials, *Actelion* changed the original indication of Bosentan. Instead of treating congestive heart failure, *Actelion* focused on pulmonary hypertension. This change increased the potential for an approved drug. Finally, *Actelion* successfully launched the product under the Tracleer® brand. After Phase III, *Roche* decided not to use the call-back option in exchange for ca. 10% of revenues (see Fig. 4.1).

Roche was able to generate income from an originally abandoned project through the spin-off. The risk of the Phase III trials and market launch was transferred to *Actelion*. *Actelion* was given the opportunity to launch a new product without taking the risk in the early stages of development (Gassmann et al. 2016, 2018; Gassmann and Bader 2017).

Call-Back: Novartis and Speedel

To further develop a project that did not fit into the portfolio, *Novartis* founded the spin-off *Speedel* in 1998. *Novartis* had stopped a project involving the substance Aliskiren for the treatment of hypertension after the preclinical phase. By out-licensing to *Speedel*, *Novartis* offloaded the Phase I and Phase II clinical trials to *Speedel* (see Fig. 4.2). In 2002, following the successful completion of the Phase I and II trials, *Novartis* used its call-back option to move the compound into Phase III trials, and finally launched the product. Both *Novartis* and *Speedel* received revenues from sales of the drug. The spin-off allowed Novartis to launch a new drug without bearing the cost and risk of the Phase I and II trials. *Speedel* was able to generate revenues from a project without early development risks, and production and marketing expenses (Gassmann et al. 2016, 2018; Gassmann and Bader 2017).

4.6 Joint Venture

By forming joint ventures, the founding companies can complement their technologies, property rights, and know-how and jointly develop and expand them. In this way, costs and risks can be shared between the associated companies, and access to new technologies and sales markets can be created. *Bayer Innovation* is an example of this approach.

Joint Venture: Bayer Innovation

Bayer Innovation used to be a part of *Bayer's* innovation strategy and worked with the aim of identifying and developing new growth areas for *Bayer*, and thereby preparing its entry into new high-growth markets. The strength of *Bayer Innovation* lied in developing innovative solutions beyond the boundaries of the subgroups and developing new products and businesses together with external partners. The technologies developed by *Bayer Innovation* were sold to interested *Bayer*

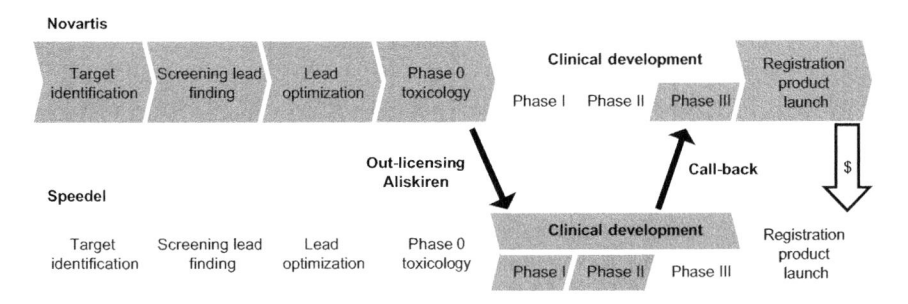

Fig. 4.2 Licensing agreement between *Novartis* and *Speedel* (Gassmann et al. 2016) (Used with kind permission by Wiley-VCH, Weinheim. All rights reserved)

subgroups for commercial integration. Technologies that were not integrated into the *Bayer Group* were commercialized externally by *Bayer Innovation*. The company still pursues a venture capital approach, i.e., industrial property rights are used as tradable assets with the aim of forming joint ventures or similar partnerships and thus maximizing the return on research and development.

4.7   Patenting for Access to Finance

In addition to the exploitation possibilities already mentioned, patents are now also used in the context of corporate financing. They can be the object of equity or debt financing, but they can also be used in hybrid (hybrid form between equity and debt) financing (Bessler et al. 2003). The following possibilities of a patent-based financing are among others available:

- Credit security through patents
- Issue of equity securities based on core competencies monopolized by patents
- Sale-and-lease-back transactions through the sale of patents
- Securitization of future cash flows generated from patents on the capital market
- Patent funds as a means of financing the further development of embryonic technologies

Patenting for Access to Finance: Uber!

Aside from being well-known, *Uber* presents an interesting case in that its patents likely played a major role in the company's ability to access capital, which eventually lead to its stock market debut in May of 2019. It is also illustrative from a commercialization perspective, in that *Uber* acquired components of its patent portfolio that were essentially unexploited by their inventors.

Legend has it that *Uber* began with a simple idea by two guys trying to hail a cab in wintry Paris whilst attending the 2008 *LeWeb*, a major tech conference. A year later those same two guys (Garrett Camp and Travis Kalanick) had filed US 26699609 P, a "System and method for arranging transport amongst parties through use of mobile devices" and a patent for "Providing user feedback for transport services through use of mobile devices"—*Alpha* testing with three cars in New York. The idea and patents (along with the fact that both of them had already sold tech 10m+ start-ups before), were enough to secure financing. In October 2010, *Uber* received its first major funding, a $1.25 million round led by *First Round Capital*. At that same *LeWeb* conference where it had all started, the CEO announced that *Uber* had raised $37 million in Series B funding from *Menlo Ventures*, Jeff Bezos (CEO of *Amazon*), and *Goldman Sachs*. It was then able to secure another $11 million in series A funding a San Francisco VC firm, *Benchmark Capital*, in February of 2012. The company took some of that money and filed 14 more utility and design patents at the USPTO just a few months later over the course of 2012, and

4.7 Patenting for Access to Finance

by June 2016, Uber was able to raise a $3.5 billion investment from *Saudi Arabia's Wealth Fund*, and had filed about 163 patents and designs.

The company used its cash pipeline to make a number of IP acquisitions. In an interview, Kurt Brash, head of *Uber's* patent transactions team, said "With patents taking on average four years to grant, we hadn't had enough time to build up our own portfolio. [A]nd we knew we needed some way to protect our business." Seeing the future in robotic rather than human drivers with pesky wages, benefits, and demands that started to plague management, *Uber* acquired *Otto*, a self-driving company founded by a former *Google* employee, for an estimated 680 million dollars.

That was a bridge too far into big player's technology portfolios, and *Google's* self-driving subsidiary *Waymo* sued *Otto/Uber* for violation of trade secrecy. *Uber* promptly then bought up some of *AT&T's* portfolio in February of 2017 to give it priority over *Lyft*, and others.

To facilitate the acquisition, *Uber* developed its "own acquisition portal to directly solicit assets, speed our team's analysis and provide *Uber* with protection against third party patent threats cloaked as purchase opportunities" (Lloyd 2018). They have a "quality" acquisition strategy. Choi continues, "For *Uber*, a quality patent is one that has applicability in an identified area of technology, reasonably broad claim scope, and an early priority date as compared to known technologies. By whittling down the number of patents at the outset, the group can concentrate on applying their sector expertise to thoroughly scrutinize claim breadth, validity, patent term, assignment information, sale price expectation, etc."

Ironically, all this IP acquisition to defend its business model put the company in the legal crosshairs of *Google* when it acquired *Waymo*, whose technology came from a former *Google* engineer who had allegedly stolen trade secrets for self-driving cars. Reuters reported *Uber* had to settle with *Google* for 245 million dollars ("*Waymo* accepts $245 million and *Uber's* 'regret' to settle self-driving car dispute," Reuters 2018)—nearly 20 times the total value of all their patents in 2018! Rather than buying technological value, *Uber* inadvertently bought a legal grenade with its *Waymo* acquisition.

In its Initial Public Offering (IPO) prospectus, *Uber* stated to the US Securities and Exchange Commission (SEC) that:

> As of December 31, 2018, we have 904 issued patents (of which 323 are international) and 1,297 pending patent applications (of which 486 are international), many of which relate to our core technology such as match optimization, pricing, routing, traffic, navigation, mapping, safety, and telematics.

Figure 4.3 shows the landscape of patents *Uber* has.

That same SEC IPO prospectus valued the patent portfolio at $12 million versus the $70 million in "developed technology." Meaning, the software and setup are worth more than the patents, which perhaps are only 5–13,000 a piece, depending on how they are counted. On the back of this prospectus, *Uber* raised another ca. $8 billion in May of 2019 through its IPO, bringing the total of capital raised to $16.2 billion. The company came public at around an 80-billion-dollar valuation. IP

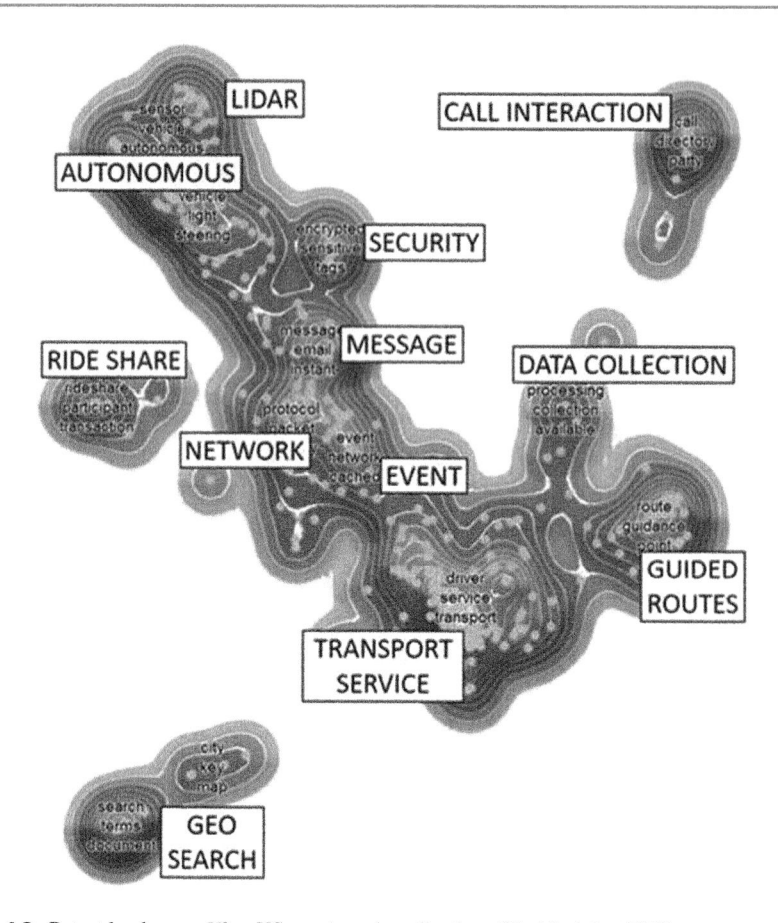

Fig. 4.3 Patent landscape: *Uber* US grants and applications (TechInsights 2018)

acquisitions may have been part of the "window-dressing" underwriters do before taking it public.

Ironically, the patents do not protect the core business; protection of the business model comes from economies of scale and self-reinforcing network effects. Many of the "inventions" are not patentable outside of the USA. Hence, valuing *Uber's* technology portfolio at $82 million seems a bit over the top considering that an Estonian high-school student and his code-savvy friends were able to re-create a similar platform, copied from the Ukraine, within about 9 months and with minimal investment. Their company, *Bolt* (formerly *Taxify*), is the go-to ride sharing app in the Baltics—not *Uber* (Treija 2016). *Yandex* was active in the East Bloc countries, another *Uber* clone, and had to be bought out by *Uber*, again showing the limits of IP protection for the business model.

As of this writing, *Uber* continues to hemorrhage cash at $1 billion per year, and is coming under pressure from competing services such as *Bolt*, *Lyft*, and others with similar technology; this may indicate that reliance on an IP moat may have been a bad idea. *Tesla* and the major automakers are likely to be far ahead in the self-driving technology race—and the *Waymo* litigation is just a taste of what is to come if any company should crack the self-driving nut, unleashing billions in idle capital sitting in driveways, and obviating the demand swathes of unskilled labor to pilot vehicles. If anything, all the companies with idle IP on self-driving, ride-sharing, and adjacent technology have been the ones to profit most from *Uber's* patent buying spree, and are finally able to commercialize their patents.

The take-aways:

- Patents signal to investors that a CEO is serious and that the technology can be appropriated.
- Most of the value accrued to companies with fragments of the ride-sharing technology could not monetize them.
- IP portfolio played a substantial role in raising capital and was a motivation for acquisitions.
- Portfolio size and foray into self-driving tech opened the company up to litigation.

4.8 Litigation for Value

In addition, new companies are entering the market with increasing frequency, no longer commercializing their patents through products but using them primarily to generate licensing income. Such non-operating companies are therefore also referred to as *Non-Practicing Entities (NPEs)* and include universities, research institutes, and research companies such as *ETH, Fraunhofer,* and *InterDigital.*

Among the NPEs, the so-called *Patent Assertion Entities (PAEs)*, which acquire patents from third parties for later exploitation, deserve special mention. Their main business purpose is to generate licensing income through patent infringement suits. They are often undifferentiatedly disreputable in the vernacular as so-called *Patent Trolls.*[1] However, PAEs often also represent individual inventors or small companies on a commission basis. They, therefore, play an important role for those inventors and companies, who do not have the competence, resources, or means to fight the protracted patent legal battles, requisite to enforce them. In this sense, NPEs fill an ecological niche in the complex and competitive IP/inventor ecosystem.

PAEs can be divided into four different groups based on the type of value they added (Krech et al. 2015):

- **Guarders**, for example, *Golden Rice, MPEG LA*
- **Shielders**, such as *Intellectual Discovery*

---

[1] Here also the term "troll" tongue-in-cheek is frequently used to refer to patent assertion entities, patent jargon for companies that do not practise their patents themselves.

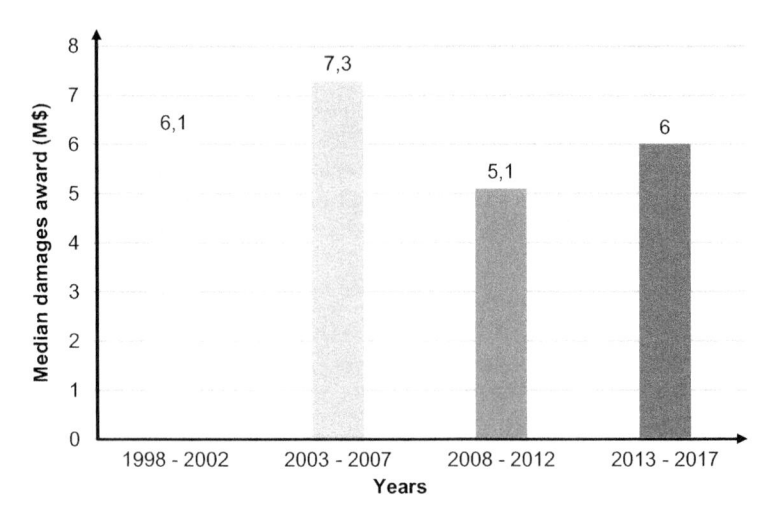

Fig. 4.4 Median damage award (based on PwC 2018)

- **Funders**, e.g., *Pete Invest*, *Patent Select*
- **Earners**, for example, *Acacia Research*, *Allied Security Trust*, *Intellectual Ventures*

For exploitation, PAEs usually resort to a very aggressive exploitation strategy, specifically searching for potential patent infringements and taking action against them (Ewing and Feldman 2012). The aim is usually not a court ruling but a settlement. This litigation focused strategy can be lucrative since the median award is about 6 million dollars according to *PricewaterhouseCoopers*; Fig. 4.4 reveals this figure having been relatively stable, even if the variance of damage awards in the USA are high.

It is estimated that the damage payments to PAEs now exceed those to manufacturing companies (Bessen and Meurer 2013). Even *IBM* faced an aggressive exploitation attack in the 1990s when *TechSearch*, a PAE, threatened the company with an injunction for infringement of a patent and asked IBM to pay a large license fee (Hess-Blumer 2009; IP Watchdogs 2013).

These new exploitation strategies received particular attention, among other things, due to the bidding competition for the patents of the Canadian telecommunications provider *Nortel* (see also Ziegler et al. 2011). When *Nortel* filed for bankruptcy in 2011, *Google* and *Rockstar Bidco*, a consortium of originally five mobile phone companies, including *Apple* and *Microsoft*, competed intensively for the 6000 patents of the telecommunications provider. Ultimately, the patents were auctioned for $4.5 billion by the *Rockstar Consortium*. The consortium used the acquired patents to conduct licensing negotiations for patent infringement with *Android* developer *Google* and device manufacturers such as *HTC* and *Samsung*. At the end of 2014, it became known that *Rockstar* had fulfilled its purpose and the 2000 most valuable patents had been transferred to its owners, while in 2015 the remaining 4000 patents had been taken over by *RPX*, a so-called defensive patent exploiter, for $900 million (Reuters 2014). In 2018, *HGGC*, a private equity firm, ended up taking *RPX* with its patent portfolio private in an all-cash transaction worth $555 million, implying a potential massive loss on the 2014 *Rockstar* purchases!

Patent Assertion Entity: Acacia Research

Picture archival and communications systems store medical images from CT scans, MRIs, ultrasounds, and similar images. A medical engineering team in Florida filed a patent for distributing medical imagery via communications networks. Not having the capacity to market the technology, they sold the patent to the *Acacia Research Corporation* in 2005. *Acacia* is a non-practicing entity. *Acacia* claimed a wider scope of coverage for its newly acquired patents, arguing that the patents covered any system that could "enable multiple, remote users to simultaneously access image data from remote display terminals over common phone and data networks, such as the Internet." This description obviously applies to a much wider range of industries and technologies than the original patent had covered. *Acacia* then launched multiple suits against some of the biggest players: *GE*, *Siemens*, and *Philips*. This had an immediate chilling effect on those companies imaging software sales, freezing millions in R&D dollars.

4.9 Complex Strategies

BT Exact (British Telecom)

The R&D department of *British Telecom (BT Exact)* defines the nature and scope of the commercialization of internal research from a specially developed exploitation matrix (see Fig. 4.5). The exploitation matrix distinguishes between informal and formal Intellectual Property (IP): *informal IP* refers to intangible knowledge, such as skills and expertise; whereas, *formal IP* refers to legal IPRs, such as copyrights and patents (see also Sect. 1.3). With regard to licenses, *BT Exact* is prepared to license patents, copyright, and knowledge to external companies. Such an agreement usually involves the transfer of knowledge and technology. However, if there is a specific market for formal intellectual property, *BT Exact* prefers to outsource it as a separate business. *BT Exact* normally holds less than 100% of the equity. Another option is to invest IP into existing businesses, such as start-ups. Licensing and "spin-ups" (company-internal start-ups) are not mutually exclusive and can even stimulate each other. In markets that are already well developed, licenses often can generate immediate profits. If a technology cannot be sufficiently patented, internal spin-up activities are preferred to licensing. If good patents meet high technical expertise, a spin-out offers the greatest benefit but is also associated with increased risk. Sharing these risks with other partners can help to reduce costs and risks. Spin-outs also have the advantage of stimulating entrepreneurial and intrapreneurial opportunities.

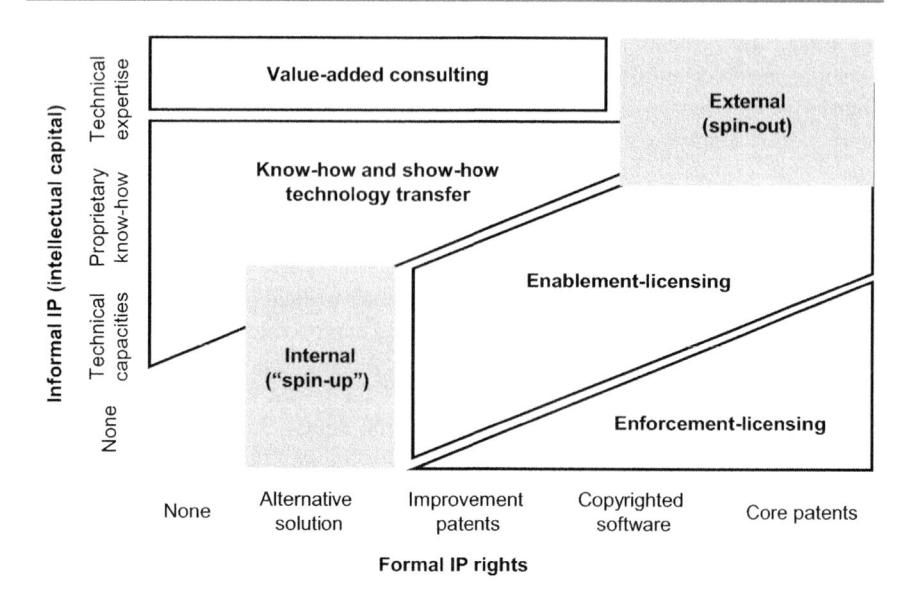

Fig. 4.5 Intellectual Property Usage Matrix of *BT Exact* (authors' own figure)

Make or Buy: Bayer

The *Bayer* chemicals and pharmaceuticals group has established a lifecycle process for intellectual property consisting of three phases: knowledge acquisition; knowledge assurance; and knowledge exploitation (see Fig. 4.6). Knowledge is acquired either internally through its own knowledge generation or externally through contract research, cooperation, and joint ventures, in-licensing, purchase, or via acquisition *(make or buy)*. Knowledge can be exploited internally, for example, through proprietary applications, products, processes, or services. Externally, the stored knowledge can be used in research cooperation and joint ventures, licensed or sold to third parties, or used as part of outsourcing or benchmarking *(keep or sell)*.

4.10 Commercialization Concepts and Conclusions

Despite the growing trend to use patents as strategic levers in management and to exploit patents and create additional value by using them internally in products and processes, companies face several challenges. The technology markets in which patents can be traded are often not transparent. In addition, there is still a need for uniform and recognized valuation methods for patents (Kamiyama et al. 2006). Negotiations on a licensing agreement often fail because the financial and nonfinancial terms are not agreed upon. High transaction costs, the identification of an

4.10 Commercialization Concepts and Conclusions

	Internal technology generation	Internal technology use
Internal	• Innovation • Business development	• Own applications • Own products • Own processes • Own services

IP-relevant sub-processes

Acquiring knowledge   Securing knowledge   Using knowledge

	External technology acquisition	External technology exploitation
External	• Contract research • Cooperation & joint ventures • In-licensing • Purchase & acquisition	• Benchmarking • Cooperation & joint ventures • Out-licensing • Selling know-how • Outsourcing

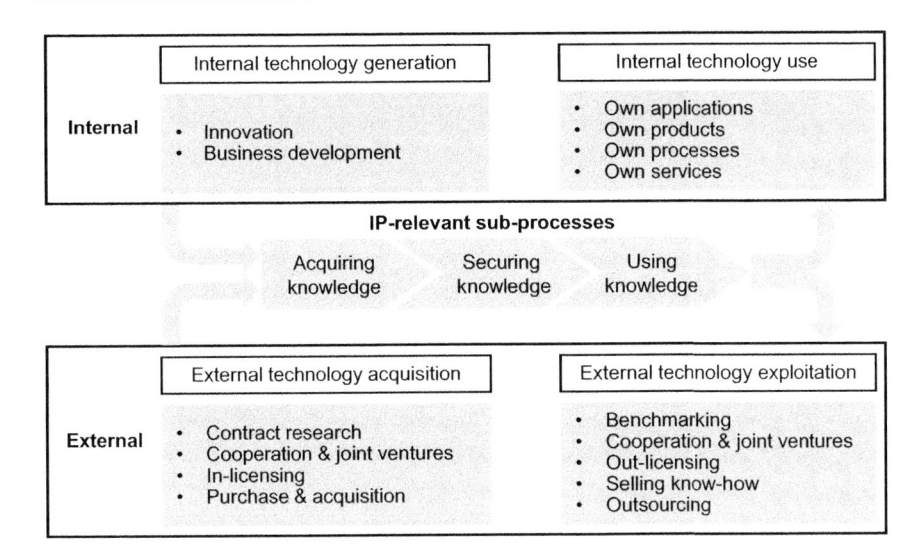

Fig. 4.6 Commercialization cycle of Intellectual Property at *Bayer* (authors' own figure)

exploitation partner, and a lack of resources also represent barriers to patent exploitation (Gambardella et al. 2007; Gassmann et al. 2010).

Within the framework of an industry consortium project, a guideline for patent exploitation was therefore coordinated by the *Competence Center for Intellectual Property Management at the University of St. Gallen (HSG)* (Ziegler et al. 2011).

The guideline for the successful exploitation of patents consists of four phases (see Fig. 4.7):

1. Identification of potential patents for exploitation
2. Evaluation of these patents and pricing
3. Search for suitable transaction partners
4. Implementation of the transaction

Each of the phases is associated with specific challenges, issues to be clarified and decisions to be taken. The key to patent exploitation is: which decisions are made and how, and what challenges these decisions entail. In the following, the individual phases of the exploitation process are therefore presented in more detail and the aspects already mentioned are addressed.

Phase 1: Identification

The challenge of this phase is to identify possible patents from the portfolio that are to be exploited on the basis of the company's internal exploitation motives, whether they are monetary or strategic.

1. Identification
Identification of patents for external exploitation

2. Evaluation
Strategic (qualitative) value   Monetary (quantitative) value
Non-monetary evaluation   Monetary valuation

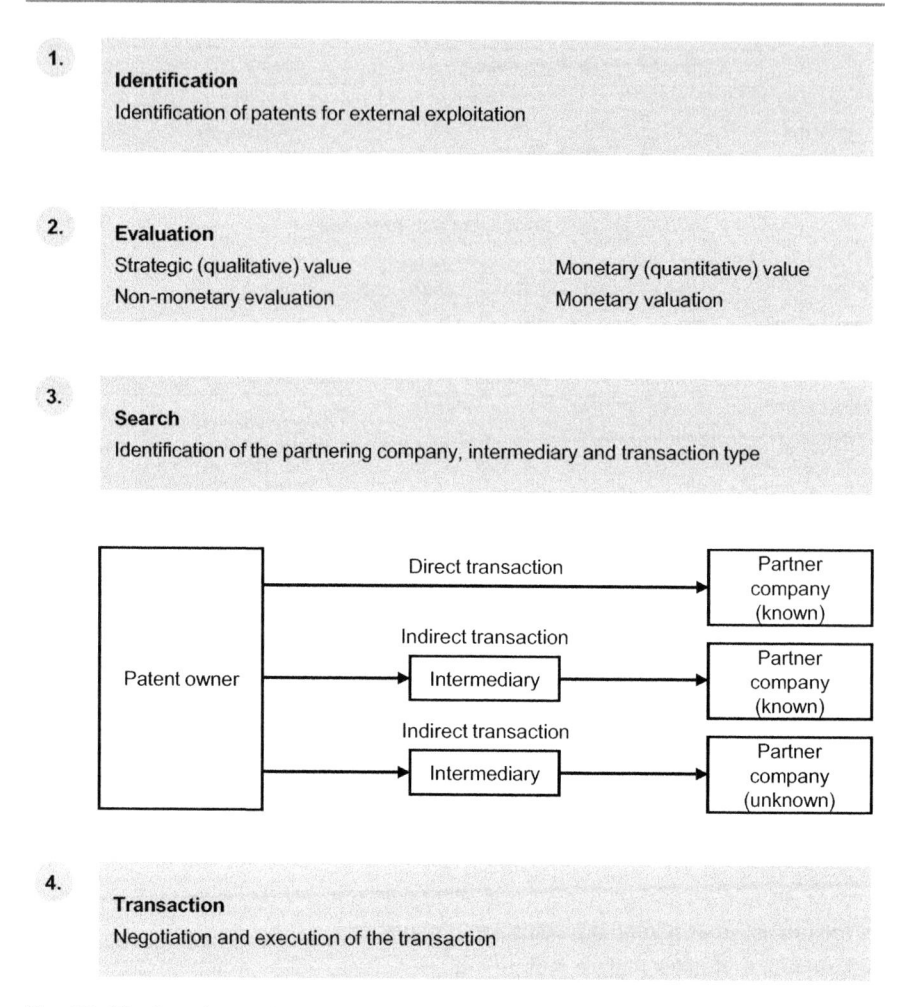

3. Search
Identification of the partnering company, intermediary and transaction type

```
                        Direct transaction          ┌─ Partner company (known) ─┐
Patent owner ──────────  Indirect transaction ──── Intermediary ──── Partner company (known)
                         Indirect transaction ──── Intermediary ──── Partner company (unknown)
```

4. Transaction
Negotiation and execution of the transaction

Fig. 4.7 The four phases of successful patent exploitation (Ziegler et al. 2011)

The following decisions have to be made:

- **Keep or Sell:** Which technologies, products or business models have the potential to be out-licensed? What should be kept, what should be sold? What kind of patents should be sold (core patents, non-core patents)?
- **Motives:** What goals does the company pursue with patent exploitation? Are they more strategic or more monetary in nature?
- **Resources:** Licensing activities require many resources. How many resources are used for the patent exploitation project?
- **Timing:** When is the right time for licensing (depending on the development phase of the technology, market situation, strategic orientation of the company)?

4.10 Commercialization Concepts and Conclusions

- **Responsibility:** Who is responsible for organizing and coordinating external exploitation and all current and future activities in this area?

Phase 2: Evaluation

Once the patents to be exploited have been identified, the company is faced with the challenge of valuing the patents appropriately:

- **Price:** What is the right price? Due to the lack of standardized, generally accepted valuation methods (qualitative, quantitative, or both?), pricing, when transferring patents, remains a major challenge.
- **Valuation method:** Should a qualitative or a quantitative method be used? (see Chap. 3).
- **Risks:** What risks are taken in relation to the company's core business?
- **Exclusion factors:** What factors speak against external exploitation (loss of market share, unprofitable cost-benefit estimates)?

Phase 3: Search

In the third phase, it is necessary to consider whether a direct or indirect transfer is being sought. Furthermore, the choice of a suitable partner company or intermediary is at the center of this phase:

- **Industry:** Should the license be granted within or outside your own industry?
- **Licensing partners:** Who is the right licensing partner? How is this partner to be found and then convinced?
- **Competition:** Is the company willing to sell to a direct competitor?
- **Utilization channel:** Will the patent be licensed out directly to a third party or should the company resort to the support of patent intermediaries (e.g., patent brokers, patent auctions)?
- **Resources:** Does the company have the resources and expertise to find a suitable partner company itself and to carry out the transaction? Is an intermediary necessary?
- **Intermediary:** Who is a suitable intermediary to support the patent exploitation?
- **Responsibility:** What tasks should the intermediary perform, what tasks are performed internally?

Phase 4: Transaction

The fourth and final phase will focus on negotiations on the terms and conditions of the patent transaction and its execution:

- **Make or Buy:** What should be self-generated, what should be in-licensed?
- **Exclusivity:** Should exclusive or nonexclusive licenses be granted?
- **Scope and content of the transaction:** Should the patent be out-licensed with or without knowledge transfer? What services are associated with the license, from pure patent exploitation to full know-how transfer and process support?
- **Regional delimitation:** For which region is the license valid, for example only in Germany or worldwide?
- **Willingness to compromise:** Which demands can be neglected in negotiations, which ideas are central?
- **Consideration:** What does the company expect in return (a lump sum, licenses, know-how)?

10 Factors of Success for Commercializing Patents

- *Corporate strategy:* The adaptation of the exploitation strategy to the corporate and R&D strategy is central to successful exploitation. Inconsistencies can lead to confusion and inefficiency.
- *Industry:* The decision as to whether patent exploitation should be pursued within the industry itself, or outside of it, must be reflected in the exploitation strategy.
- *Market know-how:* For a successful patent exploitation it is essential to know the characteristics and market structures of the target industry in order to identify a possible demand for the patent.
- *Target definition:* Only with a clear target definition of the patent exploitation strategy can the right patents for the exploitation process be identified and selected.
- *Commercialization channel:* The path of commercialization must be chosen with regard to the external resources and competencies required, for example, direct or indirect transfer with the help of an intermediary.
- *Partner companies:* The choice of companies to which the patent rights are to be transferred must be made carefully in relation to the objectives of patent exploitation. The competence of the partner company is particularly important for projects with know-how transfer.
- *Evaluation model:* There is no perfect method for patent evaluation. The choice of valuation and evaluation methods always depends on the occasion, and the objective and must be chosen accordingly.
- *Organizational structure:* A successful exploitation strategy requires appropriate organizational structures, such as organizational units specialized in patents and with clear resource allocation.
- *Management:* A successful exploitation strategy requires the strong and active support of the management.
- *Organizational culture:* External patent exploitation is an exception for many companies. In order to enable successful exploitation in the long term, incentives must be created within a company not only for patent generation but also for external exploitation.

References

Bader, M. A., & Liegler, F. (2013). Ein europäischer (Finanz-)Markt für Geistiges Eigentum? *Mitteilungen der deutschen Patentanwälte, 104*(1), 25–26.

Bader, M. A., Gassmann, O., Jha, P., Liegler, F., Maicher, L., Posselt, T., Preissler, S., Rüther, F., Tonisson, L., & Wabra, S. (2012a). Creating an organised IP rights market in Europe. In: *Intellectual Asset Management Magazine*, No. 26, pp. 33–38.

Bader, M. A., Gassmann, O., Jha, P., Liegler, F., Maicher, L., Posselt, T., Preissler, S., Rüther, F., & Wabra, S. (2012b). *Creating a financial market for IPR*. European Commission: Brussels.

Bessen, J., & Meurer, M. J. (2013). Direct costs from NPE disputes. *The Cornell Law Review*, No. 99, p. 387.

Bessler, W., Bittelmeyer, C., & Lipfert, S. (2003). Zur Bedeutung von wissensbasierten immateriellen Vermögensgegenständen für die Bewertung und Finanzierung von kleinen und mittleren Unternehmen. In J.-A. Meyer (Ed.), *Unternehmensbewertung und Basel II in kleinen und mittleren Unternehmen* (pp. 309–334). Cologn: Eul.

Ewing, T., & Feldman, R. (2012). The giants among us. *Stanford Technology Law Review, 1*, 1–61.

Gambardella, A., Giuri, P., & Luzzi, A. (2007). The market for patents. *Europe Research Policy, 39*, 1163–1183.

Gassmann, O., & Bader, M. A. (2017). *Patentmanagement: Innovationen erfolgreich nutzen und schützen* (4th ed.). Berlin: Springer.

Gassmann, O., Ziegler, N., Bader, M. A., & Nowak, R. (2010). *IP management in practice*. St. Gallen: University of St. Gallen (ITEM-HSG).

Gassmann, O., Krech, C.-A., Bader, M. A., & Reepmeyer, G. (2016). Out-licensing in pharmaceutical research and development. In A. Schuhmacher, M. Hinder, & O. Gassmann (Eds.), *Value creation in the pharmaceutical industry – The critical path to innovation* (pp. 363–380). Weinheim: Wiley-VCH.

Gassmann, O., Schuhmacher, A., Reepmeyer, G., & von Zedtwitz, M. (2018). *Leading pharmaceutical innovation – How to win the life science race* (3rd ed.). Berlin: Springer.

Hess-Blumer, A. (2009). Patent Trolls – Eine Analyse nach Schweizer Recht. *sic!*, pp. 851–865.

IP Watchdogs (2013). *Why bash individual inventor owned or controlled companies?* http://www.ipwatchdog.com/2013/06/30/why-bash-individual-inventor-owned-or-controlled-companies/id=42613/

IPXI. (2015). *Corporate announcement*. Chicago: Intellectual Property Exchange International. https://www.ipxi.com/corporate-announcement.html.

Kamiyama, S., Sheehan, J., & Martinez, C. (2006). Valuation and exploitation of intellectual property. *OECD Science, Technology and Industry Working Papers*, No. 5. Paris: OECD.

Krech, C.-A., Rüther, F., & Gassmann, O. (2015). Profiting from invention: Business models of patent aggregating companies. *International Journal of Innovation Management, 19*(3), 1–26.

Lloyd, R. (2018). Uber's patent transactions head explains how the company built its portfolio through savvy deal-making. *Intellectual Asset Management (IAM)*.

Parr, R. L., & Sullivan, P. H. (1996). *Technology licensing. Corporate strategies for maximizing value*. New York: Wiley.

PricewaterhouseCoopers. (2018). *2018 Patent litigation study*. https://www.pwc.com/us/en/forensic-services/publications/assets/2018-pwc-patent-litigation-study.pdf

Reuters. (2014). *RPX buys Apple-backed Rockstar patents for $900 million*. http://www.reuters.com/article/2014/12/23/us-rpx-rockstar-ip-idUSKBN0K11AI20141223

Reuters. (2018) *Alexandria Sage, Dan Levine, Heather Somerville*.

TechInsights. (2018). *What does Uber's patent landscape look like?* https://www.techinsights.com/blog/what-does-ubers-patent-landscape-look

Treija. (2016). Uber, what? Taxify is the most popular taxi startup in the Baltics. *EU Start-Ups*.

Ziegler, N., Bader, M. A., & Rüther, F. (2011). *Handbook: External patent exploitation: Motives, forms, the role of intermediaries, and a guideline*. St. Gallen: University of St. Gallen (ITEM-HSG).

Organizing Patent Management

5.1 Governance vs. Service Patent Department

As internal service providers, patent departments operate in constant tension between strategic control and governance on the one hand and providing services on the other (based on Loebbert 2000). Internal customer relationships are maintained at three levels (see Fig. 5.1):

- *Executive and strategic level:* Management's mandate concerning the patent department must be clear and unambiguous. The widespread requirement of only regarding the number of patents is far from sufficient. Clear statements on the strategic thrust are important (see Chap. 2).
- *Operative level:* The provision of services for the internal client must be balanced (give and take, duties and rights).
- *Project level:* The moderation and alignment role of the patent department between the strategic client and the internal business line and staff department clients must be balanced.

The tasks of a patent department therefore include:

- Clarification of inventions
- Productive promotion of inventions
- Litigating patents and other intellectual property rights plus monitoring of external law firms
- Advice, support, searches, due diligence (methodology, analysis, support, patent strategy)
- Inventor remuneration for employees and incentive systems
- Standardization issues
- Patent portfolio management (database and information management)
- Administration of patent processes (deadlines, fees)

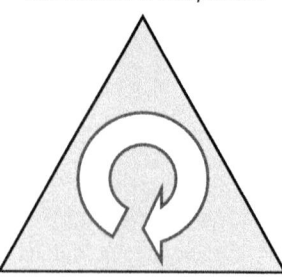

Fig. 5.1 Levels of the customer relationship of an internal patent department (authors' own figure)

- Suggestions for improvement
- Knowledge management (idea management, state of the art overview, invention disclosures, own patents, patents of competitors)

The services provided by central patent departments often come under continual criticism in a lot of companies because the service aspect is forgotten in many companies. Instead, some patent departments act as censors and inhibitors rather than as catalysts of innovation. Those responsible often find it difficult to take timely measures based on the benefits and costs of providing services and having to balance them between the different groups of interest. It is important to keep and see Research and Development (R&D) and business units as customers. Three levels can be distinguished:

1. *Executive and strategic level:* Mission statement from the executives should be clear and definite.
2. *Operative level:* Services for internal clients must be adequate and valuable.
3. *Project level:* Balance between the strategic principal and the service clients (see Fig. 5.1).

> **Factors for Successfully Managing a Patent Department**
> The management of a patent department is highly dependent on the interaction within the entire company. It requires:
>
> 1. Full backing and support from top management, line management, and project managers
> 2. Internal networking: availability of internal specialists as well as decentralized, supporting coordinators that are, for example, embedded in the R&D department
>
> (continued)

3. Cooperation between the Intellectual Property, R&D, and Marketing/Sales departments
4. Regular patent awareness training and further education for R&D, management, and marketing/sales as well as in the patent department
5. Clear evaluation and selection system for inventions and patent portfolio with corresponding processes, taking into account cost/benefit aspects
6. Defense against warnings and patent infringement proceedings through the rapid availability of a centrally coordinated core team, which can also draw decentrally on specialists and decision-makers
7. Licensing and enforcement of intellectual property rights, taking into account the availability of suitable intellectual property rights, financial resources, and in-house capabilities
8. Promoting an appropriate invention culture, including an adequate incentive system
9. Controlling both material and immaterial incentives for all parties involved, for example, for inventors or licensing experts
10. Determination of resources concerning headcounts and financial framework

5.2 Costs and Benefits of a Patent Department

The pressure in companies to optimize costs and benefits has led to greater attention being paid to intellectual property issues while at the same time improving processes. Our studies show that 75% of companies pursue legal protection strategies and have a well-formulated patent strategy that is aligned with the company's strategy, implemented across the organization, and regularly reviewed and updated. R&D departments, in particular, are actively involved in the strategy process.

Those studies also show that the main thrust of patent strategies is becoming increasingly directed not only toward pure defense and the protection of intellectual property but also toward the generation of license revenues through external exploitation of industrial property. In general, patents are already being marketed externally by every second company. Here, however, a differentiated approach is necessary since, as a rule, the core competencies and comparative competitive advantages of companies are affected.

The direct costs of an existing patent department are relatively easy to determine. In addition to personnel costs, infrastructure costs and costs of external services such as search costs, office costs and fees must also be taken into account. However, it is relatively difficult to always see the costs of the entire patent management process, taking into account all internal and external stakeholders.

It has therefore proved advantageous in numerous companies to introduce cost transparency on the basis of individual activities or process steps. These must be accounted for internally according to the polluter-pays principle. The overall performance is divided into performance groups. This results in a regulatory between the expected benefit, the effort, and the associated costs of service provision.

Within the framework of the settlement of individual services, various settlement models exist:

- Allocation
- Hourly billing
- Flat-rate billing on a case-by-case basis

In allocation accounting, the costs incurred are allocated to the various stakeholder groups, e.g., business units. Cost centers are often used for allocation. The criteria for the distribution key can be the sales of the enterprise areas, their R&D budget, or the number of R&D employees. The advantage of this type of allocation is that it is very simple. In practice, the low influenceability and lack of transparency of the allocation keys are often seen as a disadvantage.

Hourly billing, analogous to external service providers, is characterized by high transparency and accuracy. The internal effort, however, is usually much higher and involves the difficulty of allocating hours that cannot be charged directly.

The flat-rate billing per case represents a compromise, since sufficient accuracy can be achieved with a justifiable effort. Particularly suitable work processes for flat-rate invoicing are the preparation of notifications, notices, and expert opinions, administrative portfolio maintenance and information. Other service processes, such as infringement matters or innovation consulting, are difficult to compute as a flat-rate due to the very case-specific expense and are therefore usually charged on a time and material basis.

The general disadvantage of settlement models consists of the dominance of particular and business interests in the sense of "who pays, creates." Even more problematic than the costs *per* se, is the benefit of a patent department, which is therefore always under increased scrutiny. In other words: what would be the opportunity costs if no patent department existed? The directly monetary measurable benefit through license revenues usually represents the smallest part. Much more important is the trouble it causes to prove that competitors were able to circumvent a good patent with difficulty and that therefore no imitator is active as a competitor (temporary monopoly profits). The extent to which competitors are effectively blocked by their own patents can only be determined in exceptional cases (e.g., *Gore-Tex* patent). In practice, however, these blockade effects cannot really be assessed in monetary terms.

Performance Evaluation
The consumer goods manufacturer Henkel uses the number of oppositions against its own patents as the indicator for assessing the quality of the patent filing activity of the patent department. This seems to be a simple and effective indicator for the purpose.

Complex Patent Department Reshuffle: Infineon Technologies

The semiconductor company *Infineon Technologies* was a spin-off from its mother entity *Siemens* in April 1999. *Infineon* was already one of the top ten semiconductor companies worldwide at the time and had a patent portfolio of over 20,000 patents and patent applications at the time of the spin-off. This case is particularly instructive since the intellectual property (IP) related arrangements were central to the success of the new company, and supporting IP organization was very complex.

Infineon's initial philosophy was to become independent of the former parent company as quickly as possible. As numerous services had previously been provided centrally by *Siemens* but had not been spun off, it was important to make greater use of externally available sources, especially in the service sector. This particularly affected the patent and trademark departments. This initial situation gave rise to different perspectives:

- *Infineon's* consideration: How can *Siemens'* previous semiconductor patent department be committed to support *Infineon's* patent and trademark department for as long as possible?
- *Siemens'* consideration: What should happen to the former semiconductor-specific patent department? → Internal absorption and independence as an external law firm.

In setting up an intellectual property service, short and long-term goals had to be balanced out. In the short term, it was necessary to completely transfer the previous intellectual property support from *Siemens* to *Infineon* until the planned Initial Public Offering (IPO), only 1 year later in April 2000. In the long term, the company wanted to build up its own competitive intellectual property support with a sophisticated range of services.

However, the conditions were very risky for the establishment of an internal patent department. A very large number of inventions and patent applications had to be processed. More than 1000 patent applications were filed annually in 1998/1999. In addition, there was a very high active file inventory with more than 10,000 patent dossiers. A large number of infringements and other legal disputes as well as a generally high need for legal advice, such as for product clearings and redesign, placed high demands on the department's advisory capacity and quality. In contrast, only a small number of freely available IP professionals were available on the labor market for the high-tech area of semiconductor technology. In addition, there was generally strong demand for freelance IP professionals.

The starting position described above suggested outsourcing the provision of services in the patent application process. In addition, it was obvious that the service package had to be divided among several external patent law firms.

A comprehensive set of measures was outlined by *Infineon* and *Siemens* to enable the independence of the intellectual property activities at *Infineon*. Approximately one-third of the specialist staff of the *Siemens'* semiconductor patent department was successfully hived off as an independent law firm. In this context, *Infineon*

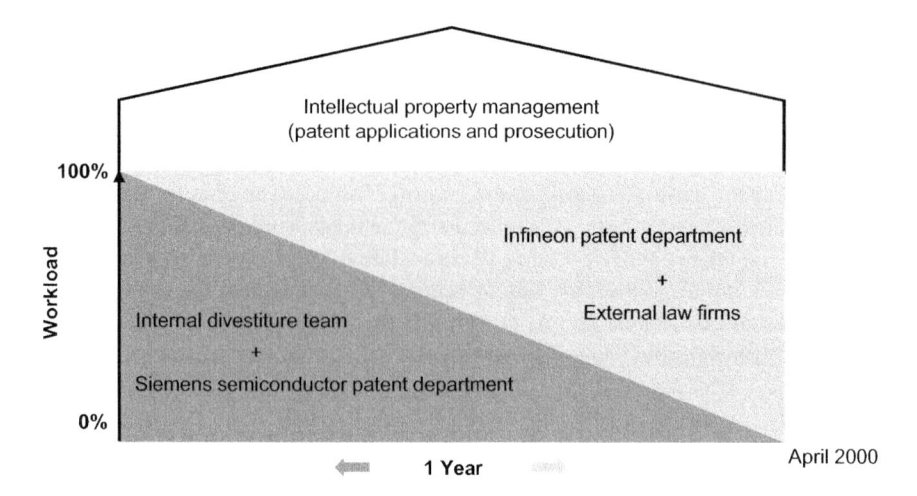

Fig. 5.2 Transition to new patent department and external providers (authors' own figure)

temporarily assured the firm of minimum reference values. In addition, the *Siemens* patent department, which had previously been responsible for the semiconductor sector, already had relationships with an external network of law firms. Peak workloads have already been outsourced as so-called "colleague work," but without the assignment of mandates. These activities resulted in relationships with about 30 law firms in Germany, which should now be increasingly accessed. A transitional arrangement between *Siemens* and *Infineon* got *Infineon* the temporary support of a handling team of the *Siemens* patent department as well as the continuity of administrative handling. At the same time, *Infineon* began setting up its own intellectual property department. The prerequisite for the outsourcing of intellectual property processes, however, was the establishment of *Infineon*-specific IT infrastructure in order to create a so-called "law firm capability" (see Fig. 5.2).

Managing Outsourcing

The goal at *Infineon* was to put in charge as few law firms as possible in order to maintain the greatest degree of controllability possible. An important selection criterion was that the law firms had sufficiently technically qualified employees and that they had the opportunity to expand this knowledge. The technically relevant areas mainly concerned semiconductor technology and communications technology, along with some security know-how. Another important factor was the general willingness of the law firms to act, for example, to achieve certain growth by hiring additional employees.

Infineon avoided relying on a single firm. Therefore, at least a second, sufficiently qualified and suitable law firm was mandated in relevant subject areas. This was intended to simplify performance and price comparisons at a later date and to make capacity shifts practicable.

A particularly decisive factor in the selection was, however, the extent to which a law firm was able to handle not only new applications but also ongoing proceedings. On average, the quantity ratio was about 1:4: for each new application, four ongoing application procedures had to be taken over. In this respect, of course, those law firms that had previously provided "colleague work" as an extended workbench for the *Siemens* semiconductor patent department were generally at an advantage. *Infineon* chose to standardize as much as possible during the selection process:

- *Infineon* created standard interfaces linking to law firms, for example by establishing:
  - Lawyer ↔ Infineon Patent Department channels.
  - Law firm ↔ inventor channels.
- Law firm ↔ inventor channels.
- Decision processes were standardized.
- Technical application fields and channels for office capacity requirements were identified.

Managing Quality
Strong, pragmatic, and consistent quality controlling was established to evaluate the quality of external patent services. *Infineon's* purchasing department was significantly involved in this process. When negotiating conditions with the law firms, price and performance, including time requirements, were an integral part of the negotiations. Framework agreements were then drawn up with law firms on this basis.

By developing a standardized quality controlling process covering quantitative and qualitative aspects and involving inventors, patent departments, and law firms, the performance of external attorneys could be better evaluated and thus taken into account when awarding further contracts.

Managing Processes
Infineon has largely outsourced the operational patent application process (see Fig. 5.3). While the *internal* focus is on strategy, coordination, and decision-making processes, the *external* focus is on ensuring that patent applications are handled quickly and in line with requirements, which has led to a minimal backlog of patent applications in progress.

5.3 Core Processes of Patent Management

Determining the correct "dosage" of freedom to operate, competitive differentiation, and license revenues that a company wants to achieve through the use of patents is also referred to as a patent strategy. If the company is divided into different business areas, a two-pronged strategy development is recommended, which is divided into company and business area levels. At the corporate level, the general patent strategy tailored to the enterprise is defined, specifying for example, how offensively or

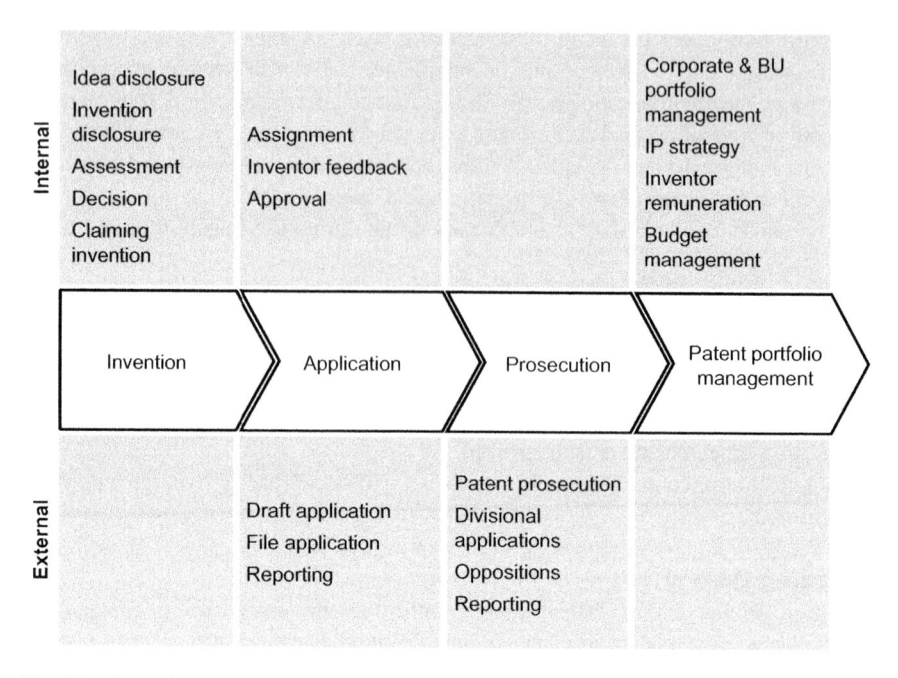

	Invention	Application	Prosecution	Patent portfolio management
Internal	Idea disclosure Invention disclosure Assessment Decision Claiming invention	Assignment Inventor feedback Approval		Corporate & BU portfolio management IP strategy Inventor remuneration Budget management
External		Draft application File application Reporting	Patent prosecution Divisional applications Oppositions Reporting	

Fig. 5.3 Internal and external processes at *Infineon Technologies* (authors' own figure)

defensively the enterprise wants to behave. At the business unit level, it is primarily the application strategy that has to be formulated, which includes the main areas of invention, selection criteria, and country portfolios.

The comparison of top-down and bottom-up strategy elements is an iterative process. The best strategy is good-for-nothing if it is not consistently implemented. This requires suitable structures and processes within the company. The following questions arise in particular:

- How do you obtain the necessary commitment from top management and other stakeholders for the formulation and implementation of the patent strategy?
- Who should be involved in the creation and evaluation of invention disclosures? How should patent applications and patents be pursued?
- How are cost/benefit aspects reviewed?
- What is the scope of the patent protection?
- What are the alternatives to patent protection?
- Which organizational forms and reporting channels should be chosen for the internal provision of services?
- What are the typical implementation measures?
- How can external service providers be involved and how can the quality provided be monitored?
- Which culturally influencing factors should be considered?

Regardless of the internal complexity, the formulation of the patent strategy must be coordinated with the respective stakeholders, at the latest, however, before processes are introduced.

> **Invention Generation Process:**
>
> 1. Stimulating and identifying of inventions
> 2. Evaluating and selecting of inventions
>
> **Procedures before Patent Offices:**
>
> 3. First filings
> 4. Divisional applications, applications abroad
> 5. Maintaining patents and other protection rights

Strategy rounds, often referred to as *Strategic Patent Committees*, are suitable for implementing the strategizing process in large companies. These are conducted regularly, for example annually, and can be prepared by the patent department. However, their general implementation requires the explicit support of the management.

An essential component of patent management is the conduct of proceedings in the patent application procedure before the patent offices *(patent prosecution)*. Typically, this is divided firstly into the process of generating inventions and secondly into the conduct of proceedings before the patent offices:

Invention Generation Process

1. **Stimulating and Identifying of Inventions:**
   This first step begins with the generation and search for suitable ideas. This includes, for example, idea generation, associated discussions with inventors and project managers as well as reviews of project milestones. In addition to the rather passive recording of patent ideas during project reviews, the patent attorney also plays an active role: he moderates and stimulates ideas for possible patent applications in order to find not only concrete product concepts but also far-reaching innovation ideas. Furthermore, the patent attorney helps to abstract from existing product concepts and to break out of familiar thinking structures. A new combination of knowledge and experience as well as a moderated change of perspective stimulate new patent ideas. The following steps have to be clearly subdivided:
   (a) Problem clarification: system delimitation and problem definition of the area to be patented.

(b) Idea generation: creativity and divergent thinking dominate; helpful here are creativity techniques, for example, the morphological box, the TRIZ, 6-3-5 method, or ordinary brainstorming. It is important to stimulate ideas in this phase, but not to evaluate them yet.
(c) Idea selection: preliminary selection of ideas that should at least be followed up. The focus here is on structuring, evaluating, and condensing the ideas into the most promising solution approaches.
(d) Implementation: creation of invention disclosures.
2. **Evaluating and Selecting of Inventions:**
An assessment is preferably made in a team in which the areas of patent function, R&D, innovation management, operations, and marketing are represented. It is an advantage if regular meetings take place. In addition to the composition of the evaluation team, it is also important that the evaluation is not carried out by individuals but by the entire team. In addition, a written individual evaluation can also be carried out according to precisely defined criteria specified by the patent department (see Chap. 3).

Procedures before Patent Offices

3. **First Filings:**
This step includes searches and filing with a patent office. Approvals should be country-specific. General prior art publications can be made by publication in journals, showcases, the Internet, or other media.

In general, before filing the first application, it should be looked into whether the attainable benefit of a later patent is at all in a reasonable proportion to the costs (see Sect. 2.4). In addition, if there is a problem that potential infringement will be difficult or impossible to prove later, consideration should be given to keeping the invention secret instead of filing a patent application. This is often the case, for example, with production processes, since these take place in production facilities that are inaccessible to outsiders and are also very company-specific.

If, however, there is a danger that third parties could obtain interfering patents in the same area, then, in order to avoid this, self-induced state of the art can be created by publishing generic improvements by means of so-called prior art publications (see Sect. 2.5).

The German multinational industrial control and automation company *Festo* has set clearly defined milestones in the development process (see Fig. 5.4). Based on this, *Festo* conducts patent searches, analyses patent information, evaluates inventions, and carries out a portfolio evaluation in order to control the patent application process. The general process of the European patent procedure and of the grant procedure at the European Patent Office are displayed in Figs. 5.5 and 5.6 (see also WIPO 2017).
4. **Divisional Applications, Applications Abroad:**
After one has already filed a first application, e.g., a national one, one can file a second application, e.g., to gain a more international patent protection, and

5.3 Core Processes of Patent Management

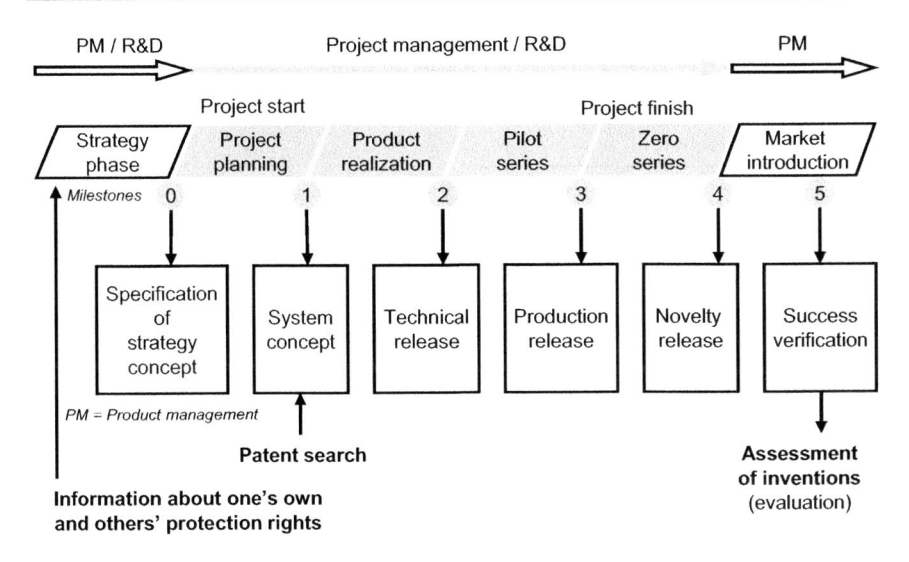

Fig. 5.4 Inclusion of the different patent processes at *Festo* (authors' own figure)

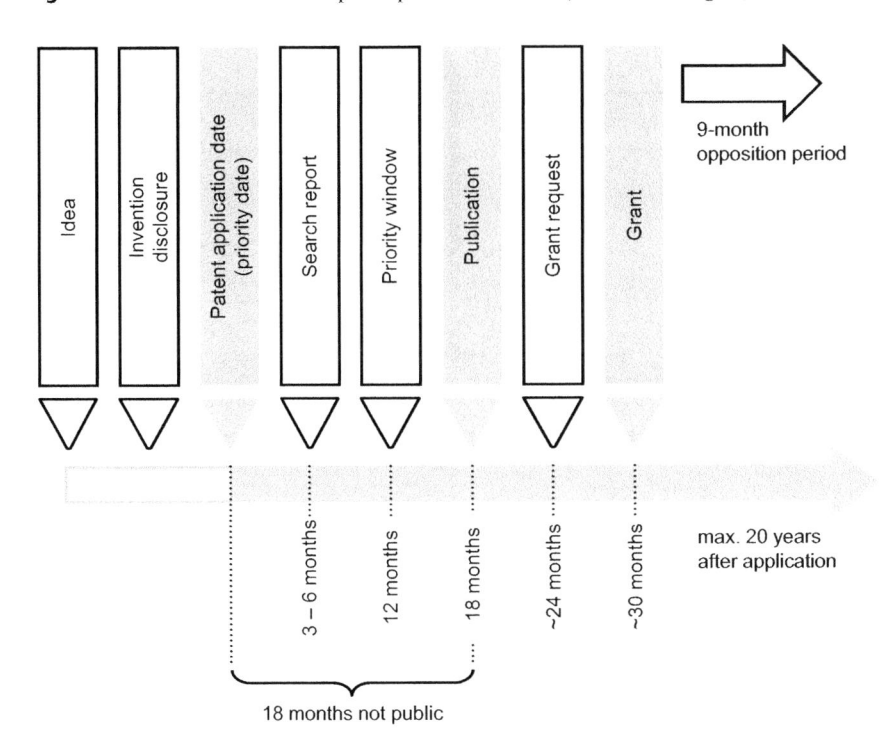

Fig. 5.5 Process of the European patent application procedure (authors' own figure)

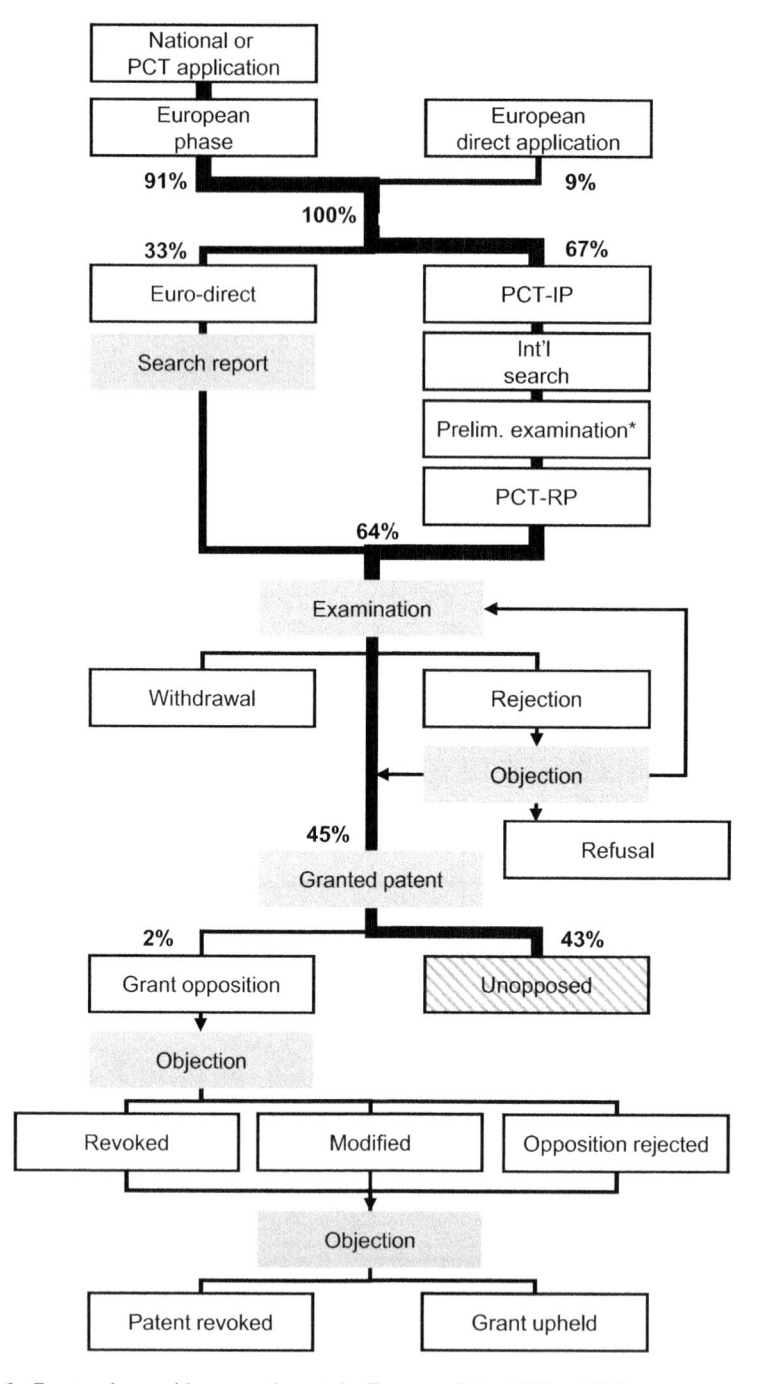

Fig. 5.6 Grant and opposition procedure at the European Patent Office (EPO)

maintain the original filing date. The filing date of that original application then becomes the priority date of the second application. The priority date applies only to elements the two applications have in common. When placing second applications, it is then ideally investigated whether the assessment criteria on which the initial application is based are still current. This phase also involves the cost-intensive selection of countries in which further industrial property rights are to be obtained. Particularly suitable criteria are the sales market countries and the countries in which the competitors' production facilities are located.

For the German chemical and consumer goods company *Henkel*, a multinational active both in the consumer and industrial sector, an important prerequisite for the identification of invention disclosures is a good understanding of the state of the art and the competition. *Henkel* uses the services offered by *Derwent* and *MicroPatent* to monitor the competition. Approximately 5000 patent specifications are processed manually each year. The focus is on the activities of the competitors. In addition, keyword searches are used to monitor the fields of technology. The responsible technology specialists are responsible for monitoring and evaluating the patent documents. As a rule, these are the heads of the R&D groups. For example, the head of development for detergent tablets is responsible for the "Tablets" search field. Although the group leaders bear the responsibility in the first instance, they can fall back on the input of other designated technology experts in their team. The R&D manager receives regular and direct reports on the patent situation from the heads of the R&D groups. At *Henkel*, great attention is paid to the regular and intensive work of the R&D specialists with patent documents and information. After reviewing the documents, the second step is to derive appropriate action measures on the basis of the new understanding.

5. **Maintenance:**
A separate process step must be dedicated to the maintenance of intellectual property rights, during which the assessment criteria are re-examined before the official fees are paid. The maturity of the costs in the individual countries plays an important role here. While annual fees are charged in European countries, in the USA they are due only every 4 years after they have been granted. As a rule, property rights are not explicitly dropped, but simply no fees are paid and thus expire. In particular, this has the advantage that in the event of a wrong decision, the property right can possibly be reactivated.

The generation of patents is usually based on individual decisions made by individuals in Small and Medium Enterprises (SMEs) and by teams of experts in larger companies. Such teams, also known as *patent liaisons* or *operational patent committees*, are composed of several experts with market, technology, and patent expertise. These teams often meet once a month or quarter to assess new invention disclosures, initial and subsequent applications, and patent maintenance. This process may take several years before the patent is granted. Patent offices worldwide have been trying to cope with the backlog, and recently have been bringing down the time previously needed for this. Patent applications before the European Patent Office, for example, are granted only after 2–3 years, and patents are held for an average of 12 years (see Figs. 5.7 and 5.8).

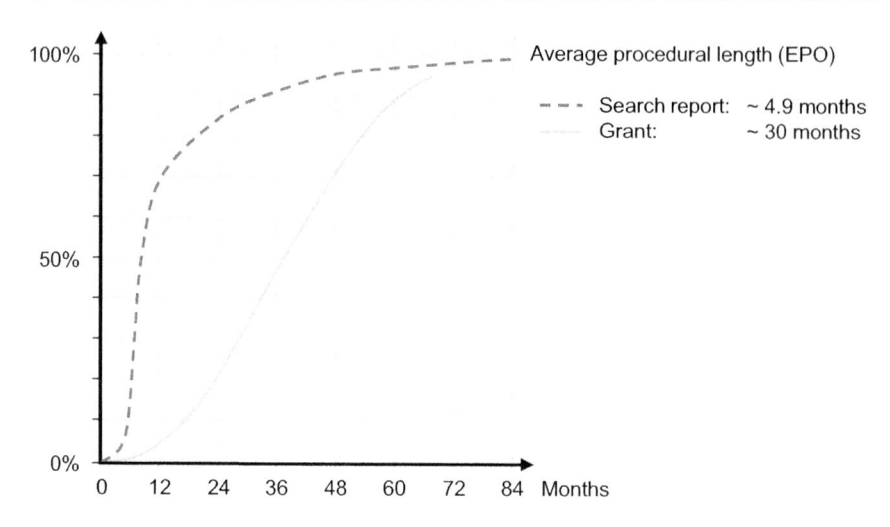

Fig. 5.7 Average procedural length at the European Patent Office (EPO)

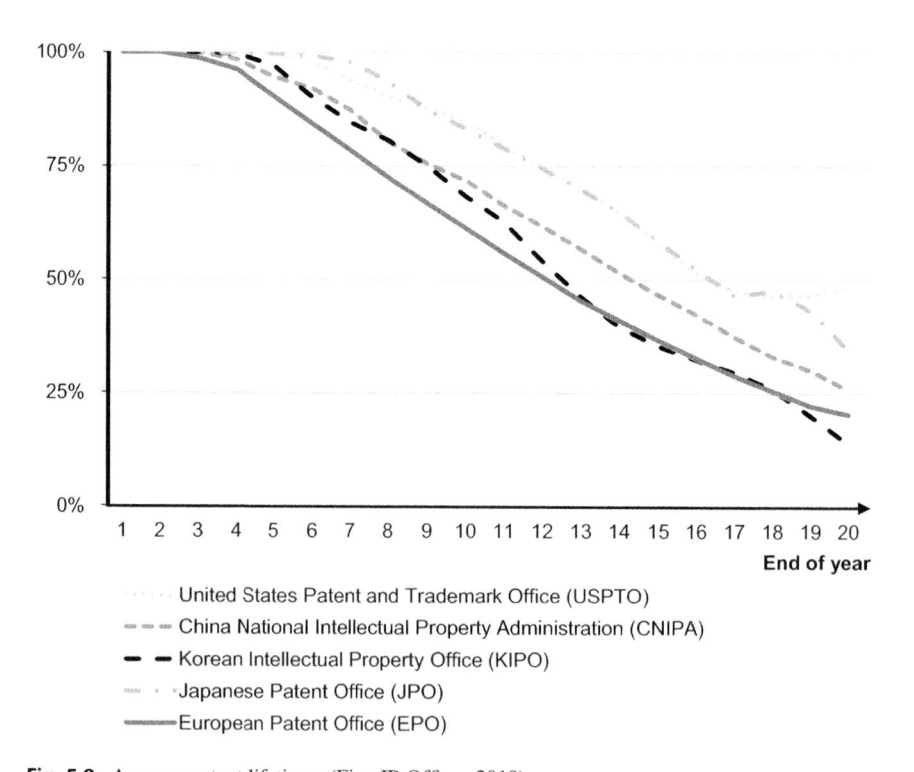

Fig. 5.8 Average patent lifetimes (Five IP Offices 2019)

The USA offers a fast-track program, which aims to grant after 1 year. Japan has drastically reduced its pendency, with time to first action down from ca. 26 months in 2011 to around 10 months now, and getting a final decision made at around month 20 (WIPO 2017).

5.4 Inventor Culture as a Catalyst

An essential component of the innovation culture is the ability of a company's employees to develop ideas and translate them into marketable technologies, products, and services. In order to implement the patent strategy, inventive activities are therefore shaped by business interests. The introduction of an incentive system that rewards those inventions, which contribute significantly is particularly suitable for this purpose. Appropriate measures can be taken to create an inventor culture:

- Ensuring broad access to all sources of information
- Clarification of communication responsibilities and roles
- Development of a common team code
- Regular feedback and reviews
- Promotion of social events for personal exchange
- Active communication of success stories
- Project debriefings at the end of the project
- Break-out sessions to distance people from day-to-day business
- Establishment of experimental rooms to promote experiments

The Swiss industrial firm, *Georg Fischer*, has opted for a purely monetary incentive system to stimulate inventions that takes account of national obligations, such as employee inventor remuneration. It is important that the incentive system is perceived as fair by those involved. This applies in particular when employees from different areas and locations of the company work together as a team on projects. A relevant starting point for comparisons is the average salaries of the locations. Furthermore, transparency, broad communication, and appropriate training are required. Support must be provided by the R&D management or a technical board if the program is to be perceived and accepted as serious and sustainable.

The reinsurance company *Swiss Re* has introduced an incentive system for inventions with monetary and non-monetary components. The inventors are listed and honored in a *Hall of Fame* on the Intranet. This is accompanied by a letter of recognition from a member of the Executive Board and, if necessary, by small gifts.

The process automation solution and services provider *Endress+Hauser* published an annual report, the cover of which had the portraits of all the company's inventors—a strong signal, on the one hand, to inventors and employees within the company and, on the other, to customers outside the company.

> **"Innovate or Perish"**
> Although it is financially in decline, *Eastman Kodak* had a strong inventor culture, one that was initiated by its inventor-founder George Eastman in the nineteenth century; four main awards got established, three of which relate to patents:
> - **1st CTO 1st Patent Award:**
>   Award for the first patent granted, including a copy of the patent certificate issued and a letter signed by the CTO.
> - **2nd 20th Kodak Patent:**
>   Award for the 20th patent granted, including a cash prize and an invitation to an annual dinner hosted by the CEO and the CTO.
> - **3rd 100th Kodak Patent:**
>   CTO Century award, including a cash prize and an invitation to the annual dinner.
> - **4th Eastman Innovation Award:**
>   Annual award related to important inventions, but not necessarily patents. However, the patent awards were not enough to prevent the eventual downfall of the Kodak corporation; Kodak did not promote enough disruptive innovation internally.

"Culture Eats Strategy for Breakfast"

Due to pressure on margins, and fierce competition, companies are facing pressure to innovate. While there are already many good solutions to the strategy and business model levels, the human factor of innovation is often overlooked. Yet, corporate culture can often be a key resource, enabling companies to use their employees as a key success factor for innovation (Gassmann et al. 2018).

An innovative corporate culture acts as a central factor in driving sustainable growth and attracting young talent. According to studies by the sociologist Richard Florida, young people can no longer be recruited and retained with a high salary and good career perspectives alone. What is more important in the competition for the world's best talent is a strong and positive organizational culture.

By looking at highly innovative companies, we focused not only on the leaders, as these do mostly not innovate, but also on the people that actually generate the innovation. We tried to identify successful practices of how to develop and promote a highly innovative company culture. In our research, we identified seven cultural aspects of innovative companies, which we call the *ANIMATE* model (see Fig. 5.9):

- ***A*** **gile implementation:** acting in fast, iterative learning cycles.
- ***N*** **urturing:** develop measures to stimulate employees and external partners to think outside the box.
- ***I*** **nspire:** give employees a purpose and inspire them.

5.4 Inventor Culture as a Catalyst

- ***M* otivate:** make employees go the extra mile by motivating them.
- ***A* lign teams:** arrange teams to achieve goals together.
- ***T* ransparency:** communicate openly so that all employees can contribute to the set goals in the most effective way.
- ***E* mpowerment:** create the feeling of being competent and in charge of one's own actions, and create confidence on all hierarchical levels. This will catalyze entrepreneurship.

To address cultural innovation, we created the St. Gallen Innovation Culture Navigator which outlines 66 practices of highly successful organizations supporting their pursuit of company innovation. Linked to an online self-assessment on www.innovationculturenavigator.com, the Innovation Culture Navigator represents a playful way of developing your organizational culture by learning from practices from leading innovation players.

A strong innovation culture is not only enabling more patents and innovation but also, las a side effect, has led to 36% more profits and 45% more sales, as Michaelis found out in 2018. The ANIMATE framework supports specific practices concerning innovation culture. It is important to understand that culture is not God-given but can be developed and designed similarly to the business model itself. It takes time, but there are practices within the seven dimensions of ANIMATE which help leaders to create a dynamic environment for a vibrant, sparkling, and energetic corporate culture—the humus for innovation in every company.

Knowledge leaves when people do. In spite of digitization, immense efforts in the field of knowledge management, and the availability of new and innovative tools such as artificial intelligence, people remain the key drivers of innovation. It is widely accepted in software engineering that a good developer can be almost a hundred times more productive than an average developer. The cause of this productivity gap has less to do with training in technology, mathematics or programming, and more to do with specific skills of intelligent assessment and reflection. The best and most innovative software developers are becoming increasingly less likely to be employed in traditional industries such as banking, industry, or commerce. Instead, most of them end up at *Google, Amazon,* or *IBM*. Even more commonly, many of them apply their skills in open-source projects outside of their jobs, because that is where they find what is lacking in their workplaces: agility, diversity, inspiration, motivational feedback, high levels of transparency, and self-development.

Successful products, such as *Sony's* PlayStation, Gmail from *Google*, the first *Apple Macintosh* or *Facebook's* famous "Like" button were developed by innovative employees on their own initiative. The first *BMW* 3 Series' Touring model the company's management never wanted. An employee acting on his own initiative developed and presented this product himself. *3M's* famous *Post-it*®s were a by-product of an experiment with adhesives that did not work out. Even Teflon was developed as a "spin-off" after searching for a new type of refrigerant. The famous *tesafilm*® (adhesive tape) from *Beiersdorf*, which today (in the German language) is used synonymously for an entire product class, is actually an unsuccessful *Hansaplast*® (band-aid).

None of these products would exist if it had not been for the tremendous commitment of creative employees, some of whom encountered a lot of resistance within and outside their organization.

It is often claimed that innovation is pure luck. Indeed, the random screening of every conceivable active substance is in fact a common method in pharmaceutical research. That is how the transplant drug Cyclosporin from *Sandoz*, now part of *Novartis*, was developed, for example. However, it is often forgotten that large amounts of determination, perseverance, and teamwork are required in order to successfully identify and develop an active ingredient. There are companies that are constantly searching for and encouraging these curious pioneers. Innovation must not only be desired but must first and foremost as a precondition be permitted and encouraged. This is not always easy, because it also means going down many dead-ends and accepting many failures. How do you measure this kind of innovation? One thing is certain: linear innovation processes, such as stage-gate processes, are not going to take you all the way. You also have to take a chance. In the end, what matters is beating the failure rate statistics for innovation projects. In other words: You have to kiss a lot of frogs to find a prince.

In retrospect, companies often mythologize their innovations and founders. There are numerous stories and legends built up around *IBM* founder and inventor *Thomas Watson*, and the same is true of *Wilhelm Conrad Röntgen*. Often employees and colleagues are left forgotten and in the background—only the lonely, heroic warriors remain. Reality, however, is characterized by team efforts, and that is all the truer of a modern innovation organization. Without teams, most innovations would never have emerged. It is important for managers to be aware of this. You are hardly going to create an innovative organization by building a culture around silos.

A strong innovation culture also clearly supports the implementation of an innovation strategy: In a study of 1000 companies, it was shown that companies, the innovation strategy of which was supported by a suitable innovation culture, experienced a growth by 33% in company value and a growth increase by one-sixth in net profit over a period of 5 years than companies that did not have a suitable innovation culture. It is not just Silicon Valley that offers successful examples of this. There are many regional hidden champions as well, such as the German multinational industrial control and automation company *Festo,* and the Swiss world-class screen printing, filtration and architectural solutions provider *Sefar*, which manage to achieve sustainable innovation thanks to their systematic striving for an innovative and inventive culture.

Nevertheless, many industry partners whose innovations we have supported in recent years see culture as an intangible construct that cannot be managed systematically. Engineers work on designing and developing their products and processes, but view the company culture as a given historic construct.

This fatalistic view is dangerous because it puts the spark of inspiration and innovation at risk. Executives and managers are especially responsible for implementing an innovative corporate culture. This can be done at all company levels and does not necessarily have to come from the executive—even though it might work better that way.

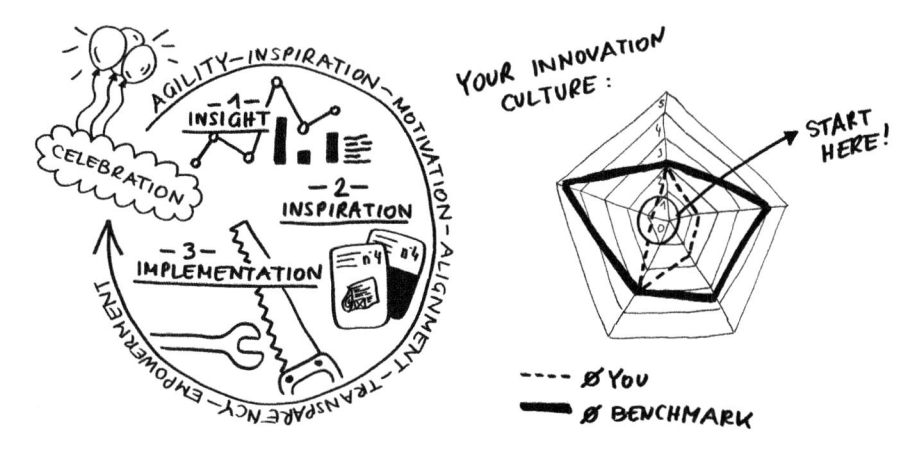

Fig. 5.9 Managing inventor culture: The St. Gallen Innovation Culture Navigator (Gassmann et al. 2018)

Seven Dimensions of Innovation Culture
"ANIMATE":

1. Agile implementation
2. Nurture and develop measures to stimulate to think outside the box
3. Inspire employees, due to diverse perspectives
4. Motivate employees to go the extra mile
5. Align teams in order to achieve goals together
6. Transparency, so that all employees can contribute in the most effective way
7. Empower employees so that they can use their innovation potential

---

Three Steps Toward An Innovation Culture Plan

1. **Insight** (first stage): In order to identify the most efficient levers for action, get a clear assessment of your organization's innovation culture.
2. **Inspiration** (second stage): Taking your assessment results into consideration, the cultural practices that fit the company's profile best are examined. Obviously, these practices also have to get adapted for your specific organizational context.
3. **Implementation** (third stage): Roll out and test the adapted cultural practices.
   Source: St. Gallen Innovation Culture Navigator (2020)

The St. Gallen Innovation Culture Navigator

The Swiss *Institute of Technology Management* at the renowned *University of St. Gallen (ITEM-HSG)* has been researching the management of innovation and has also been investigating the success factors of the most successful innovative organizations for almost 20 years. The Institute has also made numerous contributions to the rankings of the most innovative companies.

A central lever is considered to be the corporate culture, which allows to capitalize on employees as a success factor for innovation. Successful products such as Liechtenstein's multinational *Hilti's* Fleet Management were initiated by innovative employees on their own initiative. However, a culture of innovation also influences the success of strategic innovation from top management, which depends on the willingness and ability of employees to implement it. At the same time, many of our industrial partners see culture as too intangible a construct to be managed systemically. Based on this feedback the *St. Gallen Innovation Culture Navigator* allows for a systematic management of innovation culture (see Fig. 5.9):

1. *Insight:* Learning what is missing
2. *Inspiration:* Seeing what is working
3. *Implementation:* Doing what is fitting

1. **Insight**

    Good management needs good data. Even an innovation culture cannot be designed efficiently on the basis of mere instinct. A precise assessment of your innovation culture will identify both the cultural strengths and the cultural possibilities, which your company can encounter if suitable cultural practices are selected. You can start developing your innovation culture by determining the most efficient drivers: Is your biggest challenge that your employees do not produce enough innovative ideas? Does your company lack the right channels to process and test ideas quickly and efficiently? Or do your employees perhaps have very little incentive to implement their innovative ideas within your company and therefore implement them externally? Systematically measuring your innovation culture and knowing your status quo both enable you to focus. You can direct your energy and time into the identified possibilities and thus achieve maximum impact. In addition, your employees can already get involved, aware of innovation culture being an important topic. To then give employees an active role as co-shapers of the company's future is a practical step toward a successful innovation culture.

    We assess the seven dimensions of your innovation culture by using a standardized measurement tool.[1] You should, however, involve employees from different departments and hierarchical levels. This is the only way to

---

[1] Self-assessment available under https://innovationskulturnavigator.ch/en

guarantee a truly valid and representative measurement of your innovation culture. In order to make employee data directly interpretable and action-relevant, your data can be compared to a benchmark. Without such a context, it is difficult to interpret a "four" in the area of agility. First, you can have internal benchmarking in which different business areas are compared with each other. Second, we enable comparisons amongst companies, which form part of our growing research database. We ultimately recommend using internal time-based benchmarking, whereby a new measurement is performed cyclically (about every 12 or 24 months) so that trends can be tracked within the company. These three reference points—especially when combined—enable us to interpret the assessment results and to select specifically those goals for the second phase *Inspiration*, which promise the greatest impact.

2. **Inspiration**
   Learn from the best and be inspired by the innovation champions' 66 cultural practices.

   The advantage of designing an innovation culture with concrete cultural practices is that tangible and visible developments quickly reach employees. The rich and varied perspectives within the 66 cultural practices help break out of familiar thinking patterns and old discussions in order to then consider completely new options for action. Numerous company examples help enliven the cultural practices and provide reference points that help convince colleagues. The cultural practices cover a very broad spectrum and let you decide how courageously the culture is to be developed: The Heroic Failure Award, which *Grey* symbolically bestows to improve the way in which failure is handled in a company, is not likely to be controversial—even in conservative companies. The payment service, *Stripe*, implemented the cultural practice known as Zero Barriers to *Users*, whereby product developers are assigned to customer support for one day a week to bring more empathy and customer-centricity into product development. This is a practice with great impact requiring, for many CTOs, a lot of persuasion.

   We recommend a workshop setting, which involves employees from different departments and an experienced (possibly external) facilitator. You should start with the results of stage one *Insight*. Present these results and reflect upon them: For example, which interpretation results from the comparisons within the benchmarking categories? Based on the analyses, the group should set a focus. Then you tackle the Innovation Culture Navigator's cultural practices, those which fit the selected focus goals and framework conditions. Yet, it is crucially important not to impulsively reject or to approve of a practice. Work through them in concrete terms: How would specifically this be understood in my company? Who would be affected? What possibilities and challenges arise? Remember that although the 66 cultural practices are excellent material for inspiration, they must often be adapted to the concrete conditions of the company. The cultural practices which are implemented must match the DNA of the company—do not merely follow just any trend. *Bosch* is a good example of this. They were inspired by

Google's well-known 20% regulation, which allowed employees to work on their innovation projects every Friday. However, in the German corporate culture, it was more appropriate to allocate innovation time slots to Tuesday mornings.

3. **Implementation**
   You have to continuously deal with your own innovation culture. It is not just a once in a lifetime operation and far from being a static element. That is why you have to anchor innovation culture in concrete routines—routines for how your employees do their work, how they adjust, how they interact with each other, and what they celebrate. We design these routines according to the results in stage two *Inspiration*. Now it is time to implement and iteratively optimize the cultural practices, which you have selected and adapted. The iterative character of the process is particularly important here. Although it is becoming more and more widespread in product design, it is still not used frequently enough in organizational and cultural design. The effectiveness of the practice can be optimized step by step via close feedback loops. Simply continue adapting them to the concrete needs and profiles of your employees. At the same time, this design integrates two important success factors of cultural development: Transparency for employees and participation of employees.

   Sweet spot thinking: We recommend that you identify and use simple, as well as promising, opportunities to create visible success stories before iteratively rolling out the practice any further. These success stories and the people behind them can play an important role, the people acting as ambassadors while the cultural practices are instantiated. An iterative rolling-out process offers several advantages (if it is organizationally feasible): On the one hand, you can simultaneously implement, learn through employee feedback, and further develop your cultural practice. On the other hand, it directly turns a short glimpse on innovation culture into an ongoing process of cultural design and development. In our experience, this enables an organic transition back to the first stage, *Insight*, which is both a measure of success and the kick-off for the next cycle of cultural design. You will have a permanent process of actively shaping your own innovation culture and constantly developing yourself as a company. ◄

5.5 Preventing Product Piracy

Counterfeit goods not only pose a risk of loss of profit but can also damage a company's image, cause an outflow of know-how, lead to a loss of market share, and inhibit growth potential. In a report, the OECD has been tracking trade in counterfeit goods (OECD 2019; see Fig. 5.10).

The renowned chainsaw manufacturer *Andreas Stihl* has been actively fighting against brand and product piracy from Asia for years. However, the company only became aware of product piracy after losing about 40% in sales in Indonesia. The

5.5 Preventing Product Piracy

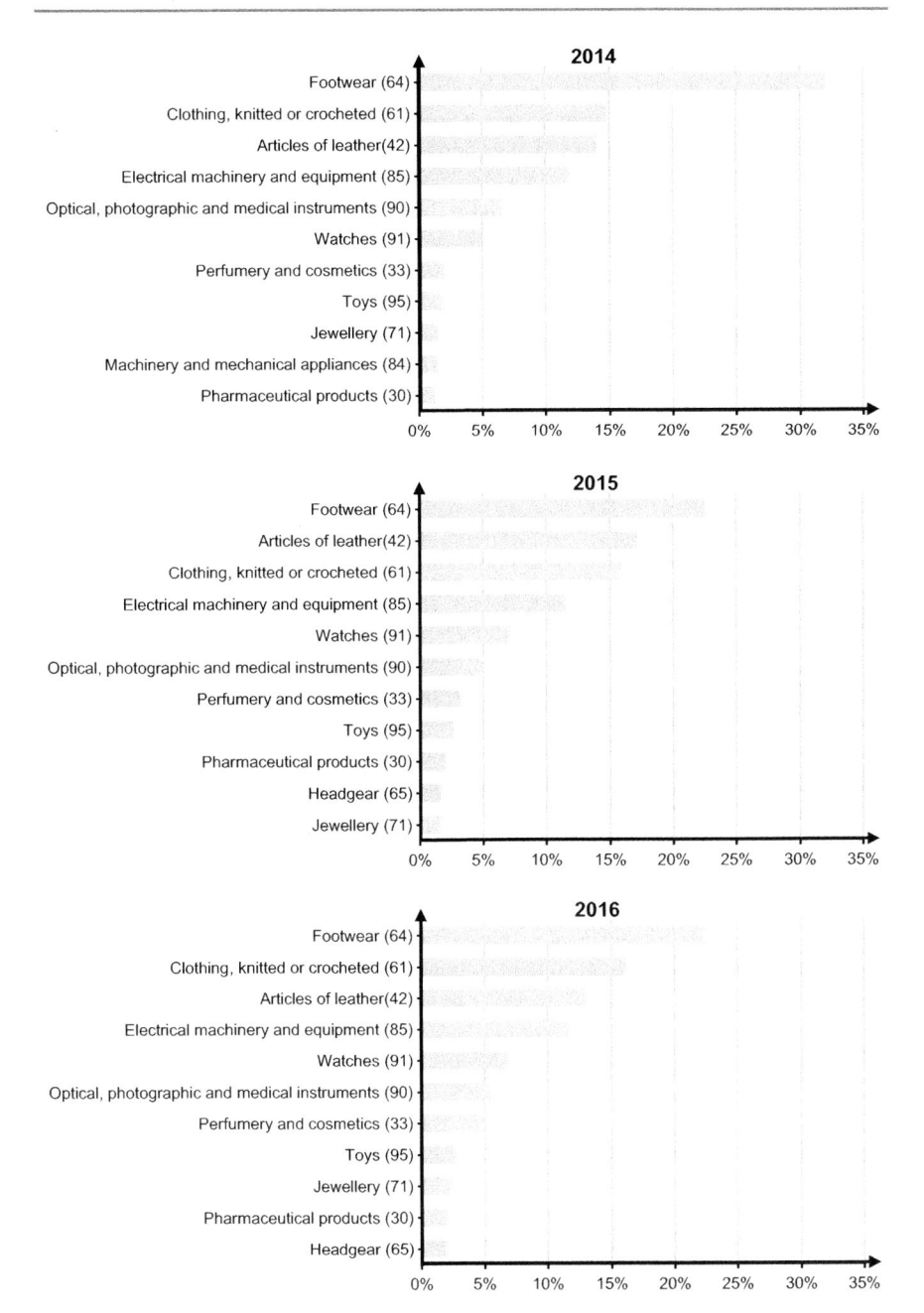

Fig. 5.10 Seizures of counterfeit and pirated goods: top industries by Harmonized System (HS) code, 2014, 2015 and 2016 (OECD 2019)

company noticed not only that spare parts for outdated models were being copied, but that complete models of the current series were also being pirated.

The case serves as a lesson showing the potential risks of why a product portfolio must consequently be safeguarded at an early stage in order to identify the causes of piracy and to counteract them. Potential risks from product piracy, which lead to considerable loss of financial returns, are:

- Loss of market share and growth potential
- Know-how outflow
- Loss of image
- Reduced product quality
- Danger of product liability

In emerging markets such as *China*, external factors such as uncertain legal certainty, cultural differences, language barriers, and lack of transparency (flow of information, provision of information, responsibilities, corruption, geographical reach) are also very important (Prud'homme et al. 2018). In order to identify possible effects in good time, the risk portfolio of individual products or product groups should be assessed. This assessment is based on the probability of imitation on the one hand and on the potential business damage of a counterfeit on the other. The imitation probability results from the significance and image of the product in the market. The potential business damage results from the significance of the product for the company, for example, margin, market penetration, and degree of awareness, complexity of the product, and then also phase of the product life cycle (Gassmann and Bader 2017).

If, for example, the question arises whether a patent should be applied for in China, always keeping an eye on the knowledge to be thereby completely protected is important. Legal measures, such as patent, design and trademark protection, alone are not sufficient to protect against piracy and the outflow of know-how. Just as important are technological business, marketing, and personnel measures. Only a holistic approach that combines both legal and factual strategies can comprehensively optimize protection against product piracy and IP infringement (see Sect. 1.2).

Siemens in China

In China, the multinational engineering and electronics company *Siemens* succeeded in reducing the leaving rate of its R&D employees to less than 10% with both monetary and non-monetary incentives. For example, employees are tied to the Western Group through international training and development opportunities. Local values and standards also play an important role, since, for example, job descriptions and corresponding titles are particularly important for the function of employees. ◄

One example of such a holistic approach is the *IP-Protection Star* (Gassmann et al. 2012). In this model, five dimensions of IP protection are addressed: *Legal,*

5.5 Preventing Product Piracy

Technology, Business, Market, and *Human* (see Fig. 5.11). In order to establish a holistic perspective of IP management, the same importance must be attached to each of these five dimensions, as this is the only way to avoid blind spots. The following describes and explains these individual dimensions:

Legal

Intellectual property must be protected legally by the application of various types of intellectual property rights, such as patents, and trade secrets. This can be supplemented by contractual protective measures, such as confidentiality agreements made with employees or confidentiality agreements made with suppliers. The legal enforcement of these protective measures is central to this: if violations are ignored and thus have no consequences for infringers, the legal protective measures lose their deterrent effect.

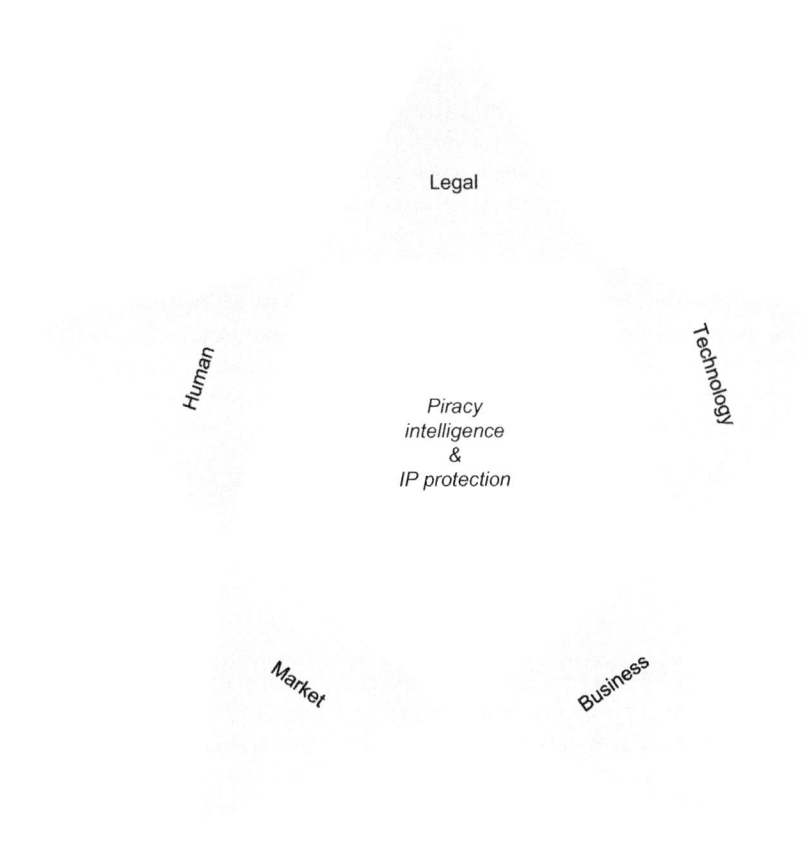

Fig. 5.11 Comprehensive protection strategy against piracy (Gassmann et al. 2012)

Technology

The aim is to prevent infringement in advance by means of various technical measures. Products can be protected with the help of various technical aids: both in a visible way, such as with holograms or security labels, and in an invisible way, such as through isotopes that can only be recognized with the help of technological devices. The complexity of the product also plays a decisive role here: the higher the complexity of a product, the more difficult it is to copy it and the higher the barriers for possible imitators. The degree of complexity is influenced by various factors, such as the degree of standardization or the number of process steps. The degree of customization can also support the protection efforts, as it is much more difficult to copy a highly individualized product. A further measure is the distribution of production to different development and production sites. In accordance with the "need-to-know" principle, only the necessary part of the know-how is passed on to the sites, thus preventing the outflow of production knowledge.

Business

In this context, the protection of competitive advantages is of central importance, such as through a unique business model or by means of targeted differentiation strategies. Possible differentiation strategies include strong corporate branding, quality, price, or product differentiation as well as an established brand. Such competitive advantages can better protect innovations, as they represent barriers for possible imitators. It also makes sense to control corporate processes. Violations often occur at certain points in the value chain, which is why monitoring and tracking products are very effective. Close cooperation with customs can also prevent the import or export of imitations. The use of your own sales staff can also play a protective role along with educating customers by convincing them of the added value of the original product. In addition, qualified sales personnel create a general added value for customers that imitation cannot offer.

Market

In order to detect or even prevent possible infringement of IP rights by competitors or suppliers at an early stage, continuous monitoring of market activities and key technologies is just as necessary as an active search for products that infringe IP rights. An additional *de facto* measure is to convince customers of the value of the company and its product portfolio. On the one hand, this can reduce the risk of customers unknowingly acquiring copies, and on the other hand, it can strengthen customer loyalty, as they also become familiar with the long-term advantages of the product, differentiating it from imitation products.

Human

This dimension concerns measures against the direct or indirect outflow of know-how. In addition to controlling access to facilities and data, it is important to create awareness among employees for the responsible handling of confidential information, for example, through internal training. Cooperation with universities can also be useful in developing the skills of employees at the local level. For example, *Philips* entered into partnerships with several Chinese universities and offered events for students on intellectual property as part of its *Philips IP Academy*. Loyalty and identification with the company, which can be promoted through career opportunities or reward systems, can also be an effective means of preventing know-how loss.

References

Five IP Offices. (2019). *IP5 statistics reports 2018 edition*. Edited by Korean Intellectual Property Office, Oct 2019.

Gassmann, O., & Bader, M. A. (2017). *Patentmanagement: Innovationen erfolgreich nutzen und schützen* (4th ed.). Berlin: Springer.

Gassmann, O., Beckenbauer, A., & Friesike, S. (2012). *Profiting from innovation in China*. Heidelberg: Springer.

Gassmann, O., Wecht, C. H., Meister, C., & Boemelburg, R. (2018). *Exploit the hidden success factor of innovation culture*. Munich: Innovationskulturnavigator. Carl Hanser.

Loebbert, M. (2000). Interne Dienstleister: Was sie alles können müssen. *Harvard Business Manager, 3*, 49–57.

OECD. (2019). *Trends in trade in counterfeit and pirated goods*. Published on March 18, 2019.

Prud'homme, D., von Zedwitz, M., Thraen, J., & Bader, M. A. (2018). Forced technology transfer policies: Workings in China and strategic implications. *Technological Forecasting and Social Change, 134*, 150–168.

St. Gallen Innovation Culture Navigator. (2020). Accessed January 6, 2020, from https://innovationskulturnavigator.ch/en

WIPO. (2017). *Patent office operations: Application processing times, examination capacity and examination outcomes*. World Intellectual Property Indicators 2017. https://www.wipo.int/edocs/pubdocs/en/wipo_pub_941_2017-chapter1.pdf

Patent Management by Industry 6

The effect of patents is strongly sector-dependent. Some industry-specific aspects of patent management are presented and discussed below.

We here give an overview of the following industry sectors, highlighting case study examples on specific aspects of patent management:

1. Pharma
2. Chemistry
3. Crop Science
4. Life Sciences
5. Consumer Goods
6. Machinery
7. Electrics and Electronics
8. Automotive
9. Information and Communications Technology
10. Computer Science
11. Financial Services and Fintech
12. Transport and Logistics
13. Start-ups and SMEs

6.1 Pharma

In the pharmaceutical and chemical industries as well as in the biotechnology sector, patents grant an effective monopoly on the active ingredients and products to be protected (Gassmann et al. 2016, 2018). In the pharmaceutical industry, in particular, products are essentially entirely dependent on patent protection. Revenues from so-called blockbuster products with sales of more than USD 1 billion each and an average annual sales growth of more than 20% can usually only be achieved with patent protection. The entire generics market is based on bioequivalent products for which patent protection has expired. The global generics market is estimated at 257.3 billion US dollars with a future compound annual growth rate of 8.8% (Visiongain 2018). In extreme cases, generic products can cause sales losses of more than 50% in the first few months after patent protection expires. Pharmaceutical companies' blockbuster drugs are especially vulnerable to drugs coming off patent, examples would be *Pfizer* (Lipitor), *AbbVie* (Humira), *GlaxoSmithKline* (Advair), *Johnson and Johnson* (Remicade), *AstraZeneca Bristol-Myers Squibb* (>40%), *Eli Lilly* (>40%), *Schering-Plough* (>50%), *Amgen* (>60%), *TAP* (>90%), or *Novo Nordisk* (>50%).

It is therefore a major challenge in the pharmaceutical industry to protect sales of successful products from rapid price erosion, to replace them with replacement products, and to operate proactively in patent management (see Fig. 6.1). Due to the time it takes to approve a drug, pharmaceutical patents enjoy special extensions, and companies derive value through:

- Supplementary protection certificates for drugs for a maximum of 5 years
- So-called orphan drug provisions for niche drugs with an additional protection of 7 years in the USA, and a maximum of 10 years in the EU
- Extension of protection for pediatric medicines for 6 months in the USA and Europe
- Continuous increase in product value through new active ingredients and new indications
- Aggressive defense of intellectual property rights against patent infringers
- Securing sales after expiration of patent protection by changing the drug status to an OTC drug or introducing a generic brand
- Reduction of dependence on key products through investments in the life cycle and portfolio management, licensing to third parties, and mergers and acquisitions

Case: Bristol-Myers Squibb vs. Gilead Sciences

Pharma is one industry where patents add a large amount of value. Society is willing to pay huge amounts in the effort to save and maintain life, and pharma meets that

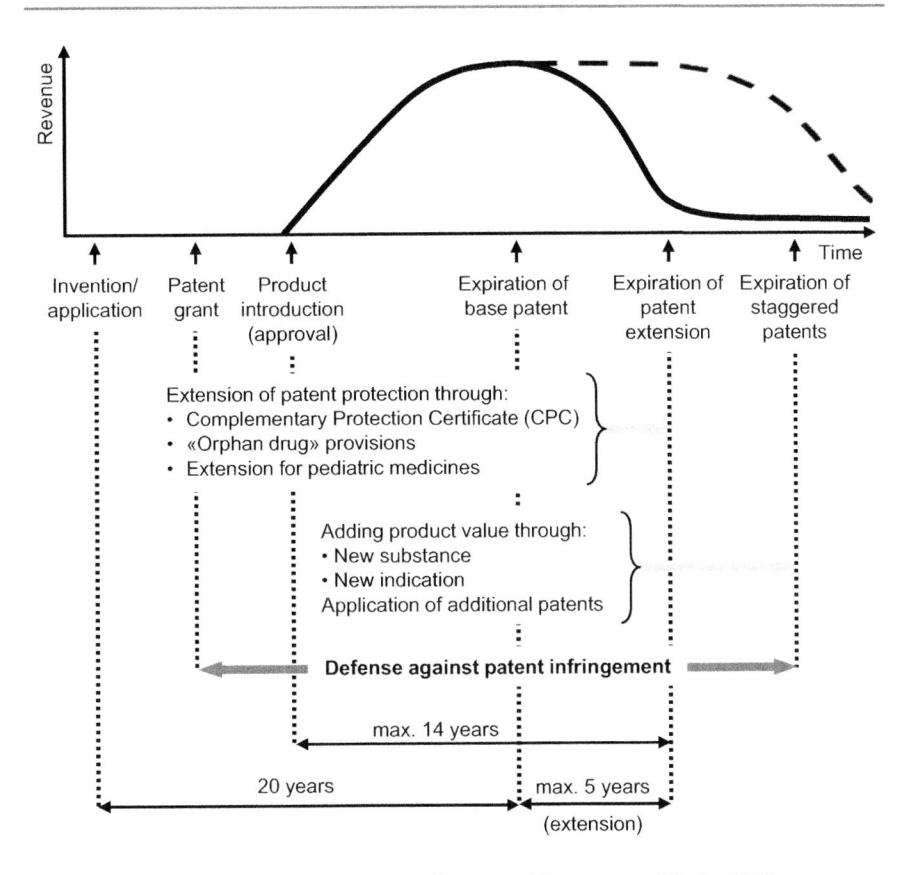

Fig. 6.1 Patent protection extension strategy in pharma (Gassmann and Bader 2017)

basic demand. In a recent court case, a Los Angelean jury found that *Gilead's* Yescarta (axicabtagene ciloleucel) cancer treatment had violated *Bristol-Myer's* licensed patent. *Bristol-Myers* was awarded US $752 Mio. in damages plus a 27.6% royalty on all future sales of *Gilead's* Yescarta. The technology licensed from the Kettering Cancer Center in New York is both novel and powerful since it reprograms the patients' immunological T cells to attack the cancer. *Gilead* asserted that "Given that *Kite* independently developed Yescarta and took all of the risk in its discovery and development, we do not believe *Sloan Kettering* and *Juno* are entitled to any level of damages" (Wolfe 2019).

> **Take-Aways Pharma**
> - The productivity paradox in pharma increases (Gassmann et al. 2018): Only 1 out of 10,000 substances tested preclinically becomes a marketed product.
> - The overall R&D pipeline output is low at the average.
> - Lower risk tolerance of both regulators and society contributes negatively to new molecular entities.
> - The pressure to commercialize the R&D investment increases as clinical studies become larger and more complex and drug discovery technologies more expensive.
> - Time that is available to monetize patents gets shortened, since the innovation process slows down.
> - Time delays are caused by licensing, co-development, and joint venture negotiations. This has to be speeded up.
> - The imperative for blockbusters (1 billion-dollar drugs) increases the importance of single patents.
> - New technologies such as artificial intelligence are starting to play a strategic role in the pharma industry.
> - New entrants in the health care sector are often data-based companies, e.g., wearables from consumer electronics.
> - Regulators play a crucial role in the value of innovation and patents: New product registration, R&D experiment regulations, price regulations, health care financing laws, but also patent protection policies in developing countries.

6.2 Chemistry

In the chemical industry, the rule is, "Whoever has the formula has the power." With regard to the handling of patents, licensing, and market structures in the chemical industry, patents are used in conjunction with other instruments, such as secrecy. This applies in particular to process innovations. Depending on the underlying field of knowledge, attempts are made to cover entire fields of technology with patent clusters. License agreements are often part of technology packages. In general, companies in the chemical industry are increasingly willing to license their products and technologies.

An important driver for technology exploitation is the commercial usability by third parties. Technologies, products, or even business models are licensed as the degree of maturity increases and the business risk decreases. A typical challenge, however, is the valuation of IP and know-how in the demand for an excessive license fee from the licensor. As a result, the licensee's market success is jeopardized due to high market prices and too low contribution margins. There is thus a risk of losing potential profits for both the licensee and the licensor. In order to maximize profits, the licensor and licensee may therefore at least strive to optimize the contribution margin jointly. While for mature products a realistic net present value risk assessment distribution for licensor and licensee is often 60% to 40%, for immature or untested products a risk value of 30% is more appropriate for the licensee.

Case: *Covestro*

Covestro was formed in September 2015 from *Bayer MaterialScience*. *Bayer* announced its intention to divest *Covestro* and float the polymer division on the stock exchange in early 2016 in order to focus exclusively on the life science businesses. In 2019 *Covestro* had sales of 12.4 billion euros in fiscal and employs about 17,200 people at about 30 sites worldwide. Its main competitors are: *Dow Chemical*, *GE Plastics/Sabic*, *BASF*, *Huntsman*, and *Wanhua*.

Covestro has a portfolio of about 2500 patent families with about 12,900 patent family members (2019). In 2019, about 290 new patent applications were filed. The initial applications are usually at first made in Germany, the USA, or China, and are filed for disclosure and protection purposes. Subsequent applications are made abroad after careful consideration. Opposition is used where appropriate.

Covestro has set itself the goal of exploiting its own technologies. The company's earnings are to be further increased through intangible assets. As a prerequisite for this, the valuable technologies are protected by legal rights. In order to achieve this and enable optimum exploitation, intangible assets, i.e., patents and know-how, are managed in a similar way to property, plant, and equipment:

- Targeted development of intellectual assets within the framework of risk-assessed R&D projects
- Professional patent portfolio management
- Prevention of misuse by third parties
- Consistent enforcement of own prohibition rights

A patent committee has been set up for each field of technology, comprising: IP Department, R&D, marketing, and process and technology. Regular meetings of the patent committee form the basis for coordinated decisions concerning intellectual property. For IP asset management, *Covestro* involves the IP Department, R&D, process, and technology as well as marketing.

R&D projects are evaluated at *Covestro* on a regular basis. As part of the innovation and R&D process, intellectual property-related aspects are taken into account at every milestone based on a stage-gate philosophy: from idea generation to product release. Technology is handled as an important asset class at *Covestro*. Technology exploitation can thus begin well before a product is even marketed. *Covestro* has even a special division for asset exploitation such as in- and out-licensing. *Covestro* mainly uses direct marketing to exploit its technologies. Though the direct sale of know-how and IP is not part of *Covestro's* core business, its importance is increasing significantly. Very valuable are technology partnerships which often result in mutual technology licensing. In addition, with a specialized litigation function, *Covestro* takes consistent action against patent infringers, where considerable difficulties exist with piracy from the Asia-Pacific region.

> **Take-Aways *Covestro***
> - IP department reflecting business units in substructures with group-wide governance.
> - Interdisciplinary patent committees with decision-makers for each technology area.
> - IP processes attuned to the R&D processes.
> - Use of R&D cooperation and technology partnerships to generate and exploit IP.

6.3 Crop Science

Research Despite Patents Possible

Plant varieties produced by traditional methods are not patentable. In the case of a patent for corn with an increased oil content, the patent was revoked on the basis of this rule. The patent filed by *DuPont* with the European Patent Office in 1995 covered corn grains with an increased oil content, the oil obtained from these corn grains, and the use of the oil in foodstuffs. The maize was obtained from a cross between two different maize varieties, one of which had been chemically modified (mutated). *Greenpeace*, the Episcopal relief organization *Misereor,* and the government of Mexico have challenged the patent. The patent was rejected, among other things, because the maize was considered bred and therefore not patentable. If the company had achieved the same result with a genetic engineering process, the patent would probably have been granted.

In Europe, patent number EP 546 090 covers a genetically engineered type of soy: The US company *Monsanto* is the owner of a transgenic soy variety that is resistant to the herbicide *Roundup*, which is also approved in Switzerland in food and animal feed. With this patent, *Monsanto* not only has exclusive rights to use for all genetically modified soy varieties that are resistant to herbicide *Roundup*, but also to all genetically modified plants containing artificially induced "Roundup-Ready" resistance, such as wheat, rice, soy, cotton, sugar beet, rapeseed, flax, sunflower, potato, tobacco, tomato, alfalfa, poplar, pineapple, apple, and grape. The patent also extends to all subsequent plant generations. In the USA and Canada, farmers who reuse patented seeds from their last crop for sowing are prosecuted by *Monsanto*.

6.3 Crop Science

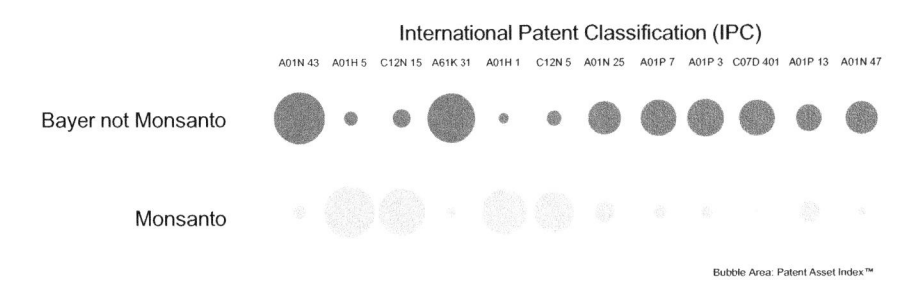

Fig. 6.2 Technology matrix *Bayer–Monsanto* (based on IPI/PatentSight 2020)

> **After the So-Called *Broccoli/Tomato Rulings* on Breeding Methods for Plants[1]**
>
> Practice before the European Patent Office (EPO): Processes of production of plants or animals which contain one or more steps of sexually crossing whole genomes are excluded from patentability. But, genetic engineering methods for introducing new traits into plants or animals are not excluded from patentability. ◄

Case: *Monsanto Canada*[2]

Bayer acquired *Monsanto* in 2016 to complement its crop science technologies and business. As a *patent* portfolio analysis confirms, *Bayer* is strong in pharma and "classic" agrochemistry, while *Monsanto* is strong in genetic plant engineering (see Fig. 6.2).

Technology Protection

Monsanto Canada ULC, now also part of *Bayer AG*, created its IP protection program in 1997 to help maintain a level playing field for Canadian farmers and ensure that farmers who have not paid for its patented technologies are not benefiting unfairly.

---

[1] EPO (2019) on the patentability of (essentially) biological processes:

EP 1 069 819 (G 2/07, "Broccoli"): Method for production of Brassica o., comprising steps of crossing and selection, wherein molecular markers are used to identify desired hybrids, and claims to plants per se;

EP 1 211 926 (G 1/08, "Wrinkled tomato"): Method for breeding tomato plants that produce tomatoes with reduced fruit water content, comprising crossing and selection steps, followed by allowing fruit to remain on the vine until it is partially dried ... and claims to plants per se.

[2] This is a redacted paraphrase taken from *Bayer CropScience Canada*:
https://www.cropscience.bayer.ca/en/Technology-Protection

Why Does Bayer Enforce Its Patents?

If someone other than the patent holder tries to make, use, or sell the patented invention without the permission of the patent holder, they may be guilty of patent infringement. *Monsanto Canada* ULC profits from its developments in crop sciences. If farmers plant and harvest *Bayer's* patented trait technologies without a *Technology Stewardship Agreement*, they would be infringing *Bayer's* patent rights. The Technology Stewardship Agreement gives farmers permission to use *Bayer's* patented trait technologies. By signing this agreement, the farmer has a license to use their patented technologies subject to certain terms and conditions. There is nothing unusual about including terms and conditions in the agreement. It is a limited use license; it does not allow farmers to distribute, transfer, or sell patented technologies and it only allows them to plant the seeds on their own farm for a single season.

Monsanto invests in the enforcement of its patent rights for three key reasons:

- No business can survive without being paid for its product.
- *Monsanto* currently invests millions of dollars per day to develop and bring new products to the market. If only some growers are paying the required technology fees, our ability to invest in research and development to create new products thereby decreases.
- *Monsanto* enforces its IP and agreements against violators as a matter of equity to those farmers who honor the agreement and respect Canadian IP law.

Seeds with the technology cannot be saved. The vast majority of farmers honor the agreement. They are prepared to purchase new patented seeds for each growing season, mainly because they are getting the benefits they want and need on their farm.

Monsanto also maintains an anti-piracy program. In 1997, *Monsanto* started enforcing its patent rights in Canada. This was after 2 years of grower education across Canada about the rules and obligations associated with growing *Monsanto's* patented seed technology on their farms were explained. It offers a technical support line, which looks into possible illicit use of *Bayer's* technology. When *Bayer* discovers issues of patent infringement, it does not immediately rush to file suit; it tries to settle matters amicably and outside the courtroom.

Take-Aways Crop Science
- Plant varieties produced by traditional methods are not patentable.
- Plants obtained from an "essentially biological process" are not patentable [EPO G3/19, 2020].
- Natural contractual incentives of licensees to enforce *Bayer's* IP.
- Easy process to flag infringement with helpline.
- Industry is highly influenced by data analytics and new platforms in agriculture; technologies around data analytics will play a more important role.

6.4 Life Sciences

Patenting in life sciences has a long history: in 1873 *Louis Pasteur* was granted a patent for purified yeast. In 1953, the DNA's structure was discovered, which led to the commercial use of genetic engineering since the 1980s. Drugs such as human insulin for the treatment of diabetes, erythropoietin for the treatment of anemia, and monoclonal antibodies for cancer therapy are based on biotechnological manufacturing processes. In agriculture, biotechnology is used to modify plants to make them more resistant to diseases, herbicides, and difficult environmental conditions or to increase yields (see also EPO 2019).

Case: *Prionics*

Prionics is a high-tech and innovative life science SME, which is now part of *Thermo Fisher Scientific*. The company was founded in 1997 as a spin-off of the University of Zurich and is based in Schlieren, Switzerland. The life science company manufactures products in the field of farm animal diagnostics, diagnostic solutions for prion diseases, and animal identification solutions. *Prionics* manufactures approximately 300 products. The majority of these are government-mandated and subsidized test systems for farm animals.

Prionics' first and best-known product is the test for bovine spongiform encephalopathy (BSE), which was launched in 1999. Today, *Prionics* is the world's number two in farm animal diagnostics, offering diagnostic solutions for the ten major farm animal diseases. *Prionics'* strategy is to expand along the food value chain with the continuous development of new diagnostic systems.

Defending One's Intellectual Property as a Small Life Science Company[3]

Prionics gained a world market share of 40–50% in the last 10 years with their antibody-based BSE tests. They could have prospered from this alone. Nevertheless, the company with Markus Moser as CEO has launched ten more diagnostic products for cattle, sheep, goats, and pigs.

At present, the *Prionics'* portfolio includes 29 international patents, and three or four more are added each year. They come either from their own 20-man strong research department or are licenses acquired from the academic world. "Basically, each of our innovation projects aims at a formal IP right," says Moser. Therefore, the Zurich-based company has built up a highly complex process that ranges from the combined patent and literature search (technology search) at the IPI as well as a bi-monthly monitoring of all projects and products to the creation of an internal database with selected third-party patents.

However, this is not enough for the life science markets because, as has been the case in the pharmaceutical industry for a long time, a kind of balance of terror

---

[3]Extract from IPI (2019).

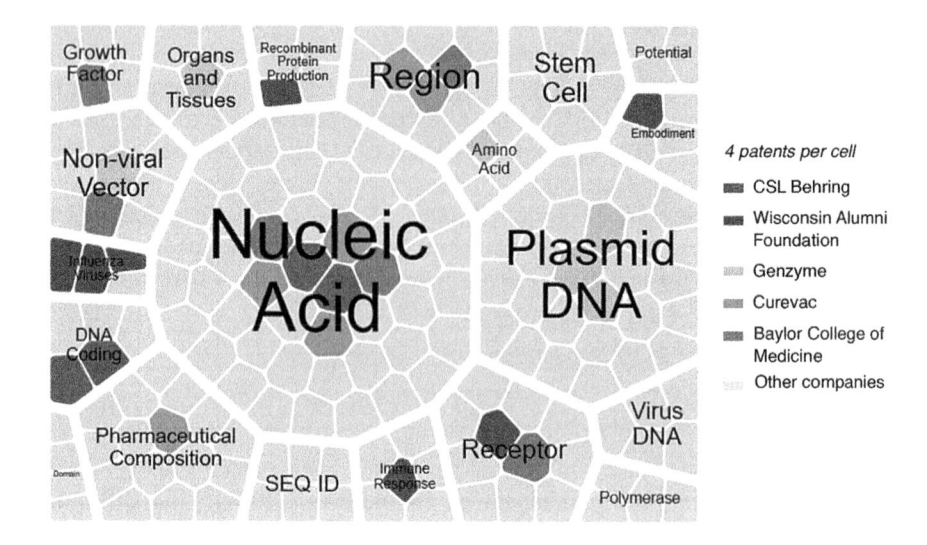

Fig. 6.3 Visualization of life sciences patenting (Picanço-Castro et al. 2020)

prevails in these markets. The market operators build up entire protective barriers around their products and fight on all relevant technological fronts for every inch of the market.

"Even we can be very aggressive when it's about our IP," says Moser honestly. For example, *Prionics* also defends its IP abroad by protecting products with a patent in every country in which a competitor could earn money with an imitation product. "It is not just a question of money, but also a matter of principle," explains Moser. *Prionics* who is serious about things when it comes to a court case. In Germany, for example, a lawsuit is currently pending because somebody tried to free ride on the back of the company.

There are years when *Prionics* is forced to spend over a million francs on its IP protection. For a company with approximately 100 employees, this is a lot of money. But Markus Moser is certain: "If we did not do so, we would soon be out of the market."

Take-Aways Life Sciences[4]
- Performing patent searches at the beginning of each invention is the best protection against later surprises (e.g., see Fig. 6.3).
- In the case of a blockade by a competitor's patent, it is initially sensible to work on workarounds.

(continued)

---

[4]Bader and Gassmann (2020).

- A best practice model is to focus on one "key" patent that is going to be the core patent of the company.
- However, effective protection is often not provided by individual patents. Innovative SMEs should, therefore, set up a systematic patent cluster to secure competitive advantages.
- While broad patents have a stronger impact, they are also more vulnerable. The application of broad patents should, therefore, be considered especially at the beginning of a technology cycle.
- In addition to basic patents, various more specific design and application alternatives can also be patented.
- In the event of a dispute, the own negotiation basis can be improved if an improvement solution is submitted based on a systematic analysis and evaluation of competing products, as this makes further development difficult for the competitor.
- In-licensing or patent license exchange enables the use of inventions and technologies patented by other parties.
- For patent invalidation actions, such as opposition or nullity proceedings, it is advisable to engage a patent attorney, as general technical–legal knowledge is not sufficiently available internally.
- Consistent and rigorous action against patent infringers has a deterrent effect and increases the imitation hurdles.
- Another option is to trade patent rights: patents are regarded as real products that are traded as assets on a marketplace, including options such as barter, sale, or licensing.
- With regard to a later partnership with, or an exit scenario to, larger corporations, consider the early implications for establishing a business case relevant patent portfolio, including a sufficient patent country coverage.

6.5 Consumer Goods

The consumer goods industry comprises sectors such as the food, beverage, cosmetics, and chemical industries as well as the textile, sporting goods, and consumer electronics industries. This industry therefore mainly produces goods that are intended for private use. Marketing and advertising therefore also play a central role in this industry in order to strengthen a brand. The annualized consumer goods market in Germany amounted to 428.11 billion euros in July 2019 (German Federal Statistics Office 2020). While *Henkel* was the strongest company in Germany with net sales of 21 billion US dollars in 2013, *Nestlé* was the European

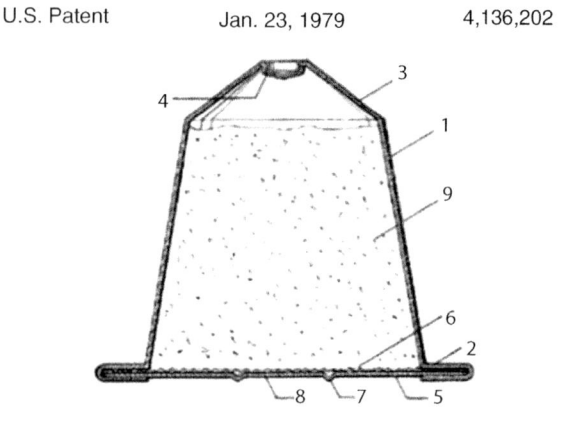

Fig. 6.4 US 4,136,202: Capsule for beverage preparation *(Nestlé)*

U.S. Patent   Jan. 23, 1979   4,136,202

leader in consumer goods with 98 billion US dollars. This makes Nestlé one of the largest consumer goods manufacturers in the world, along with *Unilever, Anheuser-Busch InBev,* and *L'Oréal,* but also American companies such as *Procter & Gamble, Pepsi,* and *Coca-Cola*.

Case: *Nespresso*, the Game Changer

In the hotly contested consumer goods market, patents therefore also play an important role in protecting innovations and differentiating oneself from competitors. For example, *Nestlé* has filed over 2000 patents for its *Nespresso* machine since 1976 to protect its innovative capsules and brewing system (Brem et al. 2016; see Fig. 6.4). There has been a long fight over whether the earlier *Battelle* patent on a capsule apparatus from the year 1972 can be seen as the first step.

Today there are over 85 competitors, only in Europe, in the coffee capsules business. Since the early patents expired *Nestlé* had to further develop and protect its business model. Through this extensive patent portfolio, *Nestlé* was able to secure its functional competitive advantages and strengthen the *Nespresso* brand through clever marketing activities.

Case: *Henkel*

Henkel sees brands as synonymous with trust and reliability. It is important for the company to have a clear understanding that customers act locally and that brands, therefore, have a local impact. The brand strategy employed by *Henkel* is caught between the need for *standardization* on the one hand and the need for *differentiation* on the other. The standardization of products and brands is advantageous for efficient and inexpensive production, low complexity, and a rapid introduction of new products. Differentiation is necessary in order to achieve the highest possible level of customer loyalty, to obtain flexible responses, and to be able to close regional markets. As a result, the brand strategy tries to do justice to both focal points. *Henkel* has come up with the made-up portmanteau word *glocal*, which is derived from combining the words, "local" and "global."

Henkel's patent strategy distinguishes between core competence and non-core competence areas. In core competence areas, inventions are pursued as best as possible as patent applications in order to achieve the greatest possible differentiation from competitors. In these core areas, *Henkel* strives to provide exclusive protection for products, technologies, packaging, and ingredients. In non-core areas of competence, *Henkel* attempts to maintain the greatest possible freedom-of-action position: Often, inventions in these areas are not filed for patent, but are published in restricted publications in order to prevent them from being patented by competitors.

Henkel coordinates both the achievable protection through trademarks and the achievable protection through patents. While trademark protection is primarily suitable for protecting the customer interface, patents are mainly used to protect products and technologies. Since the protective effects of trademarks and patents have complementary effects in this sense, it is, therefore, necessary to coordinate the protective alternatives in such a way that an optimal overall effect is achieved on both the customer and the technology side.

Take-Aways *Henkel*
- Coordinated, complementary brand, and patent strategy
- Determination of the permissible filing period depending on the potentially achievable scope of protection
- Interdisciplinary teams to evaluate inventions in terms of market relevance and technical relevance
- Four-stage decision-making and selection process, aligned to the patent application process
- Supply exclusivity agreements in R&D cooperation as compensation for nonexclusivity in patent and trademark rights

6.6 Machinery

Case: Patent Management Processes at *Schindler & Inventio*

The Swiss manufacturer *Schindler* is a global leader in the market for elevators and escalators and today employs over 55,000 people, around 430 of whom work in central research and development. Its main sales markets are Europe, the USA, and Asia, with the Asian market showing high growth rates. The main competitors are *OTIS*, *ThyssenKrupp*, *Kone*, and *Mitsubishi*. There is a major price war going on in the industry. In addition to the development and production of elevator systems, maintenance and service as well as modernization are considered important areas of activity and sources of income. The vertical integration is still relatively high. Software development is playing an increasingly important role.

Schindler has a total patent portfolio of over 9000 active patents. About 80% of the patents come from the R&D department. About 80 new patent applications are made every year. In the event of a patent infringement of strategic importance, the Group Board Committee decides whether or not to take legal action.

Inventio AG is a separate company responsible for *Schindler's* global intellectual property business. The main features of the global intellectual property strategy are approved by the Board of Directors of *Inventio*. The head of central R&D is a member of the *Inventio* Board of Directors. This ensures that the R&D strategy is regularly aligned with the business strategy. The global implementation of the IP strategy is the responsibility of *Inventio's* management in coordination with product line management and R&D. Developmental cooperation exists with various technology partners and is initiated and implemented by R&D or the Board. Make-or-buy decisions are made by *Inventio* together with R&D and the market organization.

Schindler allows market changes and changes in internal goals to guide the strategy. Strategic building blocks that do not contribute to the desired success are redefined. The patent strategy is developed top-down, formulated in writing and communicated internally. In order to implement the patent strategy, the patent portfolio must be aligned with *Schindler's* main activities. Core process steps for patent generation are shown in Fig. 6.5.

Schindler applies four basic core process steps for patent generation (see Fig. 6.5):

Boost ideas to IP values & ensure freedom of action

Trend team	Exploitation	Portfolio management	Invention process

• Anticipate trends
• Trend mapping
• Propose studies
	• Encourage ideas
	• Assess ideas
	• Exploit ideas
	• WS
	• Study proposal
		• Portfolio analysis
		  • Infringements
		  • Morphology
		  • Alternatives
		• Portfolio synthesis
		  • IP-Opportunities
		  • Extension to cluster
		• Competitor survey
		• Make or buy
			• Integrated PCP
			  • Invention workflow
			• IP-Manager
			  • First level support
			• Education
			• Classification
			• Incentives

Invention database and patent database

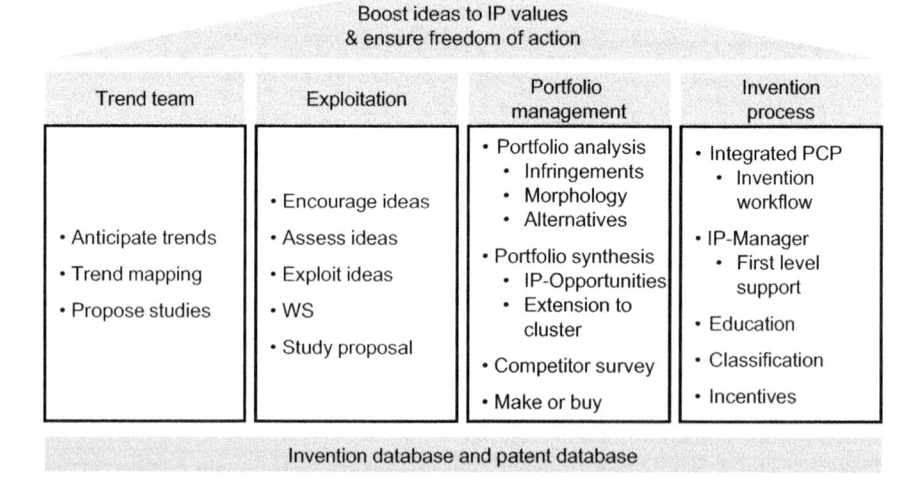

Fig. 6.5 Core process of patent generation at *Schindler* (authors' own figure)

- Trend Team: Market analysis and technology scouting
- Exploitation: Promotion and use of internal ideas
- Portfolio management: Performing patent portfolio analyses, identifying opportunities and risks, monitoring competition, make-or-buy decisions
- Invention Process: Continuous invention disclosure process with classification

In addition, patent analyses are used to generate new ideas. Patent analyses represent one of several sources of information on competitive activities. Schindler also uses patent analyses to expand its technological leadership and thus influence the industry technologically. The main general objective is to maintain the company's own freedom to operate.

Invention Process

The generation of invention disclosures is an important Research and Development (R&D) goal at *Schindler* and is therefore strongly weighted in the personal target agreements. The necessary decisions are made exclusively by *Inventio*, a separate company responsible for *Schindler's* global intellectual property business. The *Schindler* Invention Process consists of two sub-processes, starting with the idea evaluation and ending with the patentability evaluation (see Fig. 6.6):

- *Disclosure Process:* ideas are developed by the inventors and evaluated according to technical and economic criteria with the involvement of the supervisor.
- *Invention Disclosure Process:* ideas are then examined for their suitability for patent application. An important criterion here is the ability to differentiate from the state of the art.

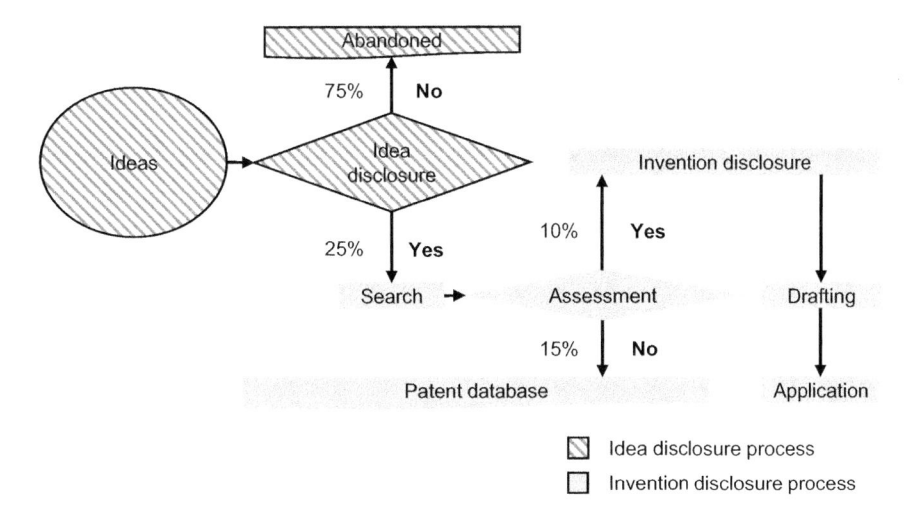

Fig. 6.6 Partial process of portfolio management at *Schindler* (authors' own figure)

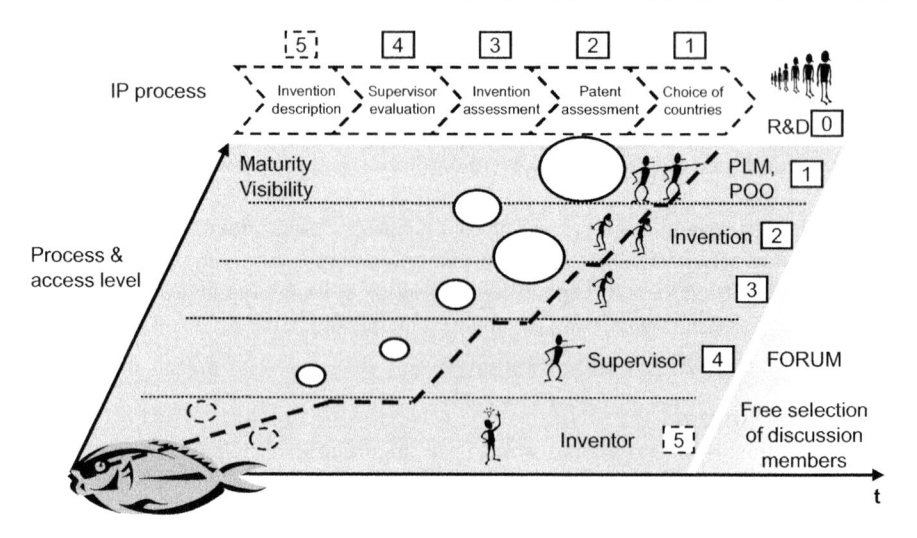

Fig. 6.7 IP process at *Schindler* (authors' own figure)

Initial registrations are initiated exclusively by *Inventio*. For subsequent applications, the relevance of the state of the art will be taken into account. *Inventio* obtains comments from *Schindler* product managers and selects the appropriate countries on this basis (see Fig. 6.7). The evaluation of such information and the investment decisions based on it requires many years of experience and foresighted thinking on the part of *Inventio's* management. As a rule, product managers are asked in writing every 2 years to maintain intellectual property rights. Ultimately, however, the decision is made by *Inventio*.

Portfolio Management
Portfolio management is closely linked to product development and marketing. With regard to the influence on idea generation, certain focal points are maintained; for example, further developments mature into invention disclosures in joint R&D and *Inventio* workshops.

Portfolio information and the associated flow of information are provided by *Inventio*. Communication with *Schindler* takes place both traditionally via forms and postal delivery, and electronically. As part of its intellectual property management, *Schindler* generally tries to prevent the launch of patent applications with a low probability of success, recognize possible infringements, and thus prevent possible legal actions.

Invention and Patent Database
A virtual invention database provides valuable criteria for an efficient and pragmatic evaluation of ideas and inventions (see Fig. 6.8). A patent mapping function

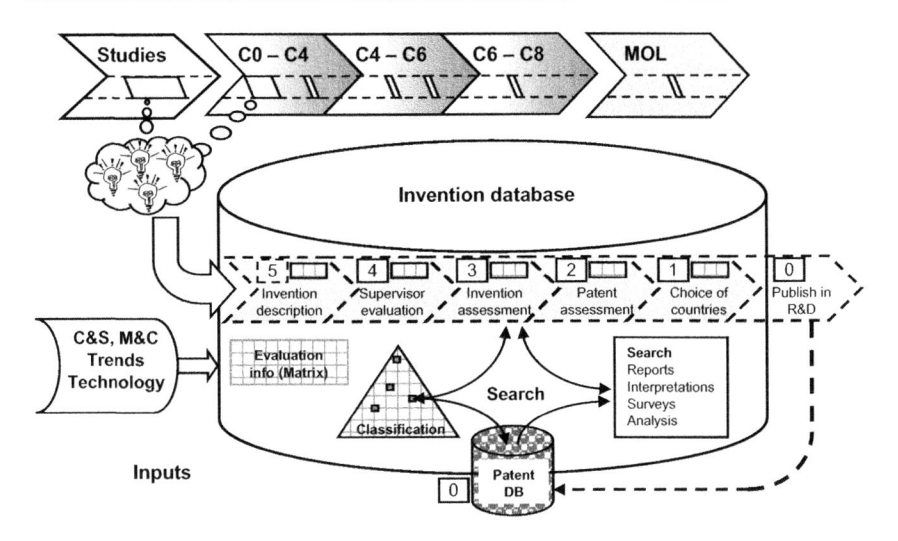

Fig. 6.8 Invention concept database at *Schindler* (authors' own figure)

implemented in the invention database enables the active design of the *Schindler Inventio* patent portfolio.

Prerequisites for the successful implementation of the idea and invention disclosure process at *Schindler* are:

- Guaranteed privacy for the inventor to a certain extent
- Simple involvement of colleagues, employees, and partners during studies and projects
- Supervisor feedback, usually from project or R&D managers on ideas in order to create further added value
- Extended information base for *Inventio*, R&D, and Product Line Managers
- Greater availability of information within *Schindler*
- Function sharing for all decision-makers
- Coordination of the value chain process
- Objective remuneration for inventions
- Management tool for patent mapping

The invention database enables a simple documentation of ideas. *Schindler* first had to solve the problem that, on the one hand, the inventor's urge to communicate and, on the other hand, the confidentiality interests of the individual and the company had to be taken into account. Data transmission and communication between the parties involved takes place within an encrypted intranet. Especially for the previously applicable requirements of US American inventor law (first-to-invent principle), all documents receive an irrevocable time stamp that "freezes" the document and makes it unchangeable. In this way, inventions can be proved to have been made at a precise time. Different levels of access authorization have made it possible to regulate accessibility for user groups and thus the level of confidentiality. Through consistent introduction and communication, *Schindler* was able to achieve a high level of acceptance among users.

Organization

The intellectual property department at *Schindler* has been outsourced to the subsidiary *Inventio*. Inventio holds all intellectual property rights and is responsible for their acquisition, enforcement, and exploitation worldwide. Inventio is internally described as customer-oriented, diverse, and cooperative and offers R&D support on important issues.

Cooperation and Licensing

Schindler is open to granting licenses. In doing so, the company works mainly with suppliers. For key technologies that can be marketed worldwide, *Schindler* consistently strives for exclusivity in order to achieve competitive advantages.

Cooperation with development partners, who conduct R&D for *Schindler*, is typical. *Schindler* also cooperates with suppliers, who customize their components to *Schindler*'s specifications, so that these components fit perfectly with existing systems. Licensing intellectual property rights in partnerships with suppliers tends to increase continuously. Cooperation with partners in research projects is rather rare. Within the framework of development projects, cooperation is also entered into where external know-how is required. The number of partnerships is large due to the number of technical areas that have to be covered: 15–20% of the R&D budget is spent on cooperation.

In R&D partnerships, *Schindler* claims generated IP in full and handles the patent application process. In special cases, suppliers are granted a right of use outside the elevator and escalator sector. *Schindler* bears the patent costs for creation, application, and maintenance. Sublicenses are possible with component suppliers.

Take-Aways *Schindler/Inventio*
- Company remains the sole proprietor of IP
- Clearly formulated patent strategy along with the core process
- Two-tiered selection and decision process for filing a patent
- Inclusion of patent experts in technological motoring and trend teams
- Inventions database as an info platform for inventors
- Generation of patent applications is an explicit part of R&D KPIs
- Almost 20% of R&D budget flowing into R&D budget goes into partnerships

6.7 Electronics and Electrical Equipment

Case: Patent Management at *ABB*

ABB is a globally active electrical engineering group with headquarters in Zurich. *ABB* was formed in 1988 from the merger of the Swedish *Allmänna Svenska Elektriska Aktiebolaget (ASEA)* and the Swiss *Brown Boveri & Cie (BBC)*. Today, *ABB* employs around 120,000 people, of whom about 6400 work in Switzerland. *ABB's* businesses are divided into five divisions: Power Products, Power Systems, Automation Products, Process Automation, and Robotics. The company has nine research centers with over 6000 researchers worldwide. In addition, the company has cooperation agreements with 70 different universities.

Patent Generation Strategy

Technologies play a key role for *ABB* in that technologies are its source of value. *ABB* applies for about 700 new patents annually and holds 16,000 patents or patent applications worldwide. Expenditure on IP protection amounts to approximately CHF 36 million per year! *ABB's* patent management is strategically focused on generating patents that add value to the company and protect its products. *ABB's* company-wide patent strategy is linked to its business strategy and forms the basis for the specific patent strategies of the individual business units.

The aim of the patent strategy is to create patents that deliver added value. *ABB* distinguishes between a business and a strategic approach to creating value through patents. The business approach focuses on sustainably increasing and maximizing return on capital employed (ROCE). Intellectual property rights enable the maximum ROCE to be increased. In addition, patents can slow down the decline of ROCE after its maximum by reducing competitive pressure, i.e., it can achieve sustainability. The strategic approach puts the market and competition in the foreground. From this perspective, patents can reduce competitive pressure, secure market share, create new market access, and optimize pricing.

Patent Generation Processes

In order to achieve the objectives of the patent strategy, *ABB* employs the following measures:

- *Gate model:* The development of new products follows a gate model in which questions and tasks relating to IP protection and the proactive avoidance of conflicts with third-party property rights are answered or processed at several gates. Without careful and complete processing and answering of these questions and tasks, it is not possible to move the development project forward.
- *Strategic patent workshops:* One-day events with an interdisciplinary group of participants to analyze the patent situation and further strategic orientation.
- *Cooperative approach:* Patent specialists are represented at all levels of the company and work closely with the internal patent attorneys.

- *Quality control*: Two-stage control concept prior to patent applications through review processes and peer reviews.
- *Patenting opinions:* Decision support for foreign applications.

ABB's goal is to create valuable patents. On the one hand, a valuable patent fulfills the claim of an optimal technical object. This means that it is an object that is in demand by the market and fits *ABB's* technology strategy. In addition, an optimal geographical scope of protection should be achieved. Depending on the area of application and market of the various technologies, priorities are set differently and a corresponding country strategy is developed. Thirdly, the optimal factual scope of protection must be ensured, i.e., when filing a patent application, the scope of protection must be examined and tailored to potential infringements.

Organizing Patent Generation

ABB has developed an organizational structure that integrates patent management at all levels of the company. As the top level, the "Chief IP Counsel" is responsible for company-wide IP management. As the next level, each business unit has an assigned patent attorney. The third level is represented by local patent attorneys. For the future, *ABB* is considering establishing a fourth level with licensing specialists and so-called patent enforcement specialists. The latter would have the task of actively searching for patent infringements by third parties. *ABB* has a total of nine IP departments worldwide with about 85 employees. *ABB* handles about 80% of its work volume through internal employees. External resources are only called upon in special cases.

Evaluating Patents

ABB stresses the importance of regular reviews and feedback in the patent management process. The company, therefore, carries out a two-stage quality control process:

- *Check the invention:* Is the patent project aligned with the business strategy?
- *Check of the patent application:* Has an appropriate country strategy been selected? Are the claims formulated broadly enough?

ABB uses a four-field matrix to implement and monitor the patent strategy and patent portfolio (see Fig. 6.9). The axes reflect the strength of relative IP protection compared with the competition and the degree of differentiation of the product or market.

With weak patent protection and at the same time a low degree of differentiation, there is a risk of being blocked by competitors with stronger patents. Weak patent protection combined with a high degree of product differentiation makes it easy for competitors to legally imitate an interesting product and thus increases the risk of being copied. Strong patent protection in a highly differentiated market means exclusivity for the patent holder. He has control over competitors and can determine the market. An opportunity for out-licensing arises from a strong patent on a

6.7 Electronics and Electrical Equipment

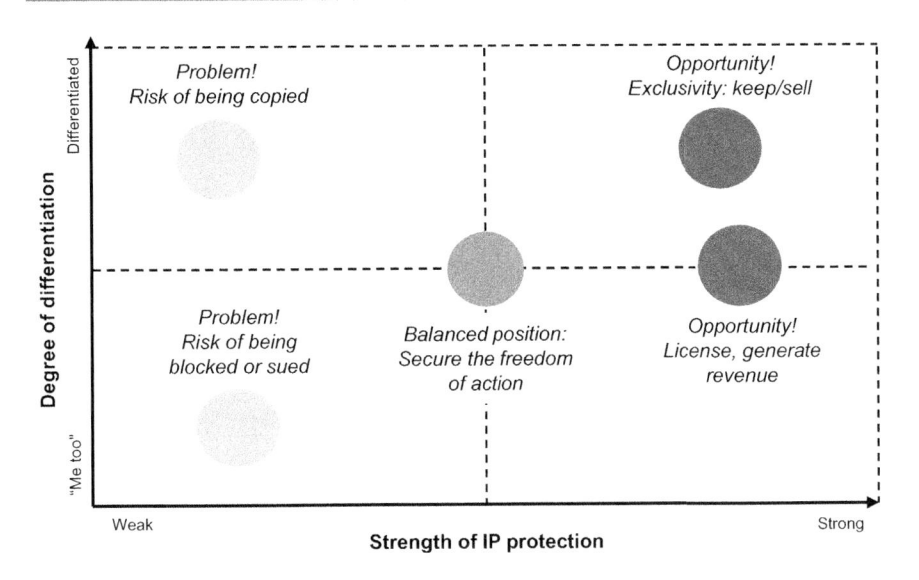

Fig. 6.9 *ABBs* patent evaluation matrix (Gassmann and Bader 2017)

medium-differentiated product. Here, an out-licensing strategy can generate additional revenues. With medium differentiation and medium patent strength, the product is in a balanced state and allows freedom to operate. Starting from the balanced position, the strength of the patent is the decisive factor. If the patent strength decreases, the product is quickly in one of the risk areas. Securing a valuable patent during the patent application process is therefore an important success factor.

ABB also uses this evaluation matrix as a tool for defining its patenting strategy. When defining the strategy of a product, it can be positioned in the matrix. The next steps are to consider which position is to be aimed for the product in the future, and by which measures this can be achieved.

Below are two examples of *ABB* products and their assignment to the evaluation matrix.

Low Voltage Products
Low voltage products such as switches or circuit breakers are mass products. There is a multitude of competitors and the margins are low. The differentiation is mainly based on price. Since there are hardly any technical possibilities for differentiating such a mass product, *ABB* has to assert itself through the strength of its intellectual property rights. As a supplement to a patent, design protection can increase the strength of protection. The aim is therefore to keep the position in the middle of the matrix stable (see Fig. 6.10).

High Voltage Products
ABB is the world market leader in the field of high-voltage products. Only a few competitors compete in this very sophisticated technological field. Market entry

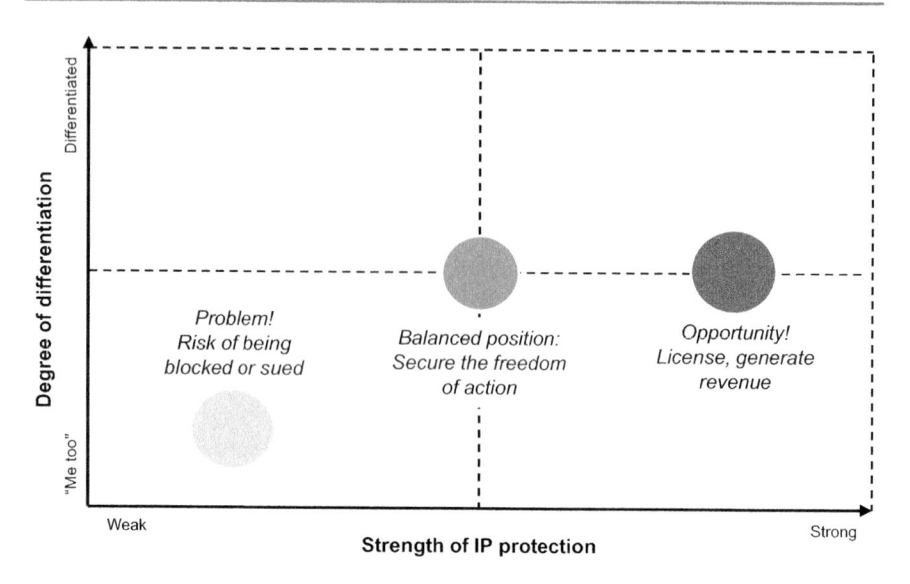

Fig. 6.10 Example from *ABB's* low voltage products (Gassmann and Bader 2017)

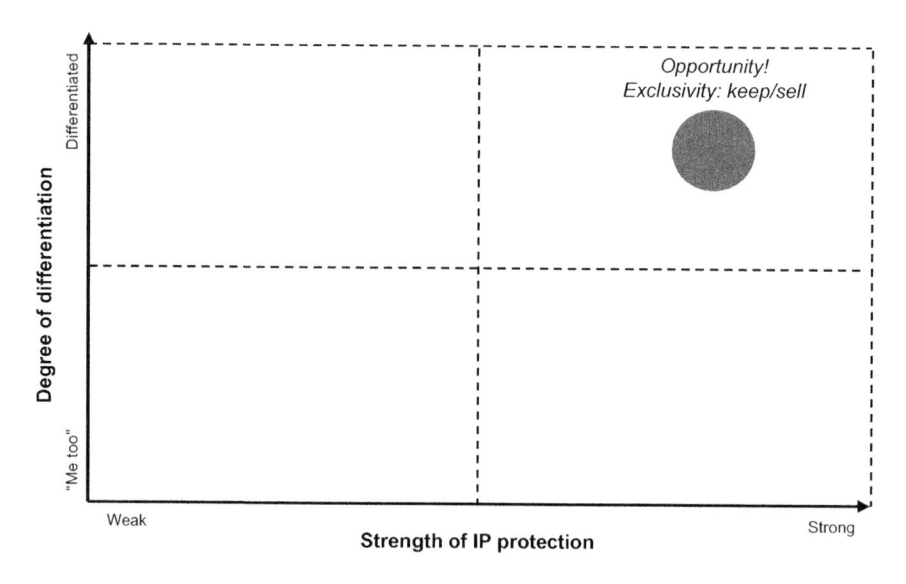

Fig. 6.11 Example from *ABB's* high voltage products (Gassmann and Bader 2017)

requires high investments and a high level of technological knowledge. *ABB* produces customized products and can generate high margins. In this example (see Fig. 6.11). *ABB* is in the top right quadrant of the evaluation matrix, with high differentiation and strong patent protection. This gives *ABB* an exclusivity advantage in the market.

Patent Commercialization

ABB's primary goal in patent filing is to protect its own products. The external exploitation of patents is therefore not the primary focus. Nevertheless, *ABB* is in principle prepared to grant licenses if it is advantageous, for example, to broaden the market penetration of a product. Patents that are not central to securing *ABB's* own competitive advantage are reviewed for their external exploitation potential and released for commercialization on a case-by-case basis. *ABB* believes that in-licensing and out-licensing of technologies will play a more important role in the future and is therefore in the process of building up corresponding competencies.

> **Take-Aways *ABB***
> - Patent strategy is embedded in the business strategy.
> - Patents must generate added value.
> - Patent management is a strategic instrument.
> - Every business unit has a defined patent strategy.
> - Organization uses a cooperative approach, where patent managers are represented at all levels.
> - Evaluation matrix for implementing the patent strategy.
> - Patents are reviewed for commercialization potential.

Case: *Philips* vs. *Google*

Beyond industrial electronics, *Google*, an advertiser, and *Philips*, a consumer electronics producer fought in Germany over patent number EP 0 888 687, a User Interface for Television (see Fig. 6.12).

The legal dispute was the overuse of the technology in the area of mobile phones. *Philips* was in dispute with various manufacturers, and *Google*, the provider of Android OS, stepped in to defend their interests against *Philips*. The battle was fought in multiple jurisdictions simultaneously with the defendants *Wiko* and *Asus* being found to be infringing on *Philips* radio technology. Originally, the Circuit Court in Mannheim, Germany, had enjoined *Asus* not to sell any devices with Android 5.0 given that the interface may violate the *Philips* patent. The German Court of Justice ruled the European patent invalid for Germany.

> **Take-Aways Electronics**
> - Non-competing players in other industries can hold relevant technologies.
> - A "small" patent can block an entirely unrelated and massive product line.
> - Value of patents is getting increasingly monetarized by litigation.

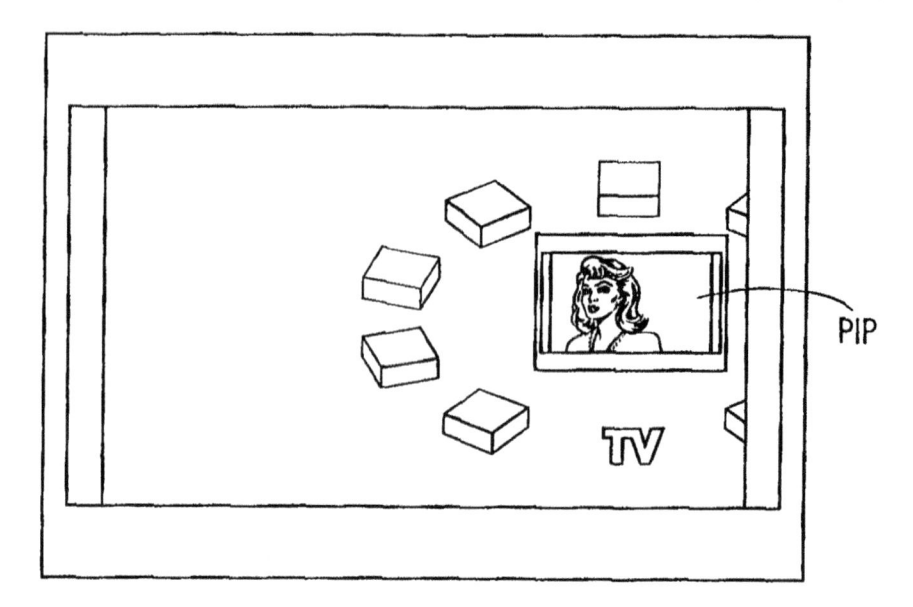

Fig. 6.12 *Philips* patent EP 0 888 687 B1: User Interface for Television

6.8 Automotive

According to the German Patent and Trade Mark Office, most patent applications in the automotive industry in Germany in both 2018 and the previous year came from the vehicle construction sector (12,273), electrical machinery and apparatus (7420), followed by machine elements (5871).[5]

Due to greater involvement and commitment on the part of automotive suppliers, vehicle components are already being largely developed and manufactured by suppliers. More than 70% of the value added in development is generated by the suppliers. The only exceptions are engines and transmissions (Wagner 2015). The outsourcing of innovation activities to automotive suppliers has the consequence that these suppliers have to apply for industrial property rights more independently. According to the Head of Technology Management at *Daimler*, the major automotive suppliers are conducting research in the same areas as the Original Equipment Manufacturers (OEMs): "*Bosch* (a supplier) and *Daimler* (a carmaker) are tough competitors in automotive research." The main focus is on the battle for new knowledge and strategically strong patents. On the other hand, the purchasing

---

[5]https://www.dpma.de/docs/presse/statistik_2018_patente_eng.pdf

departments of automobile manufacturers are exerting strong cost pressure on suppliers. In principle, attempts are being made to find several suppliers, so-called second or third sources, for components. In practice, the respective suppliers can then only achieve exclusivity secured by patents on a temporary basis, and at best get it for the luxury class vehicles. Only innovative and strong suppliers are able to maintain truly independent positions. The automotive suppliers *Bosch, Continental, Delphi, Mann+Hummel, Schäffler, Valeo,* and *ZF Friedrichshafen* have built up strong patent positions in the past and use them to strengthen their negotiating position with OEMs.

For example, the 6-speed transmission by *ZF Friedrichshafen* for *BMW* launched in 2002 had exclusivity for *BMW* only for a short period. This means that there is hardly enough time left for a sustained differentiation from automotive competitors. The leading OEMs, such as *Daimler* and *BMW*, therefore explicitly cooperate with technology-intensive non-suppliers (such as high-tech spin-offs from universities) in the early innovation phases in order to develop strategically important patents for the automotive sector. This is particularly relevant for system innovations. One example is the replacement of conventional steering systems by brake-and-steer-by-wire systems.

The development of various new drive forms, such as hybrid or electric drives, poses a challenge for automobile manufacturers. This effect is reinforced by political and social pressure to reduce CO_2 emissions and therefore improve the powertrain. Consequently, research activities for electric cars, for example, will be intensified. This is also reflected in a rapid increase in patent applications worldwide for electric cars in 2012, twice as many as for hybrid vehicles in the same period.

However, this development is also accompanied by a change in the automotive industry. More and more core technologies for electric cars are coming from other industries, and the automotive industry sees itself increasingly pushed onto the defensive. While over 80% of applications for hybrid technology still come from the classic automotive industry, this figure is just over 40% for electric drives (Grünecker 2013). Such developments, as well as the research on autonomously driving cars, lead to a completely new market with participants pushing into the automotive sector. In some cases, these new market participants even own numerous patents in future-relevant areas such as infotainment systems *(Google, Apple, Sony)* or battery technologies and hybrid/electric drives *(LG, Samsung)*. An analysis of patent applications for automotive business processes also confirms this trend. Among the top 15 applicants in the field of automotive business processes in the period from 2001 to 2013, there was not a single automobile company. The patent landscape is dominated by companies from outside the industry like *IBM, American Express Travel, Amadeus,* who offer scientific and technical services alongside travel services (Niemann 2014).

Electronics and connectivity have become integral to the automotive industries, and traditional automakers are now having to play ball with electronics firms. *Daimler* went to EU-mandated arbitration with *Nokia* and its standard essential patents that the carmaker required to achieve connectivity. Talks fell through in March of 2019, and a *Daimler*-led consortium seeking *Nokia's* patents started to file suit, alleging a violation of anti-competition law. Since the EU anti-trust commission takes years to act, it tried to toss the dispute back into mediation, though with no success. Some of the dispute revolves around the practice of charging royalties based on the value of the product—*Nokia* wants *Daimler* to take the license and to assess it based on the value of the car, and *Daimler* maintains that it is part of a modular subsystem and that royalty should be set based on that. *Nokia's* patent is being challenged in court in a separate attack with other carmakers and suppliers (Juve 2020). The dispute remains unresolved, but it is illustrative of how the automotive industry is an ecosystem of suppliers, which is discussed in more detail further on in the chapter.

R&D Cooperation with Suppliers

The strength of automotive suppliers can hence be seen in the extent to which they are able to keep their own innovations exclusive in development cooperation with automobile manufacturers. This is currently only possible with the major suppliers. SME suppliers have less bargaining power: Automotive suppliers try to develop and patent inventions for fundamental innovations as independently as possible. Since, however, development work often only takes place in close cooperation with and on behalf of automobile manufacturers, the latter usually succeed in securing the development results as "contract developments" (see Fig. 6.13). Inventions and the resulting industrial property rights must then generally be transferred to the automobile manufacturer. The automotive supplier Z1 retains at most a simple right of use. The automobile manufacturer A1 can license the rights of use to further suppliers Z2 in order to secure second and third suppliers for the development results achieved.

If the automotive supplier Z1 also wishes to supply A2 to another car manufacturer on the basis of its remaining usage rights, it is forced to pay licenses to A1. Frequently, it is also tied to an exclusivity period, usually 3–5 years, during which it may only deliver to the original car manufacturer A1. In return, it is guaranteed, for example, minimum purchase volumes.

If, on the other hand, the automotive supplier Z1 has industrial property rights, which it alone can dispose of, the automotive manufacturer A1 generally demands a sub-licensable right of use which can be passed on to the second and third supplier Z2. As compensation, the car manufacturer, A1, then pays quantity or turnover-dependent license fees to the owner of the industrial property right Z1, which are passed on to the second and third suppliers Z2 benefiting from the license through correspondingly reduced part costs. As a rule, the license fees are not of a magnitude to compensate for the development costs incurred.

It is possible, however, that automotive supplier Z1 will be forced to use intellectual property rights against license payments from third parties, for example from a 2nd tier subcontractor $Z1^2$, even without the "mediation" of the automotive manufacturer. These include in particular very large automotive suppliers such as *Bosch* or *Schaeffler*. The 1st tier automotive supplier Z1 then has no choice but to try to pass on the license fees to the automobile manufacturer A1 in some way. In this

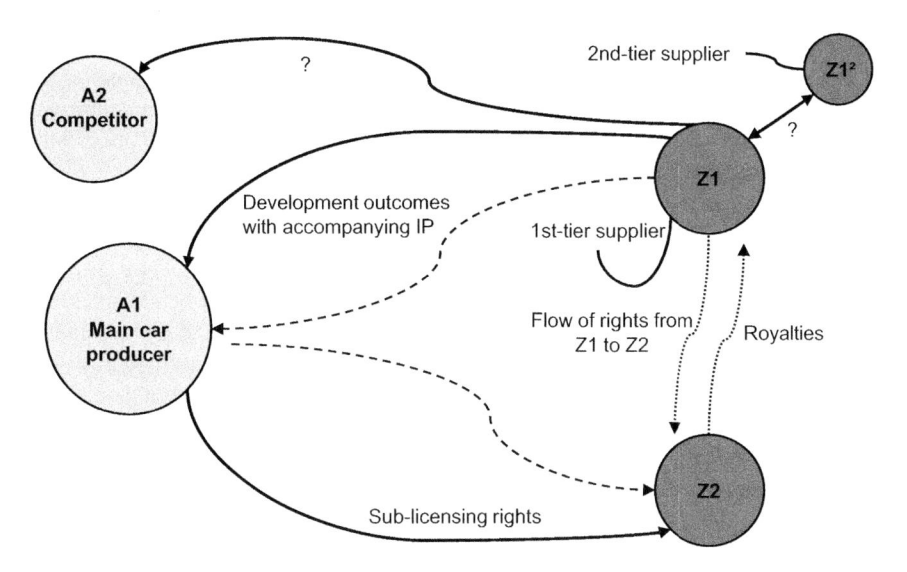

Fig. 6.13 Usage and licensing rights in the automotive sector (authors' own figure)

scenario, however, the automobile manufacturer A1 has the risk that its second and third supplier Z2 may not be able to take licenses from the 2nd tier subcontractor $Z1^2$ or not at the same conditions. This may be the case, for example, because usage licenses are tied to the purchase of $Z1^2$'s subcontracted products. However, there are increasing efforts by 2nd tier subcontractors $Z1^2$ to enter directly into license negotiations with the automobile manufacturers A1. However, this has not yet been implemented in practice.

Case: *Tesla*, the Pacemaker

Leapfrogging by Declaring Commons

One of the most interesting patent strategies of a very high profile and a large company is that of *Tesla*. *Tesla* renounced its IP in favor of any open innovation strategy. The following is an ungrammatically titled explanation from Elon Musk himself—it is not all that common for a CEO to directly discuss an IP strategy beyond a few platitudes.

"All Our Patent Are Belong to You"[6]

Yesterday, there was a wall of Tesla patents in the lobby of our Palo Alto headquarters. That is no longer the case. They have been removed, in the spirit of the open-source movement, for the advancement of electric vehicle technology.

---

[6]Elon Musk, CEO June 12, 2014.

Tesla Motors was created to accelerate the advent of sustainable transport. If we clear a path to the creation of compelling electric vehicles, but then lay intellectual property landmines behind us to inhibit others, we are acting in a manner contrary to that goal. *Tesla* will not initiate patent lawsuits against anyone who, in good faith, wants to use our technology.

When I started out with my first company, *Zip2*, I thought patents were a good thing and worked hard to obtain them. And maybe they were good long ago, but too often these days they serve merely to stifle progress, entrench the positions of giant corporations and enrich those in the legal profession, rather than the actual inventors. After *Zip2*, when I realized that receiving a patent really just meant that you bought a lottery ticket to a lawsuit, I avoided them whenever possible.

At *Tesla*, however, we felt compelled to create patents out of concern that the big car companies would copy our technology and then use their massive manufacturing, sales, and marketing power to overwhelm *Tesla*. We could not have been more wrong. The unfortunate reality is the opposite: electric car programs (or programs for any vehicle that does not burn hydrocarbons) at the major manufacturers are small to non-existent, constituting an average of far less than 1% of their total vehicle sales.

At best, the large automakers are producing electric cars with limited range in limited volume. Some produce no zero emission cars at all.

Given that annual new vehicle production is approaching 100 million per year and the global fleet is approximately 2 billion cars, it is impossible for Tesla to build electric cars fast enough to address the carbon crisis. By the same token, it means the market is enormous. Our true competition is not the small trickle of non-Tesla electric cars being produced, but rather the enormous flood of gasoline cars pouring out of the world's factories every day.

We believe that *Tesla*, other companies making electric cars, and the world would all benefit from a common, rapidly evolving technology platform.

Technology leadership is not defined by patents, which history has repeatedly shown to be small protection indeed against a determined competitor, but rather by the ability of a company to attract and motivate the world's most talented engineers. We believe that applying the open-source philosophy to our patents will strengthen rather than diminish Tesla's position in this regard.[7]

The Why

Beyond Elon's high-minded explanation lies actually some very savvy business acumen. By allowing others to use Tesla's technology, he helped roll-out the charging stations needed. Moreover, Musk's vision and attitude coincides with the *Tesla* brand. In short, the brand-value may be. It is also worth noting that Musk's phrase "initiate patent lawsuits against anyone who, in good faith, wants to use our technology" would not exactly convince legal experts at a major car company to allow cars to go into production. Most of Elon's value-added lies not in an ancient

---

[7]https://www.tesla.com/about/legal#patent-pledge

motor technology, but rather in the car's software, especially in the sophisticated AI and self-driving features—all of which is a trade secret and copyrighted...

Case: *Avanci*—Traditional Automotive Players Under Attack

Avanci is a patent pool in the ICT space (cf. section for an explanation). *Volvo* along with 14 others, including major automotive brands, have signed patent licensing agreements with *Avanci* to get access to its patent pool. Cars increasingly rely on wireless connectivity.

The *Avanci* patent pool was conceived both to monetize patents, but also to eliminate a lot of the legal challenges in the space. Some of the *Avanci* members *(Nokia, Sharp, Conversant)* have sued *Daimler* to coax the company to agree to its licensing terms. The case went into mediation, which eventually failed. *Continental Automotive Systems,* argued that *Avanci* in acting for its members violated (Fair, Reasonable, and Non-Discriminatory) FRAND principles. *Avanci* would prefer to license to the end-user automotive company, but *Daimler* has resisted this since the royalty rates are then assessed not on the components, which suppliers like *Continental* make, but instead on the end product. To use a concrete case: *Continental* needs a 20-dollar baseband chip—and *Avanci* wants 15 dollars per car—meaning the royalty would be a 75% markup on the cost of that component—the complete connectivity module, which *Continental* sells, is only 75 dollars. *Continental* thus asserts this is not reasonable or fair, considering that patent royalties conventionally have constituted only a 5–15% markup, perhaps 2 dollars—so, whether the parties can close the gap remains to be seen (Ropes and Gray 2019; Juve 2020). European case law is still developing in the area of FRAND and Standard Essential Patents (SEPs) (cf. infra "Smartphone Patent Wars").

> **Take-Aways Automotive**
> - Complex supply chains mean that there is lot of cooperation across firms vertically and horizontally.
> - Design patents play a major role.
> - More and more value is coming from the software side rather than from hardware.
> - Business model thinking is becoming essential in the automotive industry, too, whereas patents play a major role in enforcing and multiplying the value of patents and technology (although this is to a high degree being questioned by the traditional players in the automotive industry).

6.9 Information and Communications Technology

Since the 1980s, the *Information and Communications Technology (ICT)* sector has been a highly innovative and rapidly changing area. These technologies include computing and telecommunications and encompass new developments in emerging technologies, e.g., Artificial Intelligence (AI). More than a third of the 165,000 applications received by the European Patent Office (EPO) in 2017 concerned ICT directly or indirectly (see Fig. 6.14). Given this importance, the EPO has even created a specialized ICT department, which brings together several of the EPO's examiners from various other technical sections like computers or semiconductors. This puts EPO examiners in the best position to assess the alleged novelty of inventions described in patent applications (EPO 2018).

In many areas of the electronics, semiconductor, and telecommunications industries, patents are interdependent. Almost no company in these sectors can still develop and sell products independently without being dependent on third-party patents. Accordingly, companies such as *IBM* or *Siemens* are increasingly forced to pursue an open licensing policy and conclude cross-licensing agreements on a broad scale.

Due to market requirements, there are often broad areas of technical overlap. On the other hand, there are usually numerous different technical solution variants that offer the same functionality but can still meet the needed requirements. Since users are demanding ever greater modularization of technical devices, international, and cross-company technical standardization initiatives have become unavoidable. These are particularly pronounced in the field of mobile communications. In the standardization committees, however, the companies involved must generally be prepared to sacrifice their patent portfolios in favor of a common standard that is then made available to all participants.

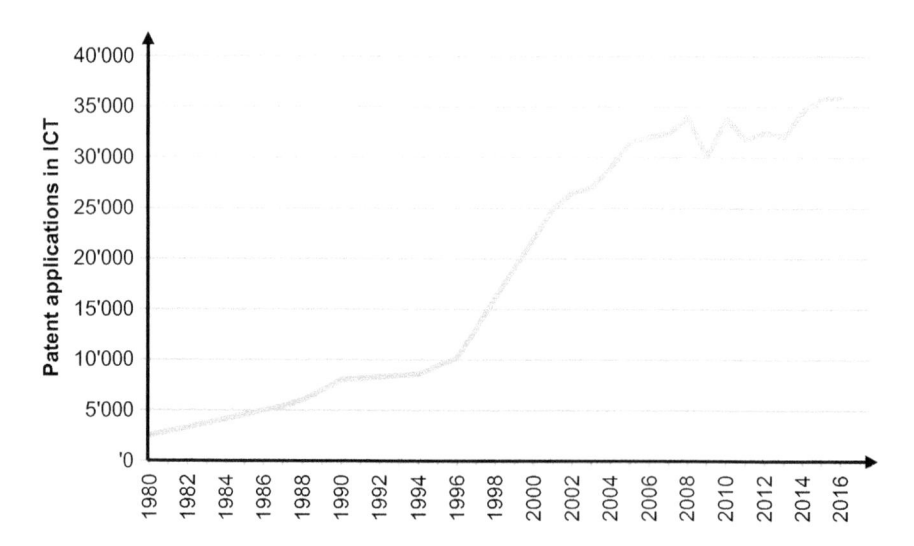

Fig. 6.14 Patent applications in ICT at the European Patent Office (based on EPO 2017)

From GSM to UMTS Standard to 5G

In the late 1980s, when the *European Global System for Mobile communications (GSM)* standard was developed, the American company *Motorola* influenced the standardization process significantly using its own relevant patents, and it pursued a licensing policy that was unusually aggressive at the time (Granstrand 1999). Thus, the GSM standard was kept away from countries in which *Motorola* pursued other interests. In addition, specific licensing conditions could be enforced, such as cross-licensing, which secured *Motorola* access to competitors' patent and technology portfolios and determined the structure of the GSM supplier market (Bekkers et al. 2002): Despite a small number of its own relevant patents, *Siemens* succeeded in joining the GSM standard at a later date. The French-German company *Alcatel* originally pursued a different technical solution, but this did not become the standard. Once the GSM standard had been defined, the company, therefore, had to build up a new patent portfolio.

The underlying patent portfolios also played an important role in the worldwide third-generation *Universal Mobile Telecommunications System (UMTS)* standard. There are significant technical dependencies on the *American Code Division Multiple Access (CDMA)* mobile communications standard. This was based on relevant patents of the American company *Qualcomm*, without which the UMTS standard could not be operated. The new race is now about who gets to be part of the new standard for the fifth-generation wireless technology for digital cellular networks "5G" (see Fig. 6.15).

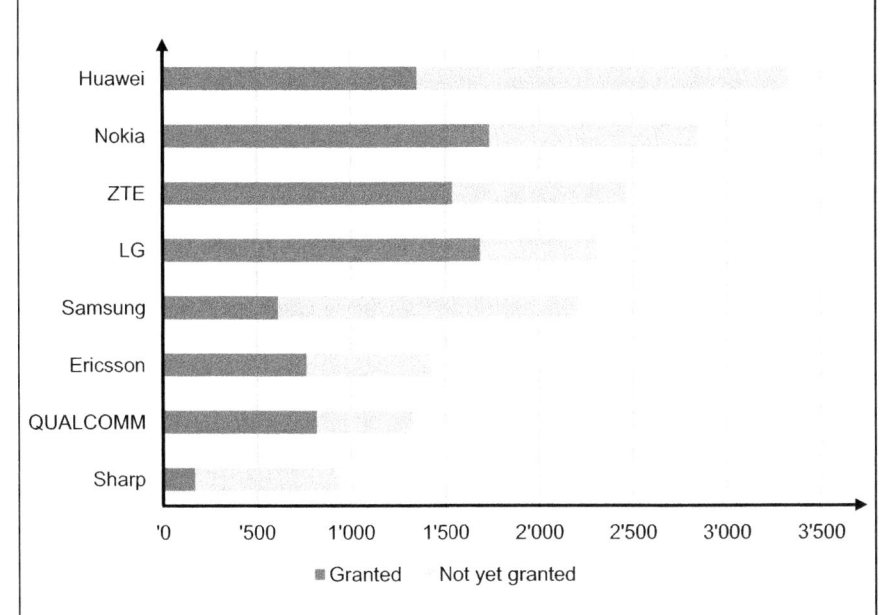

Fig. 6.15 The 5G patent owners' race: companies which have filed the most 5G SEP patent families as of November 2019 (based on Statista/IPlytics 2019)

(continued)

> Patent portfolios are increasingly getting used to keep previously uninvolved newcomers out of the market through raising high barriers to market entry. Technical standards supported by patent portfolios and their licensing regulations force newcomers to disclose their own relevant intellectual property rights and make them available to standard participants. In return, a license to the standard is acquired. Such trade, however, comes up against its limits when standard-relevant patents exist but their owners themselves have no intention of marketing their own, standard-compliant products, but are instead primarily aimed at licensing revenues.

The Smartphone Patent Wars

One of the more epic struggles in patenting took place around the so-called smartphone patent wars. As the smartphone was coming into its own the various players in the industry realized the size and potential of the market. What ensued were dozens of lawsuits between *Apple, Sony Mobile, Google, HTC, Motorola, Microsoft, Nokia, Huawei, LG Electronics, Samsung,* and *ZTE*. This big battle entailed hundreds of thousands of patents ranging from the seemingly simple icon design, to sophisticated high-frequency modem chips and it included everything in between. The iPhone was released mid-2007, marking a new era in connectivity—*Nokia*, a key player in the cell phone industry, kicked the war off by filing suit against *Apple* in late 2009, when the revolutionary device started to gain traction. The Nordic telecommunications equipment provider contended that Apple had not contributed to the patent pool surrounding the GSM, UTMS, and Wireless LAN standards, and thus owed a royalty of 6–12 dollars per phone. *Apple* promptly countersued, alleging *Nokia* stole some of its technology in 13 patents, the licensing terms of *Nokia* were not *FRAND (Fair, Reasonable and Non-Discriminatory)*, and some of the patents in the standards were not enforceable (iam 2015, 2016).

The enmity also brought other players, not even involved in consumer technology, like *Oracle*, to attack *Google* over the use of *Java* in *Android*. It underscores how patent infringement comes out of the woodwork when there is a lot of money at stake; *Java* had become widespread for the very reason that the language was considered an open technology after *Sun Microsystems* had become defunct, and perhaps this is the main reason it had become so popular.

The antagonism did not just involve the major big players of the industry, *EMG Technology*, a small Santa Monica company, alleged *Google* had violated its patent (US 7,441,196 B2) for an "apparatus and method of manipulating a region on a wireless device screen for viewing, zooming and scrolling internet content." The method patent offers simplified navigation in a sister site. While numerous lawsuits were filed in Eastern Texas (a patent-friendly circuit court) over the technology—it never got invalidated, perhaps because the holder was willing to settle for a small sum. On its face, it is not clear that this patent would not be obvious for a skilled web-developer in view of the state of the art in general. It is common for the core patent never to be invalidated. For reasons of game theory, neither the owner nor the infringer typically have an incentive to invalidate it (Thompson 2013). As an IP manager, it is often a good strategy to settle an invalidity suit rather than go to court because 1/2 of a monopoly is more than 1/2 of no monopoly profit. It is thus often very hard to know the extent of a company's IP strength by legal action.

In the ICT sector *Standard Essential Patents (SEPs)* play a key role. SEPs are often subject to compulsory licensing terms under *FRAND* conditions *(Fair, Reasonable and Non-Discriminatory)*. The FRAND idea has had to be—and currently still is—interpreted by several courts as having to come up with an operationalizable concept. The main European FRAND case law comes from: *Unwired Planet vs. Huawei* (UK High Court); *Huawei vs. ZTE* (European Court of Justice—ECJ); and *Sisvel vs. Haier* (German Higher Regional Court Dusseldorf).

The ECJ formalized the FRAND concept in its *Huawei* vs. *ZTE* case, wherein it outlined a general procedure to be taken when injunctive relief is sought under FRAND-committed SEPs (Kastler 2019):

- Before seeking an injunction, the SEP-holder must give notice to the alleged infringer by designating the SEP in question and specifying how it has been infringed
- The alleged infringer must express its willingness to take a license on FRAND terms

The SEP holder must:

- Provide a written license offer on FRAND terms, specifying the royalty and how it should be calculated.

There is no universal formula for this, but the German courts have ruled that it should include a "claim chart" or a "proud list" to facilitate negotiates.

The alleged infringer must:

- Respond to the SEP holder's offer in good faith by accepting the SEP holder's offer; or
- Make a counter-offer on FRAND terms
- Provide appropriate security
- Be able to render an account of its acts of use[8]

---

[8]What it is, exactly, that constitutes security, is still a bit ambiguous. The court in *Sisvel vs. Haier* held that requiring secured royalties which are due in the future as being excessive and not FRAND-compliant. Again, the idea of good faith is the guiding principle.

[9]Trade dress deals with the visual presentation of the product, such as colors, shape, markings, fonts, a presentation which shows the consumer the source of the product (Sect. 1.3).

Confidentiality and the obligation to conclude a *Non-Disclosure Agreement (NDA)*: in *Sisvel vs. Haier*, the court held that an SEP is required to produce comparable license agreements under an NDA.

Case: *Apple* vs. *Samsung*

Apple sued *Samsung* in 2011; this case was launched in the broader context of the smartphone war (cf. supra). The lawsuit is a big conflict involving: trademarks, patents, designs, trade dress,[9] technology standards, FRAND licensing, anti-trust law, and the patent doctrine of exhaustion.

While the lawsuit was centered around many software elements, trial documents show that these are very complex. The jury had to decide whether *Samsung* had violated rules surrounding "trade dress." It argued that *Samsung* copied its famously minimalistic packaging and design when marketing its devices in violation of its trade dress rights. The jury had to decide whether *Apple's* trade dress was famous, and by extension protectable.

Apple also invoked its design rights, alleging *Samsung* had copied its industrial designs filed for the iPhone. In the same suit, *Samsung* had alleged violation of several of its utility patents. The burden of proof in the case was whether it would be "proven by clear and convincing evidence that *Apple's* infringement was willful."

Apple had even claimed trademark violation under USC §1114 and general trademark law. This intellectual property right was used to cover its icons, design, user interface, and look and feel.

On top of those types of rights, *Apple* had claimed various anti-trust violations by *Samsung* for certain Universal Mobile Telecommunications Service (UMTS) patents in violation of the US Sherman Anti-Trust Act of 1890. Furthermore, *Apple* claimed that *Samsung* had not offered its standard-essential patents at a fair, reasonable, and non-discriminatory royalty (FRAND) rate.

Apple also invoked a more obscure defense against *Samsung's* claims. A doctrine of patent law is the concept of "exhaustion," which means that once the patented product has entered into commercial circulation—the patent right becomes exhausted. This reason for this doctrine is simple—it would be far too complex in an economy to manage a patent royalty right extending beyond the first sale. *Apple* alleged that *Samsung* had granted licenses to baseband chip suppliers and that once they had done this, *Samsung* had "exhausted" its patent rights on the technology, and could not then come after *Apple* for violation of these same patents, even if it incorporated *Samsung's* technology via these chips.

---

[9]Trade dress deals with the visual presentation of the product, such as colors, shape, markings, fonts, a presentation which shows the consumer the source of the product (Sect. 1.3).

Dealing with the Anti-commons

One of the academic debates that have been taking place for quite a long while is whether patents are actually harmful and in balance with certain technological areas where there are many players, or where a technology requires dozens of different inventions to be viable. This economic situation is known as the *tragedy of the anti-commons* where too many owners of scarce resources mutually exclude other actors to the point that there is no longer any production taking place. There are a couple of sectors, like ICT or consumer electronics, where this is more likely to be the case because many players own a tiny slice of the technology needed to put a product together—a cell phone is a wondrous device, requiring many patents to make. In a study done for the WIPO, there Reidenberg et al. (2015) identified some 314,000 *entities* with even more patents on everything from Liquid Crystal Displays (LCDs), software, on to modems. Any player trying to operate in this technological space is walking into an extensive legal minefield.

In the face of such obstacles, new entrants not only have to perfectly identify what is patented and what is not, a bewildering task in and of itself (cf. Freedom-to-Operate), but they also have to negotiate with potentially dozens or even hundreds of entities. The transaction costs and asymmetries of information are so high that for some technologies and products this is prohibitively expensive—and this is a "tragedy" since the product could be made but is not.

That is the pessimistic economic perspective, a more optimistic take is that where there is profit to be made economic actors will organize to capture it. This *invisible hand* is precisely what will overcome the predicament. This is just what has happened for years in patent pools, where multiple inventors allow their innovations to be used by members of the pool—this legal cartel then can extract additional value from their inventions. These patent pools are sometimes very opaque, but a new entity, *Avanci*, has created a new type of open licensing platform in the space of wireless connectivity for the internet of things. "*Avanci* streamlines this process by offering a single license to patents owned by many companies, claiming fair, reasonable, and non-discriminatory (FRAND) terms". Just as theory predicts, *InterDigital*, a producer/patent troll entity, signed a patent agreement with Google in 2019 using this new platform (Google 2019).

Though there is cause for optimism, the internet of things is still in its infancy, unlike the mobile space, so there is not much downside if the players toss their patents into a patent pool with a circumscribed objective. Moreover, we are much more likely to observe a patent pool rather than some forlorn inventor dead from exhaustion having tried to comprehend the legal implications of the patent record for her new invention.

Take-Aways Information and Communications Technology
- Patents are extremely critical for patent pool negotiations.
- Patents and technologies directly determine capital expenditures as standards are formed.
- The ICT industry is characterized by several cross-licensing agreements on the one side and tough patent wars on the other.
- The acquisition of entire companies because of patents—as happened in the *Motorola* acquisition by *Google*—can be a strategic step to enter the connected world.
- ICT has a big influence on several industries, driven by the IoT (internet of things) economy.
- Several industries should pay close attention to the ICT sector and the patent behavior since there is a spill-over as soon as connectivity enters the industry—and today nearly every sector is driven by the strategic trend of connectivity.

6.10 Computer Science

The computer science industry is characterized by rapid growth and a high rate of change. The high-tech sector is typified by the following challenges and risks (see also Fig. 6.16):

- Rapidly growing number of patents on software and business method applications requires a lot of monitoring effort.
- The quality and legal validity of numerous patents is questionable due to a lack of awareness of sufficient and relevant state of the art among applicants and patent offices.
- High-risk of third parties getting involved in a costly and time-consuming patent infringement process, especially in the US market.
- The enforcement of own patents is associated with a high financial risk, especially in the USA.
- Heterogeneity regarding the general legal development in the various legislations regarding the patentability of software applications. Unlike more technical inventions, these patents are often subject to a wide variety of different national types of legislation.

Case: *Microsoft*

Like other large software technology companies, *Microsoft* is now patenting its inventions. In 2004, Bill Gates announced that *Microsoft* was estimated to register

6.10 Computer Science

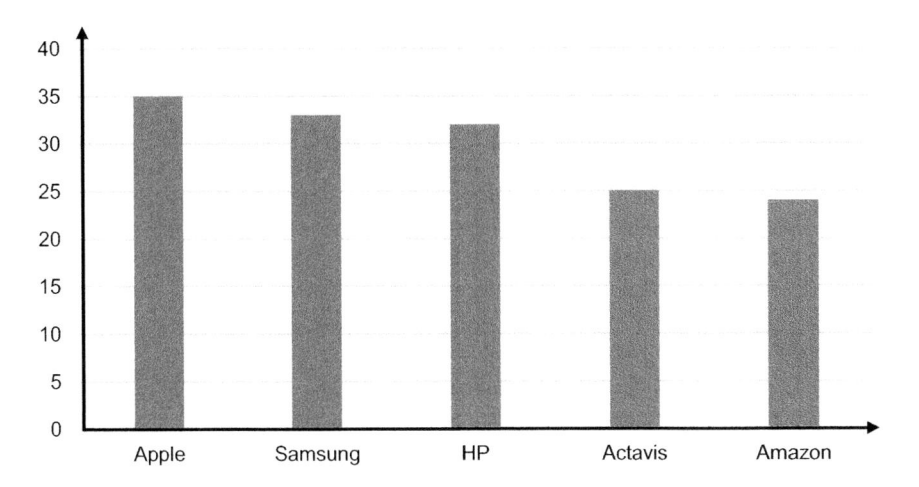

Fig. 6.16 The companies sued the most over patents: number of US patent litigation cases against companies in the first half of 2015 (based on Statista/Unified Patents 2015)

twice as many software patents the following year than in the previous year. The announcement was made against the background that it became increasingly necessary for *Microsoft* to have its own patent portfolio: on the one hand to negotiate cross-licenses and generate license income, and on the other hand to transfer knowledge. At the venture capital conference in 2005, CEO Steve Ballmer once again underlined the great importance of patent management for *Microsoft* by announcing that the group often spends more money on the purchase or generation of patents than on the development of the actual technologies, *Microsoft* invests more than $9 billion annually in research and development and, according to its own statements, now holds the largest and strongest patent portfolio in the software industry. *Microsoft* held nearly 60,000 patents in 2013; in 2019, *Microsoft* boasted another record year with 3083 patents (Seattle Times 2020)!

One reason for the change in direction of the software company, which was previously inactive in the patent sector, is probably that *Microsoft* has faced around three dozen patent infringement lawsuits since 1998. The legal proceedings could often be ended in settlements, such as with *Time Warner* and their *Netscape* browser, with mergers as with *AT&T*. Nevertheless, these were not necessarily cheap solutions, as can easily be seen when looking at the example given by *Sun Microsystems*. *Microsoft* had to pay the *Java House* a severance payment of US $1.95 billion. Small businesses also took action against *Microsoft*, such as *Inter Trust Technologies* in Santa Clara, California, which has patented approximately 30 patents with *Microsoft* regarding DRM (Digital Rights Management) technology. The settlement ended with a US $440 million payment to *Inter Trust Technologies* and a license to use the patent portfolio for *Microsoft* extending to end-users of Windows operating systems. In a recent case, an American Court of Appeals upheld a ruling that allowed *Microsoft*, starting in 2010, to sell only a modified version of Microsoft Word 2007. The reason for this is the infringement of a patent by the small Canadian software company *i4i*. The patent relates to a method with which the architecture and content of documents can be processed independently of each another. *Microsoft* has been ordered to pay damages of US $290 million. *Microsoft's* patent strategy has changed fundamentally in recent years; the company is now more interested in getting to balanced patent license exchange contracts (Bader 2006). Two companies license each other their respective technologies in exchange for corresponding back licenses from the contractual partner. *Microsoft* currently has such agreements with *Cisco Systems, Hewlett Packard, IBM, SAP, Siemens, Sun Microsystems, Unisys*, and *Xerox*. Prior to this, *Microsoft* primarily employed an aggressive strategy (offensive patent enforcement).

In addition to the offensive strategy, *Microsoft* introduced an IP licensing program in 2003 with (technology) licensing programs and the *Microsoft IP Ventures Program*, which among other things was aimed at awarding ventures to technologies developed by *Microsoft* but not used by the company. *Microsoft* offers start-ups and small business owners a special license for these technologies. In return for its technology, *Microsoft* gets a share of the licensee's equity. If a new, internally developed technology has earnings potential of less than $1 billion or does not fit into your own product portfolio in any other way, it is available to the IP Ventures program. According to David Kaefer, General Manager of *Microsoft's* Intellectual Property Licensing Team, the licensing terms are specifically agreed on a case-by-case basis. The licenses are granted nonexclusively. *Microsoft*, therefore, reserves the right to assign technology to different licensees.

Since its introduction, more than 600 license agreements have been made with the help of the IP license program, which is available to customers, partners, and competitors. Analysts rate *Microsoft's* licensing program as an intelligent move. The company has invested billions of dollars in research and development, which has led to a host of good ideas—probably more than *Microsoft* is able to turn into marketable products for itself. By making unused technologies available to the market, the shareholders' equity shares in return enable them to participate in their success without the need for further investments made in the licensed technologies themselves. In summary, *Microsoft's* patent strategy consists of four components:

- Building a larger patent portfolio as a starting point
- Patent license exchange contracts for risk minimization and as technology access
- Defense of one's own patent portfolio against patent infringers
- Awarding technology licenses to ventures in return for company shares for sustainable technology exploitation

Microsoft has developed a sophisticated patent strategy over the past decade that goes beyond a purely offensive enforcement strategy. In addition to this, *Microsoft* also attaches particular importance to human resource management, product development, and market launch, as well as organizational learning in the innovation process. *Microsoft* has also played a pioneering role in the latest developments in R&D, inside of global innovation networks. To meet this demand, *Microsoft's* Intellectual Property Team is led by *IBM* veteran Marshall Phelps, who was largely responsible for the licensing success of "Big Blue."

Eolas vs. Microsoft

Due to patent infringement, *Microsoft* had to pay more than half a billion US dollars in August 2003. A US federal court awarded the software company *Eolas Technologies* in Chicago and the University of California damages of around 520 million dollars. *Microsoft* appealed, but then withdrew the lawsuit when the Federal Court of Appeals in Washington dismissed the claim to the lower court due to a procedural error but did not overturn the verdict. *Microsoft* then settled out of court with *Eolas* and paid an unknown amount to settle the dispute.

The court ruled that Microsoft had infringed a patent that *Eolas* boss Michael Doyle had co-developed at the *University of California* with his browser *Internet Explorer*. The patent concerns a technology that enables access to interactive programs embedded in Internet pages. *Eolas* was founded in 1994 to distribute the software; the university holds the corresponding patent. Eolas and the university have accused *Microsoft* of having integrated their development into their Internet browser Explorer. The patent has since been upheld several times by courts and the USPTO. The original patent was even extended in 2002 to cover newer applications. This extension of the patent protection now serves *Eolas* as a starting point from which to sue more illustrious names such as *Amazon*, *eBay*, or *Google* for patent infringement or non-payment of license fees. A total of 24 companies worldwide are affected by the mass action.

Critics want to exclude software and basic principles, such as *Eolas'*, from patent protection in order not to hinder technological progress. Michael D. Doyle, founder of *Eolas*, explains the matter to Spiegel: "We developed this technology more than 15 years ago and demonstrated it publicly, years before the market heard of web-enabled applications that remotely tap into powerful resources. To profit from the inventions of others without paying for them is deeply unfair. We only want what is rightfully ours" (Spiegel Online 2009). ◄

Take-Aways Computer Science
- Software eats the world—there is hardly an industry without softwaretization.
- Software is de jure not patentable in Europe, it is their part of copyright law. But is de facto, in combination with a technical apparatus, one of the most patented areas.
- Software and methods portfolios are typically built around "mass" rather than quality.
- Software and methods patents are nuanced and complicated to soften and monitor.
- Software and methods patents are not necessarily patentable everywhere.

6.11 Financial Services and Fintech

The financial services industry has been idle for a long time with respect to its own intellectual property activities compared to other lines of business and only at a late stage did it begin to patent its developments (Glazier 2003). This may seem unusual at first, since it is a highly developed industry in which software and system solutions, in which a lot is invested, play a central role. The emerging possibility of patenting business models could provide additional competitive advantages over competitors by preventing them from using the protected business model (Möhrle and Walter 2009).[10] Also in the financial sector, a number of players had therefore begun to deal consistently with patents (Bader and Bischof 2005; Bader 2007, 2008; Bader and Cuypers 2008).

The trigger for the incipient rethinking among financial service providers lay in particular legal disputes, which also met with a great response in the media due to their scope and novelty:

- *Data Treasury vs. JP Morgan Chase et al.*: The lawsuit pertains, *inter alia*, to the recording, data processing, and storage of cheques and credit card receipts;
- *LML Payments Systems vs. U.S. Bancorp et al.*: The lawsuit concerns, among other things, methods of converting paper cheques into electronic transactions;
- *NetMoneyIn vs. Bank One, Citibank, Wells Fargo*: The complaint relates, *inter alia*, to methods of accepting credit card payments over the Internet.

In the last decade, protection against lawsuits has also been the basic driving force behind the patent strategies, particularly in the finance and insurance sectors. The main thrust of which was to be able to prevent legal disputes with third parties by means of own patents. The banking sector's patenting has originally been driven in particular by institutions such as *Bank of America, Barclays, BNP Paribas, Capital One, Citibank, Credit Suisse, Deutsche Bank, Goldman Sachs, HSBC, JPMorgan Chase, Lehman Brothers,*[11] *Merrill Lynch, Royal Bank of Scotland, UBS*, and *Wells Fargo* (see Fig. 6.17). However, traditional tech companies, like *Alphabet, Amazon, Apple, IBM, Oracle*, and *Microsoft* have started building up specific Fintech patent portfolios to protect their engagement in financial and payment services (see Fig. 6.18).

---

[10]Cf. Changes caused by *In re Bilsky* decision. See the info-box *Patentability of Business Methods in the USA on Trial*.

[11]As part of the bankruptcy proceedings against *Lehman Brothers*, the patent portfolio went to *Barclays* in 2008: the industry breathed a sigh of relief that the portfolio didn't go to a PAE.

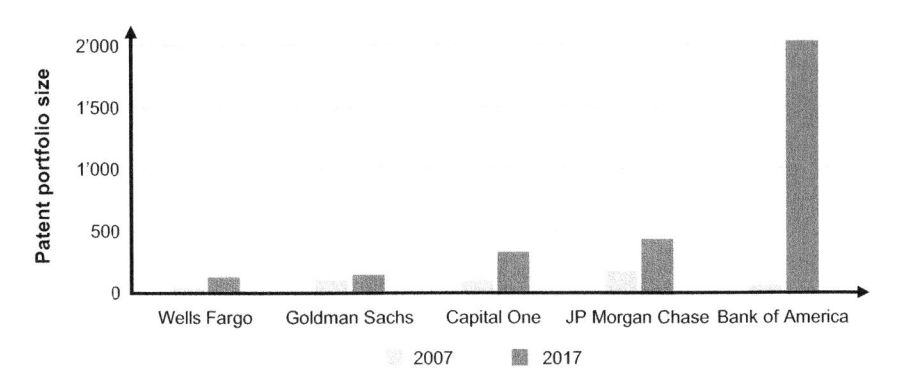

Fig. 6.17 Patent portfolio growth of largest US banks, 2007 versus 2017 (based on Bördin 2019)

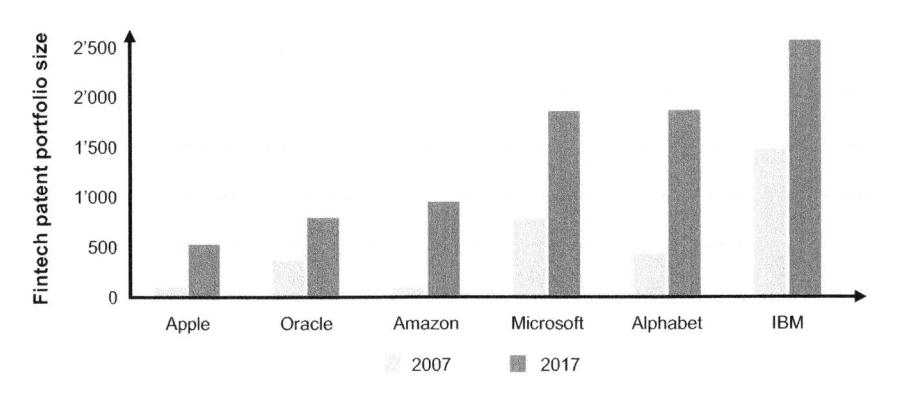

Fig. 6.18 Fintech patent portfolios of major tech companies (based on Bördin 2019)

Case: MasterCard

Also, payment solution providers have significantly increased their patent filing activities. Hot spot patenting areas are especially blockchain, data security, and machine learning. The two market leaders, *Mastercard* and *Visa*, have increased their annual patent filings by six times since 2010, reaching a peak of about 650 filings in 2016 (Bördin 2019; see Fig. 6.19).

MasterCard recently got a patent granted on a "Method and system for partitioned blockchains and enhanced privacy for permissioned blockchains" (US 10,097,344 B2, granted in 2018; see Fig. 6.20). The claimed concept allows multiple, different types of transactions to all be stored on a single blockchain. For instance, transactions for several different cryptocurrencies can all be stored in the single blockchain (see also Sect. 7.6).

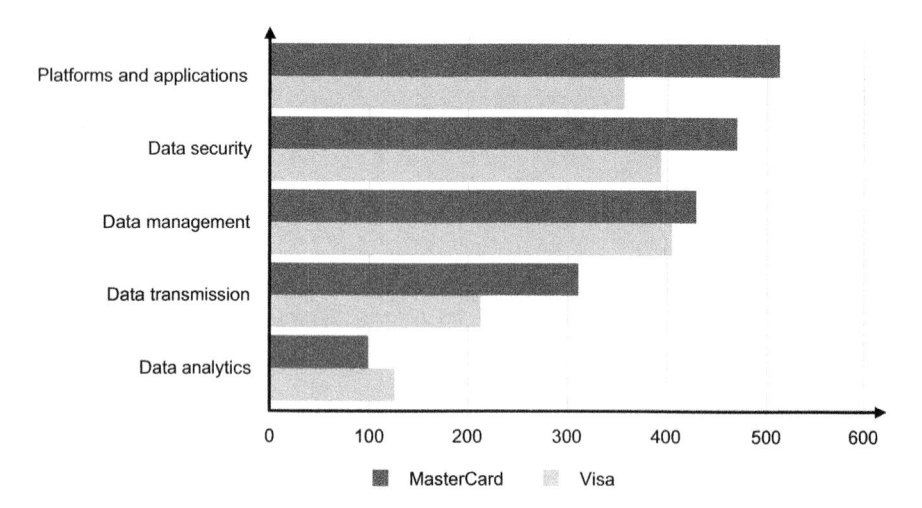

Fig. 6.19 *Mastercard* and *Visa's* technology distribution (based on Bördin 2019)

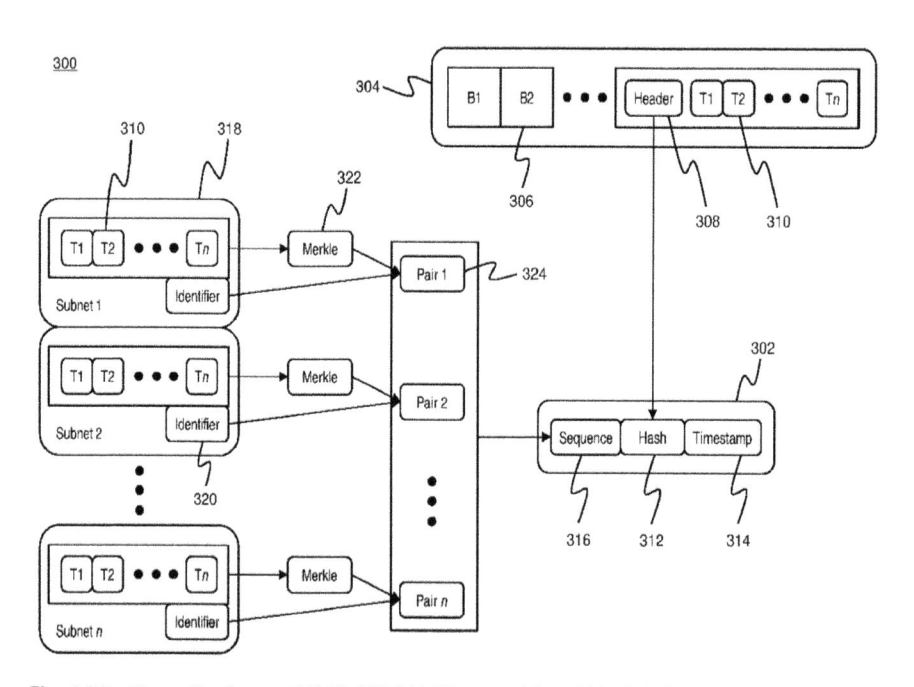

Fig. 6.20 *MasterCard* patent US 10,097,344 B2 on partitioned blockchains and enhanced privacy

> **Take-Aways Financial Services**
> - Finance is plagued by the same pitfalls of methods patents that the computer industry is, where the invention is often less definite than in other fields.
> - The financial sector started quite late with patenting activities. Early starts have been done by US companies, namely the City Bank which has been one of the most active banks, patenting at the European Patent Office.
> - Innovation has not been a strong domain of the financial sector but fintech companies are changing the rules and behavior of the industry.
> - Customers are becoming more hybrid, loyalty is lower, user experience plays an important role for customers.

6.12 Transport and Logistics

The transport and logistics sector comprises companies that directly or indirectly dispatch or transport people and goods and "intelligently distribute" them. Companies in the sector are increasingly competing on the basis of services, which increases the importance of managing service innovation in general and logistics innovation in particular. The management of logistics innovations encompasses and refers to the planning, control, and monitoring of novel logistics products or processes in supply chains or within companies. Logistical production innovations crystallize through technologies such as "hardware" (e.g., new load carriers), and "software" (e.g., new advanced planning and scheduling systems) or a combination of the two (e.g., radio-frequency identification RFID use). Logistical process innovations, on the other hand, are primarily based on innovations in the area of process knowledge and the structure of the network of relationships. Logistics innovations also come from IT service providers as well as in industrial and commercial enterprises.

The logistics industry is therefore increasingly developing from a cost factor to a differentiation factor that promises sustainable competitive advantages. This trend is in line with the development of the industry into a knowledge or service society. Although numerous advances have been made in logistics in terms of increasing customer satisfaction, improving delivery services, or reducing costs, these achievements have little protection against imitation by competitors compared with other industries. Only a few companies in the logistics services sector systematically and comprehensively manage their intellectual property rights (Bader and Hofmann 2006). Almost 15 years ago, there were no patent applications at all in the logistics services sector. Only in the last 10 years has there been a significant revival in patenting activities, with the major players playing a pioneering role. More than 180 new patent applications were published by *UPS* during this period, followed by *Deutsche Post DHL* with over 160, *UPS* with about 125, *FedEx* with about 20, and *La*

Poste with about 10. Of these, most patents are filed not only nationally, but more than a third internationally. Nevertheless, it can be stated that logistics companies still make far too little use of the possibility of patenting business models and thus run the risk of losing innovative know-how and risking freedom-to-operate (Niemann et al. 2013).

Case: *FedEx* and *United Parcel Service (UPS)*

UPS was founded in 1907 as a courier service in the USA and is today the world's largest express and parcel delivery service. Over the years, *UPS* has expanded its service portfolio tremendously and today not only coordinates the movement of goods but also the information and financial flows that result from this. *UPS* has always placed great emphasis on innovation, standardizing customer service, and increasing reliability. *UPS* sees this as a sustainable way of differentiating itself from the competition. *UPS* applies three principles of innovation: first, business activities are continuously redefined, which *UPS* successfully implements with the strategic reorientation from "serving the small package delivery needs of our customers" to "enabling global commerce" and the entry into the service business. Second, the importance of the long-term time horizon of innovation and third, the important role of the corporate brand in communication during change are recognized.

Despite the fact that the *UPS* business model is enabled by a lot of logistics infrastructure, it has not been immune to patent lawsuits. It was sued by *Mobile Technology Technologies (MTel)* for infringement of U.S. Patent No. 5,786,748. The patent claims "to provide prompt notification of delivery of an express mailing to the addressee thereof, the page number of a person to be notified upon delivery of the express mailing is communicated to an express mail tracking network and to an operations center of a wireless paging service." The court applied the *Alice* Doctrine in its examination of the patent and found that the patent did not have the requisite inventive concept. *MTel* appealed to the court, arguing that the court had engaged in temporal bias—while the concept of notifying a sender of reception via telecommunications seems laughably trivial in 2016—it was not when the patent was filed in 1996. The court dismissed the appeal for reconsideration, holding that at its core the patent is simply an implementation of an abstract idea and that the patent's very subject was ineligible for patent protection under US law (*Mobile Telecommunications Technologies, LLC vs. United Parcel Service*, US District Court for the Northern District of Georgia, Atlanta Division, October 21, 2016).

Enlarging Logistics to Cloud Computing: *Amazon*

Although *Amazon* is commonly known as a major logistics player, it has substantial patent portfolios in logistics, drones, and aircraft technology.[12] As a recent analysis from Forbes points out (Forbes 2019):

---

[12] As a side note, *Amazon* is now offering an *Amazon IP Accelerator* service, with pre-vetted legal professionals that can companies help to quickly accelerate IP and brand protection: https://brandservices.amazon.com/ipaccelerator

6.12 Transport and Logistics

- Since 2010 *Amazon* has grown its patent portfolio from less than 1000 active patents in 2010 to nearly 10,000 in 2019, a tenfold increase in less than a decade.
- *Amazon* heavily cites *Microsoft*, *IBM*, and *Alphabet*.
- *Amazon's* patent portfolio is dominated by Cloud Computing, with the majority of the patents contributing to *Amazon Web Services (AWS)* current and future services roadmap.
- *Amazon's* ongoing developments in alternative delivery methods in Urban Logistics and Drones are mirrored by strong patents (see Fig. 6.21). ◄

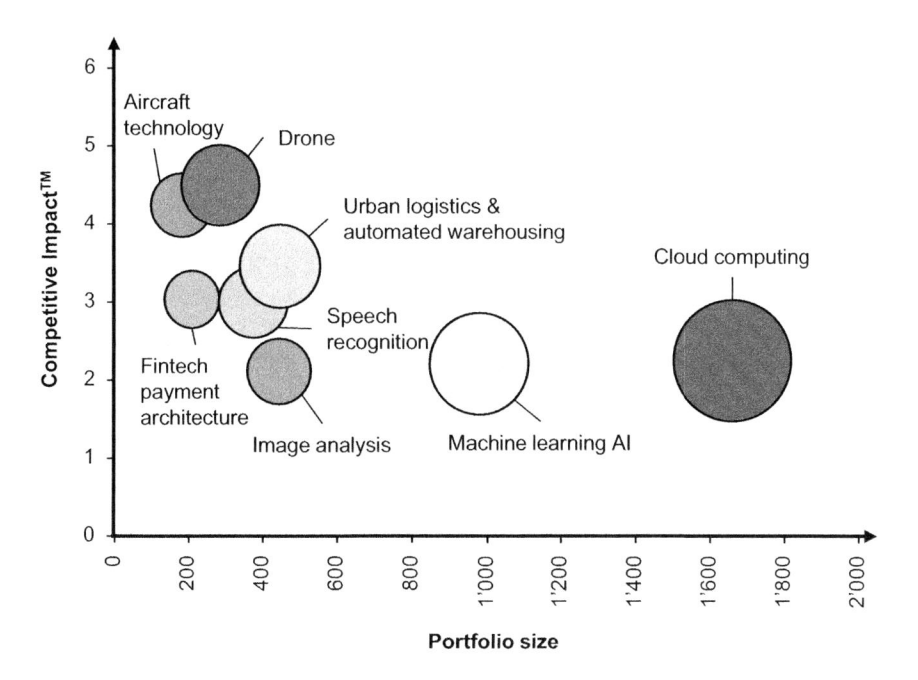

Fig. 6.21 *Amazon* patent portfolio report in selected technology fields (based on Forbes/PatentSight 2019)

Take-Aways Transport and Logistics
- The logistics sector is changing from a traditional low-tech sector to a data-based high-tech industry.
- Location-based services and traceability are becoming more important in the industry.
- The future of autonomous driving systems will revolutionize the logistics sector.
- Technologies as sensor systems, connectivity, 5G, data analytics with neural networks drive the change of the industry.

6.13 Start-Ups and SMEs

In contrast to large companies, SMEs across industries have no differentiated processes, fewer research activities, and often no software tools to manage their patents. SMEs often focus on clear cost/benefit aspects of a patent. As a consequence, small companies apply more stringent criteria when selecting inventions for patent applications. They usually have a widely networked but very lean internal structure. Frequently, the managing director or the R&D manager coordinates all patent management-related activities. The patent filing process, including file management and search activities, therefore usually involves a high degree of outsourcing to external patent law firms and consultants. In addition, the problem of patent enforceability may arise with regard to available resources and high costs. In contrast to large companies, small companies are often disadvantaged and therefore generally prefer to keep a patent application confidential.

However, the creation and use of industrial property rights also has advantages for SMEs (see Fig. 6.22):

Strengthening the Negotiating Position SMEs are more active in the business-to-business sector, where large companies dominate as customers. Without patent protection, their bargaining position vis-à-vis their large corporate customers would be extremely weak, as they can often adopt an innovation themselves or have it produced more cheaply by third parties. Patent protection can make a significant contribution to securing follow-up orders that are needed to amortize previous R&D investments.

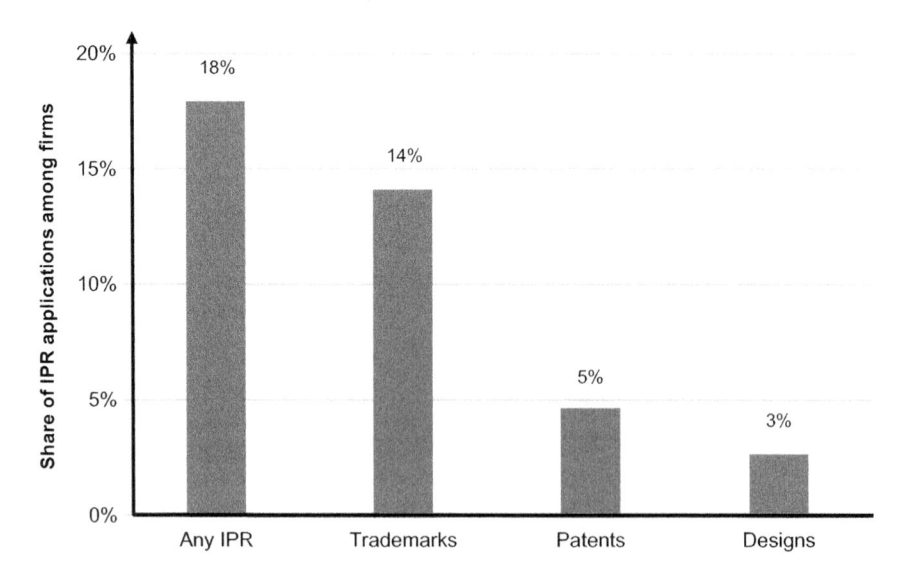

Fig. 6.22 Frequency of IPR use by European SMEs (based on EPO and EUIPO 2019)

6.13 Start-Ups and SMEs

Raising Capital Venture capitalist firms often require collateral for their investments. Patents, patent applications, utility models, and trademarks are increasingly accepted as indicators for the business plan and as some measure of protection for innovations against imitators. Patents can now even be used directly as collateral for loans.

Particularly in the case of SMEs, which have so far had a not very consistent patent management, the core tasks of IP rights often still lie with the managing director. In some cases, the coordination of patent activities is delegated to a member of the development department, who is supposed to perform this task alongside other activities. The consequences of this type of informal arrangement are:

- Little strategic orientation of patent management
- Little time for questions of industrial property rights
- Few systematic methods of evaluation or valuation
- Little or no structure or formalization
- No official contact person
- Lack of technical or legal expertise

There is a risk that patenting is not completed on time and that there is little overview of the many different procedures involved—payment of fees, examination deadlines, international filing, etc. On the other hand, there are SMEs that have grown rapidly in a short time and are globally active based on patenting activity. Our research on these so-called *"Born Globals"* has shown that very often patent management has played a central role in their rapid growth. Strategic patents were generated, systematically defended, and commercialized globally.

Practical Tips for Patent Management in Start-Ups and SMEs

1. Carrying out patent searches at the beginning for each invention is the best way to protect yourself against surprises later on.
2. In the case of being blocked by a patent of a competitor, it is useful to develop workarounds.
3. Effective protection is often not provided by individual patents. Innovative SMEs should, therefore, set up a systematic patent cluster to secure their competitive advantages.
4. Broad patents have a greater impact but are also easier to attack. The application for broad patents should, therefore, be considered especially at the beginning of a technology cycle.
5. In addition to basic patents, various concrete design variants can be patented.
6. The own negotiating basis can be improved in the event of a dispute if an improvement solution is filed based on a systematic analysis and

(continued)

evaluation of competing products, as this makes further development more difficult for the competitor.
7. In-licensing or patent cross-licensing enables the use of foreign, already patented inventions.
8. In patent law steps, such as opposition or nullity proceedings, it is advisable to engage a patent attorney, since technical knowledge is not sufficient in such cases.
9. A consistent and rigorous approach to patent infringers acts as a deterrent and increases the barriers to imitation.
10. Another option for action is the trade in patent rights: Patents are regarded as real products that are traded on a marketplace, including options such as barter, sale, or licensing.
Source: Gassmann and Bader (2017)

References

Bader, M. A. (2006). *Intellectual property management in R&D collaborations*. Heidelberg: Physica.
Bader, M. A. (2007). Extending legal protection strategies to the service innovations area: Review and analysis. *World Patent Information, 29*, 122–135.
Bader, M. A. (2008). Managing intellectual property in the financial services industry sector: Learning from Swiss Re. *Technovation, 28*(4), 196–207.
Bader, M. A., & Bischof, D. (2005). Intellectual property management in der finanzdienstleistungsbranche. In O. Gassmann & S. Albers (Eds.), *Handbuch technologie- und innovationsmanagement*. Wiesbaden: Gabler.
Bader, M. A., & Cuypers, F. (2008). Swiss Re: Global intellectual property management in the financial services industry. In R. Boutellier, O. Gassmann, & M. von Zedtwitz (Eds.), *Managing global innovation* (3rd ed.). Berlin: Springer.
Bader, M. A., & Gassmann, O. (2020, forthcoming) Patents in the biomedical sciences and industry – the case of the Swiss life science company Prionics. In: Hinder, M., Schuhmacher, A., & Goldhahn, J. (Eds.), *Principles of biomedical science and industry*. Weinheim: Wiley-VCH.
Bader, M. A., & Hofmann, E. (2006). Intellectual property management in der Logistik. *Supply Chain Management, 6*(4), 7–13.
Bekkers, R., Duysters, G., & Verspagen, B. (2002). Intellectual property rights, strategic technology agreements and market structure: The case of GSM. *Research Policy, 31*(7), 1141–1161.
Bördin, J. (2019). Born from business need. *iam magazine*, autumn 2019. Accessed 2020-04-11, from https://www.iam-media.com/patents/born-business-need
Brem, A., Maier, M., & Wimschneider, C. (2016). *Competitive advantage through innovation: The case of Nespresso. European Journal of Innovation Management, 19*(1), 133–148.
EPO. (2017). *Patents and the fourth industrial revolution. The inventions behind digital transformation*. Munich: European Patent Office.
EPO. (2018). *Information and communications technology patents at the EPO*. https://www.epo.org/news-issues/issues/ict/about-ict.html. Accessed on December 30th, 2019. Munich: European Patent Office.

References

EPO. (2019). *Patenting biotechnological inventions at the EPO*. Brussels: Dr. Harald Schmidt-Yodlee. European Patent Office.
EPO and EUIPO. (2019). *High-growth firms and intellectual property rights. IPR profile of high-potential SMEs in Europe, May 2019*. A joint project between the European Patent Office and the European Union Intellectual Property Office, Munich and Alicante.
Forbes/PatentSight. (2019). *10 Charts that will change your perspective of Amazon's patent growth*. Accessed 2020-04-11, from https://www.forbes.com/sites/forbespr/2020/04/09/forbes-releases-23rd-annual-major-league-baseball-valuations/#4b7277557eeb
Gassmann, O., & Bader, M. A. (2017). *Patentmanagement: Innovationen erfolgreich nutzen und schützen* (4th ed.). Berlin: Springer.
Gassmann, O., Krech, C.-A., Bader, M. A., & Reepmeyer, G. (2016). Out-licensing in pharmaceutical research and development. In A. Schuhmacher, M. Hinder, & O. Gassmann (Eds.), *Value creation in the pharmaceutical industry – The critical path to innovation* (pp. 363–380). Weinheim: Wiley-VCH.
Gassmann, O., Schuhmacher, A., Reepmeyer, G., & von Zedtwitz, M. (2018). *Leading pharmaceutical innovation – How to win the life science race* (3rd ed.). Berlin: Springer.
Glazier, S. C. (2003). *E-patent strategies*. Washington, DC: LBI Law & Business Institute.
Google. (2019). *Q3 earnings call*, October 31st.
Granstrand, O. (1999). *The economics and management of intellectual property. Towards intellectual capitalism*. Northampton, MA: Edward Elgar.
Grünecker. (2013). *E-Auto-Patentindex 2013*. Grünecker Patent- und Rechtsanwälte.
iam. (2015). *In search of the next patent war*. Accessed 2020-04-11, from https://www.iam-media.com/litigation/search-next-patent-war
iam. (2016). *Innovation and survival: Lessons from the smartphone wars*. Accessed 2020-04-11, from https://www.iam-media.com/innovation-and-survival-lessons-smartphone-wars
IPI. (2019). *Pulling no punches – how Prionics, a life science company in Zurich, defends its intellectual property*. https://www.ige.ch/en/intellectual-property/sme-portal/smes-report/detailseiten/prionics-ag.html.
IPI/PatentSight. (2020). *Patent analytics as a support to business decisions*. Bern: IPI.
Juve. (2020). *Collision course set for Nokia and Daimler*. Accessed 2020-03-18, from https://www.juve-patent.com/news-and-stories/cases/collision-course-set-for-nokia-and-daimler/ & *Hopes dwindle for peaceful settlement between Nokia and Daimler*. https://www.juve-patent.com/news-and-stories/cases/hopes-dwindle-for-peaceful-settlement-between-nokia-and-daimler/
Kastler, H. A. (2019). *FRAND Case Law in Europe After Huawei vs. ZTE*. https://www.mofo.com/resources/insights/190405-frand-case-law-europe.html, accessed 20-03-14.
Möhrle, M. G., & Walter, L. (2009). *Patentierung von Geschäftsprozessen. Monitoring – Strategien – Schutz*. Dordrecht: Springer.
Niemann, H. (2014). *Corporate Foresight mittels Geschäftsprozesspatenten: Entwicklungsstränge der Automobilindustrie*. Wiesbaden: Springer.
Niemann, H., Moehrle, M. G., & Walter, L. (2013). The development of business method patenting in the logistics industry—Insights from the case of intelligent sensor networks. *International Journal of Technology Management, 61*(2), 177–197.
Picanço-Castro, V., Pereira, C., Covas, D. T., Porto, G., Athanassiadou, A., & Figueiredo, M. L. (2020). Emerging patent landscape for non-viral vectors used for gene therapy, *Nature: Biotechnology*, 38, 151–157. Graphic released to public by Purdue University: https://www.purdue.edu/newsroom/releases/2020/Q1/novel-techniques-for-mining-patented-gene-therapies-offer-promising-treatment-options-for-cancers,-other-diseases.html
Reidenberg, J. R., Cammeron Russel, N., Price, M., & Mohand, A. (2015). *Patents and the Small Participants in the Smartphone Industry*. Fordham Center on Law and Information Policy & the World Intellectual Property Organization.
Ropes and Gray. (2019). *Continental automotive v. avanci: Wireless SEP licensing presents challenges for automotive industry*. https://www.lexology.com/library/detail.aspx?g=2e0a83b4-6e78-4faa-8311-9b6e4a0c945f.

Seattle Times. (2020). *Microsoft, Amazon, and China's Huawei among top 10 recipients of U.S. patents in 2019*, 2020-01-15.
Spiegel Online. (2009). *Microsoft-Bezwinger greift Web-Wirtschaft an*. http://www.spiegel.de/netzwelt/netzpolitik/software-firma-eolas-microsoft-bezwinger-greift-web-wirtschaft-an-a-653659.html
Statista. (2015). *The Companies Sued The Most Over Patents In 2015. Number of US patent litigation cases against companies in the first half of 2015*. Accessed 2020-04-11, from https://www.statista.com/chart/3699/the-companies-sued-the-most-over-patents-in-2015/
Statista. (2019). *Who is leading the 5G patent race? Companies which have filed the most patents for 5G technology as of November 2019*. Accessed 2020-04-11, from https://www.statista.com/chart/20095/companies-with-most-5g-patent-families-and-patent-families-applications/
Thompson. (2013). Costs of Swiss Patent Litigation. *Sic!* June, 2013.
VisionGain. (2018). *Generic drugs market forecast 2019-2029*. London.
Wagner, R. (2015). Wichtige Trends in der Automobilindustrie. In R. Wagner & G. Hab (Eds.), *Projektmanagement in der Automobilindustrie* (pp. 3–9). Wiesbaden: Springer Fachmedien.
Wolfe, J. (2019). *Bristol-Myers wins $752 million in US patent case against Gilead Reuters*.

Patent Management in New Technology Environments

7

The intellectual property system dates back several hundred years to when the first patent was issued in Florence, Italy, in 1421 for a barge hoist. This concept of privileged use of this slowly spread throughout Europe. But the patent system in its modern incarnation goes back to the industrial age of the nineteenth century, and is increasingly at odds with the physicality of the originally designed system. Throughout all this time, technology has undoubtedly progressed, but inventions have become less physical, and more ethereal as well.

Contemporary inventions are starting to exert pressure against the legal framework of the patent system conceived in an age of steel. Knowledge about which genes control which biological function is certainly a discovery on par with, if not more powerful, than any physical invention of the industrial age, but biotechnology raises deep bio-ethical questions, and questions about where invention ends and discovery begins. Artificial intelligence is already pushing the legal boundaries of human agency in the creation of IP. The following is a selection of these technologies, which are likely to be both relevant commercially and where there are implications for intellectual property.

The following chapter covers:

1. Biotechnology
2. Nanotechnology
3. Industry 4.0 and Internet of Things
4. Software and Business Methods
5. Artificial Intelligence-based Business Models
6. Blockchain and Distributed Ledger Technologies

A selected portion of this chapter, i.e., "Artificial intelligence-based business models," was previously published in the chapter Bader MA and Stummeyer C (2019) The role of innovation and IP in AI-based business models; in: Baierl R, Behrens J and Brem A (eds): Digital Entrepreneurship – Interfaces Between Digital Technologies and Entrepreneurship; Springer: Heidelberg, pp. 23–56. Used with permission.

© Springer Nature Switzerland AG 2021
O. Gassmann et al., *Patent Management*, Management for Professionals, https://doi.org/10.1007/978-3-030-59009-3_7

7.1 Biotechnology

In recent decades, biotechnology has been one of the faster-growing fields as well as being amongst the top ten technical fields in terms of the number of patent applications filed with the European Patent Office (European Patent Index 2019); this is a volatile area (see Table 7.1). About half of these applications come from scientific institutes and universities. As this field of science covers a wide range of fields from microorganisms to agriculture and medical applications and covers publicly controversial techniques and products, such as genetically modified plants, animal cloning, or the use of human embryonic stem cells, patents are discussed more vividly here than in other technical fields.

Patenting biotechnological inventions raises a host of questions, not only legal or economic ones but also ones that are ethical and social in nature. Patenting is polarizing, although numerous studies have dealt with this controversial issue (OECD 2003; Straus 2003; Thumm 2001, 2003; Dutfield 2003): for some, patents are important for economic and scientific development, for others, they represent an inadmissible commercialization of life or a barrier to the free exchange of knowledge. In collaboration with the Swiss Federal Institute of Intellectual Property (IGE) and the Group for Science and Research (GWF), the Science et Cité Foundation has illustrated various points of view in this regard (Stiftung Science et Cité 2004):

Examples of Patentable Biotechnological Inventions

- Genes and nucleic acid molecules (e.g., disease-related genes for diagnostics or for the antisense procedure, siRNA molecules for therapy)
- Proteins (e.g., insulin, erythropoietin for therapy, cell receptors for drug screening)
- Enzymes (e.g., proteases for washing powder, cellulose-degrading enzymes for the production of biofuels)
- Antibodies (e.g., for cancer treatment, pregnancy tests or diagnostics)

Table 7.1 Number of patent applications filed with the European Patent Office in biotech

Year	EPO biotechnology patent applications	Growth (%)
2009	5154	
2010	7723	50
2011	5870	−24
2012	5539	−6
2013	5269	−5
2014	5754	9
2015	5724	−1
2016	5477	−4
2017	6013	10
2018	6689	11.2

Source: EPO (2020)

- Viruses and virus sequences (e.g., hepatitis C virus and HIV for blood tests and for the development of vaccines and therapies)
- Cells (e.g., hematopoietic stem cells for the treatment of leukemia)
- Microorganisms (e.g., bacteria for bioremediation, yeast for food production)
- Plants (e.g., herbicide-resistant soybeans, "golden rice" with a high content of provitamin A, drought-resistant plants and algae that extract CO_2 from the atmosphere)
- Animals (e.g., disease models for research purposes such as the genetically modified "cancer mouse," donor animals for xenotransplantation, milk-producing animals that excrete medicinal substances in their milk) ◄

Examples of Non-patentable Biotechnological Inventions

- DNA sequences without known function (e.g., expressed sequence tags (ESTs) as a result of automatic sequencing)
- Genetically modified animals that have to suffer without there being a significant medical benefit, e.g., a genetically modified animal that is only used for cosmetic tests
- Plant varieties (already protected by the International Convention for the Protection of New Varieties of Plants, e.g., apples of the "Golden Delicious" variety)
- Animal breeds (e.g., Holstein cattle)
- Human embryos
- Procedures that inevitably involve the use and destruction of human embryos
- Human germ cells (sperm, ova)
- Human–animal chimeras ◄

Research Despite Patents Possible
In biotechnology, the use of basic procedures, for example, for the isolation of genes, is essential for research. If such processes are not available or only available at a high cost because of patents, research can suffer as a result. The polymerase chain reaction (PCR) is an elementary process in genetic engineering with which very small amounts of DNA can be amplified at will. Duplication solves the problem that genetic material is often only available in extremely small quantities and thus eludes direct detection or analysis.

The PCR method has been the subject of numerous patents. These patents have made the research possible, as the granting of licenses has allowed the technology to be used by others. This is evidenced by the exponential increase in the number of scientific publications referencing PCR technology between 1987 and 1997, which appeared after the publication of the PCR patent. In general, when licenses are granted, the costs of research projects may increase because license fees have to be paid. Especially in basic research, costs are an important factor.

> **Biotechnological Inventions and Patents**
> According to the European Patent Convention (EPC), "biotechnological inventions" are inventions which concern a product consisting of or containing biological material—such as DNA sequences, genes, or proteins—or a process by which biological material is produced, processed, or used (Rule 26(2) EPC).
> "Biological material" means any material containing genetic information and capable of reproducing itself or being reproduced in a biological system (Rule 26(3) EPC). This includes living organisms and DNA.
> "Biotech patents" are patents for biotechnological inventions and may also cover plant, animal or human cells, tissues, organs, or genetically modified animals and plants, as well as genetically modified seeds.

Biotechnology Patents at the EPO

In the following, excerpts from the EPO on the legal requirements on *biotechnology patents* (EPO 2017a) are displayed:

As with all other technologies, inventions in biotechnology are generally considered patentable under the law, and the same general patent examination rules and processes apply to all inventions.

At the EPO, biotechnology represents about 4% of all patent applications filed: 6048 of the total number of 160,022 European patent applications received in 2015 concerned biotechnology.

In the vast majority of cases, patent applications in this field are uncontroversial. Public debate concerns a very small number of patent applications related specifically to animals and plants.

The EPO examines all patent applications diligently. Across all technologies, fewer than half of the applications filed become a patent. In biotechnology, the grant rate is significantly lower: less than 30% of the patent applications filed become a European patent.

Respecting Traditional Knowledge

The EPO uses powerful tools and very comprehensive databases when performing a search to determine whether the invention claimed in a patent application is new or not.

To avoid undue privatization of traditional knowledge already in the public domain, the EPO also searches specialized databases, such as the Indian Traditional Knowledge Digital Library, which provides information related to Indian traditional medicine for patent offices. In 2009 the EPO signed an agreement with the Indian government granting EPO examiners online access to this database. The EPO also consults databases relating to other traditional knowledge, in particular databases describing Chinese and Korean traditional knowledge.

Ethics

The EPO grants patents in strict accordance with its legal basis, the European Patent Convention (EPC) and takes ethical considerations into account when granting patents. Inventions whose exploitation is deemed to be contrary to Article 53 EPC are not patentable. The law lists exceptions to patentability for ethical reasons, among them human cloning, modification of the human genome, and commercial uses of human embryos.

For patents in biotechnology, the rules of the EU's Directive on the legal protection of biotechnological inventions ("Biopatent Directive") also apply. The Directive for instance clarifies that human genes, plants, and animals are patentable when all conditions for a patent are fulfilled. The Directive became part of the EPC in 1999.

The EPO voluntarily follows the rulings of the European Court of Justice on the correct interpretation of the Directive and has incorporated such rulings into its practical work in biotechnology.

The EPO engages with stakeholders of the patent system and the public in open and transparent discussions. It closely cooperates with the EU institutions and informs them on important developments in the field of biotechnology patents. It recently began a close cooperation with the Community Plant Variety Office on questions relating to patents on plants.

Animals and Human Genes

Patents for a human gene often form the basis for many life-saving drugs. The EPO does not grant patents for genes without a known activity, or for unidentified gene fragments. For a patent to be granted for a human gene, its activity must have been described in the patent application and not be obvious.

Patents for human genes do not confer any rights to the human body. Applicants tend to withdraw their applications when they receive negative reports from the EPO on the patentability of their invention. The number of patent applications refused by the EPO, therefore, is generally quite low. However, there are many examples of rejected patent biotech applications.

In the area of human genes, numerous applications were refused because the function of the gene had not been convincingly demonstrated in the application. Examples include application 97930715 and 01981441, both concerning human gene sequences said to be promising targets for the manufacture of medications. Application 96903521 was refused on ethical grounds because it was based on the use of human embryonic stem cells which at the time of filing could only be isolated by destroying human embryos, which is not allowable under the EPC.

Like plants, animals are patentable according to the law. The patent applications filed with the EPO mostly concern transgenic (genetically modified) mice and rats used in medical research. However, the EPO takes ethical considerations into account: If the transgenic invention is found to make the animal suffer, it may only be patented if it brings a substantial medical benefit to humans (or animals).

As with plants, conventional breeding methods for animals are not patentable either. No patents for farm animals produced by such conventional breeding methods have been granted by the EPO.

Patenting of the First Mammal in the USA

In 1988, the US Patent Office granted the first patent on a mammal, the Harvard mouse.[1] This genetically modified mouse was not a great success in practice and in economic terms. But since the patent was granted, the effects of patenting living matter have been the subject of controversial debate worldwide. In fact, biological matter was considered patentable a few years earlier in the USA, Europe, and Japan. Until then, however, patents had only been granted for microorganisms or plants. It was only with the granting of a patent for an animal that the fundamental discussion on the patenting of biological material, especially in Europe, was launched. In Canada, the patent was revoked by the highest court because higher life forms could not be considered inventions.

Different Views in the USA, Europe, and Japan[2]

Before 1980, living matter other than plants was not patentable in the USA. With a decision of the US Supreme Court in 1980, this view was thrown overboard and patentability was basically extended to any man-made biological material ("anything under the sun that is made by man"). In the US Patent Act there are no general reservations with regard to public order or morality, as is the case in Europe and Switzerland and to some extent also in Japan. In the USA, therapeutic, diagnostic and surgical procedures on humans are also patentable, which are excluded from patenting in Europe, Switzerland, and Japan. The European Patent Convention defines specific exceptions to biotechnological inventions that are not patentable, such as processes for cloning human beings or the use of human embryos for industrial or commercial purposes. Such specific exceptions are not listed either in the US Patent Act or in the Japanese Patent Act.

---

[1] US 4,736,866 ("Harvard-Maus"/"Oncomouse").
[2] Stiftung Science et Cité (2004).

CRISPR-Cas9 Patent Dispute

CRISPR-associated protein 9 (Cas-9)[3] is an enzyme, which uses CRISPR genetic sequences to cleave DNA (Deoxyribonucleic acid) at specific points. The system comes from a prokaryotic bacteria immune response to nucleic attacks from virii and plasmids. The immune-response mechanism gets the foreign agents to integrate the sequences into their own sequence, and then the Cas-9 enzyme cleaves the subsequent RNA (Ribonucleic acid)—disrupting the virus or plasmid.

This obscure biological mechanism is now at the epicenter of the biggest advance in biotechnology since the advent of PCR DNA amplification because it allows scientists to tailor how and where the CRISPR sequences get inserted into another sequence, and to then cleave it in a precise way.

The Universities in *Berkeley* and *Vienna* filed a patent in 2012 which was where Jennifer Doudna and Emmanuelle Charpentier had worked to discover the application of the naturally occurring biological mechanism. US201261652086P "provides methods of modulating transcription of a target nucleic acid in a target cell, generally involving contacting the target nucleic acid with an enzymatically inactive Cas9 polypeptide and a DNA-targeting RNA. Kits and compositions for carrying out the methods are also provided. The present disclosure provides genetically modified cells that produce Cas9; and Cas9 transgenic non-human multicellular organisms."

A competing team, led by Feng Zhang, at *Massachusetts Institute of Technology (MIT)* filed a similar patent just a few months later. This triggered an interference procedure. The *Berkeley–Vienna* group showed how CRISPR could be used in an in vitro experimental system to alter DNA (Jinek et al. 2012); the *Cambridge group (MIT and Harvard)* showed in US patent No. 8'697'359 about 1 year later how it might be used in eukaryotic cells, of the type found in humans. In contrast the *Berkeley–Vienna group* showed and based their findings on prokaryotic cells, the type found in bacteria—but the patent claims were left vague as to which cell type was meant.

The *Berkeley–Vienna* then triggered an interference at the US patent office claiming their patent covered what the *Cambridge group* had claimed. America at the time, before the "America Invents Act" granted the patent to the first party to invent—and not necessarily the first to file. So, there is a period in which inventors can present evidence as to which party invented it.

Interference Proceeding

At the US Patent and Trademark Office (USPTO), an interference proceeding is conducted by a quasi-judicial panel of administrative patent judges to determine which applicant has a legal claim to the patent:

---

[3]CRISPR = Clustered regularly interspaced short palindromic repeats.

(a) Two or more pending patent applications; or
(b) At least one pending patent application and at least one patent issued within a year of the pending application's filing date.

Appeals are heard by the United States Court of Appeals for the Federal Circuit or the United States District Court for the District of Columbia. ◄

The *Cambridge group* moved to have the interference quashed, arguing that a person of ordinary skill in the art would not have had a reasonable expectation of success in applying the CRISPR-Cas9 system in eukaryotes. For both patents to be upheld, to subject matter must be "patentably distinct." The USPTO panel has a two-way test. They apply this test by asking the questions, "Whether a person of ordinary skill in the art would have been motivated to modify or combine teachings in the prior art, and whether he would have had a reasonable expectation of success"; see In re Stepan Co., 868 F.3d 1342, 1345–46 (Fed. Cir. 2017).

The expert testimony and the panel concluded that the eukaryotic and prokaryotic systems are so distinct that applications in one cell type cannot be directly applied to the other with any certainty. Ironically, one of the lead inventors in the *Berkeley–Vienna group*, Jennifer Doudna, experienced many "frustrations" while getting CRISPR-Cas9 to work in human cells. For these reasons, the United States Court of Appeals for the Federal Circuit held that the Cambridge CRISPR patent was not anticipated by the *Berkeley–Vienna group's* patent.

In this epic battle, the scientific community was in luck because both breakthroughs had been made in publicly funded laboratories. All the universities involved have since then licensed the technology, which has advanced genetic engineering and biotechnology. Had such an advance been discovered and patented by a private lab, a king's ransom could have been charged for the breakthrough, and the story of this amazing technology-propelling medicine and crop science could have been a lot different.

In the latest conflict of the CRISPR important story, one of the European patents (EP 2 771 468) was declared invalid. The reason is legally highly technical. Patents filed abroad depend on a so-called priority document, which is the first patent application for a given invention. EP 2 771 468 cites a US application, US 2012/61736527 P, as its priority document. The priority invention exists as an independent legal right, but the inventor. Article 87(1) of the European patent convention states:

Any person who has duly filed, in or for (a) any State party to the Paris Convention for the Protection of Industrial Property or (b) any Member of the World Trade Organization, an application for a patent, a utility model or a utility certificate, or his successor in title, shall enjoy, for the purpose of filing a European patent application in respect of the same invention, a right of priority during a period of 12 months from the date of filing of the first application.

The EP 2 771 468 cites 12(!) priority documents, but the earliest documents are the essential ones because the novelty of the invention was subsequently destroyed as several researches had made their publications shortly afterward. In these cases, the initial US 2012/61736527 P applicant had to legally transfer the right within that period to the subsequent EP 2 771 468 applicant. This was not done within the time window of that year, legally it meant that the EP 2 771 468 was then void. In any many other cases, this legal technicality might have gone unnoticed—but here there was a lot at stake scientifically and commercially, and thus the patent was challenged at the EPO by nine different opponents. Upon reviewing the case, the Opposition Board at the EPO ruled the patent invalid; the applicants lost their appeal in January 2020. The invention is now free to be used in Europe (see also IPStudies 2019; Ledford 2019; ScienceMag 2017; Sherkow 2015).

Aside from being highly relevant to biotechnology, the presented case is an example of bad patent management—letting such a legal technicality slip through cost millions of dollars in revenue potential. It is also the exact type of arcane detail that might get lost if a company does not have good patent management in place. Moreover, as the value of a patent goes up, it will be subject to more and more legal scrutiny and challenge. This is why it is important for management to strategically weigh the risks and rewards of a given IP right.

Figure 7.1 offers a visual depiction of the frenzy of cross-licensing activity that has taken place round the CRISP technology.

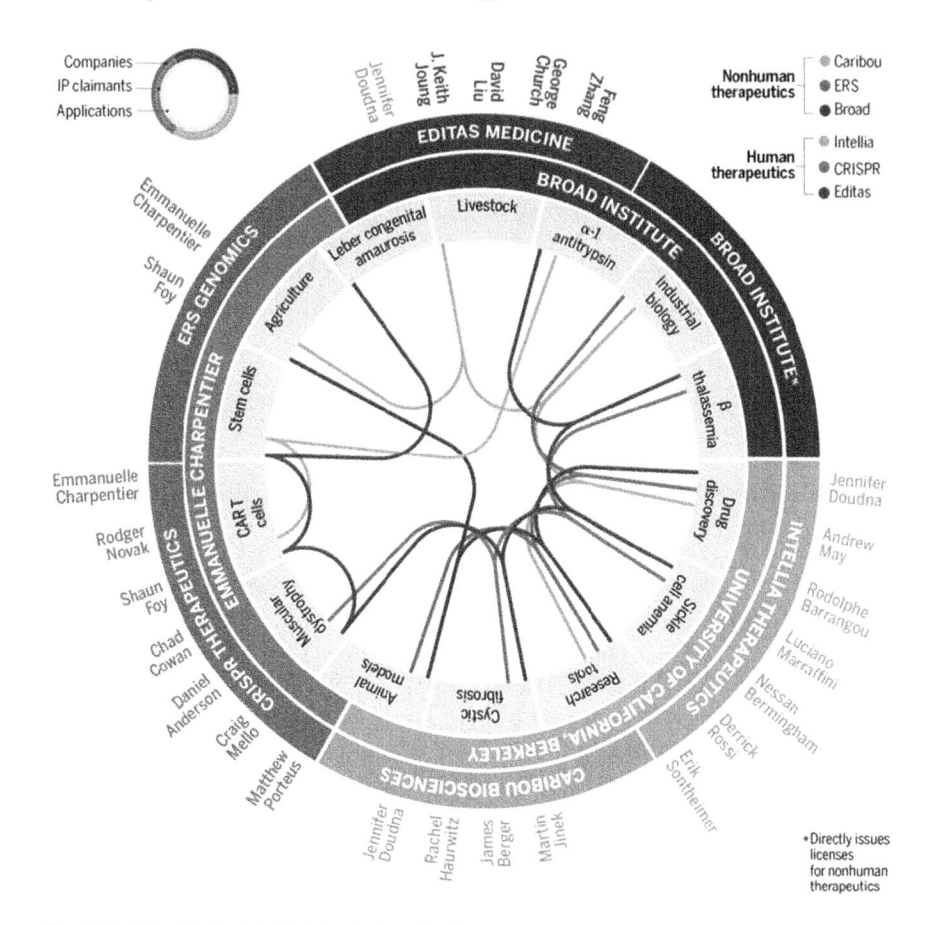

Fig. 7.1 "The Birth of CRISPR" (Cohen 2017)

Take-Aways CRISPR-Cas9

CRISPR/Cas9 promises to be one of the most significant scientific and medical breakthroughs in modern history:

- Its precision and relative ease-of-use have already transformed how scientists study disease and the human genome.
- Use for therapeutic and diagnostic development, plant and animal breeding.
- The concept of using the CRISPR/Cas complex in animal and human cells is expressed in patent (applications) and disputed.

CRISPR IP battle falls mainly into two camps: *UC Berkeley* and the *Broad Institute at Harvard* and *MIT* (see Fig. 7.1).

- Both claimed IP rights to CRISPR technology shortly after its initial discovery in 2012.
- CRISPR technology results in more than 5000 patent families and 140 licensing agreements (IPStudies 2019).
- EP family member was invalidated in 2020 during opposition on the legal technicality of entitlement.

For licensors (patent owners):

- Who is interested in my technology?
- Do I grant a license?
- How do I get paid for a license agreement (e.g., in cryptocurrency)?
- Will I be informed about changes in the IP landscape?
- How can I inform other parties and competitors about my other related projects to avoid double work and future IP problems?

For licensees (researchers, universities, companies):

- Do I need a license?
- Do I get a license?
- How do I pay for a license (e.g., with cryptocurrency)?
- Will I be informed about changes in the IP landscape?
- Is my project anonymized?
- How can I inform other researches about my project to avoid double work and future IP problems?
- How can interested parties contact me to cooperate?

Source: BGW (2019)

7.2 Nanotechnology

Nanotechnology is the field of engineering of matter at the scale of less than 1 ten-millionth of a meter. It is a rapidly growing field and is regarded as one of the key technologies of the twenty-first century. In contrast to other domains, much of the research and development has been financed by state policy. In a Harvard law review done for the WIPO, Lisa Ouellete asserts that nanotechnology belongs to IP's "negative space," i.e., a domain where innovation takes place regardless of intellectual property rather than because of it (Ouellette 2015). Many of the requisite technologies comprise basic research and physics. So, it is an interesting counterpoint to other domains where patents are the primary policy tool and incentive for innovation.

Given the fact that nanotechnology often relies on the discovery of something underlying it that is physical, some legal scholars have begun to question which parts of nanotechnology are actually patentable. Smalley (2014) writes, "The rules articulated in *Prometheus* and Myriad [US Supreme Court cases] may ultimately be applicable to nanotechnology. Compositions of matter that fall into the category of nanotechnology may already exist in nature or be a small-scale version of something that already exists in nature. For example, carbon nanotubes are naturally created in soot, but are the subject of thousands of patents. Further, the usefulness of nanotechnology inventions often comes from the unique properties of matter at the nanoscale, such as increased magnetism, conductivity, reactivity, or reflective ability. The 'product of nature' doctrine, as articulated in *Prometheus* and *Myriad*, may have substantial effects on the patenting of nanotechnology-related inventions because many such inventions involve discovering and harnessing the properties of material at the nanoscale or processes involving the use of nanoscale materials." As a concrete example, physicists Wang et al. (2008) have shown that the quantum tunneling effect can be used to drive an arrangement of carbon atoms to make a nanomotor. Their discovery begs the question of whether this is an invention, law of nature, or discovery, raising a fundamental question about patentability. Moreover, it raises another questions, namely whether a person sufficiently trained in the art would be able to create such a motor since presumably any quantum physicist would/should be able to predict the behavior of such an arrangement of atoms using the quantum and physical equations known to all—as they did using computer modeling. Such legal arguments might be used to attack many active patents in the nanotechnology space.

The role of state-sponsored R&D and legal patentability notwithstanding, numerous experts see nanotechnology as the major growth market after biotechnology. A volume of over 75 billion US dollars is forecast for 2020. Against this background, it is not surprising that nanotechnology-related patent applications are growing at an above-average rate internationally. Korea leads with over 70%, followed by India, Poland, and China, which still show more than 40% growth (OECD 2009). Between 1990 and 2016, there has been a veritable explosion in the number of articles being published on nanotechnology. Among the top applicants are companies such as *IBM, Eastman Kodak, Micron, Hewlett-Packard, Xerox,* and *3M* but also *L'Oréal,*

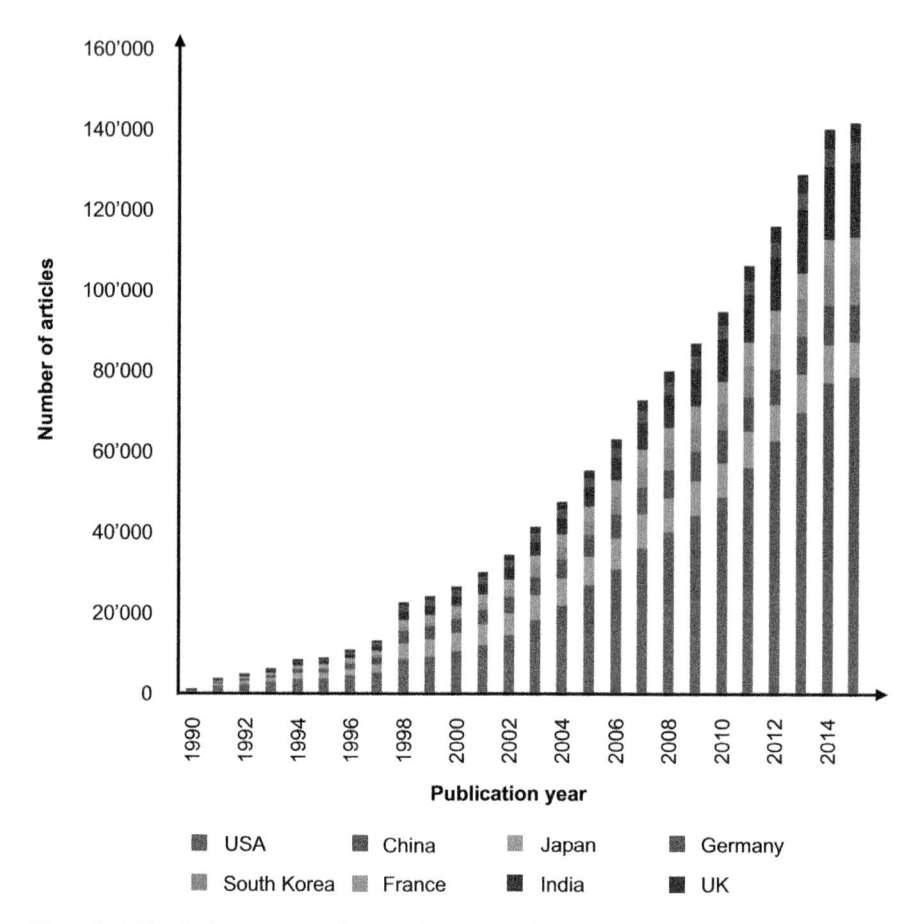

Fig. 7.2 Web of science growth of nanotechnology publications (based on Youtie et al. 2016)

BASF, Samsung as well as the Japan Science and Technology Agency and *Matsushita* (Chen et al. 2008). The search database of the European Patent Office has already classified more than 90,000 patent documents worldwide that can be attributed to nanotechnology.

Figure 7.2 shows the growth in nano-tech publications identified in the Web of Science, a former product of the Intellectual Property and Science business of Thomson Reuters.

As with all new technologies, the patenting process often first had to develop and adapt (Miller et al. 2005; Huebner 2008). One of the central questions regarding the patentability of nanotechnologies was whether already the miniaturization of a device known *per se* can be regarded as something new. As a rule, this is to be denied. If, however, a technical effect is reinforced by miniaturization, the practice of the European Patent Office assumes that the order of magnitude constituted an explicitly chosen path and that the novelty is thereby generally affirmed. If a sub-area of a larger area is selected three criteria must be met to meet the novelty requirement (Kallinger et al. 2008):

- The defined scope/scale must be narrow in comparison to the known range.
- The defined scope must be sufficiently distant from scope/scale which is known from examples known from the state of the art.
- A purely randomly selected subscale is not sufficient; rather, a new technical effect must occur that only occurs in the subscale.

It is also necessary for the inventive step to be substantiated that the specific or additional technical effect produced by the miniaturization is not obvious. Furthermore, it is important that the invention is sufficiently detailed and clearly described by the patent applicant in order to meet the requirements for patentability.

Despite the emerging case law in this field, there are already patent disputes. The US nanotech company *Nanosys*, which was only founded in 2001, filed a patent infringement suit against the British company *Nanoco* at the beginning of 2009, a kind of spin-off from the University of Manchester suit. *Nanosys* claims to have a portfolio of more than 500 patents and patent applications in the field of inorganic high-tech performance nanostructures, including five US patents which *Nanosys* had previously exclusively in-licensed from the *Massachusetts Institute of Technology (MIT)* (Nanosys 2009). The in-licensed patents relate to luminescent quantum dot nanocrystals (based on a CdSe/ZnS core structure) that can be used in various areas, such as flat panel displays. In mid-2009, *Nanosys* and *Nanoco* already compared themselves without compensation payments, but on the condition that *Nanoco* withdraws from the US market with heavy metal-based quantum dot nanocrystals. *Nanoco* patent disputes in the USA were too costly, as it sees its focus on heavy metal-free quantum dot nanocrystals.

Practice of the European Patent Office (EPO)

In the following, excerpts from the EPO are displayed concerning the legal requirements on *nanotechnology patents* (EPO 2013):

> **Basic Requirements for European Patent Applications**
> All European patent applications, including those relating to nanotechnology, have to meet the requirements of the European Patent Convention (EPC). To get your nanotechnology patent granted:
>
> - Invention must be new (the principle of "novelty").
> - It must involve an inventive step.
> - It must be susceptible to industrial application.
>
> Furthermore, the invention must be adequately disclosed and the claims of the application must be clear, concise, and supported by the description.
>
> When trying to determine whether or not your invention is new, it can be useful to look at catalogs and trade journals to see what is already on the market.
>
> However, the single most important source of information for seeing what inventions already exist has to be the vast collection of published patent documents describing the relevant state of the art. A search of the patent literature using, e.g., *Espacenet* will help to give you an indication of whether or not the invention is new (see Sect. 8.5).

1. **Novelty and size**
   For an invention to be regarded as patentable it must be *new*, i.e., there must be no evidence that the same invention has ever been described before.

   With regard to nanotechnology, the question is whether making a known device smaller is in itself novel. Generally speaking, this is not the case. Patent applications directed toward the downscaling of an entity have to meet additional criteria if they are to comply with the requirement of novelty.

   A smaller version of a known device is considered new if it shows the same effect as the bigger one but to a greater extent, such that it is reasonable to assume that the size was selected on purpose.

   In general, if there is a technical effect that is enhanced in a selected subrange, the device is new and not just a part of the prior art.

Example Novelty

In nanotechnology, inventions are often defined by a parametric range. For example, particle A has a diameter in the range of 20–30 nm. What if a particle B of the same material is known and has a diameter of less than 1 μm? At first sight, it seems that particle A is not new because the claimed range of 20–30 nm is already included in particle B's range of less than 1 μm. However, A will be considered as new provided that the selected subrange is—narrow compared with the known range—sufficiently far removed from any specific examples disclosed in the prior art and from the endpoints of the known range—not an arbitrary miniaturization of a known particle. ◄

2. **Inventive step**

To be patentable, an invention must also be the product of an *inventive step*.

Novelty and inventive step are different criteria. Novelty basically exists if there is any difference between the invention and any prior art. The question—"Is there an inventive step?"—only gets raised if there is novelty. The answer to this question is positive if a person who is skilled in the technical field of the invention and familiar with the prior art would not—on his own—have arrived at the solution provided by the invention.

When assessing whether or not a nanotechnology invention involves an inventive step, the key question is often whether the miniaturization of a known device is inventive. Is it just a random selection, or is there a new technical advantage to be had from making it smaller?

If the inventor has simply taken the known prior art and made it smaller, without showing any particular technical advantage to making the invention this particular size, it is not inventive. In other words, there is no inventive step when the mere reduction of dimensions shows no additional or surprising effect and is arrived at arbitrarily.

However, if the invention provides a new technical advantage that was not to be found in the prior art, and it was not an obvious thing for a skilled person with a thorough knowledge of the state of the art to arrive at, then the miniaturization could be considered inventive.

Example Inventive Step

One of the features of an invention relating to a field-effect transistor was that it had an insulating layer with a thickness of 3–18 nm.

When assessing whether this feature involved an inventive step, it was decided that the thickness range for the dielectric film merely followed a trend toward miniaturization in semiconductor devices.

The applicant also failed to demonstrate any particular effects produced by the film having this specific thickness. The thickness in this case was deemed to be an arbitrary selection, and the patent was not granted. ◄

3. **Disclosure**

In many cases, nanotechnology is the product of highly sophisticated preparation methods and tools for manipulating materials in the nanometer or even molecular range. Some of these methods when applied to a highly specific problem go beyond the knowledge of the person of average skill in the field, and even beyond that of experts.

Sufficiency of disclosure, i.e., providing the skilled person with sufficient information as to how the invention is performed, is therefore a very important requirement for nanotechnology applications. The application as filed has to enable the skilled person to carry out the invention over the whole of the (broad) field claimed. To this end, the skilled person needs detailed information about the processes and tools used.

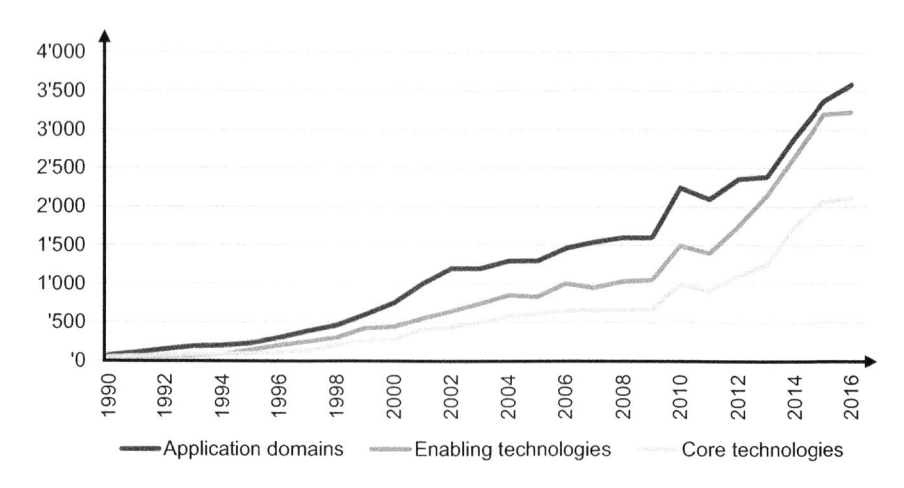

Fig. 7.3 4IR patent applications at the EPO by technology fields (based on EPO 2017b)

Example Disclosure

It is not sufficient to say "nanoelectrodes with a diameter of 5 nm were deposited onto a substrate," since this cannot be done with commonly known methods. The precise conditions for carrying out the method have to be described. ◄

Take Aways Nanotechnology Patent Applications
- Clarity can be a problem in nanotechnology applications, particularly if relative terms or unusual terminology are used. It is important to use terminology that has a well-recognized meaning or to word the application more precisely.
- The application as a whole must disclose the invention in such a way that a person skilled in the art can carry it out.
- Making something smaller does not automatically make it new or inventive. Miniaturization-based inventions should always demonstrate an enhanced technical effect derived from the size.

7.3 Industry 4.0 and Internet of Things

The *Fourth Industrial Revolution* or, in some regions known as *Industry 4.0* or *Industrial IoT (Internet of Things)*, refers to inventions that can be assigned to three broad classes:

- *Core technologies* (hardware, software, and connectivity) that make it possible to transform any object into a smart device connected via the internet

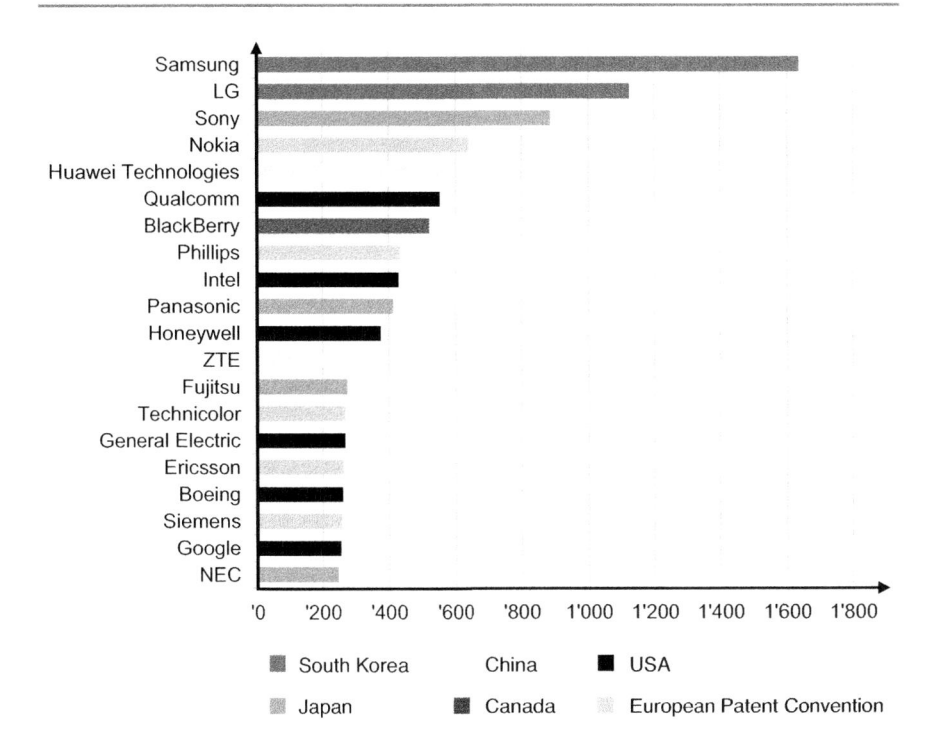

Fig. 7.4 Top 20 Industrial IoT patent applicants at the EPO 2011–2016 (based on EPO 2017b)

- *Enabling technologies* (analytics, security, artificial intelligence, locating, power supply, 3D systems, user interfaces) that are used in combination with connected objects
- *Application domains* (home, personal, enterprise, manufacturing, infrastructure, vehicles) where the potential of connected objects can be exploited.

Industrial IoT Innovation Is Taking Off

More than 5000 patent applications for inventions relating to autonomous objects were filed at the European Patent Office (EPO) in 2016 alone and in the last 3 years, the rate of growth for Industrial IoT patent applications was 54% (see Fig. 7.3), outstripping the 7.65% overall growth of patent applications over the last 3 years. Connectivity and the application domains personal and enterprise have attracted the largest numbers of such patent applications so far, while the fastest-growing fields are 3D systems, artificial intelligence, and user interfaces.

The rise in IoT inventions has been across all three main subsectors (Fig. 3.2). However, the actual number of inventions varies depending on the subsector to the sector. Application domains and core technologies capture a larger share of inventions, with the number of inventions relating to enabling technologies being significantly smaller. In recent years, the number of inventions involving core technologies has been increasing at a faster rate, almost catching up with the application domains.

Top 4IR Applicants Active in Different Industries

Twenty companies, most of them located in Asia, accounted for 42% of all Industrial IoT patent applications filed with the EPO between 2011 and 2016. Innovation in core technologies is mainly led by a limited number of large companies focused on *Information and Communication Technologies (ICT)* (see Sect. 6.9). Inventions in enabling technologies and application domains are less concentrated, and the top applicants in these sectors originate from a larger variety of industries (see Fig. 7.4).

Europe, the USA, and Japan have been the main principle centers of innovation of Industrial IoT technologies since the mid-1990s. Large US, European, and Japanese companies from various sectors comprise the dominant applicants in the IoT enabling technologies. IoT innovation started to later in China and Korea, which is dominated by a few ICT companies. *LG* and *Samsung* control 90% of the IoT applications in Korea; *Huawei* and *ZTE* control 70% of the 4IR patents in China.

In Europe, 4IR innovation tends to cluster in Munich and Paris. France and Germany are the dipoles of 4IR technological development. Germany has been the leader since the late 1990s, and it excels in the fields of manufacturing, vehicles, and infrastructure. The technological profile of France, along with the Benelux, Nordic countries, are specialized more in AI, user interface, 3D processing, and security. *Philips*, *Nokia*, and *Ericsson* are key innovation players in those locations. Some forecast project that developments in the IoT will accelerate the advent of the fourth industrial revolution. If anything, the software and social organization to organize the underlying technology have been developing in these regions and organizations. Technology is outstripping the legal paradigm's ability to cope. For example, it has raised what legal and liability changes will be needed in order to allow for self-driving cars, which are arguably statistically safer than human drivers already, but where culpability and liability have not been clarified legally. Taken one step further, society has to consider legally when software and networked devices might allow each one to be its own economic agent using distributed ledger technology, such as the IOTA protocol from the *IOTA Foundation* (EPO 2017b).

The Fourth Industrial Revolution

The so-called *Fourth Industrial Revolution (4IR)*[4] describes a major technology trend that is being observed across a whole range of technical fields. This trend is primarily driven by the emergence of the *Internet of Things (IoT)* or *Industrial IoT* (which is close to the Industry 4.0 concept). It also encompasses a number of other technologies, such as cloud computing and artificial intelligence, technologies that make it possible to fully exploit the potential of smart connected objects in nearly all sectors of the economy.

The term "industrial revolution" reflects the pervasiveness and the disruptive potential of the latest technological developments. While previous industrial revolutions have led to the increasing automation of repetitive physical work, 4IR goes much further: it leads to the large-scale automation of whole groups of tasks, including repetitive intellectual tasks previously performed by human beings. 4IR can significantly enhance the efficiency and flexibility of production processes and augment the value of products and services (MGI 2015). The transition toward "smart" factories operating autonomously has already been recognized as an important challenge by industry and policy-makers in Europe[5] and beyond. Likewise, the deployment of connected objects in transport (autonomous vehicles), energy (smart grids), cities, healthcare, and agriculture profoundly changes to the way these sectors are organized.

Like previous industrial revolutions, 4IR raises major economic and social issues (OECD 2017). Increasing the automation of routine intellectual tasks changes the nature of human work, and hence the balance of the labor market. It obliges companies to rethink their business models and to adapt to new forms of competition. Besides investing in the training of the 4IR workforce, policy-makers face the challenge of supporting and regulating new digital infrastructures and of creating appropriate legal frameworks to safeguard competition, cybersecurity, and consumer rights in the digital age.

Source: Definition extracted from EPO (2017b)

---

[4]Fourth Industrial Revolution is the term used by Klaus Schwab, founder and Executive Chairman of the World Economic Forum, in his recent book on this subject (Schwab 2017).

[5]See, e.g., "Industry 4.0" (Germany), "Nouvelle France Industrielle" (France), "Fabricca Intelligente" (Italy), "Industria Conectada 4.0" (Spain), "Made Different" (Belgium), "Prumysl 4.0" (Czech Republic), "Smart Industry" (Slovakia), "Production 2014" (Sweden), "MADE" (Denmark), "Produktion der Zukunft" (Austria), and "Smart Industry" (The Netherlands).

7.4 Software and Business Methods

Ninety percent of developments since the beginning of this century have been software-related (EPO 2007). So-called computer-implemented inventions have become omnipresent and can be found in almost all technical fields. This is also reflected in patent applications. The inventive share is increasingly based on software-based developments.

The development of software goes back to the 1960s (Boehm 1976). In the past, software development was mainly focused on mainframe and minicomputer computing, whereas today a distinction is already made between software development for personal, pervasive, and embedded computing. Whereas in the past the legal protection of software was mainly covered by copyright in practice, numerous companies now also strive to protect software innovations by means of patents (see Table 7.2). It is interesting to note that the *SAP* software group did not start setting up its own patent department until 1998 and only held four software-related patents in May of 2001. The reason for establishing the patent department was the growing international competition in which patents played an increasingly important role.

The trigger for the "software patent boom" was a groundbreaking court decision, which in 1992 led to the so-called *Freeman–Walter–Abele Test*, which enabled the patenting of algorithms applied in practice and thus of software in the USA. In 1998, this test was replaced by the so-called *State Street Bank* court decision in the USA, which was affirmed in 1999. Mathematical algorithms thus became patentable if the invention led to a concrete and tangible result. This heralded the start of the business method patents era in the USA. As a result, the number of patent applications and granted patents in the software sector skyrocketed internationally at the turn of the millennium (Hall and MacGarvie 2010) to such an extent that there was increasing public criticism of patentability in this sector (Coriat and Orsi 2002). One of the most (in)famous patents was *Amazon*'s so-called *"1-Click"* patent, which concerns a technology that makes it possible to make online purchases with a mouse click. *Amazon*'s patent was granted in the USA in 1999 and was confirmed with some limitations after a reexamination procedure by the US Patent and Trademark Office (USPTO) in March 2010. In Europe, however, the application from the same patent family was not granted by the European Patent Office. While the procedural practice of the European Patent Office in the field of computer-implemented inventions has

Table 7.2 Four types of protection for software (table compiled by authors)

Results of software development	Right
Documentation Screen appearance Code	Copyright/Design Patents/Trade Dress
Processes Algorithms	Patents
Branding	Trademarks

largely consolidated after some confusion in the mid-1990s. The practice was again confirmed by the Enlarged Board of Appeal of the European Patent Office in mid-2010.

The emerging patenting numbers gained considerable relevance in the software industry after the first patent infringement suits. Initially, mainly large companies were affected that generate large sales volumes and profits with a few product variants, such as *Apple*, *eBay*, *Google*, *Microsoft*, *SAP*, and *Oracle*. The Internet auction house *eBay* had to pay US $29.5 million in damages to *MercExchange* in 2003 after a patent infringement lawsuit, as *MercExchange's* patented proprietary auction technology also covered *eBay's* "buy now" feature. The damages were 30% of *eBay's* goodwill at the time. At the end of 2009, the Walldorf-based software group *SAP* was ordered to pay nearly US $140 million in damages to US competitor *Versata* following 2 years of patent infringement proceedings.

In addition to this, it is becoming increasingly clear that software, as a cross-sectional technology, has become a central factor in the convergence of technologies: The Taiwanese smartphone manufacturer *HTC* acquired a license from *Microsoft* after *Microsoft* accused the *Android* operating system, which now belongs to *Google*, of infringing several patents in areas of the user interface and the underlying system. The license agreement between *Microsoft* and *HTC* was concluded against the background that both companies' main competitor *Apple* had also sued *HTC* for infringing the *Linux*-based open-source operating system *Android* from *Google* out of 20 patents at the beginning of 2010. So even users of open-source software are not immune to patent infringement allegations. *Microsoft* in particular accused *Linux* that its operating system core infringes more than 230 of its patents and has already entered into license agreements with *Apple*, *Hewlett Packard*, *Novell*, and *Amazon*. In the latter case, *Microsoft* also received licenses to *Amazon* patents in return, which gave the software group easier access to the tablet computer market. This includes e-bookstore solutions that *Amazon*, among others, has at its disposal.

Computer-Implemented Inventions (CII) at the European Patent Office (EPO)

Computer-implemented inventions are treated differently by patent offices in different regions of the world (see Table 7.3). In Europe, Article 52 of the European Patent Convention (EPC) excludes computer programs "as such" from patent protection. This exclusion does not mean that all inventions involving software are excluded from patenting; what it does mean is that tighter scrutiny of the technical character of these inventions is required.

Over the years, the case law of the EPO boards of appeal has clarified the implications of Article 52 EPC, establishing a stable and predictable framework for the patentability of computer-implemented inventions.

Like all other inventions, in order to be patentable, computer-implemented inventions must meet the fundamental legal requirements of novelty, inventive step and industrial application. In addition, it must be established that they have a technical character that distinguishes them from computer programs "as such." In other words, they must solve a technical problem in a novel and non-obvious manner.

The normal physical effects of the execution of a program, e.g., electrical currents, are not in themselves sufficient to lend a computer program technical character, and a further technical effect is needed. The further technical effect may result, for example, from the control of an industrial process or the working of a piece of machinery, or from the internal functioning of the computer itself (e.g., memory organization, program execution control) under the influence of the computer program.

The EPC thus enables the EPO to grant patents for inventions in many fields of technology in which computer programs make a technical contribution. Such fields include medical devices, the automotive sector, aerospace, industrial control, communication/media technology, including automated natural language translation, voice recognition, and video compression, and also the computer/processor itself.

Source: Extract from EPO (2017b)

Table 7.3 Comparison of the term "invention" at EPO/CNPO/JPO (EPO and JPO 2018; EPO and CNIPA 2019)

European Patent Office (EPO)
Under Article 52(2) and (3) EPC, the following are not regarded as "inventions" if claimed as such: • Discoveries, scientific theories, and mathematical methods • Esthetic creations • Schemes, rules, and methods for performing mental acts, playing games, or doing business, and programs for computers • Presentations of information
Japan Patent Office (JPO)

The following are subject matters not corresponding to statutory "inventions" described in JPGL, Part III, Chap. 1, 2.1:
• A law of nature as such
• Mere discoveries and not creations
• Those contrary to a law of nature
• Those in which a law of nature is not utilized, e.g.,
   (i) Any laws other than a law of nature (e.g., economic laws)
   (ii) Arbitrary arrangements (e.g., a rule for playing a game as such)
   (iii) Mathematical formula
   (iv) Mental activities of humans, or
   (v) Those utilizing only (i) to
   (vi) (e.g., methods for doing business as such)
• Those not regarded as technical ideas, e.g., personal skill, mere presentation of information or mere aesthetic creations
• Those for which it is clearly impossible to solve the problem to be solved by any means presented in a claim

China National Intellectual Property Administration (CNIPA)
Under Article 25.1 Chinese Patent Law, patent rights shall not be granted for any of the following: • Scientific discoveries • Rules and methods for mental activities • Methods for the diagnosis or treatment of diseases • Animal or plant varieties • Substances obtained by means of nuclear transformation; and designs that are mainly used for marking the pattern, color, or the combination of the two of prints

Practice of the European Patent Office (EPO)

In the following excerpts from the EPO are displayed on *computer-implemented inventions (CII)* and so-called *software patents* (EPO 2019):

The term "software" is considered to be ambiguous, because it may refer to a program listing written in a programming language to implement an algorithm, but also to binary code loaded in a computer-based apparatus, and it may also encompass the accompanying documentation. So, in place of this ambiguous term the concept of a computer-implemented invention has been introduced.

A computer-implemented invention is one which involves the use of a computer, computer network, or other programmable apparatus, where one or more features are realized wholly or partly by means of a computer program.

Under the European Patent Convention (EPC), a computer program claimed "as such" is not a patentable invention (Article 52(2)(c) and (3) EPC). Patents are not granted merely for program listings. Program listings as such are protected by copyright. For a patent to be granted for a computer-implemented invention, a technical problem has to be solved in a novel and non-obvious manner (see Table 7.3).

The starting point for assessing the patentability of computer-implemented inventions is the fundamental provision that a patent should be granted for any invention, in any field of technology, provided that it is new, involves an inventive step, is susceptible of industrial application and is not expressly excluded from patent protection (Article 52 EPC).

Patent Protection for Technical Creations
Whilst the EPC sets out the patentability requirements of novelty, inventive step, and industrial application in some detail (Articles 54, 56 and 57 EPC), it does not contain a legal definition of the term "invention." It has, however, been part of the European legal tradition since the early days of the patent system that patent protection should be reserved for technical creations. The subject matter for which protection is sought must, therefore, have a "technical character" or, to be more precise, involve a "technical teaching," i.e., instruction, addressed to a technically skilled person as to how to solve a particular technical problem using particular technical means. The problem solved by the invention must thus be technical, in contrast for example to a purely financial, commercial, or mathematical one. This must be satisfied in order for the invention not to be excluded from patentability (see Fig. 7.5).

Although the law does not define the term "invention," it does contain a list of subject matter or activities that are not to be regarded as "inventions." Among the particular examples mentioned in this list are "programs for computers." It should be emphasized that the subject matter or activities on the list are excluded only if the European patent application or patent relates to them "as such." Therefore, inventions having a technical character that are or may be implemented by a computer program are not excluded from patentability.

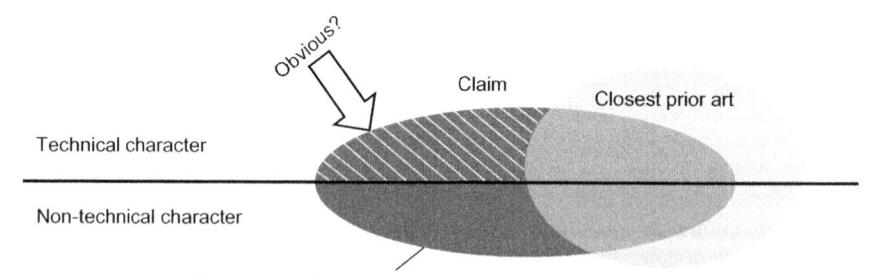

Fig. 7.5 How the inventive step for mixed inventions is assessed at the EPO (based on EPO and CNIPA 2019)

7.4 Software and Business Methods

The Case Law of the Boards of Appeal
In the field of computer-implemented inventions, many decisions have developed the interpretation of the EPC provisions relating to the term "invention," providing guidance on what is patentable and what is not.

EPO case law says that controlling or carrying out a technical process is not excluded from patentability, irrespective of whether it is implemented by hardware or by software. Whether the process is carried out by means of special circuits or by means of a computer program has been found to depend on economic and technological factors; patentability should not be denied on the grounds that a computer program is involved.

A specific claim form for the protection of computer-implemented inventions is the "computer program/computer program product." It was introduced in order to provide better legal protection for computer programs distributed on a data carrier and not forming part of a computerized system. This claim form should not be confused with the term "computer program" as a list of instructions. Subject matter claimed under this form is not excluded from patentability if the computer program resulting from the implementation of the corresponding method is capable of bringing about, when running on a computer or loaded into a computer, a "further technical effect" going beyond the "normal" physical interactions between the computer program and the computer hardware on which it is run.

The normal physical effects of the execution of a program, e.g., electrical currents, are not in themselves sufficient to lend a computer program technical character, and a further technical effect is needed. The further technical effect may result for example from the control of an industrial process or the working of a piece of machinery, but also from the internal functioning of the computer itself (e.g., memory organization, program execution control) under the influence of the computer program.

For instance, a method of encoding audio information in a communication system may aim to reduce distortion induced by channel noise. Although the idea underlying such a method may be considered to reside in a mathematical method, the encoding method as a whole is not a mathematical method "as such," and hence is not excluded from patentability by Article 52(2)(a) and (3) EPC. Similarly, a method of encrypting/decrypting or signing electronic communications may be regarded as a technical method, even if it is essentially based on a mathematical method.

On the other hand, "schemes, rules and methods for (...) doing business" are not patentable; but a new method which solves a technical, rather than a purely administrative, problem may indeed be patentable.

Patents for Computer-Implemented Inventions
Patents for CII may comprise claims to computers, computer networks, or other programmable apparatus, whereby at least one feature is realized by means of a computer program. If the invention concerns software which can be loaded into memory, transmitted over a network, or distributed on a data carrier, a claim to a "computer program" or "computer program product" may also be present in addition

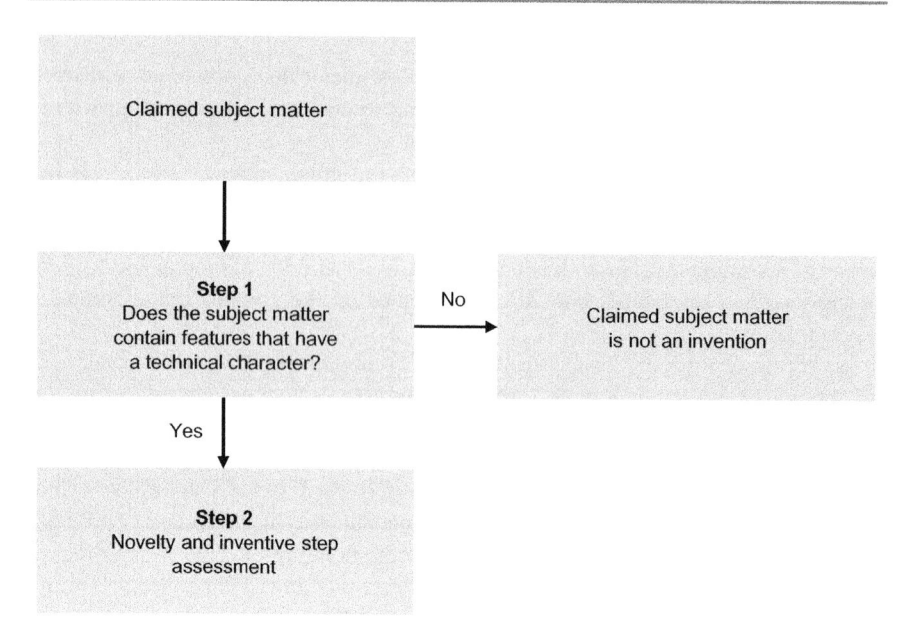

Fig. 7.6 The two-step approach for assessment of CII applications at the EPO (based on EPO and CNIPA 2019)

to a computer-implemented method. However, in such inventions, although different claim structures are possible, the set of claims usually starts with a method claim, defining the steps performed by a computer, or other data processing means capable of running software, to achieve the desired technical effect (see Fig. 7.6).

A common type of CII patent relates to subject matter where all the method steps can be fully carried out by computer program instructions running on, e.g., a personal computer, the processors in a smartphone or printer, etc. Other types of CII patents concern inventions where some method steps are performed outside a computer, and require specific technical means, such as a sensor. For example, in a method for automatically braking in a self-driving vehicle, sensors measure the distance to the vehicle in front, and the signals received and produced by the sensors are used to control the braking process. Physical devices like sensors provide inputs and outputs for the invention, but the decisions as to how the devices operate are taken by a computer according to parameters and instructions, i.e., software. Any patent for such an invention would protect the combination of devices and computers carrying out the novel method.

Whereas mechanical inventions are represented with technical drawings in patents, for CII the patent will often feature a flow diagram for the method, showing the decision steps in the process, and any interactions with devices and external inputs and outputs.

Patentability of Business Methods in the USA

In 1997, the two applicants, Bernard L. Bilski and Rand A. Warsaw, applied in the USA for patent protection for a business method relating to a method of hedging risks in commodities trading. After the patent application had been rejected twice, first by the Board of Patent Appeals and Interferences, and by then the United States Court of Appeals for the Federal Circuit (CAFC), the U.S. Supreme Court took up the issue of patentability of business method claims, which in particular also include business methods and software. The Supreme Court upheld the lower court's ruling that "concrete and tangible result" test is not necessarily a sufficient test of business method patentability. The so-called "machine-or-transformation" test introduced by the CAFC was not confirmed by the U.S. Supreme Court as the only test for patentability, but only as a "useful tool for investigation."

Until the *Bilski*, patentability of business methods was based on the *State Street Bank* decision (delivered by the CAFC), where implemented procedures were patentable if they led to an applicable, concrete, and tangible result. As a result, a large number of patents on pure business methods were granted in the USA. With *State Street Bank*, the CAFC now questioned not only these earlier criteria in general but also the Freeman–Walter–Abele Test (delivered by the Court of Customs and Patent Appeals, a predecessor of the CAFC), which had been previously applied to software patents to examine the patentability of mathematical principles and algorithms.[6]

The legal validity of patents of business methods and software-based processes was therefore no longer questioned in principle in the USA—but then came the so-called *Alice* decision that changed everything again.

---

[6]Source: In re Bernard L. Bilski and Rand A. Warsawk, 545 F.3d 943, 88 U.S.P.Q.2d 1385, Mayo v. Prometheus and Funk Bros. Seed Co. v. Kalo Inoculant Co.

The Alice Case—2014

Several years later, in *Alice v. CLS Bank*, the Supreme Court readdressed the patent-eligibility of a business method. It held patent ineligible a method of securing intermediated settlement—a form of electronic escrow. In invalidating *Alice's* patent, the Court announced a two-step test based on the Court's earlier decisions in *Mayo v. Prometheus* and *Funk Bros. Seed Co. v. Kalo Inoculant Co.* This test first determines whether the claimed invention is directed to an abstract idea, law of nature, mathematical formula, or similar abstraction. If it is, the court is to proceed to the second step—determining whether the way the claimed invention implements the abstraction contains an inventive concept, as contrasted with being routine and conventional. Under the Alice test, the claimed invention is patent-eligible only if it contains an inventive concept.

The US Patent and Trademark Office (USPTO) business method examining work groups responded quickly to the Alice decision. Allowances per month for patents related to finance dropped to 10% of their pre-Alice value. The Patent Trial and Appeal Board has reacted in a similar manner. Only about 20% of the appealed business method rejections by patent examiners are getting reversed by the board (see Fig. 7.7). ◀

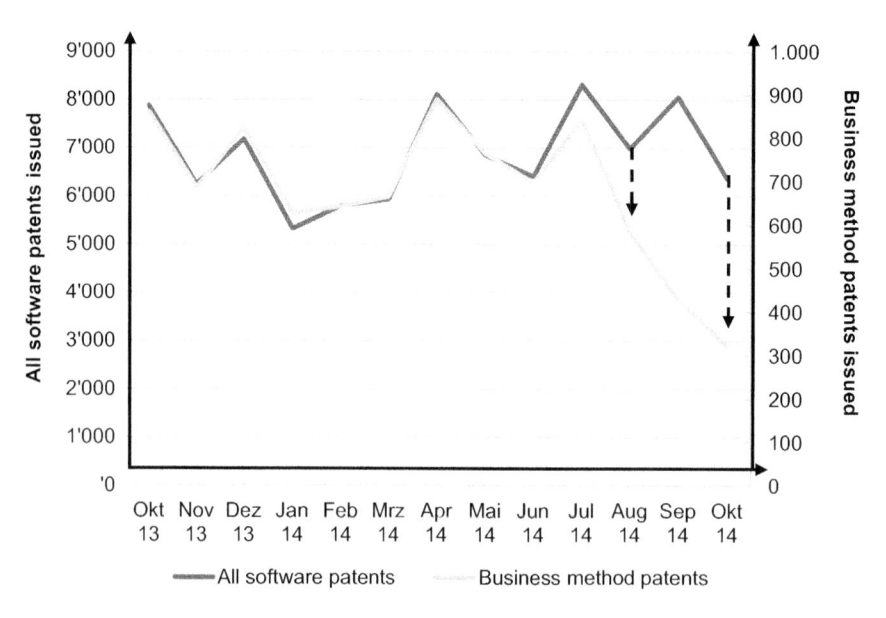

Fig. 7.7 Drop of business method related patents after the Alice decision compared to software (based on Stellbrink 2016)

7.5 Artificial Intelligence-Based Business Models

Formal and informal Intellectual Property (IP) protection strategies also play a big role in Artificial Intelligence (AI)-based business models, taking into account the challenges given by an open innovation approach. Existing literature already distinguishes between formal and informal protection strategies and has tried to understand their influence on value capture for different business models. However, their application to the new field of AI is still a white spot. Therefore, this research aims at how formal and informal protection strategies can be applied in the field of AI-based business models, taking into account an open innovation environment that is relevant and current practice in AI-based innovation regimes. The managerial implications also cover how to balance open and proprietary innovation with a focus on entrepreneurship and start-up environments. Methodology: qualitative research based on own empirical resources and analysis of empirical reports (see for this chapter also Bader and Stummeyer 2019).

Protecting that kind of intellectual property has become a relevant aspect depending on which business model is being operated and which elements of the value creation should be protected to gain high-value creation leverage. In a recent study based on an evaluation of different business model types, it could be emphasized that different business models need different optimization and complementation of formal and informal IP protection strategies (Bonakdar et al. 2017).

Challenge to Apply Formal IP Strategies to AI

Applying formal IP strategies to AI-based innovations faces a challenge when it comes to patenting AI-based inventions. The two main reasons are that, on the one hand, algorithms play a major role when designing AI concepts; as algorithms "as such" are seen as mathematical methods, they are per se excluded from patentability under the main patent legislation regimes. On the other hand, AI concepts are often directed at automating or conducting tasks and activities that are currently performed by the human mind—another reason for patent-ineligibility; either for being just considered as a theoretical concept or due to lack of novelty.

However, many of the current AI-based inventions are based and implemented as software. As is the case in other fast-developing technical growth sectors. For example, more than 80% of the value added in the ICT sector is based on software and related services (OECD 2017). So, patent legislation and practices relating to this have been built up during the last decades having to do with how to deal with software-based inventions:

In Europe, under the European Patent Convention AI as a mathematical method per definition is excluded from patentability when claimed as such. However, if a method involves technical means (e.g., a computer) or a device, its subject matter may have a technical character when seen as a whole and for that reason is not excluded from patentability (so-called computer-implemented inventions, CII): "The element in the technology which is new and inventive is actually a changed computerized algorithm or control mechanism which is responsible for bringing about an improved technical effect" (EPO 2013, 2017a, b, see also Glossary for CII). When assessing patentability, the European Patent Office (EPO) applies the so-called two-hurdle approach for "mixed-type inventions" and checks whether "the AI method (steps) contributes to the technical character of the invention?" (EPO 2018a). In this context the EPO also recently updated their Guidelines for Examination with a specific section on "Artificial intelligence and machine learning," providing guidance on the assessment of whether an invention on AI and machine learning is based on the necessary "technical character" to be patentable and would feature examples relating to AI as well as detailed information on the technicality of CII based on decisions by the EPO's boards of appeal (EPO 2018b).

The US patent-eligibility so far presents a challenge, too, but due to a different legal philosophy. This is because, in the USA, abstract ideas are not considered patentable. Furthermore, the mere use of a computer to implement an abstract idea is not sufficient to gain patent-eligibility (EPO 2018a).

As the law firm Baker McKenzie elaborates (Flaim and Chae 2019): In the USA, the biggest legal hurdle to obtaining a patent on an AI invention is arguably 35 United States Code (U.S.C.) §101, which limits patent-eligible subject matter to a "process, machine, manufacture, or composition of matter," and is interpreted by the courts as excluding abstract ideas, laws of nature and natural phenomena. The standard on this patent subject matter eligibility requirement became more stringent for software and "computer-implemented" inventions with the U.S. Supreme Court's 2014 decision in *Alice Corporation vs. CLS Bank International*, which employed an intensified two-step test:

1. Determining whether the invention is directed to a patent-ineligible concept, such as an abstract idea; and if so
2. Determining whether the claimed elements provide any "inventive concept" that would transform the abstract idea into a "patent-eligible application."

The Alice Court held that the patent claims on "intermediated settlement" are directed at an abstract idea lacking any inventive concept because each of their elements is a "well-understood, routine, conventional" activity, unable to do more than "require a generic computer to perform generic computer functions." Lower court decisions, such as *DDR Holdings, LLC vs. Hotels.com, LP, Enfish, LLC vs. Microsoft Corp., BASCOM Global Internet Services, Inc. vs. AT&T Mobility LLC*, and *Berkheimer vs. HP Inc.*, among others, provide meaningful insights into the application of Alice's two-step test, and the United States Patent and Trademark Office's guidelines, particularly the "2019 Revised Patent Subject Matter Eligibility Guidance," which can bring further clarity on subject matter eligibility (USPTO 2019).

"Abstract idea" in U.S. jurisprudence: courts' invalidations of patent claims for covering subject matter that could be performed through an "ordinary mental process" "in the human mind" or by "a human using a pen and paper" under the *Alice Corporation vs. CLS Bank International* test. This puts a strain on patenting AI inventions because the goal of AI is often to automate or better perform human tasks and activities.

Other jurisdictions have different standards on subject matter eligibility, as discussed in the USPTO's "Patent-Eligible Subject Matter: Report on Views and Recommendations from the Public," issued in July 2017:

- In Japan, a software invention is patentable if its information-processing aspects are required to be "specifically implemented by using hardware resources." Many view software inventions as being patent-eligible, as long as their claimed inventive steps are expressly tied to hardware.
- In China, according to the examination guidelines revised in April 2017, "the computer program-related invention" that has "technical characteristics will not be excluded from patentability." This revision is viewed by many as a broadening of the scope of patent-eligible subject matter.
- The Korean Intellectual Property Office's guidelines state that computer programs per se are not patent-eligible, but they also "indicate that if computer software is claimed in conjunction with hardware, then the combination, the operating method of the combination, and a computer-readable medium containing the software that implicates the combination is patent eligible." The Republic of Korea recently introduced an accelerated examination for patent applications pertaining to AI and other specified emerging technology fields.

Generally speaking, software inventions can be patented in these non-U.S. offices if they are implemented with or sufficiently tied to hardware. Thus, some believe that the patent subject matter eligibility standard outside the USA might be less stringent than the Alice framework, although others believe that the recent developments indicate a convergence of the Alice framework, particularly with respect to its second prong, and the European practice.

Status Quo in Patenting AI-Related Innovations

As already indicated, AI-related innovations are often based on software and computer-implemented inventions, respectively. They might be directed to one or more specific AI application fields. Based on earlier and current legislation, various companies and research organizations have started filing patents also in the field of AI. As displayed in Fig. 7.8 (AI related patent families and scientific publications by earliest publication year), nearly 340,000 patent families[7] have been filed and

---

[7]The terms "patent family," "patent application," "patent filing," or "invention" may be used interchangeably, referring to the representative patent family member and the corresponding invention. A patent family may include members for which patents have been granted, others not granted or still under patent examination. A patent family includes all those patents in different offices that relate to the same or similar technical content. The earliest application in the family has what is known as the priority number, and other applications in the family share one or more pieces

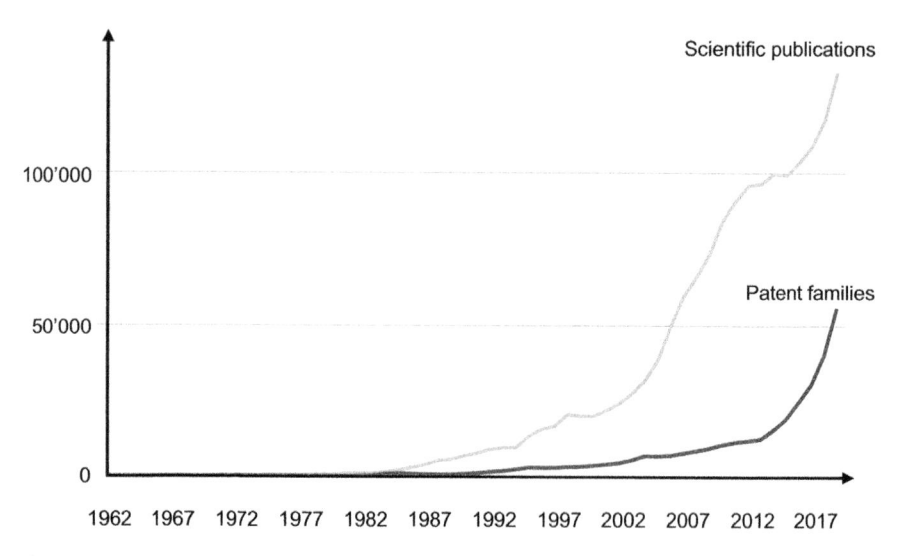

Fig. 7.8 AI patent families/scientific publications by the earliest publication year (based on WIPO 2019)

published since the 1960s. One can also see that AI has become a major field in science with a total of more than 1.5 million papers published up to mid-2018. While the number of scientific publications increased significantly by the beginning of the 2000s (with an average annual growth rate almost doubling to 18% between 2002 and 2007), it took another 10 years for the patent publications to lift-off (with an average annual growth rate of 28% between 2012 and 2017). A reasonable interpretation is that basic research primarily results first in scientific publications, while development efforts with regard to industrial applications take some time and result in patent publications.

Patent applications directed to specific application fields have been emerging since the mid-1990s (see Fig. 7.9).[8] The application fields for which patent protection is mainly sought are transportation and telecommunications. Please note that AI-related inventions are regularly directed to several application fields.

IP Protection Strategies for AI-Based Business Models

Current AI research and innovation is based on large monetary investments. Just the European Union alone wants to increase the overall investments (public and private

---

of priority data for the purposes of novelty and inventive step. There are different definitions of patent families; for the displayed data and charts patent families are used that are grouping together the same invention sharing the exact priority data seeking patent protection in different jurisdictions (WIPO 2019).

[8]Note: A patent may refer to more than one category.

7.5 Artificial Intelligence-Based Business Models

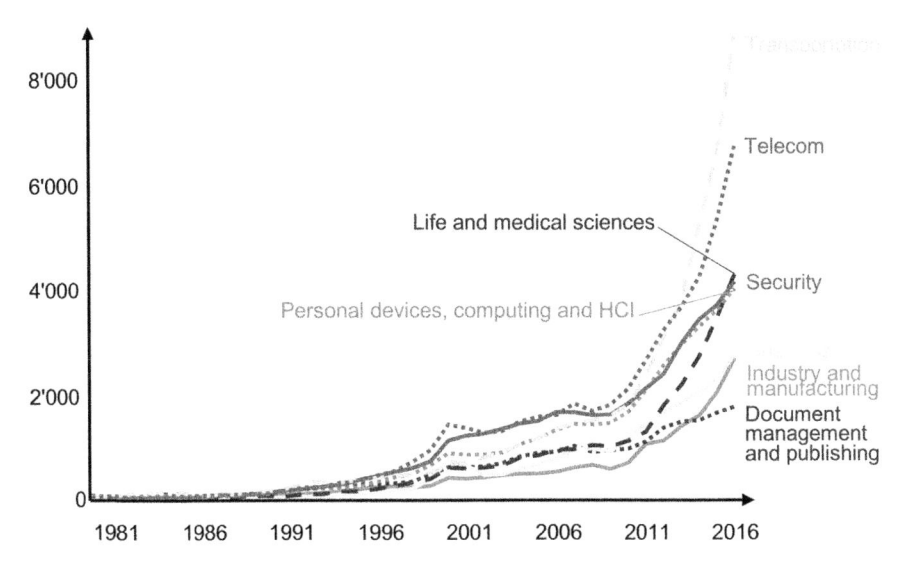

Fig. 7.9 Patent families for application field categories by earliest priority year (based on WIPO 2019)

sectors) within the EU region in AI to at least 20 billion euros per year beyond 2020 (European Commission 2018).

According to WIPO data, almost 3000 companies active in AI have received funding (almost half of all AI active companies), representing about US $46 billion in funding. Also, M&A has become a means of acquiring AI-based technologies, data access, and related patent portfolios. Almost 500 companies have been acquired, with more than half of them since 2016. This represents a great exit and co-funding environment for start-ups. Given the high investments in AI technologies and their applications, it is obvious that companies and investors are attempting to protect and monetarize their investments. While over 1.6 million publicly available scientific publications have emerged out of research, 340,000 AI-related inventions have been claimed for patent protection since artificial intelligence emerged in the 1050s. Enforcing patents has also made inroads into the field of AI, with thousands of AI-related patent families being mentioned in litigation cases (WIPO 2019).

Also, in the field of AI IP protection, mechanisms are used and enforced to secure and to monetarize investments. Below, some of the applied key protection strategies for formal and informal AI-related IP are presented:

1. Protectability of AI-based inventions and innovations with *formal IP* means:
   (a) *AI algorithms → Patents:* There are typically three types of AI-related inventions (EPO 2018a) that are eligible for patent protection (provided that the general legal requirements for patentability of software can be met, e.g., the two-hurdle approach to testing the technical character of the invention before the EPO in Europe or the passing of the *Alice Corporation vs. CLS Bank International* test in the US):

Core AI, including the challenge that algorithms as such, may not be patentable (e.g., if not implemented in an applied field and are then consequently considered as non-patent-eligible mathematical methods).

Trained models/machine learning, including the challenge to claim variations and ranges.

AI as a tool in an applied field, defined via technical effects.

(b) *AI code → Copyright:*

AI software program code is generally considered as non-patent-eligible subject matter but is eligible for copyright protection.

2. Protectability of AI-based inventions and innovations with *informal IP* means:

(a) *AI data → Trade secrets:*

Datasets (e.g., categorized training data for supervised learning may be classified and kept secret)

Data protection rules (e.g., the General Data Protection Regulation (GDPR) in the European Union, which may limit the exchange of or access to data)

In contrast to the above-mentioned IP protection strategies that aim to gain differentiation by gaining exclusivity, there is a second applied approach that is based on a standardization by access from and to the public domain. In the recent models of innovation management, both approaches have been practiced by innovation champions parallel to optimizing innovation speed and getting access to standards, while still monetarizing their own R&D investments (Bader 2007; Gassmann and Bader 2017).

However, when developing AI techniques there are two major challenges: (a) to develop the AI systems and algorithms from a technical point-of-view; and (b) to have access to qualified datasets (e.g., to optimize the AI algorithms or to train the AI systems). Access to datasets is already considered as a major competitive advantage between legal systems (e.g., China compared to the USA), but also for investors that invest in start-ups: which dataset is available? How much of the investment needs to first get burned for qualifying raw data? For public research organizations, it might be even more difficult to get data access due to limited financial budgets or data protection rules (e.g., in the field of life sciences).

Within the public domain, there might be open access to algorithms and software code (e.g., TensorFlow and scikit-learn, which are available on the collaborative developer platform GitHub) (Stone et al. 2016), but also to datasets (e.g., for training purposes). Furthermore, public research organizations might dedicate their outcomes to the public domain (e.g., for fundamental research, like *MIT-IBM Watson AI Lab*, US $240 million funding in 2017, or due to a philanthropic approach, like *MILA*, US $3.4 million funding from *Alphabet/Google* in 2016).

For entrepreneurial companies it is, therefore, a comparative advantage when researching and/or innovating in the field of AI to practice both: standardization in the open-source public domain (e.g., to speed up development or to centrally collect and enlarge datasets), and (!) differentiation by exclusivity applying formal and informal IP protection strategies to capture value (e.g., to leverage competitive advantages or to get access to VC investments).

Managerial Implications

AI has emerged not as a single technology mantra but rather as multiple sets of techniques, e.g., machine learning or deep learning based on multi-layered neuronal networks being specifically used within certain application fields, e.g., for speech processing, computer vision, or robotics.

Although basic research is still ongoing and scientific publications have significantly increased since the 2000s, industry-sector-specific and cross-industry AI applications have become increasingly common since 2012, as patent application numbers clearly suggest. AI is increasingly being used and applied in business models, ranging from weak AI and narrow AI for limited tasks to strong AI in the (potentially near) future.

There has been various research and practical evidence that complementary formal and informal protection strategies are necessary for effective value capture in business model innovation. For AI-based business models, especially formal IP protection means [patents (e.g., for applied AI algorithms), copyrights (e.g., for AI code)] and informal IP protection [trade secrets (e.g., for AI datasets)] play a significant role. As the current systems primarily clarify how AI can be patented as being considered as software, applying AI algorithms, it is still up to legislation and professionals to tackle the remaining legal, practical, and ethical challenges, especially when it comes to patent protecting AI-based methods and systems.

From an innovator's point-of-view, the main challenge is how to balance public commons (e.g., getting access to specific datasets and/or specific AI algorithms), while the innovators' basic question is how and where to capture value/comparative differentiation (e.g., to monetarize the ownership/access to specific datasets). Figure 7.10 summarizes integrates our findings from R&D cooperation and cooperation models and practices, as well as the above outlined formal and informal complementary protection strategy.

Concerning entrepreneurship and start-ups, the accelerating progress of AI technologies has made it necessary to cope with a new and higher level of acceleration in business development, requiring a tremendous concentration of activities—attracting funding, attracting AI software engineers—at a rate not seen before, while still constructed around the comparatively and traditionally slow decision taking and reluctant adoption processes of large corporations (Šrámek 2019). Especially when it comes to funding or direct investments, the critical questions of how to deal with public contribution and value capturing have become an important premise setting the pace for applying formal and informal protection strategies and balancing these.

To quote the Silicon Valley-based private American venture capital firm, *Andreessen Horowitz* (Frank Chen 2019): "When investing in startups, we think about where the pockets are that can make money in the shadow of the giants (i.e.,

Proprietary innovation:	Open innovation:
• Exclusive ownership • Who pays owns case • Owner can license, sell, sue, use, etc. • No shared income	• Jointly own • Who pays controls case • All owners license to public for free

Bought Control Model:
- No loss of ownership, regardless of payment
- Full right to use, license, etc.
- No accounting problems
- Lower admin overhead

  → Differentiation

Free Public Commons Model:
- Ownership supports commons
- Full right to use, license, etc.
- No accounting problems
- For academic and commercial use

  → Standardization

<u>AI Specifics:</u>

Means:
- Proprietary datasets, a/o
- Proprietary algorithm strategies, a/o
- Proprietary source code & libraries, a/o

Means:
- Access to common datasets & pooling of datasets to increase learning bias, a/o
- Publication of algorithm strategies, a/o
- Publication of source code & libraries, a/o

Effect:
+ Proprietary position, e.g. exclusive dataset, as basis to receive funding, investments, exit strategies
+ Application specific IP possible
+ Basis to financially leverage competitive advantage
- Potentially limited innovation progress
- Potentially unclear ethical standards

Effect:
+ Acceleration of innovation progress
+ Free flow of information
+ Open discussion
+ Foster publications
- Pressure to gain intrinsic R&D, public funding or philanthropic investments

Applied by (not limited to):
- Companies that want to tie specific innovation to their business model and keep exclusivity
- Start-Ups with need for external investment

Applied by (not limited to):
- Public institutions and research institutes, e.g. MILA Montréal
- Companies and institutions that need access to (also specific) datasets or want to accelerate their innovation progress

→ **Entrepreneurial AI pioneers use both models in parallel**

Fig. 7.10 Balancing proprietary innovation and open innovation (Bader and Stummeyer 2019)

7.5 Artificial Intelligence-Based Business Models

Amazon, *Google*, *Microsoft*, and *Facebook*). These large companies are investing a lot in AI, so startups need to be thoughtful about what will differentiate them in a valley of giants. For instance, when we're looking at a company in the AI space, we look for startups that:

1. have smart, ambitious teams ready to think outside the box;
2. have access to a dataset that the giants don't (i.e., partnering with companies who may not want to give Google their business transaction data); and
3. are not over-rotated on AI. In the computer industry, we've got dozens of billion-dollar companies and a lot of opportunities ahead. AI is not a panacea."

Potential AI-enabled systems are upcoming based on AI technologies that are already starting to affect urban life, with autonomous transportation as the currently most visible AI application (Grosz and Stone 2018). The *Stanford One Hundred Year Study on Artificial Intelligence*, generally referred to as "AI100," is dedicated to assessing AI's influences on people, communities, and society, and recently published their first forward-looking assessment on life in 2030: AI, in the long run, might challenge human cognitive jobs while enhancing the benefits of owning intellectual capital (Stone et al. 2016).

Therefore, innovation in AI-based business models combined with value capturing based on formal and informal IP protection strategies retains its relevance. However, this approach is likely to be challenged by the public's appreciation of fairness and equitableness with regard to public goods and commons and the innovator's striving for appropriability.

AI as Inventor (DABUS)

One of the futuristic uses of AI may be to create intellectual property itself! Companies have long used genetic algorithms to optimize technological parameters, and thus come up with new inventions and innovations that are better, but where computers decide on the final form. The AI future is already here—there is already an invention for a flashlight gripping system invented by *"Dabus" (Device for the Autonomous Bootstrapping of Unified Sentience)*. This raises massive legal questions because if someone invents an AI system are all subsequent inventions owned by the system developer? Moreover, AI systems could conceivably use file applications on their own and spam the entire system. For example, letting an AI system loose to fill in technological gaps unseen or unexploited by normal patent record mining could create an impenetrable legal barrier to entry for subsequent firms. *Novartis* already uses machine learning and AI in its search for active compounds ("Can an AI System Be Given a Patent," *Wallstreet Journal* 2019-10-11). Dabus' inventorship was rejected by both the UK patent office and the EPO, both stating that only natural persons can be the inventor (for the Dabus patent application see example in Sect. 8.2). ◄

7.6 Blockchain and Distributed Ledger Technologies

Society often needs a canonical record of ownership, legal, and administrative transactions. In the past, this function has typically been assumed by a trusted party, such as a (central) bank or governmental land registry. In that system, each change in status or ownership is recorded and executed by the trusted party, who maintains all those canonical records. The advantage of this system is that it is not technically complex—land registries still keep simple paper records in some parts of the world. There is no external validation required and transactions can happen very quickly as soon as the registry or trusted party makes a change in the ledger. This trusted party system has been the only real practical one until recent technological developments.

Cheap computational power and software has made distributed ledgers feasible. *Distributed Ledger Technologies (DLTs)* are typically databases where multiple participants have access to the records in their respective locations. They distinguish themselves from centralized ledgers in that each participant has a copy of the records or a unique hash of the records. All participants can typically view all the records, and observe all of the changes made to the registry. Those same agents also act as guarantors of the registry integrity through cryptographic or chain of custody algorithms. Currently, there are many technologies vying for a place in our collective distributed ledger future. The "blockchain" is just one subtype of a distributed ledger system. Figure 7.11 presents a synopsis of some of the key features of new DLTs.

DLT is not explained in detail here, but its implications for IP, which are many, are explored. In the field of IP, the WIPO has recognized the huge potential of this technology and hosted a 2-day conference in 2019 to scan the horizon and explore the meaning of the technology for intellectual property. In this section, there is a look first at DLT as the object of IP, then how it might be used to secure innovation, and

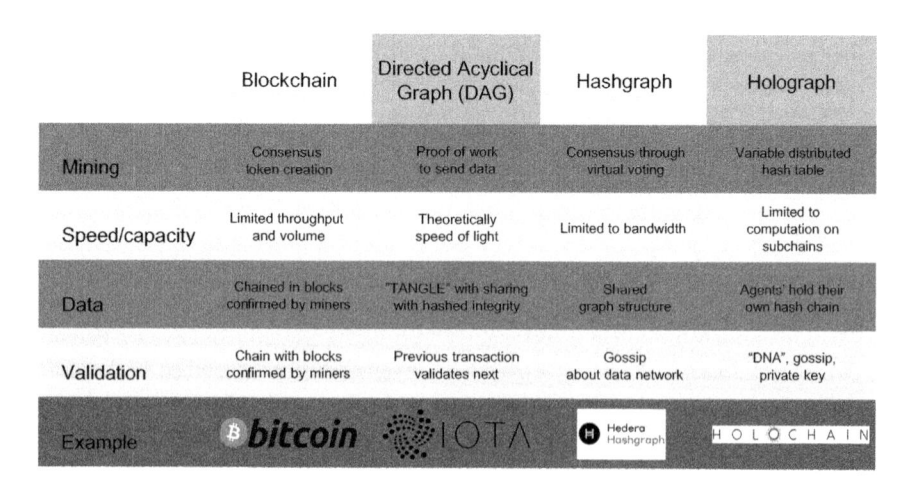

	Blockchain	Directed Acyclical Graph (DAG)	Hashgraph	Holograph
Mining	Consensus token creation	Proof of work to send data	Consensus through virtual voting	Variable distributed hash table
Speed/capacity	Limited throughput and volume	Theoretically speed of light	Limited to bandwidth	Limited to computation on subchains
Data	Chained in blocks confirmed by miners	"TANGLE" with sharing with hashed integrity	Shared graph structure	Agents' hold their own hash chain
Validation	Chain with blocks confirmed by miners	Previous transaction validates next	Gossip about data network	"DNA", gossip, private key
Example	bitcoin	IOTA	Hedera Hashgraph	HOLOCHAIN

Fig. 7.11 Examples of distributed ledger technologies (authors' own figure)

lastly at how it might be used to fundamentally alter the fabric of global patent administration and marketplace.

Blockchain as the Object of IP

The most obvious intersection of blockchain and intellectual property is the patenting of blockchain and DLT itself. Starting in 2013, blockchain and distributed ledger patents started to appear in the patent record; there are currently about 2500 of these patent families published already, of which about 500 have been granted thus far. Many of the usual suspects, *Goldman Sachs*, *Qualcomm*, and *Intel*, are among the assignees of these patents. In the face of this growth in patenting and the novelty of the technology, there have been a number of mediocre legal articles written on the patentability and legal implications of the blockchain.

But, at its core, the blockchain and DLT are really software with a source code base like any other program; it defines a protocol. As such, it is software and is protected by copyright. There is no mystery about the patentability of such a technology: the same rules that apply to software and business methods apply to these patents, which was discussed above (see Sect. 7.4).

The practical bottom line with blockchain patents has been that patenting the technology is often at fundamental odds with free use of the technology (Yanisky-Ravid and Kim 2019). Since the economic and social value of a network is proportional to the number of nodes connected to it, DLT in most cases benefits from more devices and agents using the network and system. Before any commercial players will use a system, they often need assurance that they will not be subject to licensing fees or lawsuits. Hence, free use is often required to achieve the network effects that enable widespread use, which DLT often aims to achieve. For this and ideological reasons, most of the major DLT projects are open-source projects or controlled by public foundations. Propriety blockchain systems, offered by *IBM* or *Amazon*, resemble much more traditional software as a service business model—even if they rely on blockchain or DLT.

Using Blockchain to Secure Innovation

Perhaps more exciting than blockchain as the object of IP is the fact that it can be used as a guarantor or compliment to IP. According to the European Observatory on Infringements of Intellectual Property Rights (EUIPO 2018), losses to counterfeiting are at least on the order of US $30 billion annually. Hence, one idea, elucidated in Clark and Burstall (2018), is the use of blockchain technology to prevent counterfeiting drugs in the pharmaceutical industry; their argument is that packaging and coding can be immutably etched into the blockchain. At each stage in the supply chain, certified actors can register events in the blockchain—for example, when the pharmaceutical compound leaves the production facility to be packaged, the packager can certify the chain of custody and record her own reception into her packaging facility. Similarly, when the drug leaves the packaging facility and goes to the shipper another entry in the blockchain could be made. Analogously, when the package is indeed received from the other recipient, the shipper records her own entry, and thus the supply chain continues via distributors and pharmacies. This record for chain of custody would go all the way to the consumer, who could in theory read all the events in the blockchain. Since all the events are recorded, counterfeit drugs introduced into the supply chains by unscrupulous distributors, and thereby not part of such a system, would be left out in the cold. Aside from the revenue losses, expiration and batch information may allow public health officials to take action, and prevent bad drugs from entering the supply.

As of February 2019, Europe has addressed this issue with a unique identifier (a two-dimension barcode) and anti-tampering device requirements for authorized drugs. Naturally, this territorial solution is not necessarily the first-best technological or global regulatory design, but blockchain was only in its infancy when the original 2011 directives came out. Currently, the blockchain is unlikely to make many inroads to protect pharmaceuticals due to the heavily regulated nature of the industry. Moreover, the amount of money at stake has meant that pharma spends about US $100–$165 million per year lobbying both the US Congress and the EU to press governments and international organizations to expend public resources to enforce its private intellectual property, which seems like a bargain when perhaps up to US $100 billion annually in global counterfeit medication is at stake. Estimates vary, but various transparency watchdog groups, like reports that the US Congress receive anywhere from 100 to 200 million a year depending on the election cycle and legislative docket. Amounts spent lobbying the EU for action are on a similar order of magnitude. According to the EU transparency register, *Bayer*, a major pharmaceutical manufacturer, has spent 4.2 million dollars lobbying in Brussels (lobbyfacts.eu, accessed 2020-01-26). According to *OpenSecrets*, the spend hit a whopping US $272 million a year where "Lobbying efforts focus on the patent system, research funding and Medicare" (opensecrets.org, accessed 2020-01-26).

Despite the predominance of traditional protection mechanisms (border enforcement, police action and interdiction, and lawsuits) in pharma, blockchain still could play both a vital, engaging, and interesting role for certain innovative products. For example, a luxury brand with an innovative product or design might use the blockchain in the same manner to protect the authenticity of a product and the embedded design patent, while, say, showing the chain of fine materials or artisanal manufacturers used to produce it. More mundane but essential products, like patented spare parts, could be tracked and validated analogously, along with their service history; this might guarantee the quality and service while protecting the intellectual property at the same time. Thus, in sum, distributed ledger technologies hold out both the promise of intellectual property protection and the potential of creating customer value. A hallmark of great IP management appropriates value to the innovator while creating an added value proposition for the customer; the reason for our faith in this type of strategy is not just that it is a good business practice, but rather that it creates a decentralized and vested interest in the end-user to help to actually enforce the IP and lessen demand for infringing products, as was seen in the case of *Bayer's* seed technology in the previous chapter.

Beyond patents and physical goods, there are some postulated uses of blockchain for copyright, which are in a similar vein as patent protection. The *Society of Music Authors, Composers, and Publishers (Sacem)* and *IBM* have been working together to track and capture creators' rights using DLT and the hyper ledger (Sacem 2019). DLT lends itself well to micro-rights and micro-residual payments, and the platform holds out the possibility to gather additional intelligence on users.

Beyond these more immediate uses, the blockchain is also being hypothesized as a way of tracking micropayments to photographers or graphical artists. Perhaps even more radical is using the technology of recording who had an innovative idea to determine prior art or ownership in collaborative pools across organizational boundaries. While the threshold to obtain a patent is quite high, by lowering the barriers to an IP system, it may be possible to better record and trace inventorship using DLT and blockchain.

Blockchain as the Solution to IP

This brings us to our final and perhaps most salient and realistic use of DLT for IP, which is the embryonic effort to deploy the technology as a way of publishing and recording administrative procedures. The following is a decision flow chart published by the *US National Institute of Standards and Technology's (NIST)* white paper for the use of Blockchain Technology Overview (Yaga et al. 2018), an oft-cited good technical reference on this new technology.

In the following, the *NIST* template is used to structure the to understand the patent office's decision to explore the use of blockchain—and to provide a decent managerial checklist (see Fig. 7.12):

1. **Are sharing and consistency necessary?** There is a need for a consistent and shared data store. Intellectual property (IP) records have to be consistent to understand ownership, and all economic agents in the system need to have easy access to that datastore in order to make informed decisions.
2. **Are there multiple authors?** Whether more than one entity needs to contribute is a bit questionable. In terms of patents, courts occasionally issue invalidity rulings—these are then passed to the patent office that registers the events. Banks will occasionally put liens on patents, which again would require an office to show that the property is collateral.
3. **Is record modification required?** Patents and their registry events are never deleted. In this sense, the blockchain is very appropriate. While we have seen that schlepping the entire transaction history has prevented blockchain from becoming a truly viable solution for payment systems, this indelible history is very appropriate for legal events and entitlement, which are integral to how the patent system operates.
4. **Does it involve sensitive information?** With the exception of some classified military technologies, most, if not all, of the patent record is and/or should be

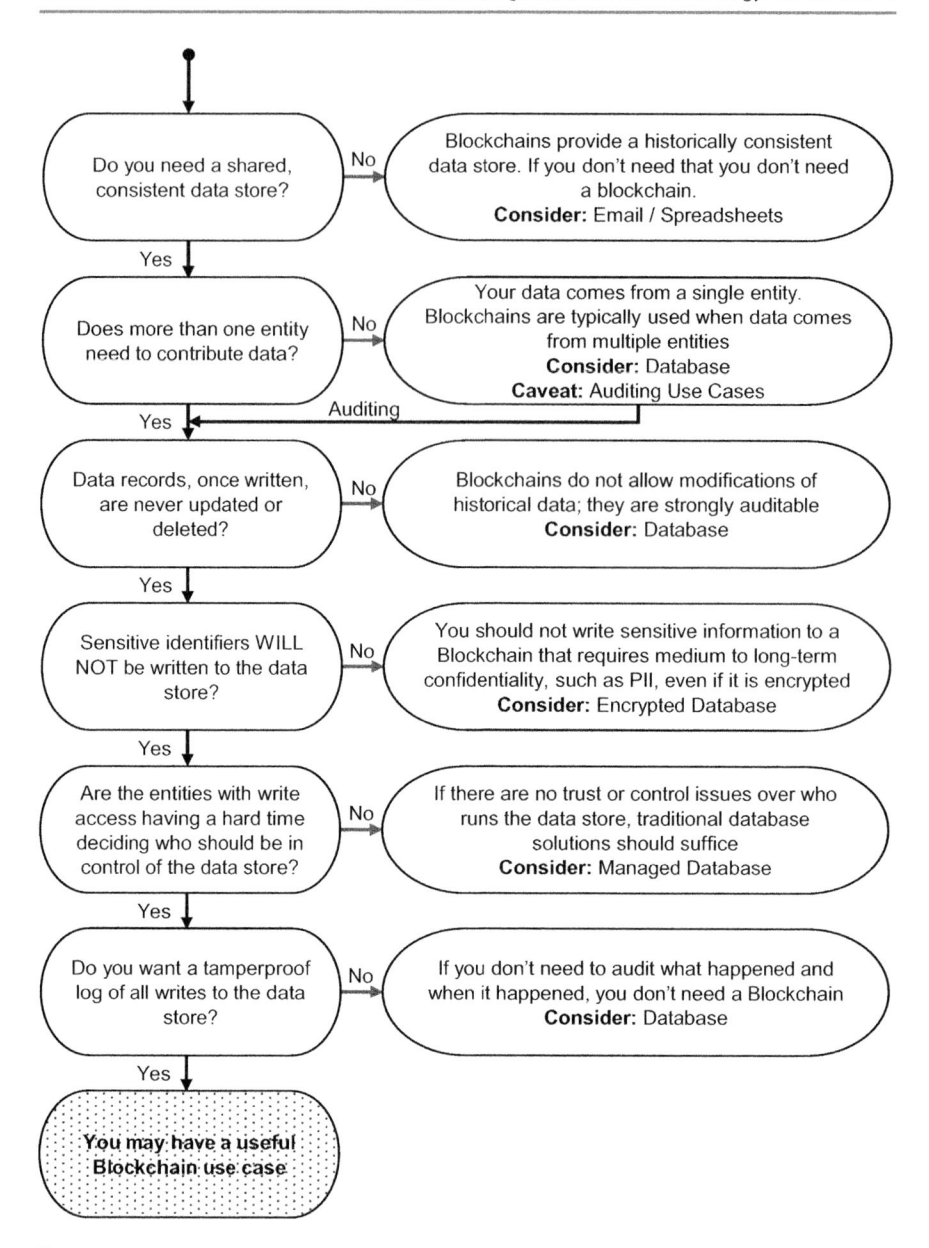

Fig. 7.12 Flowchart for deciding whether the use of Blockchain is appropriate (Yaga et al. 2018)

7.6 Blockchain and Distributed Ledger Technologies

publicly available. In this sense, there are few, if any, sensitive identifiers in the patent record.

5. **Are there control issues?** In general, IP and patent offices around the globe are trustworthy institutions. They tend to be outside of the main political fray and are staffed with highly specialized technical, and legal personnel. There is not necessarily a trust or control issue in this sense, and this is perhaps one reason why IP offices have not had to cede control over their own data.
6. **Is auditing required?** There is not a massive need to audit IP registry data. Some IP offices have been keeping records longer than even land registries. There has been no great concern about the integrity of the registry entries, thus obviating one of the major benefits of blockchain technology.

Those last two dubious reasons notwithstanding, after making this type of assessment, the WIPO and some offices, notably Russia and the Australian patent office, are pushing ahead with DLT. The Russians are making good use of their famed cyber skills, and have already set up the *IPchain*, a consortium of Russian governmental agencies, that maintains a prototype system. *Rospatent* has been experimenting with a patent record that is mirrored in the blockchain. The idea is that applications would be recorded, along with grant and examination data, which would then subsequently enable commerce to take place on the backend of the process. The country has had a blockchain gazette service for patents since October of 2019, and a prototype for IP management of trademarks since November of 2018. The Russian *IPchain* is built on the hyper ledger.[9] Russia has moved quickly on the legal front with the Russian IP court also supporting the administration's foray into DLT.

While Russia has moved ahead on the technical side, *IPAustralia* has been working, as co-leader of the *CWS Blockchain Task Force*, to map the needs of WIPO members. *IPAustralia* is also working to develop a common vernacular to discuss the issue and is spearheading the effort to achieve a standard around which the Russians can build the technological platform.

There is absolutely no reason that such a comprehensive solution need be privately run. In theory, there could be some enabling legislation that would allow the patent system to be moved to the "chain" without a supervisionary patent office, but whether that could get off the ground without serious coordination and backing is dubious.

Aside from these public initiatives, one of the privately run, visionary technologies based on DLT, comes from *IPwe*. Their platform is based on *IBM's* hyperledger blockchain technology. Their value proposition is to drastically lower the cost of transacting in patents. One of the main differences between patents and

---

[9]https://www.hyperledger.org. This effort is part of a broader Russian initiative to advance blockchain technologies, spearheaded by the *IPchain Association* (https://ipchain.global/association/). This system can be accessed using the blockchain node at: peer-1.ipchain.ipchain.ru (specialized software required).

other realia is that the price and contractual terms on the sale and licensing of intellectual property change depending on who is buying and licensing since there is often a balance of power considerations to make.

Aside from facilitating transactions, this *IPwe*'s technology holds out the possibility of offering a collective legal shield—patent owners on the platform can, through technology, instantaneously summon a massive patent portfolio to deter other legal aggressors. This would certainly alter the balance of power in the patent space—especially if any agent in the system through the use of AI and smart contracts, could summon a massive IP shield dynamically as a response to litigation, possibly deterring patent trolls.

Since ownership is tracked, inventors can also pledge patents quickly and legally through special purpose vehicles traced by the chain. This would also possibly solve another one of the liquidity issues of patents in that, as an inventor, there is a lengthy search process to find investors and/or lenders to finance inventions and, once found, there are still complicated legal arrangements to fix mutually agreeable terms. The cost of all this prohibits transacting in all but the most valuable inventions. With *IPwe*'s technology, each license could be securely recorded, and payments automated via smart contracts. This would enable complete and efficient controlling and due diligence of such assets by, say, tax authorities.

Making patents more liquid, administratively tractable, and transparent, is undoubtedly in the economic interest of the public. Whether this is in the economic interest of the major actors in the patent space, who also essentially dictate the political economy of patent policy, remains to be seen.

References

Bader, M. A. (2007). Managing intellectual property in a collaborative environment: Learning from IBM. *International Journal of Intellectual Property Management, 1*(3), 206–225.

Bader, M. A., & Stummeyer, C. (2019). The role of innovation and IP in AI-based business models. In R. Baierl, J. Behrens, & A. Brem (Eds.), *Digital entrepreneurship – interfaces between digital technologies and entrepreneurship* (pp. 23–56). Heidelberg: Springer.

BGW. (2019). *IP management in distributed ledger technology and in food technology*. St. Gallen: BGW.

Boehm, B. W. (1976). *Software engineering. IEEE Transactions on Computers, C-25*(12), 1226–1241.

Bonakdar, A., Frankenberger, K., Bader, M. A., & Gassmann, O. (2017). Capturing value from business models: The role of formal and informal protection strategies. *International Journal of Technology Management, 73*(4), 151–175.

Chen, F. (2019). The investors' view. In WIPO (2019) *WIPO technology trends 2019: Artificial intelligence*. Geneva: World Intellectual Property Organization, p. 105.

Chen, H., Roco, M. C., Li, X., & Lin, Y. (2008). Trends in nanotechnology patents. *Nature Nanotechnology, 3*(3), 123–125.

Clark, B., & Burstall, R. (2018). Blockchain, IP and the pharma industry—how distributed ledger technologies can help secure the pharma supply chain. *Journal of Intellectual Property Law and Practice, 13*(7), 531–533.

References

Cohen, J. (2017). The birth of CRISPR. The American Association for the Advancement of Science, License Number 4803211490911. *Science, 355*(6326), 680–684. https://doi.org/10.1126/science.355.6326.680.

Coriat, B., & Orsi, F. (2002). Establishing a new intellectual property rights regime in the United States: Origins, content and problems. *Research Policy, 31*(8–9), 1491–1507.

Dutfield, G. (2003). *Intellectual property rights and the life science industries. A twentieth century history*. Hampshire: Ashgate.

EPO. (2007). *Scenarios for the future. How might IP regimes evolve by 2025? What global legitimacy might such regimes have?* Munich: European Patent Office.

EPO. (2013). *Nanotechnology and patents*. Munich: European Patent Office.

EPO. (2017a). *Biotechnology patents at the EPO*. Munich: European Patent Office. https://www.epo.org/news-issues/issues/biotechnology-patents.html.

EPO. (2017b). *Patents and the fourth industrial revolution. The inventions behind digital transformation*. Munich: European Patent Office.

EPO. (2018a). *Patenting artificial intelligence. Conference summary*. Munich: European Patent Office.

EPO. (2018b). *Guidelines for examination: Artificial intelligence and machine learning (G-II 3.3.1)*. Munich: European Patent Office.

EPO. (2019). *Patents for software? European law and practice*. Munich: European Patent Office. Accessed December 28, 2019, from https://www.epo.org/news-issues/issues/ict/hardware-and-software.html#tab1

EPO. (2020). *Patent Index 2019*. In *Statistics at a glance*. Munich: European Patent Office.

EPO and CNIPA. (2019). *Comparative study on computer implemented inventions/software related inventions – Report 2019 I EPO and CNIPA*. Munich: European Patent Office. Accessed December 28, 2019, from http://documents.epo.org/projects/babylon/eponot.nsf/0/979CF38758D25C2CC12584AC004618D9/$File/comparative_study_on_computer_implemented_inventions_software_related_inventions_EPO_CNIPA_en.pdf

EPO and JPO. (2018). *Comparative study on computer implemented inventions/software related inventions – Report 2018 I EPO and JPO*. Munich: European Patent Office. Accessed December 28, 2019, from http://documents.epo.org/projects/babylon/eponet.nsf/0/346e6018b0445380c12583cb002fdb34/$FILE/comparative_study_on_computer_implemented_inventions_software_related_inventions_EPO_JPO_en.pdf

EUIPO. (2018). *2017 situation report on counterfeiting and piracy in the European Union*. Alicante: European observatory on infringements of intellectual property rights. from https://euipo.europa.eu/ohimportal/en/web/observatory/observatory-publications.

European Commission. (2018). *Artificial intelligence: European strategy*. Brussels: European Commission. Accessed March 1, 2019, from https://ec.europa.eu/jrc/sites/jrcsh/files/23112018-artificial_intelligence-huet_en.pdf

Flaim, J. G., & Chae, Y. (2019). Subject-matter eligibility in the United States, Europe, Japan, China and Korea. In: *WIPO Technology Trends 2019: Artificial Intelligence*, p. 96. Geneva: World Intellectual Property Organization.

Gassmann, O., & Bader, M. A. (2017). *Patentmanagement: Innovationen erfolgreich nutzen und schützen* (4th ed.). Berlin: Springer.

Grosz, B. J., & Stone, P. (2018). *A century long commitment to assessing artificial intelligence and its impact on society*. December 2018. Communications of the ACM (CACM).

Hall, B. H., & MacGarvie, M. (2010). The private value of software patents. *Research Policy, 39*(7), 994–1009.

Huebner, S. R. (2008). The validity of European nanotechnology patents in Germany. *Nanotechnology Law and Business, 5*(3), 353–357.

IPStudies. (2019). *CRISPR patent landscape*. In *Les Paccots*. https://www.ipstudies.ch/.

Jinek, M., Chylinski, K., Fonfara, I., Hauer, M., Doudna, J. A., & Charpentier, E. (2012). A programmable dual-RNA−guided DNA endonuclease in adaptive bacterial immunity. *Science, 337*(6096), 816–821.

Kallinger, C., Veefkind, V., Michalitsch, R., Verbandt, Y., Neumann, A., Scheu, M., & Forster, W. (2008). Patenting nanotechnology: A European patent office perspective. *Nanotechnology Law and Business, 5*(1), 95.

Ledford, H. (2019). Bitter fight over CRISPR patent heats up: Unusual battle among academic institutions holds key to gene-editing tool's future use. *Nature, 529*(7586), 265. Gale OneFile: Health and Medicine, Accessed December 26, 2019.

MGI (McKinsey Global Institute). (2015). *The internet of things: Mapping the value beyond the Hype*.

Miller, C., Serrato, R. M., Repressas-Cardenas, J. M., & Griffith, A. K. (2005). *The handbook of nanotechnology: Business, policy, and intellectual property law*. Hoboken: Wiley.

Nanosys. (2009). *Nanoco Settles Patent Infringement Lawsuit with Nanosys, Inc. for Quantum Dot Technology*. Manchester: Nanosys. http://www.nanocotechnologies.com/media/press-releases/nanoco-settles-patent-infringement-lawsuit-nanosys-inc-quantum-dot-technology

OECD. (2003). *Genetic inventions, iprs and licensing practices: Evidence and policies*. Paris: OECD.

OECD. (2009). *Nanotechnology: An overview*. Paris: OECD.

OECD. (2017). *Key issues for digital transformation in the G20. Report prepared for a joint G20 German Presidency/OECD conference*. Paris: OECD.

Ouellette, L. L. (2015). Nanotechnology and innovation policy. *Harvard Journal of Law and Technology, 29*(1), Fall.

Sacem. (2019) *Ascap, Sacem, and PRS for Music Initiate Blockchain Project to Improve Data Accuracy for Rightsholders*, press release dated 2019-03-12.

Schwab, K. (2017). *The Fourth Industrial Revolution*, 1st edition, New York Crowne Business (2017). Originally published by World Economic Forum, Geneva, Switzerland 2016.

ScienceMag. (2017). *How the battle lines over CRISPR were drawn*. Accessed December 27, 2019, from https://www.sciencemag.org/news/2017/02/how-battlelines-over-crispr-were-drawn

Sherkow, J. S. (2015). Law, history and lessons in the CRISPR patent conflict. *Nature Biotechnology, 33*, 256–257.

Smalley, L. W. (2014). Will nanotechnology products be impacted by the federal courts' 'Product of nature' exception to subject-matter eligibility under 35 U.S.C. 101? *Marshall Review of Intellectual Property Law*, 397.

Šrámek, P. (2019). AI startups in Europe. In: *WIPO technology trends 2019: Artificial intelligence*, p. 108. Geneva: World Intellectual Property Organization.

Stellbrink. (2016). *Life after Alice. Stellbrink & Partner on Twitter*: Accessed on December 28, 2019, from https://twitter.com/sp_patent/status/742705881851252737

Stiftung Science et Cité. (2004). *Streitfall biotechpatente*. Bern: Stiftung Science et Cité.

Stone, P., Brooks, R., Brynjolfsson, E., Calo, R., Etzioni, O., Hager, G., Hirschberg, J., Kalyanakrishnan, S., Kamar, E., Kraus, S., Leyton-Brown, K., Parkes, D., Press, W., Saxenian, A. L., Shah, J., Tambe, M., & Teller, A. (2016). *'Artificial intelligence and life in 2030.' One hundred year study on artificial intelligence: Report of the 2015-2016 study panel*. Stanford, CA: Stanford University, September 2016. Accessed September 6, 2016, from http://ai100.stanford.edu/2016-report

Straus, J. (2003). *An updating concerning the protection of biotechnological inventions including the scope of patents for genes*. Munich: Special edition of the Official Journal of the European Patent Office on Gene Patenting.

Thumm, N. (2001). Management of intellectual property rights in European biotechnology firms. *Technological Forecasting and Social Change, 67*, 259–272.

Thumm, N. (2003). *Research and patenting in biotechnology – A survey in Switzerland*. Swiss Federal Institute of Intellectual Property: Bern.

USPTO. (2019). *2019 Revised patent subject matter eligibility guidance*. Alexandria, VA: United States Patent and Trademark Office.

Wang, B., Vuković, L., & Král, P. (2008). Nanoscale rotary motors driven by electron tunneling. *Physical Review Letters, 101*, 186808.

WIPO. (2019). *WIPO technology trends 2019: Artificial intelligence*. Geneva: World Intellectual Property Organization. (The user is allowed to reproduce, distribute, adapt, translate and publicly perform this publication, including for commercial purposes, without explicit permission, provided that the content is accompanied by an acknowledgement that WIPO is the source and that it is clearly indicated if changes were made to the original content.)

Yaga, D., Mell, P., Roby, N., & Scarfoneet, K. (2018). *Blockchain technology overview*. National Institute of Standards and Technology, U.S. Department of Commerce. https://doi.org/10.6028/NIST.IR.8202

Yanisky-Ravid, S., & Kim, E. (May 2019). *Patenting blockchain: Mitigating the patent infringement war*, Albany Law Review.

Youtie, J., Porter, A., Shapira, P., & Newman, N. (2016). *Lessons from ten years of nanotechnology bibliometric analysis*. Paris: OECD. http://www.oecd.org/sti/080%20-%20Blue%20Sky%20STIP%20final%20submission.pdf.

Useful Information for Practitioners

Following are some useful information, facts, and trends for the practitioner:

1. Patent Growth Worldwide
2. Structure of a Patent
3. Patent Document Codes
4. Patent Classification
5. Notes on Patent Search
6. Member States of the European Patent Organisation
7. EUIPO/Unitary Patent/Unified Patent Court
8. IP Tax Regimes
9. Brief Comparison of Patent Legislation
10. The World Intellectual Property Day

8.1 Patent Growth Worldwide

The request for commercial IP rights has increased dramatically in the last two decades. A bigger growing number of companies have recognized the advantage that formal IP rights can bring. The five largest intellectual property offices—the so-called *IP5 Offices*—namely the European patent Office (EPO), the Japan patent Office (JPO), the Korean Intellectual Property Office (KIPO), the China National Intellectual Property Administration (CNIPA), and the United States Patent and Trademark Office (USPTO) count the following statistics (Five IP Offices 2019a):

- At the end of 2017, 13.6 million patents were in force in the world (+15.9%).
- Ninety-one percent of these patents were in force in one of the IP5 Office jurisdictions.
- In 2017, 2.8 million patent applications were filed worldwide, either as direct national, direct regional or international phase PCT applications, of which 94% originated from the IP5 Blocs.
- In 2017, 89% of the worldwide patent applications were filed as direct national applications. The proportion of applications filed via the PCT remained stable.
- In 2018, 2.8 million patent applications were filed at the IP5 Offices (+6.0%).
- Together the IP5 Offices granted 1.2 million patents in 2018 (+1.4%).

In the wake of the 2009 recession, there was a strong decline in the number of patent applications worldwide. In the meantime, this trend has reversed into a continual increase. Especially noticeable in is that China (CNIPA) and South Korea (KIPO) have established themselves among the five largest application countries (Five IP Offices 2019b); *China* now finds itself in the pole position (see Fig. 8.1).

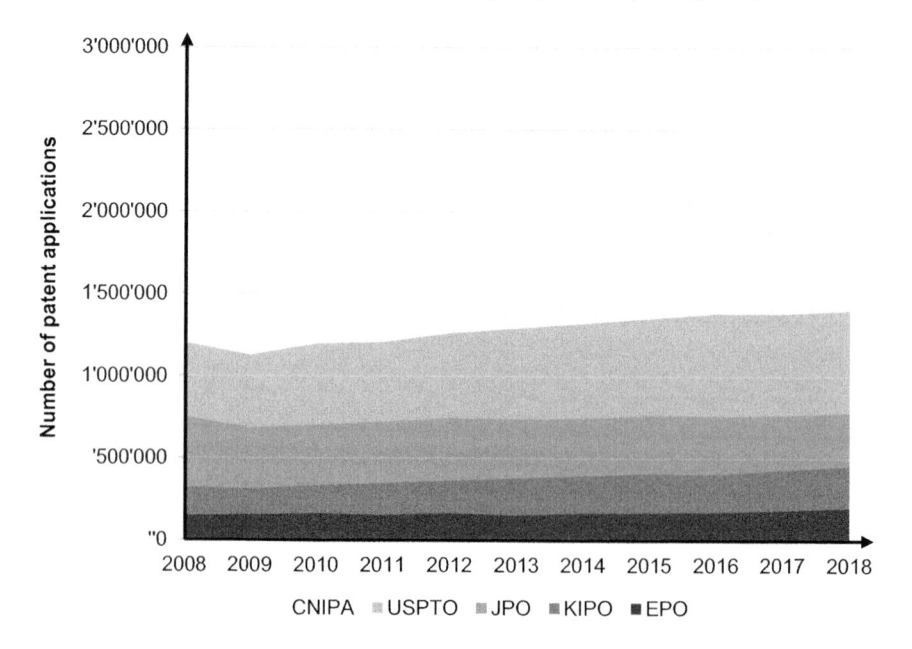

Fig. 8.1 Patent applications worldwide at the IP5 Offices (Five IP Offices 2019a, b)

8.2 Structure of a Patent

A *patent document* typically has the following structure and content:

I. Title page (example, see Fig. 8.2):
   - Country
   - Publication number
   - Classification
   - Bibliographic data (priority date, application date, publication date, grant date, evaluated state of the art)
   - Applicant, inventor, representative/agent
   - Title/description
   - Summary
II. Description:
   - Circumscription of the technical field
   - Discussion of the state of the art and its disadvantages
   - Task
   - Presentation of the invention (generally the first claim), including a description of the advantages; various solutions
   - Captions for drawings
   - Description of the invention referencing the drawings
III. Independent and dependent claims,[1] written in unitary or two-part[2] claim form ("characterized in that" or "characterized by")
IV. Drawings

> **Example of a *title page* of a patent document (see Fig. 8.2)**
>
> - Country, publication number
>   (19), (10)
> - IPC classification
>   (51)
> - Priority date
>   (30)
> - Application date
>   (22)

---

[1] *"Independent claim:* A claim that does not rely on any other claim for its content, structure, or validity and is usually considered on its own for purposes of determining validity or infringement. The opposite type of claim is a *dependent claim.* One factor in evaluating independent claims that does relate them to other claims is the doctrine of claim differentiation." (source: www.ipglossary.com).

[2] *"Two part claim:* A type of patent claim common in Europe, where the first part of the claim describes what is recognized as existing in the prior art or as being obvious and the second part, following the use of the terms of art "characterized in that" or "characterized by" constitutes the claimed invention. In the US such a claim is known as a Jepson Claim" (source: www.ipglossary.com).

- Publication date/Grant date
  (43), (45)
- Applicant, Inventor, Representative
  (71), (72), (74)
- Title/Description
  (54)
- Summary
  (57)
- Drawing ◄

8.2 Structure of a Patent

(19) Europäisches Patentamt / European Patent Office / Office européen des brevets

(11) **EP 3 564 144 A1**

(12) **EUROPEAN PATENT APPLICATION**

(43) Date of publication:
06.11.2019 Bulletin 2019/45

(21) Application number: 18275163.6

(22) Date of filing: 17.10.2018

(51) Int Cl.:
B65D 6/02 (2006.01)   B65D 8/00 (2006.01)
B65D 6/00 (2006.01)   B65D 13/02 (2006.01)
B65D 21/02 (2006.01) B65D 1/02 (2006.01)

(84) Designated Contracting States:
AL AT BE BG CH CY CZ DE DK EE ES FI FR GB GR HR HU IE IS IT LI LT LU LV MC MK MT NL NO PL PT RO RS SE SI SK SM TR
Designated Extension States:
BA ME
Designated Validation States:
KH MA MD TN

(71) Applicant: **Thaler, Stephen L.**
St. Charles MO 63303 (US)

(72) Inventor: **The designation of the inventor has not yet been filed**

(74) Representative: **Williams Powell**
11 Staple Inn
London WC1V 7QH (GB)

Remarks:
•The designation of inventor does not meet the requirements laid down in Article 81 and Rule 19 EPC.
•Amended claims in accordance with Rule 137(2) EPC.

(54) **FOOD CONTAINER**

(57) A container (10) for use, for example, for beverages, has a wall (12) with and external surface (14) and an internal wall (16) of substantially uniform thickness. The wall (12) has a fractal profile which provides a series of fractal elements (18-28) on the interior and exterior surfaces (14-16), forming pits (40) and bulges (42) in the profile of the wall and in which a pit (40) as seen from one of the exterior or interior surfaces (12, 14) forms a bulge (42) on the other of the exterior or interior surfaces (12, 14). The profile enables multiple containers to be coupled together by inter-engagement of pits and bulges on corresponding ones of the containers. The profile also improves grip, as well as heat transfer into and out of the container.

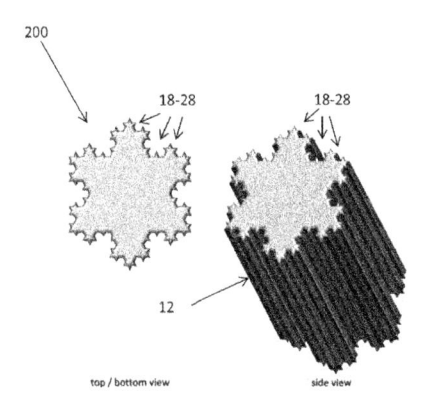

Fig. 6

Fig. 8.2 Example of patent application title page (EP 3 564 144) ["EPO refuses *DABUS patent applications* designating a machine inventor: The EPO has refused two European patent applications in which a machine was designated as inventor. Both patent applications indicate

8.3 Patent Document Codes

(11) **EP 3 564 144 A1**

For the unique identification of different types of patent documents, e.g., publications, patents, utility patents, the World Intellectual Property Organization (WIPO) has developed a standard (ST.16) way of classifying such documents.[3] The codes consist of a letter and often a number, which is printed along with the document number. Unfortunately, not all countries adhere to this standard, and such codes have changed in various countries over time. It is important to know that each jurisdiction employs its own variant of the standard. Here are some of the more common codes:

- **A1** Patent application with search report (EPO)
- **A2** Patent application without search report (EPO)
- **A3** Search report (EPO)
- **B1** Granted patent (EPO)
- **B2** Granted patent (USPTO)
- **B2** Modified patents, typically after an opposition (EPO)
- **C** Reexamination documents (USPTO)
- **E, F, G** Other sui generis rights and documents (rare)
- **M** Medical claims and patent documents
- **L** Bibliographic, figures, drawings, claims, etc. (rare)
- **N** Non-patent literature documents
- **H, I** Special requirement documents (rare)
- **P** Plant-breeders' rights and patents
- **R** Separately published search reports
- **S** Design patent documents
- **T** Translation documents of applications, granted patents, etc.
- **U, W, Y, Z** Utility model documents
- **X** Restricted documents, documents for country-specific usage

---

Fig. 8.2 (continued) 'DABUS' as inventor, which is described as 'a type of connectionist artificial intelligence'. The applicant stated that they acquired the right to the European patent from the inventor by being its successor in title. After hearing the arguments of the applicant in non-public oral proceedings on 25 November the EPO refused EP 18 275 163 (published as EP 3 564 144) and EP 18 275 174 on the grounds that they do not meet the requirement of the EPC that an inventor designated in the application has to be a human being, not a machine." (EPO 2019)]

---

[3]WIPO-Standard ST.16 und ST.50: www.wipo.int/standards/en/part_03_standards.html

8.4 Patent Classification

The entire worldwide patent literature comprises more than 115 million documents issued by more than 60 worldwide patent-issuing authorities. A structured categorization of the documents allows a simplified search. To that end, the International Patent Classification (IPC) has established itself as a taxonomy for patents and utility models based on their field of application. It is used by patent offices in over 100 countries. The USPTO and EPO have developed a more refined classification, called the Common Patent Classification (CPC), but it retains the structure of the IPC. Patent classifications (e.g., IPC/ECLA/CPC/USPC) are organized hierarchically (see Tables 8.1 and 8.2).

Table 8.1 Sections from the CPC (https://www.wipo.int/classifications/ipc/ipcpub)

CPC section	Description
Section A	Human necessities
Section B	Performing operations; transporting
Section C	Chemistry; metallurgy
Section D	Textiles; paper
Section E	Fixed constructions
Section F	Mechanical engineering; lighting; heating; weapons; blasting engines or pumps
Section G	Physics
Section H	Electricity
Section Y	General tagging of new technological developments; general tagging of cross-sectional technologies spanning over several sections of the CPC; technical subjects covered by former USPC cross-reference art collections (XRACs) and digests.

Table 8.2 Example of CPC Classification for B65D1/0223 (EP) (B65D1/02—IPC)

Section	Letter		B	TRANSPORTING
Subsection	Number (2-digit)		65	PACKING; STORING
Class	Letter		D	CONTAINERS FOR STORAGE OR TRANSPORT OF ARTICLES OR MATERIALS
Subclass	Number		1	Containers having bodies formed in one piece
Main group	Number	/	02	... Bottles or similar containers with necks or like restricted apertures
Sub-group	Number		23	... characterized by shape

8.5 Notes on Patent Search

(Tables 8.3 and 8.4)

> **When is a patent search using the Internet possible?**
>
> - Finding a single document.
> - Looking up specific information. When was this document published?
> - Answering simple questions, e.g., is there a JP application for this US patent?
>
> **When is a patent search with a professional advisable?**
>
> - When you need to ensure freedom to operate.
> - When the patent technology comprises multiple subdomains.
> - When a specific competitor or technology is not known.

Table 8.3 Overview of free internet search webpages (table compiled by authors)

Patents	Address
Canadian Patents Database	https://www.ic.gc.ca/opic-cipo/cpd/eng/search/number.html
Austria *(see.ip)*	seeip.patentamt.at
Australia *(AusPat)*	pericles.ipaustralia.gov.au
Switzerland *(Swissreg)*	https://www.swissreg.ch/
Germany *(DEPATISnet)*	https://depatisnet.dpma.de/
Germany *(DPINFO)*	register.dpma.de
EPO *(esp@cenet)*	https://worldwide.espacenet.com/
Asian patent information from EPO (incl. e.g. China, Chinese Taipei, Gulf Cooperation Council, India, Japan, Korea, Russian Federation)	https://www.epo.org/searching-for-patents/helpful-resources/asian/china/search.html
USPTO *(PatFT/AppFT)*	patft.uspto.gov
Google Patent Search	google.com/patents

Last updated: January 2020

Table 8.4 Other useful IP Links (table compiled by authors)

Subject	Address
IP Glossary (WIPO)	https://www.wipo.int/tk/en/resources/glossary.html#p
IP Glossary	http://www.ipglossary.com/
IP Portal WIPO	ipportal.wipo.int
IPI SME Portal (E, DE, FR, IT)	https://www.ige.ch/en/intellectual-property/sme-portal.html
IP Management Advisory	https://www.bgw-sg.com/

esp@cenet
Strengths:

- CPC-classification → also via Internet
- Most comprehensive collection (including technical non-patent literature)
- Documents available relatively soon after publication (often the next workday)
- Good for monitoring rights
- Simple search with keyword or word stem
- PDF download of documents, easy and fast
- Possibility of simultaneous search in the three official languages in full text
- Direct link from individual documents to the family members, legal status, machine translations, and citing and cited documents

Weaknesses:

- Limited statistical evaluations
- Maximum of 20 search items per query and 10 terms in the same search field
- Neither full text nor abstracts are available for some countries

DEPATISnet
Strengths:

- Documents available within 1 week of publication
- Ideal for monitoring
- Second biggest collection (about 28 m documents)
- Combines Boolean search with more than 40 search fields, including full text
- Search by word stem possible
- Free arrangement of search result lists (e.g., by applicant and IPC)
- Multilingual search possible
- Complete PDF files for saving and printing

Weaknesses:

- Relations are not as wide as Espacenet's word search, and sometimes limited (to title, abstract, or IPC).
- Complex query language when using advanced or Ikofax mode.

8.6 Member States of the European Patent Organisation

European patents provide protection in the 38 member states of the European Patent Organisation but also in two extension states and four validation states. This represents an area with some 700 million inhabitants (as of November 1, 2019; see Fig. 8.3).

Fig. 8.3 Jurisdictional scope of European patent protection (EPO 2020a)

8.7 EUIPO/Unitary Patent/Unified Patent Court

European Union Intellectual Property Office

The European Union Intellectual Property Office (EUIPO), which was known as Office for Harmonization in the Internal Market (OHIM) until March 23, 2016, was created as a decentralized agency of the European Union (EU) to offer IP rights protection to businesses and innovators across the 28 member states of the EU. Since its foundation in 1994 it has been based in Alicante, in Spain, where it manages the registration of the EU Trade Mark (EUTM), formerly known as the Community Trade Mark (CTM), and the Registered Community Design (RCD). EUIPO registers around 135,000 EU trademarks and close to 100,000 designs annually (EUIPO 2020).

Unitary Patent

The "European Patent with Unitary Effect" (EPUE), more commonly known as "Unitary Patent," will make it possible to get patent protection in up to 26 EU Member States by submitting a single request to the EPO. They will build on European patents granted by the EPO under the rules of the European Patent Convention (EPC), so nothing will change in the pre-grant phase, and the same high standards of quality search and examination will apply. After a European patent is granted, the patent proprietor will be able to request unitary effect, thereby getting a Unitary Patent which provides uniform patent protection in up to 26 EU Member States in addition to Morocco, Moldova, Tunisia, Cambodia, and Georgia, which are "validation states" (i.e., patent has effect, but countries do not belong to EPO).

Today, an inventor can protect an invention in Europe via a national patent or a European patent. The EPO examines applications for European patents centrally, saving inventors the costs of parallel applications while ensuring a high quality of granted patents.

However, granted European patents must be validated and maintained individually in each country where they take effect. This can be a complex and potentially very costly process: validation requirements differ between countries and can lead to high direct and indirect costs, including translation costs, validation fees (i.e., fees due in some member states for publication of the translations) and associated representation costs, such as the attorney fees charged for the administration of the patent (i.e., payment of national renewal fees). These costs can be considerable and depend on the number of countries where the patent proprietor wishes to validate the European patent (extracted from EPO 2020b).

Unified Patent Court

The Unified Patent Court (UPC)[4] is an international court set up by 25 of the participating Member States to deal with the infringement and validity of both Unitary Patents and European patents. Its rulings will apply in all Member States that have ratified the Agreement on a Unified Patent Court (extracted from EPO 2020c).

There will be three locations of the Court of First Instance (Paris, London, and Munich), a common Court of Appeal (Luxembourg), two patent mediation and arbitration centers (Lisbon and Ljubljana) and, in addition, several local and regional divisions of the Court of First Instance. Since the UK has left the European Union, it also decided to leave the Unified Patent Court; some of that decision could be to keep the UK at the center of international patent litigation and arbitration.

---

[4]Entry into force for the UPC will take place after 13 states, including Germany, France, and the United Kingdom as the three states with the most patents in force, have ratified the Agreement.

8.8 IP Tax Regimes

Intellectual Property (IP) regimes—also known as *"Patent Box," "IP Box,"* or *"Innovation Box"*—allow income from the exploitation of IP to be taxed at a lower rate than the standard statutory tax rate. IP regimes can be regimes that exclusively provide benefits to income from IP, but some preferential regimes categorized as IP regimes are "dual category" regimes. These regimes also provide benefits to income from other geographically mobile activities or provide benefits to a wide range of activities and do not necessarily exclude income from IP. The so-called *"Nexus Approach"* is the substantial activity requirement developed for IP regimes. The nexus approach requires a link between the income benefiting from the IP regime and the extent to which the taxpayer has undertaken the underlying R&D that generated the IP asset (extracted from OECD 2020).

IP regimes are used to incentivize research and development by taxing patent revenues differently from other commercial revenues. However, they have also been used as so-called *base erosion and profit shifting (BEPS)* tools, to avoid corporate taxes (Wikipedia 2020) and have therefore been investigated by the OECD (2017). Table 8.5 gives an overview of different Patent Boxes currently being installed in Europe.

Table 8.5 Patent boxes in Europe (table compiled by authors)

Country	Patent box tax rate (standard statutory tax rate)	Comment (type of IP)
Switzerland	As of 9%	Since 2020, canton specific (max. tax advantages of box are limited to 70%)
France	10% (33%)	IP income; IP: patents, SPCs, plant varieties, topography, (since 2020)
Belgium	3.8% (25%)	IP income; IP: software if copyright, patents, SPCs, plant varieties, (since 2020)
Netherland	7% (25%)	IP income; IP: software, patents, SPCs, plant varieties, utility models, ... (since 2019)
Luxemburg	5.2% (26%)	IP income; IP: software if copyright, patents, SPCs, plant varieties (since 2019)
Portugal	10.5% (21%)	Since 2019
Spain	10% (25%)	Since 2019
UK	10% (19%)	IP income; IP: patents, SPCs, plant varieties (since 2013)
Ireland	6.25%	Since 2016
Hungary	4.5% (9%)	Since 2019

Last updated: January 2020 (Sources: King and Zhu 2019; Botschaft STAF 2018)

8.9 Brief Comparison of Patent Legislation (Table 8.6)

Table 8.6 Comparison of different patent jurisdictions (table compiled by authors)

	Europe (EPO)	USA
Priority	First-to-file	First-to-file/first-to-invent—*Leahy-Smith America Invents Act (AIA)*: Since the 16th of March 2013 the USA underwent a comprehensive patent reform. This caused, *inter alia*, the following changes: (a) change to first-to-file scheme, (b) change to the publication conditioned grace period practiced since 1952, (c) opposition (new: *inter partes* review/post-grant review/covered business method; old and new: *ex parte* reexamination)
Grace period	No—Exceptions: in case of abuse or officially recognized exhibition up to a max. of 6 months before the national application day (Art. 55 EPÜ)	Up to a year before filing a national application
Publication	18 months from priority date	18 months from priority date—For US patent applications filed after 1999-11-28 applicants can elect to file a non-publication request if no foreign application is filed *(American Inventor Protection Act, 1999)*
Duration	Max. 20 years from filing	Max. 20 years from filing—For patent applications filed on or after June 8, 1995; Applicants filed before that date have a 17 years term as of the issue date
Examination request	Up to 6 months after publication of search report	No separate request possible (already included when filing the application)
Language	German, English, French—Official languages the European Patent Office. Patents can be submitted in the official languages of member states, but translations must be delivered after the fact (Art. 14(2) EPÜ)	English

(continued)

8.9 Brief Comparison of Patent Legislation (Table 8.6)

Table 8.6 (continued)

	Australia	**Canada**
Priority	First "real and reasonably clear disclosure of the subject matter of the claim"	First-to-file
Grace period	12 months for pre-April 2002 applications	One year, from Canadian or PCT (designating Canada) filing date
Publication	18 months from priority date	Open to public inspection after 18 months from the priority date
Duration	Max. 20 years from filing	20 years from filing
Examination request	Within 5 years of filing	Yes, 4 years from filing
Language	English	English and French
	Japan	**Korea**
Priority	First-to-file	First-to-file
Grace period	Max. 6 months before national application	6 months before application
Publication	18 months from priority date	18 months from priority date
Duration	Max. 20 years from filing	Max. 20 years from filing
Examination request	Up to 3 years from filing—For all JP patent applications since October 1, 2001; earlier applications had a period of 7 years	3 years from filing
Language	Japanese, English	Korean
	China/Hongkong	**Taiwan**
Priority	First-to-file	First-to-file
Grace period	No	No—Exceptions: Publications for the purpose of research and experimentation, or at international trade fair, until max. 6 months before the date of application
Publication	18 months from priority date	18 months from priority date
Duration	Max. 20 years from filing	Max. 20 years from filing
Examination	Up to 3 years from priority date	Up to 3 years from filing
Language	Chinese—Limited application for Chinese text from Taiwan	Taiwanese, English—Taiwanese translation must be delivered within 60 days
	Russian Federation	**Eurasia (EAPO)**
Priority	First-to-file	First-to-file
Grace period	6 months before application	12 months before priority
Publication	18 months from filing	18 months from filing
Duration	Max. 20 years from filing	Max. 20 years from filing
Examination request	Up to 3 years from filing	Up to 6 months after search
Language	Russian	Russian

Sources: Gassmann and Bader (2017), BCF (2020), Slater and Matsil (2020)

8.10 The World Intellectual Property Day

Every **April 26**, the World Intellectual Property Organization (WIPO) celebrates the World Intellectual Property Day to learn about the role that intellectual property (IP) rights play in encouraging innovation and creativity (see Fig. 8.4):

- #worldipday
- wipo.int/ipday
- youtube.com/wipo

Fig. 8.4 The World Intellectual Property Day: April 26th (WIPO 2020)

References

BCF. (2020). Montréal: BCF Business Law.

Botschaft STAF. (2018). *Botschaft zum Bundesgesetz über die Steuervorlage 17 (SV17)*. Schweizerische Eidgenossenschaft.

EPO. (2019). *EPO refuses DABUS patent applications designating a machine inventor*. News, 20 December 2019. Munich: European Patent Office. Accessed January 3, 2020, from https://www.epo.org/news-issues/news/2019/20191220.html

EPO. (2020a). *The EPO at a glance*. Accessed January 7, 2020, from https://www.epo.org/about-us/at-a-glance.html

EPO. (2020b). *Unitary patent*. Accessed January 7, 2020, from https://www.epo.org/law-practice/unitary/unitary-patent.html

EPO. (2020c). *Unified patent court*. Accessed January 7, 2020, from https://www.epo.org/law-practice/unitary/upc.html#tab1

EUIPO. (2020). *About EUIPO*. Accessed January 7, 2020, from https://euipo.europa.eu/ohimportal/en/the-office

Five IP Offices. (2019a). *IP5 statistics report 2018 edition*. Daejeon: Five IP Offices.

Five IP Offices. (2019b). *Key IP5 statistical indicators 2018*. Daejeon: Five IP Offices.

Gassmann, O., & Bader, M. A. (2017). *Patentmanagement: Innovationen erfolgreich nutzen und schützen* (4th ed.). Berlin: Springer.

King, C. C., & Zhu, S. (2019). *Patentboxen im Europäischen Vergleich und steuerliche Forschungsförderung in Deutschland*. In: VPP-Rundbrief No. 4/2019. Frankfurt/Main and Ludwigshafen: VCI und BASF.

OECD. (2017). *Harmful Tax Practices – 2017 Progress Report on Preferential Regimes*. In: OECD/G20 Base Erosion and Profit Shifting Project. Paris: OECD.

OECD. (2020). *Intellectual property regimes*. Accessed January 7, 2020, from https://qdd.oecd.org/subject.aspx?Subject=IP_Regimes

Slater & Matsil. (2020). Dallas: Slater and Matsil.

Wikipedia. (2020). *Patent box*. Accessed January 7, 2020, from https://en.wikipedia.org/wiki/Patent_box

WIPO. (2020). *World intellectual property day*. Accessed April 26, 2020, from https://www.wipo.int/ip-outreach/en/ipday/

Glossary

AIA Leahy–Smith America Invents Act
CNIPA China National Intellectual Property Administration
CPC Cooperative Patent Classification
CTM Community Trade Mark
ECLA European Patent Classification
EPC European Patent Convention
EPO European Patent Office
EU European Union
EUIPO European Union Intellectual Property Office
EUTM EU Trade Mark
IGE/IPI Swiss Federal Institute of Intellectual Property
IPC International Patent Classification
JPO Japan Patent Office
KIPO Korean Intellectual Property Office
OHIM Office for Harmonization in the Internal Market
R&D Research and Development
RCD Registered Community Design
SMEs Small and Medium Enterprises
SPCs Supplementary Protection Certificates
UPC Unified Patent Court
USPC United States Patent Classification
USPTO United States Patent and Trademark Office
WIPO World Intellectual Property Organization
XRAC Cross-Reference Art Collection

Index

A
Access to finance, 102–105
Additional profit method, 70
African Regional Intellectual Property Organization (ARIPO), 39
Alice, 186, 220
Alice Corporation *vs.* CLS Bank International test, 222, 225
Alternative techniques of value appropriation, 48, 49
Analogy method, 66, 67
Anti-commons, 177–178
Appellation d'Origine Controlée (AOC), 21
Artificial Intelligence (AI), 194–236
Assertion, 95–113
Automotive, 166–171

B
Bilski, 219
Biotechnology, 194–202
Blockchain, 183–185, 230–236
Brand strategy, 154–155
Broccoli EPO Ruling, 149
Business methods, 212–220

C
Call-back, 101
Chemistry, 146–148
China, 138, 242
'1-Click' patent, 212
Cloud computing, 186
Code Division Multiple Access (CDMA), 173
Commercialization, 95–112, 165
    access to finance, 102–105
    complex strategies, 107–108
    cross-licensing, 97–98
    guideline, 108–112
    joint venture, 101–102
    licensing, 96–97
    litigation, 105–107
    sale, 98–99
    spin-off, 99–101
    strategic alliance, 99
    success factors, 112
Commons, 169
    anti-commons, 177–178
Computer science, 178–181
Computer-implemented inventions (CII), 214
Consumer goods, 153–155
Cooperation, 168–169
Copyright, 15, 22
Cost of patents, 39–42
Costs, 117–121
    patent department, 117–121
CRISPR-Cas9, 199–202
Crop science, 148–150
Cross-licensing, 36, 97–98
Culture, 129–136

D
Dabus, 246
DABUS, 229, 245
Decision-tree analysis, 73
Defensive disclosure, 43, 45
Defensive publication, 43, 45
Design access, 35
Design Patent, 15, 17
Designed complexity, 47
Direct cashflow forecast method, 69
Disclosure, 207
Discounted Cash Flows (DCF), 68
Distributed Ledger Technologies (DLT), 183–185, 230–236

Domain names, 21
DRM-Technology (Digital Rights Management), 179

E
Electrics, 161–165
Electronics, 161–165
Enforcement, 96–112
Erfindungen, 196
Eurasian Patent Organization (EAPO), 39
Europäisches Patentübereinkommen (EPÜ), 196
European Patent Application, 206
 disclosure, 207
 inventive step, 207
 novelty, 206
European Patent Convention (EPC), 16
European Patent Office (EPO), 39, 196–198, 205–208, 215–218
 biotechnology, 196–198
 computer-implemented inventions (CII), 215–218
 member states, 250
 nanotechnology, 205–208
 patentability, 15
European Patent Organisation, 250
European Union Intellectual Property Office (EUIPO), 251–252
Evaluation, 52–61
Evaluation of patents
 bivariate portfolio evaluation, 56, 58, 59
 monovariate portfolio evaluation, 52–55
 trivariate portfolio evaluation, 59, 61
Exploitation, 96–112
Exposure, 56

F
Fair, Reasonable and Non-Discriminatory (FRAND), 174, 175, 177
Financial services, 182–185
5G, 173
Fourth Industrial Revolution, 208, 211
Freedom-to-operate, 33, 156, 163, 177
Freeman-Walter-Abele-Test, 212, 219

G
Geographic Designation of Origin, 15, 21
Global System for Mobile communications (GSM), 173

H
Hague Model Convention (HMA), 19
Harvard-Mouse/Oncomouse, 198

Historical cost method, 64, 65
Huawei *vs.* ZTE, 175

I
Industry 4.0, 208
Industry sectors, 143–190
 chemistry, 146–148
 crop science, 148–150
Information and Communications Technology (ICT), 172–178
Innovation box, 253
In re Bilsky, 182
Intellectual Property (IP), 107
 formal IP, 107, 221, 225
 informal IP, 107, 221, 226
 Protection Star, 138
Intellectual property rights, 1–23
 copyrights, 22
 design patent, 17
 overview, 14–23
 patents, 14, 15
 plant breeders'/variety rights, 19
 supplementary protection certificate, 16
 topography, 19
 trade dress, 21
 trade secrets, 22, 23
 trademarks, 19, 20
 utility model, 17
Interference proceeding, 199
Internet of Things (IoT), 208–211
Invalidation, 37
Invention, 123
Inventive step, 207
IP Box, 253
IP5 Offices, 242
4IR, 208–211

J
Joint venture, 101–102

K
Korea, 242

L
Leahy-Smith America Invents Act, 254
License price analogy method, 69, 70
Licensing, 96–112
 assertion licensing, 97
 carrot licensing, 97
 cross-licensing, 36
 enablement licensing, 97
 enforcement licensing, 97
 opportunity licensing, 97

stick licensing, 97
Licensing guillotine approach, 98
Life sciences, 151–153
Litigation, 179

M
Machine-or-Transformation Test, 219
Machinery, 155–160
Market price method, 66
Mission, 76
Monte Carlo method, 74

N
Nanotechnology, 203–208
Nanotechnology patents, 205
Non-Disclosure Agreement (NDA), 49
Nexus approach, 253
Non-Practicing Entities (NPE), 105
Novelty, 206

O
Opposition, 37
Organisation Africaine de la Propriété Intellectuelle (OAPI), 39
Organization, 115–141, 160, 162
Outsourcing, 42, 119–121

P
Patent, 14, 15
  alternatives, 42–49
  complementary actions, 42–49
  core processes of patent management, 121–129
  costs, 39–42
  first filing, 124
  growth applications worldwide, 242
  invention, 123–124
  legislations – comparison, 254
  maintenance, 127
  nullity procedure, 37
  opposition procedure, 37
  patent box, 253
  patent classification, 247
  patent document codes, 246
  patent management, 8, 10, 11
  prosecution, 124–129
  reexamination, 37
  searching, 248–249
  second application, 124
  strategic management, 11, 12
  structure of patent document, 243–246
  unitary patent, 251–252
Patent Assertion Entities (PAE), 105
Patent box, 253
Patent classification, 247
Patent Clearing, 34
Patent Cooperation Treaty (PCT), 16, 39
Patent department, 115–117
  costs, 117–121
  organization, 115–117
  outsourcing, 119–121
  performance indicators, 118
  processes, 121
Patent management, 8, 10, 11
  alternative techniques of value appropriation, 48, 49
  defensive publication, 43, 45
  designed complexity, 47
  evaluation of patents, 51–91
  secrecy, 45, 46
  speed, 46, 47
  valuation of patents, 51–91
Patent quality, 56
Patent strategy, 27–29, 180
Patent troll, 30, 105
Performance indicators, 118
Petty patents, 17
Pharma, 144–146
Piracy, 136–141
Plant Breeders'/Plant Variety Right, 15, 19
Polymerase Chain Reaction (PCR), 195
Portfolio
  differentiation, 37, 38
Portfolio management, 51–91, 158, 162–163
  The St. Gallen Patent Portfolio Management Model, 75, 81, 90
Prior art, 43
Processes, 117–121, 155–162
  core processes, 121–129
  freedom to operate, 156
  ideation, 157–158
  invention disclosure, 157–158
  patent generation, 156
Product Clearing, 34
Product piracy, 136–141
Prosecution, 124–129
Protected Appelations of Origin (AOP), 21
Protected Geographical Indications (IGP), 21
Protection strategies
  formal protection strategies, 6
  informal protection strategies, 6
Publication, 43, 45

Q
Quality management, 121
Quality of patents, 10, 56

R
Real option method, 73
Relief From Royalty, 69
Reproduction cost method, 64, 66
Residual value method, 71, 72
25%-rule, 76

S
Searching, 248–249
Secrecy, 45, 46
SEP, *see* Standard Essential Patents (SEP)
Small and medium-sized enterprises (SMEs), 151–153, 188–190
Smartphone patent wars, 174–176
Software, 212–220
Software patents, 215
Spin-off, 100, 119–121
Standard Essential Patents (SEP), 175
Start-up, 151–153, 188–190
State-Street-Bank, 219
St. Gallen Approach to Managing Technologies and Patents, 75
St. Gallen Innovation Culture Navigator, 134
St. Gallen Patent Index (SGPI), 53
St. Gallen Patent Portfolio Management Model, 75, 81, 90
Strategic management, 11, 12
Strategy, 27–29
  branding, 154–155
  patent generation, 161
Success factors
  managing a patent department, 116
Supplementary Protection Certificate, 15, 16

T
Technologies, 193–236
Technology Stewardship Agreement, 150
Territoriality principle, 39
Tobin's q, 67
Tomato EPO Ruling, 149
Topography, 15, 19
Trade Dress, 15, 21, 212
Trade secrets, 15, 22, 23, 103
Trademark, 15, 19, 20
Transport and logistics, 185–187

U
Unified patent court, 251–252
Unitary patent, 251–252
Universal Mobile Telecommunications System (UMTS), 173
USA
  interference proceeding, 199
Utility Model, 15, 17

V
Valuation, 61–76, 162–163
Valuation by appraisal, 72
Valuation by share of profit, 72
Valuation by technological factor, 73
Valuation of patents
  additional methods of patent valuation, 72–76
  additional profit method, 70
  analogy method, 66, 67
  cost-oriented procedures, 63
  cost-oriented valuation, 64–66
  decision-tree analysis, 73
  direct cashflow forecast method, 69
  historical cost method, 64, 65
  income-based approach, 68–72
  income-oriented procedures, 63
  license price-analogy method, 69, 70
  market-based approach, 66–68
  market-oriented procedures, 63
  market price method, 66
  Monte Carlo method, 74
  overview, 76
  real option method, 73
  Relief From Royalty, 69
  reproduction cost method, 64, 66
  residual value method, 71, 72
  valuation by appraisal, 72
  valuation by share of profit, 72
  valuation by technological factor, 73
Value
  value capture, 4–14
  value creation, 1–4
Value of patents
  evaluation of patents, 52–61
  patent portfolio management, 75–91
  valuation of patents, 61–76
Vision, 76

W
World intellectual property day, 256
World Intellectual Property Organization (WIPO), 256

Printed by Printforce, the Netherlands